Living Vegan

FOR

DUMMIES®

by Alexandra Jamieson, CHHC, AADP

Wiley Publishing, Inc.

Living Vegan For Dummies®
Published by
Wiley Publishing, Inc.
111 River St.
Hoboken, NJ 07030-5774
www.wiley.com

WILEY

About the Author

Alexandra Jamieson, CHHC, AADP, has been seen on *Oprah, The Final Word, 30 Days,* and *The National Health Test with Bryant Gumbel.* She even was featured in the award-winning documentary *Super Size Me* (2004).

Why? Because Alex has proven herself to be a wise and profound voice for holistic nutrition and healthy living. In her book, *The Great American Detox Diet* (Rodale, 2005), Alex offers remarkably sane — and tasty — advice on how to detox, live healthfully, and feel fantastic.

Her knowledge of nutrition has been artfully developed through years of both professional and self-study. As the daughter of natural health advocates, Alex crafted a unique personal mission to spread the word about the power of healthy food and the astounding ways in which it can positively transform everyday life. Alex now commands a matchless repertoire of nutritional wisdom and food savvy.

Alex is a professionally trained healthy gourmet chef, having studied at New York City's Natural Gourmet Institute for Health and Culinary Arts. She refined her techniques by cooking professionally in Milan, Italy, as well as at a variety of popular New York City restaurants.

In addition, Alex is a certified health and nutrition counselor. She studied with groundbreaking pioneers in the field of nutrition at the Institute for Integrative Nutrition, which is accredited by Columbia University's Teacher's College and by the American Association of Drugless Practitioners.

Alex also traveled the world, visiting more than 20 countries while premiering *Super Size Me,* an Oscar-nominated documentary, and acting as a messenger for the power of holistic nutrition and healthy detoxing. Though she readily and ably shares her message with all, her passion is helping professional women enhance their ability to excel and achieve using healthy food as a catalyst.

A healthy and energetic vegan herself, Alex lives in New York City with her family, including her vegan son, Laken, and a lively male cat named Sue.

For more information, please visit www.nutritionforempowered women.com.

Dedication

This book is dedicated to my son, Laken, a shining example of a healthy vegan human being. And to everyone considering living as a vegan, or supporting someone who is on this path, I applaud your efforts to make this world a better place, one bite at a time.

Author's Acknowledgments

My heartfelt thanks and acknowledgements to the wonderful folks at Wiley Publishing, Inc. who made this book possible: Copy Editor Jessica Smith, Acquisitions Editor Lindsay Lefevere, Senior Project Editor Chrissy Guthrie, and all the Composition Department folks who helped with the layout and design work. Thanks also to Rachel Nix for the technical review, to Emily Nolan for the recipe testing, and to Patty Santelli for the nutritional analysis.

Publisher's Acknowledgments

We're proud of this book; please send us your comments at `http://dummies.custhelp.com`. For other comments, please contact our Customer Care Department within the U.S. at 877-762-2974, outside the U.S. at 317-572-3993, or fax 317-572-4002.

Some of the people who helped bring this book to market include the following:

Acquisitions, Editorial, and Media Development

Senior Project Editor: Christina Guthrie

Senior Acquisitions Editor: Lindsay Lefevere

Copy Editor: Jessica Smith

Assistant Editor: Erin Calligan Mooney

Editorial Program Coordinator: Joe Niesen

Technical Editors: Rachel Nix, Emily Nolan, Patty Santelli

Editorial Manager: Christine Meloy Beck

Editorial Assistants: David Lutton, Jennette ElNaggar

Art Coordinator: Alicia B. South

Cover Photos: Crystal Cartier

Cartoons: Rich Tennant (`www.the5thwave.com`)

Composition Services

Project Coordinator: Kristie Rees

Layout and Graphics: Ashley Chamberlain, Joyce Haughey, Melissa K. Jester, Mark Pinto

Special Art: Illustrations by Elizabeth Kurtzman

Proofreaders: Melissa Cossell, Jessica Kramer, Penny Stuart

Indexer: Becky Hornyak

Publishing and Editorial for Consumer Dummies

 Diane Graves Steele, Vice President and Publisher, Consumer Dummies

 Kristin Ferguson-Wagstaffe, Product Development Director, Consumer Dummies

 Ensley Eikenburg, Associate Publisher, Travel

 Kelly Regan, Editorial Director, Travel

Publishing for Technology Dummies

 Andy Cummings, Vice President and Publisher, Dummies Technology/General User

Composition Services

 Debbie Stailey, Director of Composition Services

Contents at a Glance

Recipes at a Glance

Entreés

Side Dishes

Table of Contents

Introduction

. . . .

*G*rowing up in the wilds of Oregon, my artist/gardener mom and teacher dad taught me many lessons that served me well over the years. I was lucky enough to be raised in a family that saw the connections between fresh food, health, people, the animals and insects, and the earth we lived on. We did eat meat, dairy, eggs, and honey from our beekeeping friends, but I had a solid education in "the web of life 101." My older brother and I were pretty healthy; we ate lots of fresh food, and we rarely ate out.

My parents canned tomatoes and set aside jars of blackberry jam, and the whole family would spend hours in local u-pick farms gathering hazelnuts or cherries when the season was right.

As I grew up and moved away from home, my eating habits strayed from freshly-made, organic foods to the standard American diet of fast-food, lots of soda with high-fructose corn syrup, regular doses of fried foods, and few fresh fruits or vegetables. By the time I reached my late 20s, I was getting sick and depressed, had frequent migraines, and started gaining weight quickly for the first time in my life. I realized that what I was eating was making me sick and that I had to make a change if I were to be a fully functioning, happy person again.

I went to a holistic doctor who diagnosed me with an underlying *Candida* yeast overgrowth and recommended a sugar- and dairy-free diet to help my body recover. As I read everything the library had to offer on natural foods, the vegan diet, and the realities of health and the food system, I realized that I had caused my own health problems with my diet and discovered that my food choices had a large impact on the world around me.

I started eating vegan, whole foods within a week and immediately started to feel better. My headaches went away, the excess weight melted off, and I was clearheaded and energetic for the first time in years. I took my newfound passion for food and enrolled in a professional chef's training program at the Natural Gourmet Institute in New York City.

I later realized I wanted to help people discover how to heal their own health problems with good food and dietary choices. Since graduating from the Institute for Integrative Nutrition, I have helped countless clients all over the world improve their health by including more plant-based options to their diets.

About This Book

As more people are exposed to the realities of how our food is produced and processed and how it affects our health, eating a vegan diet becomes more popular as a way to follow a healthier, more vibrant path through life. World-class athletes and popular musicians, actors, and artists achieve incredible levels of human fitness and create amazing works of art all while living a vegan life.

This book is for new vegans and the people who love them. It's also for vegetarians who want to make the switch and lifelong carnivores who are curious about what a vegan is and what they eat. This book also can help comfort your friends and family by providing the information to quiet the fears of you wasting away to nothing by "living on lettuce."

Even if you aren't sure a vegan diet is right for you, this book can help you understand the amazing benefits of a plant-based diet. Including more vegetables, fruits, whole grains, beans, nuts, and seeds is something we're all encouraged to do by the FDA, USDA, and the ADA! Even Mom says so! If you want to improve your health, reduce your health concerns, lose weight, improve your energy and stamina, prolong your life expectancy, protect the environment, and save the lives of countless animals, this book is for you.

Living Vegan For Dummies provides an incredible amount of information that can be useful whether you read it from start to finish or not. Every chapter is written in easy-to-understand language and has distinct parts with helpful references and lots of tips and real-world strategies. The recipes can help you enjoy vegan food even if you aren't a trained chef. And most important, every chapter helps you get closer to a cruelty-free life.

Conventions Used in This Book

Following are a few conventions I've used that you should be aware of:

- Whenever I introduce you to a new food or term, I put it in *italics*.
- Keywords in bulleted lists or the action parts in numbered steps appear in **boldface.**
- Web sites appear in `monofont`.

When this book was printed, some Web addresses may have needed to break across two lines of text. If that happened, rest assured that I haven't put in any extra characters (such as hyphens) to indicate the break. So when using one of these Web addresses, just type in exactly what you see in this book, pretending as though the line break doesn't exist.

What You're Not to Read

For Dummies books are full of useful extras that pop out at you while you're reading. Fun facts and useful sidebars give you inspiration and ammunition for the vegan road ahead. You'll notice this extra information highlighted with gray shaded boxes or Technical Stuff icons throughout the chapters. You can commit these items to memory to remind yourself and others of why this lifestyle is so amazing, or you can skip them and just dive into the information that seems most important to you at the time. Just remember that this extra information is just that — extra. You don't have to read it in order to understand the topic at hand.

Foolish Assumptions

In writing this book, I made a few assumptions about you, the reader:

- ✔ You like to eat food, but you want to stop eating animal products.
- ✔ You like to wear clothes, but you want to stop wearing animal products.
- ✔ You like to wash and pamper your body, but you want to stop using products that contain animal ingredients or products that were tested on animals.
- ✔ When you buy something to use or consume, you often ask yourself or someone else "where did this come from?" or "what is this made of?" or "what am I contributing to when I buy this?"
- ✔ You have cooked a little or none at all, but you know you would like to start making some if not all your own food.
- ✔ You're curious about how to maintain proper health while eating a vegan diet.
- ✔ You aren't afraid to take a risk or be considered "weird" by the rest of society — most cool vegans are a little outside the mainstream, but that's what we like to be!

If these assumptions spoke to you, you found yourself nodding your head while reading this list, or you can easily picture your loved one who wants to become a vegan, you're reading the right book.

How This Book Is Organized

Living Vegan For Dummies is divided into seven parts. Each part covers a different area of vegan living. Read through the description for each part and then go to the chapters that excite you the most. Every part works in conjunction with the others to help you build a vibrant, conscious, and deliciously healthy life.

Part I: "Ve-gan" at the Beginning

Part I lays out what a vegan diet and lifestyle encompasses. It details the reasons people choose to become vegan in the first place and covers the ways in which choosing a vegan diet can lead to better health for yourself and can protect animals and the planet. This part also discusses the ways to make the switch from a vegetarian or omnivorous diet to a healthy, plant-based, vegan diet.

Part II: Building a Healthy Vegan Diet

This part serves as your nutritional guide to creating a healthy meal plan. I show you how to include proper protein, calcium, iron, B12, and other nutrients along with delicious vegan ingredients to ensure a well-rounded diet. An important feature of Part II is the lists of healthy, whole vegan foods. These lists help you choose foods to ensure that you're getting the nutrition you need while eating a vegan diet.

Part III: Sticking to Your Guns: Staying Vegan

The nuts and bolts of making a vegan diet work for you and your family are found in Part III. Here you can find all sorts of information, including cooking tools you need to buy, tips on how to shop for and store food items, and guidelines for planning your meals for ease and success. This part also includes handy snack and shopping lists as well as ways to cook your old favorite foods in new, vegan ways. Finally it takes you beyond the kitchen to your bathroom and closets to help you find hidden animal ingredients and products that you want to avoid.

Part IV: Tasting Is Believing: Vegan Recipes

This part is where you find delicious, mouthwatering recipes for every part of the day. I include breakfasts for school and workdays, brunch ideas for leisurely weekend meals, smaller side dishes, one-pot meals for the beginner or time-pressed chef, and delicious desserts for everyone. For all these recipes, I call for vegan ingredients and provide you with simple-to-follow instructions.

Part V: Living Vegan in the Real World

In this part, you take your first tentative steps outside of the happy vegan bubble you've created for yourself at home. The chapters here can help you make travel plans to see the rest of the world and remain a happily social vegan bon vivant even if you're the only salad eater at a table full of steak lovers. This part also can help you throw your own vegan parties so you can share your newfound love of cruelty-free food with friends and family.

Part VI: Veganism for All Walks of Life

Read this part to help plan and prepare for those special times in life that may require unique nutritional needs. This part describes how you can manage a healthy pregnancy, raise a fit baby and toddler, feed a growing athlete as well as deal with the special challenges of older vegans. It explains the benefits of a vegan diet for each phase of life and offers sound nutritional advice and strategies for success.

Part VII: The Part of Tens

Commit these lists to memory! The information in this part comes in handy when you're getting grilled by some meathead at a party, and it also offers handy lists that serve every person on the vegan path. In this part, you discover ten reasons for living vegan as well as ten exciting and inspiring ways to take your commitment out of the kitchen and into the great big world. You also receive answers to the most common questions you'll hear as a vegan.

Icons Used in This Book

As you go through the chapters of this book, you'll find the following friendly icons that are designed to draw your attention to different bits of information, from useful tidbits to satisfying trivia. Here's what each of the icons mean:

Be sure to pay attention to the information next to this icon. This advice can help you make good choices and eliminate risks.

When you see this icon, you're sure to find handy bits of guidance that will inspire, help, and ease your way along the vegan path.

Pay close attention to information featuring this icon. It will help you avoid common pitfalls as well as costly mistakes.

This icon points out information where I've gone into the science of things. You don't have to read this info to understand the topic at hand, but it is interesting stuff.

Where to Go from Here

If you aren't sure where to begin your exploration of vegan living, start your journey at the beginning of this book and read every bit until you reach the back cover. On the other hand, if you can't wait to eat great vegan food, skip ahead to the recipes in Chapters 12 through 15 and start cooking!

The great thing about this book is that you can choose the topics that are most important or interesting to you right now and jump into those areas — you don't have to read this book from the beginning for it to work for you. This book covers every area of vegan living, but you don't have to follow the information in order. Skip around, fast-forward, and rewind; do what works best for you. All the information is here for when you need it, in the order that you need it.

Whether you choose to go 100 percent vegan or just integrate several vegan meals a day, Chapters 9 through 11 can help you make better purchases. If you're already shopping in health food stores, you can still find out more about the different labels given to vegan and cruelty-free products as listed in Chapter 7. You can start snacking and eating vegan meals on the fly with the snacking and shopping lists provided in Chapter 9.

A vegan life is full of fun, passion, and ethical consciousness made real with every meal, purchase, and product. Enjoy the journey of discovery, and take heart knowing that you've committed to one of the most responsible paths available in life! Be well, and here's to your health!

Part I
"Ve-gan" at the Beginning

The 5th Wave   By Rich Tennant

"This isn't some sort of fad diet, is it?"

In this part . . .

1f your whole life could be drawn on a map, vegan living encompasses not only the roads, intersections, and detours, it's also the inspiration for your journey in the first place. Knowing what you're going to encounter on this trip ensures that you don't end up in the wilderness friendless and starving!

In this part, you can find the basics on what vegan living means. These chapters explain the solid logic of choosing this lifestyle and how to transition to it, including what you can eat and buy, the health and environmental benefits associated with it, and how to make the necessary changes from your current lifestyle.

Chapter 1

The Lowdown on Vegan Eating and Living

A vegan is the ultimate, hard-core vegetarian. Someone who follows a vegan diet avoids eating, drinking, wearing, using, or otherwise consuming *anything* that contains animal ingredients or that was tested on animals. This means a vegan eats pretty much everything except dairy from cows, sheep, or goats, (or horses, if you're ever visiting Mongolia), cheese, milk, butter, eggs, meat, poultry, fish, shellfish, or honey.

In this chapter, you discover the vast health benefits of a vegan diet, what vegan living entails, and how to deal with the common (and often ignorant) questions that people will likely ask you about your lifestyle choice.

You Are What You Eat: The Health and Food Connection

If you want to be vibrant, healthy, and full of energy, you should eat fresh, healthy, vibrant foods. If you feel bloated, tired, sluggish, and full of aches and pains, you should look to your diet first to see whether the culprits are hiding on your plate. Answer these questions to get a better sense of what's really going on in your body:

✔ Do you feel tired and unfocused during the day?

✔ Do you use caffeine to help you wake up in the morning?

✔ Do you have sugar, caffeine, or salt cravings?

✔ Do you drink regular or diet soda?

✔ Do you have high blood pressure or high cholesterol (or both)?

✔ Are you overweight or obese?

✔ Do you get bloated or have stomach cramps after eating?

✔ Do you often have headaches, depression, or moody outbursts?

✔ Do you eat most of your food from fast-food joints, packages, or boxes?

✔ Do you have problems with constipation or diarrhea?

✔ Do you eat fried foods often?

✔ Do you have skin problems like acne, eczema, or rashes?

If you answered yes to even a few of these questions, your diet needs a serious cleanup.

Moving to a vegan diet that's based on whole, unprocessed grains, beans, vegetables, and fruits, with some nuts and seeds thrown in, will give your body everything it needs to heal and recuperate from years of abuse. The benefits are clear, and it isn't difficult to figure out how to eat this way.

If you want to live a life of high-energy, peak experiences, and accomplish your biggest goals and dreams, you need a diet that will fuel your body to meet those challenges. Meet the challenges without meat!

Heart-healthy, low-fat, cholesterol-free foods

Place your hand over your heart and feel it beating. Say out loud, "Thank you, heart, for always beating even though I don't always treat you so well. From now on, I promise not to be so hard on you."

Vegans, as a group, have healthier blood pressure levels and a lower risk for heart disease. Several major studies have shown that vegans and vegetarians are 15 to 20 percent less likely to die from heart disease than meat eaters.

If you have high blood pressure, just use a whole-foods, vegan diet for two weeks, and then get retested — you'll most likely show an improvement. Plant foods are lower in fat and sodium and higher in potassium (a mineral that helps to lower blood pressure) than meat- and dairy-based foods. These are key reasons why switching to a vegan diet will improve your heart health.

Because vegan foods are naturally free of cholesterol, your arteries are less likely to get clogged up with the stuff. Humans do need cholesterol for many different functions, but the human body produces what it needs. Animal products are the biggest sources of cholesterol in modern diets, so eating a diet rich in whole, vegan foods cuts out the clogs pretty quickly. Not only will eating a low-fat, high-fiber vegan diet help you avoid heart disease, it's also been proven to reverse *atherosclerosis,* or the hardening of the arteries.

Feeling fine with fiber

Fiber is the part of plant foods that our bodies can't digest. Not being able to digest something sounds bad, but it's actually excellent! All that fiber gets mashed up by your chewing and fills up your stomach, leading to a feeling of fullness when you eat more of the healthy complex carbohydrates. Simple carbohydrates, like white bread, rice, pasta, and sugar, have little fiber, so they get digested quickly and you don't fill up on them.

Not only does fiber fill you up quickly, but it also cleans you out when it moves through your intestines. Moving things out fast is a must for overall health! This "fiber brush" effect scrapes out the food particles that can get stuck in the nooks and crannies of your gastrointestinal system. All this fiber means more elimination, which is a great way to keep the body clean and devoid of rotting material. One of the negative effects of a diet heavy in simple carbohydrates and meat is the huge amount of leftover rotting flesh and pasty glue stuck in people's colons. The fiber brush effect is one of the main reasons why vegans have less colon cancer.

As vegans avoid the modern, processed diet and go for the veggie-based one, they get abundant vitamins, *phytochemicals* (chemical compounds found in plant foods that have health-promoting properties), and fiber associated with lower cancer rates.

If you're eating a whole-foods based diet, you're already taking in more fiber than the average person. The vegetables with the highest amounts of fiber are artichokes, beans, broccoli, Brussels sprouts, cabbages, carrots, eggplant, leafy green vegetables, mushrooms, potatoes with the skin, pumpkin, peppers, rhubarb, spinach, and sweet potatoes. High-fiber fruits include apples, avocados, bananas, berries, dried fruit, guava, kiwi, oranges, pears, and prunes. Whole grains, nuts, and seeds also are good sources of fiber.

The American Heart Association and the Institute of Medicine recommend that adults consume 14 grams of fiber for every 1,000 calories eaten. For vegans, this level is no problem to achieve: 1 cup of peas has almost 9 grams; 1 cup of black beans has 19 grams; 1 banana has 3 grams; ½ cup of blackberries has more than 4 grams; and 1 tablespoon of shredded coconut has more than 3 grams. Vegan food is fiber-rific!

Raw foodists and macrobiotics

Just when you thought veganism couldn't get any more specific, here come the raw foodists and macrobiotics. Two distinct sects of the "vegan religion," raw foodists and followers of the macrobiotic diet choose to eat plant-based diets that are prepared a certain way and avoid even more ingredients than a straight-up vegan.

A raw foodist eats uncooked or slightly prepared foods that can be warmed in dehydrators to only as much as 118 degrees Fahrenheit. While some raw foodists do eat raw fish such as sushi, or even raw chicken, eggs, or meat, a majority of these folks are vegan.

Macrobiotics eat a diet based on traditional Japanese foods, which can be slightly adjusted to include local ingredients. As with raw foodists, many Macrobiotics include fish in their diets, but a good percentage avoid all animal foods and are vegans. These vegans tend to eat mostly cooked food with a focus on whole grains like brown rice, and tend to avoid tropical and raw fruits.

People tend to choose one of these diets for health, spiritual, or environmental reasons, and many documented cases from both diets have been shown to cure diseases, including cancer, diabetes, heart disease, obesity, arthritis, digestive problems, and depression. While the two diets seem to be in complete opposition to each other (one is almost 100 percent raw and the other is almost 100 percent cooked) they're both rich in health-promoting plant foods and can be useful to people experiencing health problems.

The power of proper protein

Vegan protein offers so much more than the building blocks for muscles. Because they have other magical components like fiber, complex carbohydrates, minerals, and vitamins, you can actually heal your body with vegan protein sources. In fact, according to the American Dietetic Association, a vegan diet "may be useful in the prevention and treatment of [kidney] disease . . ."

So while you're getting all the amino acids you need from your well-planned and diverse vegan diet, you can feel confident that you're also adding the natural healing components of plant foods. Eating truly healing and nutritionally dense foods — now that's smart!

The healing power of plant foods

Food was the first medicine, and a vegan's "kitchen pharmacy" can be well planned to help prevent and treat illness. Traditional healers and doctors used willow bark to treat fevers and inflammation for centuries before science discovered that the bark was teeming with *salicylic acid,* which is the inspiration and foundation of aspirin. This drug has been prescribed to people with cardiovascular problems for decades.

Here are a few foods that have been studied medicinally over the years:

- **Green leafy vegetables from the** *cruciferous,* **or cabbage, family:** These vegetables are known to help the body fight cancer growth. Broccoli, bok choy, Brussels sprouts, cabbage, cauliflower, and kale are all part of this group, so dig in. Not only do these greens offer great cancer-fighting properties, they're also rich in vitamins, minerals, and fiber. Eating these veggies is a win-win-win!

- **Ginger and turmeric:** These spices have been the most studied botanicals in recent years. They have incredible healing properties and can easily be worked into your daily diet. Ginger is used for nausea, digestion disturbances, gas, and reducing the effects of chemotherapy. Turmeric, a spice common in Indian cooking, is used for improving liver function, arthritis pain, reducing inflammation, and heartburn as well as in cancer treatment and prevention.

- **Garlic:** This powerful food can be used as a natural antibiotic and antifungal agent. As well as having anticarcinogenic and antibacterial attributes, garlic is used to treat ear infections, sinus problems, high blood pressure, and cholesterol.

- **Mushrooms:** Edible mushrooms aren't just a great meat replacement for vegans. They're a powerful class of medicinal foods. Mushrooms and their extracts are used to treat cancer, strengthen the immune system, and reduce inflammatory conditions.

These foods are only a few of thousands of plants, herbs, and spices used for centuries to heal and protect human health. By relying on these powerful plant-based foods, your kitchen truly can be a natural pharmacy.

Living Vegan Beyond Your Diet

Veganism doesn't stop at the dinner table — it leaps out of the kitchen and transforms your whole life. From what you wear to the products you buy to beautify yourself and your home, vegan living encompasses every aspect of your daily life.

Fierce, fabulous, fur-free fashion

A full vegan lifestyle not only includes a diet of solely plant-based foods, it also is dedicated to avoiding harming any living creature for any type of fashion product, whether it be handbags, shoes, sweaters, belts, or coats. Most vegans don't buy new leather, wool, or silk. Chapter 11 shows how vegan fashion can be fun and fabulous without being cruel.

Keepin' it real at home

Home is where the heart is, and a vegan home takes every purchase to a deeper level. Your home should reflect your beliefs by offering sanctuary, entertainment, and space to nourish and nurture yourself and your family according to your values.

Learn to express your individual style as a vegan at home using cruelty-free materials and decorations. Cleaning your home, making up your face, and washing your hair take on new significance when you use products that are nontoxic and not tested on animals. The labels and brands discussed in Chapter 11 can help you choose fantastic products that work for your home, body, and morals.

Staying vegan in a nonvegan world

After you know that you want to live a vegan life full of integrity, you may find areas of cruelty-free living that you just don't know anything about. Part III illustrates the nuts and bolts of daily life as a plant-food lover. Knowing how to shop for food, cook it, and make it delicious are the most important, basic, vegan skills a person can have. Even if you can't boil water or your cupboards are as bare as Mother Hubbard's, Chapter 7 can walk you through the steps of creating a basic vegan kitchen.

Living in a vegan bubble with vegan friends who love to make vegan food would be ideal, but many of us live in "mixed families" of meat and veggie heads. The combining of food ethics at home can be tricky, but Chapter 8 helps you navigate the choppy waters of sharing a kitchen with a carnivore.

Living a vegan life can be challenging if you don't map out a plan in advance. So, like a five-star general plotting a path through enemy territory, wise vegans ensure their success by learning how to strategize. Chapter 9 shares menu suggestions, healthy vegan snack lists, and shopping and meal planning guides. Integrating these blueprints on a regular basis takes the stress out of shopping, cooking, and living a busy, modern life.

Energetically Speaking: The Spiritual Side of Veganism

Various religions around the world have specific dietary rules to demonstrate their faith. Some religions avoid pork products or alcohol and others set aside certain days for fasting. The spiritual side of food has a long history that vegans can adopt to create a deeper connection with other people and animals.

Here are just a few of the many religions that have adopted vegan or vegetarian lifestyles:

- **Buddhism:** Buddhists believe that every person should try to minimize the harm that they inflict on all beings. This belief has led several Buddhist sects to live vegan lifestyles. Cultivating a "pure heart" by making the extra effort to be as compassionate as possible easily translates into avoiding eating meat and other animal products.

- **Jainism:** Jainism is an ancient religion from India that has conscious nonviolence at the center of its dinner plates. Even though most of the Jain are vegetarians and do eat dairy or eggs, growing numbers are becoming vegan. Spiritual followers of this dharma religion believe that to be truly nonviolent, they must avoid enslaving or mistreating animals in order to take their milk or eggs.

- **Seventh-day Adventism:** Seventh-day Adventists are Christian vegetarians who have been well-studied for their dietary choices and health. These religious vegetarians and vegans believe that "demonstrating reason and restraint in daily life" by avoiding meat, tobacco, alcohol, and illicit drugs brings them closer to God. These Bible passages often are quoted to justify their food choices:

  - "I have given you every herb that yields seed which is on the face of all the earth, and every tree whose fruit yields seeds; to you it shall be for food." (Genesis 1:29)

  - "And you will eat the plants of the field." (Genesis 3:18)

  - "But flesh with the life thereof, which is the blood thereof, shall ye not eat." (Genesis 9:4)

  Following these Biblical guidelines, most Seventh-day Adventists are vegetarian, but many are becoming vegan as they further develop their spiritual beliefs.

For the rest of us vegans who don't belong to a specific religious group, the spiritual side of a plant-based diet encompasses many traditions. Every meal or bite brings with it an awareness of the pain and suffering that we're preventing for other creatures. Vegans know they're making a difference every day in the lives of others, and they take much pleasure and happiness in that. By constantly cultivating compassion, vegans protect the lives of other humans, animals, and the wide world around us.

Tackling Common Questions about Veganism

Vegans answer questions on a weekly basis about their choice to avoid animal products — so get familiar with the facts and get comfortable explaining your logic and actions. Chapter 26 even lists the most common questions you'll hear along with plenty of information to stop your inquisitors in their tracks!

Why on earth would you live like that?

Vegans see the bigger picture when it comes to making a difference with small, daily actions. For those who may not readily understand this concept, you can just brag about how much healthier you're eating with a vegan diet.

Besides, most Americans are just sick and tired. According to the National Center for Health Statistics, more than 34 percent of Americans are obese, and another 32 percent are overweight — that means 66 percent of the adults in this country could stand to lose more than a few pounds! The numbers of children that are obese and overweight are just as bad. According to the Centers for Disease Control, 32 percent of children in the United States are overweight, and 16 percent are obese. A whopping 11 percent of children are extremely obese.

All those extra pounds cause more problems than just making it difficult to find jeans that fit right. The top causes of death in America are heart disease, cancer, stroke, chronic lower respiratory diseases, accidents, and diabetes. If you're overweight but wearing your seat belt and a helmet, you're still more likely to die because you're eating a high-fat, refined diet.

The good news is that lettuce-loving vegans tend to be on the skinnier side without much effort. Some vegans are overweight, but it's a much smaller percentage of the population, consisting of around 11 percent. Membership in the vegan club has its privileges!

Not only are vegans less likely to be overweight or obese, they're also healthier overall compared to the general meat-eating population. Modern dairy and meat products have been proven to contribute to the growing numbers of people with colon, breast, ovarian, and prostate cancers. A study from

Harvard University showed that regular meat consumption increased a person's risk of developing colon cancer by about 300 percent. Eating a diet high in fat causes the human body to produce more estrogen hormones, which have been linked to breast cancer.

The good news for vegans is clear: Even if you're choosing to eat a cruelty-free diet for ethical or environmental reasons, you'll still gain substantial health benefits. And improving your own health gives you the stamina needed to create a healthier, more positive world for the rest of life's creatures!

What can a vegan eat?

As you transition to veganism, you're bound to hear people say, "You don't eat dairy? Or meat? What *do* you eat?" For strangely deep, emotional reasons, people will get passionately weird about your eating choices, but don't let this scare or deter you.

The world is ripe with vegan options if you know how to look for them. And more than 300 vegan cookbooks are on the market, so you'll never be at a loss for inspiration or delicious recipes. Table 1-1 provides a sample of vegan foods that most people eat regularly without realizing it. Included in the table are the nutrients that those vegan dishes provide.

To get started with your vegan culinary skills, check out Part IV. These chapters offer delicious, healthy vegan recipes to get you through breakfast, lunch, and dinner as well as snacks and desserts.

Is it a balanced diet?

At first you and your family may question whether you can get all the nutrition you need from a plant-based diet. The answer is absolutely! Protein, calcium, iron, and B12 are the main nutrients that newbie vegans need to pay attention to — and it's so easy to get enough from whole grains, beans, nuts, seeds, vegetables, fruit, and a couple of supplemental foods or vitamins.

Not only do vegans get enough protein, calcium, and iron, they get more fiber, vitamins, antioxidants, and phytochemicals than nonvegans. That's because they tend to eat more fresh fruits and vegetables! Chapter 4 uncovers the truths about bone health, the mysteries behind common diet-induced diseases, and options for nutritional healing.

Table 1-1 Common Vegan Foods and Their Nutrients

Food	Nutrients
Beans and rice	Protein, fiber, and complex carbohydrates
Garden salad with oil and vinegar	Fiber, phytonutrients, and monounsaturated fats
Coconut curry with vegetables and rice	Healthy fats, vitamin C, calcium, complex carbohydrates, and fiber
Hummus, pita bread, and olives	Protein, complex carbohydrates, and monounsaturated fats
Black bean dip, salsa, and guacamole with tortilla chips	Iron, protein, complex carbohydrates, fiber, vitamin C, and lycopene
Gazpacho and grilled corn on the cob	Vitamin A, and lycopene
Three-bean salad	Protein, fiber, and complex carbohydrates
Lentil soup with whole-grain bread	Protein, fiber, iron, and complex carbohydrates
Oatmeal with almonds, raisins, and maple syrup	Protein, complex carbohydrates, iron, and fiber
Steamed broccoli, tofu, and brown rice	Calcium, iron, protein, and complex carbohydrates
Stir-fried vegetables with udon noodles	Complex carbohydrates, vitamin C, iron, and calcium
Peanut butter and jelly sandwich on whole-grain bread	Protein and complex carbohydrates
Couscous with chickpeas, parsley, garlic, and lemon	Complex carbohydrates, protein, iron, vitamin K, vitamin C, and fiber
Pasta primavera with white beans, olive oil, and basil	Fiber, complex carbohydrates, protein, and monounsaturated fats

Chapter 2

Understanding the Impact of Vegan Living

In This Chapter
▶ Understanding the environmental effects of raising animals for food
▶ Looking at what really happens to animals raised for consumption
▶ Avoiding circuses and zoos

*F*our main areas of thinking inspire people to become vegan: health and environmental reasons, treatment of animals, and spiritual beliefs. These four main points have something grand in common — a deep, empathetic caring for others.

If you've chosen to live a vegan lifestyle, you've probably thought a lot about the impact your choices have on the world around you. As a conscious consumer and citizen of the world, you've begun to understand that everything you eat, do, buy, and use has an effect on someone else beside yourself. This understanding is what makes vegans the ultimate eco-warriors and agents of change.

In this chapter, I discuss the basic truths about the negative impacts that factory farming and animal consumption can have on people's health, on the environment, and, of course, on the animals themselves. This chapter also sheds light on how a vegan lifestyle helps to counteract these negatives.

Straight Talk about the Ecological Impact of Animal Protein

The practice of raising animals for human consumption is nothing new. The earliest trace of livestock being kept for slaughter dates back several thousand years and continues today around the world. However, only in the last 200 years has large-scale animal agribusiness been taking place in huge feedlots and ranches across the globe. These factory farms are called *concentrated animal feeding operations,* or CAFOs. This animal agribusiness has created systems of raising, slaughtering, and transporting animals so that the production of flesh foods can reach ever-higher quantities to satisfy the growing appetite for meat, poultry, fish, and dairy.

Tied together with rising animal production comes the rising ecological impact of these industries. Massive swaths of land are required to raise cattle, chickens, pigs, and other food animals. Countless tons of clean water are needed for these animals to drink, bathe in, and wash away their waste. Air quality is degraded in ranching and farming communities because of the huge amount of waste created by animals housed so closely together. This section details the effect that animal farming has on water and air quality.

By choosing to live a vegan life, you're sending a clear message that you understand how your choices affect the world around you, and you choose to be a force for positive change! Food production can be accomplished with less dangerous methods and more humane treatment of animals and people.

Before eating your vegan meals, say a heartfelt prayer of hope for every living critter on earth. The animals could use the psychic blessings, and even our meat-eating friends need a little spiritual support in this day and age.

Water pollution and water scarcity

When large numbers of animals are kept in a contained area, something has to be done with their waste. Many factory farms use huge man-made pools or lagoons to store the animal-made waste. These cesspools, as big as 7 acres and containing 20 to 45 million gallons of wastewater, break or overflow all the time, allowing dangerous pollution, fecal microbes, hormones, drug-resistant bacteria, and antibiotics into the local water supply. Often these pools are close to natural waterways, so the escaped sludge simply gets washed downstream into the nearest river, lake, or ocean. The laws protecting our water supplies, especially where it comes to factory farming, are weak, so little enforcement is available to protect the land and waterways.

The huge quantities of manure in the waterways contain dangerous amounts of salts, heavy metals, phosphorus, and nitrogen. Enormous *dead zones* are created when these lagoons burst into local waterways. After being released into open water, these contaminants feed algae blooms, which rob the water of oxygen, killing fish, plants, and other wildlife. Farm-animal waste also can carry dangerous microorganisms that have been linked to massive fish kills in coastal waters around the United States.

The connection between livestock production and global warming

In 2006, the United Nations' Food and Agriculture Organization (FAO) published a report titled "Livestock's Long Shadow — Environmental Issues and Options." In this report, Henning Steinfeld, the senior author of the report and head of FAO's Livestock Information and Policy Branch said, "Livestock are one of the most significant contributors to today's most serious environmental problems. Urgent action is required to remedy the situation." Livestock production was deemed to be a bigger threat and contributor to global warming than pollution from cars. So, it's true: It's more environmentally friendly to be an SUV-driving vegan than it is to be a Prius-driving meat eater!

Factory-farm manure not only causes water pollution, but it also causes water scarcity. Industrial animal agriculture requires massive amounts of groundwater for cleaning facilities, cooling animals in hot weather, and providing drinking water for the animals. According to the United Nations' Food and Agricultural Organization (FAO), countries around the world and large areas of the United States are seeing reduced water capacity for food production as well as industrial and human consumption. The main culprit is industrial agriculture and the animal factory farms, which account globally for 70 percent of all water usage. In short, we're running out of clean drinking water and irrigation water because we're using it to raise animals for slaughter. Vegan diet, anyone?

Fish farms have been hailed as the answer to overfishing the oceans. Sadly, these contained areas are creating pollution and abuse issues of their own. Up to a million fish, including salmon and trout, can be farmed in one penned area. The fish waste is concentrated and allowed to settle like untreated sewage into the surrounding ocean. The pollution is so bad that most other fish and marine life are forced from the area, creating an ocean desert. The farmed fish carry diseases like sea lice, which then infect other free-swimming fish, destroying wild stocks.

The most absurd part of this equation is that fish farms grind up so many wild fish to feed to the farmed fish that more fish are destroyed than are created. It takes more than 2 pounds of wild fish to produce 1 pound of farmed salmon. This math shows that fish farms exacerbate the very problem they were created to solve.

Toxic odor and air pollution

Smell something funny? It's probably the animal farm down the road. CAFOs jam together huge numbers of large animals that produce lots of odor. These odors from animal gas, waste lagoons, and waste treatment methods combine to form pollution clouds that threaten human health and the surrounding environment. Sadly the Environmental Protection Agency (EPA) and most states have done little to regulate these emissions. Being vegan means being part of the solution instead of part of the problem — keep choosing that tofu scramble over the eggs Benedict!

Odors from all this waste can be stifling. The unbearable smells from large-scale animal agriculture cause a wide range of respiratory illnesses, fatigue, and depression. They also affect land values, leaving some homeowners stuck with property they can't sell.

What if, like CAFOs, you had millions of pounds of waste to dispose of every year? One method these farms use is to simply spray the liquid and solid waste into the air like a volcanic fountain in hopes that the wind and weather will disperse it. Hardly. Instead, surrounding humans are being showered in fine particles of waste.

People who live near waste disposal fountains experience breathing problems, asthma, and bronchitis as a direct result of exposure to the high concentration of particulates in the air. Animal waste contains ammonia, which is released into the air from lagoons, spray-field applications, and barns.

As you can see, besides helping spare their four-legged friends from becoming dinner, vegans also score high humanitarian points for protecting their fellow two-legged friends from being negatively affected by these nasty practices, too!

Mountains of manure

Some CAFOs pile animal manure into areas where it can then be used or redistributed. The laws governing waste-use on the land are too gray to really protect the environment and humans living around these large-scale operations. These manure piles can cause massive fly outbreaks and attract coyotes and rats if dead animals are in the piles. When placed near residential homes, the air quality is of course intensely affected.

Disease is spread through animal waste, and all humans are in danger of getting sick, even if they don't eat meat. Dairy cow operations have discharged manure onto piles of hay; that manure can then leach into the soil and surrounding water table and into county drains, contaminating large areas with dangerous levels of E. coli bacteria. The massive spinach recalls in 2006 due to E. coli were ultimately linked to animal waste from a nearby CAFO. Many health experts agree that a majority of intestinal reactions that humans have are caused by campylobacter, E. coli, listeria, and salmonella.

Bacteria in and on our foods are a health concern, but so are the man-made chemicals that are used to produce those foods. According to the EPA, more than 160 chemicals are found in and around manure from confined animal feeding operations. Growth hormones used to increase milk production in dairy cows, antibiotics, cleaning solvents to sanitize the barns, blood, oils and chemicals used to clean and maintain equipment, and copper sulfate are just a few of the possible contaminants found in animal manure.

When you're vegan, you can rest assured that your veggie burgers and fries aren't adding to this distasteful situation.

Having Reverence for All Life

Living a vegan lifestyle makes real the respect you hold for the well-being of all animals, including humans. Eating a vegan diet goes a long way toward providing every living creature with enough food to eat, clean water to drink, and clean air to breathe.

The deepest eco-consciousness is reached when no creature is killed or harmed for your lifestyle. By choosing not to eat animals or their products, or pay to watch them perform, vegans choose to live in ways that respect all life. It's soul-satisfying to look at the natural world around you and feel at peace with your place in it.

Taking action against food injustice and malnutrition around the world

Malnutrition is a major killer of infants and children around the world. The saddest part of this tragedy is that many of these deaths are totally preventable. We have plenty of food to go around, but that food is unequally distributed. While many humans go hungry because of corrupt governments, war, and famine, we also feed too much grain and other vegetable food to animals being raised for meat. If we all stopped eating meat, we would have enough food for all the humans on this planet, and then some.

Not only would more calories be available for human consumption, but more land would be available to raise more food. *Arable land,* or land that's suitable to grow crops, is often used to raise animals instead.

Pigs, cows, chickens, and fish need to eat in order to become dense enough for slaughter and to become our food. These animals naturally eat grains, grasses, fruits, and vegetables — the same foods that humans can live on. But in order for a cow to get big enough for us to eat or milk it, the cow must eat many more calories than it will produce for us to consume.

Estimates vary, but it could take anywhere from 3 to 16 pounds of grain to produce one pound of beef. According to the United States Department of Agriculture's educational pamphlet for children, cows eat up to 100 pounds of mixed feed a day and drink up to 30 to 50 gallons of fresh water a day. This equation doesn't add up in a world where so many humans are starving for food and thirsting for clean drinking water.

The beauty of veganism is that you get to enjoy healthy, delicious food while knowing that your choices aren't harming anyone else. Eating lower on the food chain means that your vegan diet increases the amount of food available for other people.

Standing up for animals

Meat eaters are often animal lovers — they love their dogs, cats, hamsters, and other pets. These companion animals are allowed to eat at the table (or at least in the house), and are even dressed up and paraded around as a source of pride. Most people would never consider eating their pets. Why then is this love and affection not extended to animals that humans raise to serve as food?

The harsh reality of how agricultural animals are treated is simply too heavy for many people to endure, so they just choose not to think about it. Others believe that animals don't feel pain or psychological trauma the way that humans do, which excuses any harsh treatment. Vegans know that animals are our companions in life and that they deserve respect and care no matter what form they take.

The laws that protect companion animals, such as dogs and cats, from inhumane treatment and mistreatment don't apply to most of the millions of farm animals that are raised as food for humans.

Saying no to animal-based food and clothing

Vegans are pretty savvy to the marketing magic that advertisers flash on screen, and we choose to confront the realities of animal agriculture by enjoying plant foods instead. Farm animals are rarely protected from modern factory-farming techniques, which inflict pain and discomfort and keep the animals from their natural social tendencies. Following are a few examples:

- **Cattle:** Cows raised for beef generally have more time outside than their female relatives. But these cows don't escape torture and pain. Beef calves are usually dehorned, males are castrated, and many of these animals are burned with searing brands. After cattle reach market weight, they're stunned with a severe knock to the head, bled, and skinned. Many wake up from being stunned during the final stages of their slaughtering.

✔ **Chickens:** Most chickens raised for consumption never see the light of day — they live their entire lives in a warehouse-style factory farm. Packed into tiny cages with several other chickens, they aren't able to raise their wings or follow their natural instincts of pecking and scratching the ground. So they peck and scratch each other. This can cause too much damage to valuable poultry, so the chickens are debeaked at a young age, which, as you can imagine, is a painful process.

✔ **Pigs:** Because of their huge size, farmed pigs are kept from hurting each other by being forced to live most of their lives in crates. They can't turn around or walk more than a few steps forward or backward. Pregnant sows are kept in farrowing crates, which gives them just enough space to deliver and suckle their litters. These incredibly inhumane crates have horrified enough voters that California, Florida, and Arizona have finally made them illegal.

Meat and dairy aren't the only items to be avoided. Leather is another one of the many products culled from the meat industry. This isn't the only animal skin that humans wear either. Fur farms raise many types of animals for their skins, including mink, chinchillas, and foxes. Kept in small, confined cages, these animals are killed as quickly and cheaply as possible. Anal electrocution, lethal injection of poisons, violent shaking, and beating are routine methods to kill these animals.

Why dairy isn't okay, and why vegans are the only true vegetarians

Dairy cows are separated from their babies within a day or two after giving birth. The female calves become dairy producers while the male calves become veal. By drinking cow's milk (even organic), humans are contributing to the death of veal calves. The mother cows bellow and cry for their babies, much like any human would. They're continually drugged with hormones to force their bodies to continue producing milk. And they're milked by machines long after they would have stopped naturally. And to top it off, they're given antibiotics to stave off infection from their poor, crowded living conditions.

They stand up in cramped stalls, in artificially lit warehouses, with little to no access to the outdoors, for most of their lives. The constant cycle of forced pregnancy and milking leads to a severely shortened lifespan. Cows naturally live to the age of 15 or 20 years old. A factory farmed cow usually lives to the age of 4 to 6. After her milk production starts to wane, a dairy cow is most often turned into hamburger. This cycle makes vegetarians (who consume dairy products) complicit in the killing of animals, even if they aren't eating the meat itself. Avoiding dairy products means vegans aren't contributing to the pain and suffering of these gentle giants.

Not only are they raised and killed with terrible methods, but these fur animals also are adding to the wave of pollution pouring out of factory farms. Fur and leather processing is a toxic industry in which the animal skins are treated with a chemical soup to keep them from shedding and rotting. Ammonia, formaldehyde, bleaching agents, acids, and chromium wastes are just a few of the chemicals that make leather tanning and fur processing an environmental disaster.

Looking amazing and feeling great about what you're wearing are secret benefits of living vegan! See Chapter 11 for tips on vegan fashions.

Staying away from circuses and zoos

Circus and zoo animals live a bizarre and trapped existence. The training necessary to create an animal circus performer often requires violence and pain. Elephants, tigers, bears, and horses can be trained with whips, muzzles, electric prods, tight collars, and sharp hooks.

The deeply held belief that we as humans are far superior to any other creature allows us to torture and abuse these thinking, feeling creatures. Many countries around the world, including Austria, Costa Rica, India, Finland, Singapore, and Sweden have either banned or restricted the use of animals for entertainment. Because you're sensitive to the realities of the world, as a vegan you'll most likely want to avoid animal circuses and zoos. Luckily, several popular and stunning human circuses like Cirque du Soleil can provide vegans with fantastic humane entertainment!

While zoos and wildlife enclosures seem to be a kind method to connect humans with the natural world, what goes on behind the scenes can be cruel. Charges have been brought against some zoos and zookeepers for the trauma, stress, physical harm, and unnecessary discomfort inflicted on zoo animals. Some zoos also sell off animals to circuses. At least one instance was documented where the Minnesota Zoo sold more than 100 animals from its petting zoo to a slaughterhouse.

There are more humane ways to enjoy watching the majesty of animals. For instance, farm animal sanctuaries can be found all over the country. These kind operations rescue farm animals that have escaped factory farms or that were given away by their owners. Some wild animal sanctuaries take care of retired circus and zoo animals as well, offering them a safe place to live until they die. Nature programs, documentaries, and the Internet can be used to research and discover the beauty of the animal kingdom. To find a farm animal sanctuary, go to www.farmanimalshelters.org and look for a shelter near you!

Chapter 3

Transforming to Veganism

In This Chapter

▶ Deciding whether giving up nonvegan foods all at once is for you

▶ Understanding why making the switch slowly may be more effective

▶ Following some basic guidelines when giving up meat and dairy

Changing your whole diet and lifestyle from the standard, modern method of doing things to a vegan way can be challenging without the proper planning. For most new vegans, their metamorphosis means more than just saying so long to hot dogs and ham and cheese sandwiches. Because this lifestyle encompasses health concerns, a deep environmentalism, and a way of caring about animals' rights that is outside the norm, becoming vegan involves every aspect of a person's life. But this way of living and being in the world will bring personal, emotional, physical, and global benefits.

No one can tell you how exactly these changes will occur in your life, because each individual has a unique set of circumstances to consider. Who you live with, where you live, what your job is like, and how much support you have all make a difference. If you're a butcher in Wisconsin, for example, you've got your work cut out for you. This chapter can help you decide when and how to make the switch from a meat and dairy diet to a vegan one. Just remember that every step forward toward a vegan lifestyle, whether fast or slow, is a positive step for yourself and the greater world around you.

Going Cold Tofurky

If going cold Tofurky is your preferred method of vegan transition, be aware that you may have some slip-ups. Don't beat yourself up over a bacon cheeseburger a few weeks in. A full transition will take time. In fact, you may find in the end that it's more difficult to live a completely vegan lifestyle with all the clothing, furniture, and products necessary than just focusing on eating a vegan diet.

Just keep in mind that staying positive and keeping a creative mindset are important character traits when trying to endure any setbacks or challenges.

The pros of converting quickly

Immediately getting rid of every morsel of meat or dollop of dairy can be a really satisfying experience on many different fronts. Consider these benefits of converting quickly:

- ✔ **You may notice the health benefits quickly.** For someone who has health problems that are exacerbated by meat, has excess weight to lose, or is sensitive or allergic to dairy, this method can yield near immediate positive feelings. Imagine that you've been having asthma, a runny nose, or allergies for years, and then all of a sudden your phlegm disappears because you stopped drinking milk and eating cheese just a few days ago — it's a terrific feeling, and you'll want it to continue. How's that for an incentive?

- ✔ **You can be relieved that you're no longer contributing to animal cruelty.** If animal rights and the moral issues behind veganism are an important part of your decision, you'll immediately feel so much better about eating food that doesn't contribute to the pain and suffering of others. When you realize how inhumanely animals are raised and feel compassion for the creatures that humans eat, it can be really heartbreaking to continue eating them yourself. So making the switch quickly will be a huge relief to your conscience.

- ✔ **You can be energized by the change in lifestyle.** Many people find it fun and exciting to have a life full of purpose and a new way of doing their daily deeds. Buying different foods, exploring new shops and Web sites, and discovering the complexities of a vegan life can feel truly energizing.

The cons of going too fast

Adopting the vegan way of doing things too quickly can be dizzying with its complexities and new rules. Keep in mind some of the drawbacks to moving too fast:

- ✔ **Your health may initially be affected and can cause you to crash and burn or get sick during a busy workweek.** Detoxing from meat and dairy foods is a possible side effect when you choose to go vegan. When the body stops storing the constant influx of unhealthy fats and proteins, it will finally have a chance to let go and cleanse. This cleansing can be physically uncomfortable and may result in headaches, acne, tiredness, or the urge to invade small countries. Your digestive system may not be accustomed to such large amounts of fiber, so you also could notice some bloating and increased bowel movements at the beginning of your transition.

✔ **You may go broke trying to replace every animal product in your home.** Donating or throwing away everything that was tested on or was once part of an animal can leave your cupboards bare and your house and closets empty. Replacing the leather sofa costs money as will filling up your refrigerator with vegan food. Think about how much you need to throw out to be truly vegan — and how much money you'll need to spend to replace it.

✔ **You may make mistakes if you don't do the proper research beforehand.** You're probably going to mess up in the first few weeks of being vegan. If you go too quickly and don't research all the foods, ingredients, and products you buy and use, you may continue using things that were tested on animals or that use animal ingredients. Still, messing up isn't a good reason to give up — if you trip going down the stairs, do you swear off stairs forever? No. You get up, dust yourself off, and start walking down again. Keep it up, and you'll figure it out. And eventually you'll be sliding down the banister!

Taking a Slow, Systematic Approach

Most new vegans find that a less abrupt, slow and steady transition approach works best for them. Changing your diet and lifestyle completely can be really challenging, and doing everything at once can be stressful. So, by taking your time, you're less likely to make major, costly mistakes.

Advantages of taking your time

Sudden changes to your diet can cause many surprising results, but making a slower switch to veganism can help reduce the consequences. Here are some reasons why:

✔ **You won't stress out trying to substitute foods for every animal product you're used to eating.** Consider giving up one nonvegan food category a week. Cheese, milk, meat, eggs, and butter can all move out of your life slowly as you figure out how to substitute for them with new vegan foods. Taking your time allows you to ask questions and discover new protein, fat, and nutrient sources as you move forward.

✔ **You'll encounter less discomfort from detoxifying side effects.** The human body has incredible systems in place to help detoxify and release harmful foods, liquids, and chemicals. The skin can sweat out impurities, the liver deals with unhealthy fats, and the bowels release waste. It's truly amazing what the human body is capable of doing to heal and cleanse itself, if given half a chance. However, this "spring cleaning" effect can manifest itself with some unwanted symptoms like headaches, fatigue, rashes, sleeplessness, fever, temporary loss of menstruation, diarrhea or constipation, increased methane emissions (if you know what I mean), and acne.

REMEMBER

People who move to a vegan diet very quickly are more likely to experience these symptoms. Taking your time will allow the body to work these processes slowly, causing less discomfort. Going cold Tofurky can sometimes be pretty painful!

✔ **You'll ease the flow of money out of your new pleather wallet.** If you throw out everything in your house that was tested on animals or that's made of leather, wool, silk, beeswax, dairy, meat, or eggs, your house may look the way it did the day before you moved in: Empty! Allowing more time to replace items that get used up, worn out, or eaten will spread the expenses out and make the cost more manageable.

Problems with pacing yourself

As you probably know, transitioning slowly to veganism isn't all daisies and sunshine. You may run into a few problems, including the following:

✔ **You may be impatient and find the waiting to be frustrating.** If you're the type who likes to make a decision and jump right into new habits, taking your time to make your whole life vegan may be too annoying for you. You may get bored or frustrated because you know what you want to do and how you want to live, but you can't afford to make all the necessary changes.

✔ **The prolonging of detoxifying effects may trouble you more than just getting it done and over with.** While the "shock and awe" method of quick detoxification can be too much for some new vegans, others may experience such painful physical problems that they're ready to get their bodies cleaned out as quickly as possible. When you've hit bottom physically, a few days of detoxification symptoms may be preferable to waiting weeks for relief.

The Nuts and Bolts of Changing Over

Whether you're going cold Tofurky or transitioning over time, going vegan is a life-changing event that requires you to do and remember a few basic things to be successful. I explain these nuts and bolts, including timing, education, planning, and experimentation with new foods, in the following sections.

Choosing your timing wisely

Whether you decide to be 100 percent vegan tomorrow or make the transition over the next few months, you'll want to make a plan to ensure that you don't make big changes during inconvenient times. Going vegan right before a rehearsal dinner at a steak house may be tough. Similarly, if you're about to go on a three-week vacation to Brazil, you'll find it much more difficult to eat a vegan diet if you're not experienced in choosing vegan foods. In other words, go vegan slowly over a few weeks where you aren't required to do something important: take finals, present a paper at a business conference, or give birth — there's no point in adding extra stress to an already stressful life.

Choose an easy week, and get started over the weekend so you have time to plan a week of meals, shop, and research your local resources. You can make a commitment to eating one or two vegan meals a day for the first week, adding vegan snacks and more meals as you go forward. Perhaps you have a three-day weekend coming up, or your job duties are going to be really relaxed at the end of a big project. These times would be excellent for starting to cook more or to switch from cow's milk to soy, rice, or hemp milk. You also can add another change at this time, such as eliminating white sugar, which is often processed with bone char from animals, and honey and replacing them with agave syrup. Keep building on these changes. As you master one major item, try another.

Making time to cook on a regular basis can bring you many benefits. Cooking your own food from scratch saves you money over time, because you can avoid relying on more expensive convenience items. Getting down and dirty in the kitchen also connects you with your food on a new level and helps you appreciate new flavors. When you have time to experiment, get creative with new produce and products to avoid getting stuck in a food rut. Or check out the many vegan cookbooks and recipes online to get inspired.

Educating yourself and enrolling your comrades

You've already chosen an excellent first step in educating yourself — reading this book! Looking at vegan Web sites, talking with other long-time vegans, discovering which ingredients to avoid, and buying a few vegan cookbooks also can help you prepare. Understanding how to feed yourself, what to eat, and where to get the foods and products you need are necessary skills. You don't have to be a doctor to understand the foundations of healthy living; it's easy to become a student of nutrition, food, and healing. Plus knowing the facts about veganism helps you explain your decision to become a vegan when you're confronted with questions and doubts.

You may be the only person you know who's brave enough to try a vegan diet, but it can't hurt to ask for support from your family and good friends. If they understand why this is important to you, what you plan to do, and what you may need from them in order to be successful, they'll likely offer their help or resources. Perhaps your father works with a vegan or your friend's sister works at a vegan-friendly restaurant. Cast a wide net and see what comes back to you! It's not often that you get to experience a major shift in life and truly rely on the wisdom of those who have gone before you.

Making healthier decisions by planning your meals ahead of time

Planning your meals in advance is the best way to make a healthy, less-stressful transition to veganism. Your diet may be changing drastically from bacon three meals a day, or you may just be eliminating dairy from your already vegetarian diet. Either way, you'll feel much better if you set your eating goals and write down a week's worth of menus. And think how great you'll feel when you stop buying bacon!

By using a meal planning guide (see Chapter 9) and working from a list of foods you know you want to eat more of, you can sketch out a good idea of what you need to buy. If you want to eat more leafy green vegetables, whole grains, or sea vegetables, choosing recipes that will incorporate those healing foods makes it more likely that you'll accomplish your goal.

Reminding yourself why you've chosen veganism

Display items that remind you of your dedication to living a vegan lifestyle. Print a quote or picture to hang on your wall or refrigerator that will inspire you and confirm your commitment. Some inspiring framed photos of farm animals enjoying a natural setting, kids frolicking with baby lambs, famous vegans, or brilliant philosophers can offer the visual clue you need to keep up your daily practice.

Try hand painting a stirring quote around the walls of your kitchen to inspire your cooking.

Albert Schweitzer, French philosopher and Nobel prize winner said: "Until he extends the circle of his compassion to all living things, man will not himself find peace." This quote from Albert Einstein can offer great pride in any home: "It is my view that the vegetarian manner of living, by its purely physical effect on the human temperament, would most beneficially influence the lot of mankind."

Knowing what you're going to make for dinner on Wednesday (or any other particular day of the week) helps you plan your daily schedule better so you're sure to have enough time allotted to cook at the end of the day. It also saves you and your family from bickering and deciding on takeout or veggie burgers yet again. Keep in mind that it's often easier to plan for bigger cooking projects on the weekend, because you'll have more free time and fewer obligations to worry about. And if you cook enough on the weekend, you can have leftovers to make the next week that much easier.

Purging nonvegan products from your life

Some of the nonvegan foods you'll be avoiding are pretty obvious: cheddar cheese made from cow's milk? Chuck it. Steaks in the freezer? Give 'em to the meat eater down the hall, or throw them away. Most vegans start avoiding these foods immediately once they set their minds to it.

Other ingredients aren't as easily avoided. You may find out a few days into your new vegan diet that your favorite crackers have honey in them or that the skin cream you love is made with goat's milk. Sitting on your leather sofa or car seats may gross you out after you comprehend their origins.

Go easy on yourself when you make your decisions about what to throw away and what to use until it's gone. If you can't afford to buy all new beauty aids this month, use what you have and replace each bottle of shampoo or lotion with a cruelty-free brand when the old one is gone. Perhaps you don't have anyone you can give your dozen eggs to and you don't want to waste them — maybe it's better to eat the rest of the package, say a prayer and blessing for the chickens, and buy some tofu next week instead.

You can stop using every nonvegan item today, or you can take your time. It's up to you, and no one should judge your decisions. You're already making more conscious actions, and you'll continue to improve as time goes on.

Getting to know your new community

Reach out and touch the faithful — vegans, that is. By joining a local vegan potluck group (or even a vegetarian one if that's all you can find), you'll meet like-minded people who have similar values to yours. Getting to know others who see the world as you do can help you feel connected and as if you're a part of something bigger. The folks who belong to these groups know where to buy the food you need, can share strategies with you, may teach you new recipes, and can even point out possible pitfalls. They also can help you find that fabulous vegan outfit you need for your high school reunion.

Local vegan groups may be involved in political actions or animal rescue work, which can bring a new level of meaning to your vegan lifestyle. Get involved and educated about the issues in your community so that your new theoretical lifestyle will have a real-world impact. Getting involved also shows the people around you how the ethics of your diet play out in everyday life. Many people are won over by the upstanding moral code of veganism after they see the passion and dedication their friend or family member pours into a local environmental or animal rights cause.

Focusing on the fun and adventure of being a vegan

Eating can become a mundane chore if you aren't careful. By focusing on the celebration of life, as displayed in a well-planned meal, vegan dining offers you the chance to return to honoring nature's bounty. Focusing on the fun and joy of real, natural, cruelty-free food can turn every meal, no matter how elaborate or simple, into a party.

The fun of sharing food together and searching out the new and different menus available for vegans is one of the best parts of adopting this lifestyle. A new world of tastes, products, and guilt-free meals awaits you. Make it your intention to share the glorious natural foods with your friends and family (whether they're vegan or not). Giving them the gift of healthy vegan recipes shows your love for them and all the world's creatures. Not to mention you'll be helping them get their daily dose of roughage.

Get adventurous with your meals. Even if you're preparing a simple salad for yourself, you can incorporate homegrown herbs and tomatoes that connect you to the season. When thinking of your family's upcoming reunion feast, ask the local farmers at your farmer's market what will be in peak season that week. By bringing luscious, fresh produce, you can share the story of your trip to the market, explain what you chose, and reveal how you prepared it. Not only will this show your own dedication to good food, it also may encourage those around you to try new, more sustainable fare.

Part II
Building a Healthy Vegan Diet

The 5th Wave   By Rich Tennant

"Nutritionally, we follow the Vegan Food Guide Pyramid. When I first met Philip, he ate from the Food Guide Stonehenge. It was a mysterious diet and no one's sure what its purpose was."

In this part . . .

A well-rounded vegan diet provides everything a human body needs for healthy growth and development and maintenance of proper body functions. Yet living in this meat- and dairy-loving culture can confuse even the most well-read herbivore. Vegans constantly are questioned about their nutritional wellness and the validity of their food choices.

That's why this part is so important! These chapters not only lay the foundation for vegan nutritional wellness, they also detail how to make the most health-supportive choices when it comes to cooking, shopping for food, and ordering meals.

Chapter 4

Essential Nutrients for Healthy Success

. . . .

In This Chapter

▶ Getting to know the B vitamins

▶ Discovering the truth about calcium

▶ Uncovering the solid facts about iron

▶ Finding out about vitamin D and zinc

▶ Maintaining good health with vegan supplements

. . . .

The human body requires special nutrients to ensure healthy growth and good energy. Vitamins and minerals are like the nuts and bolts that keep the human machine held together and running properly.

In this chapter, I discuss where to get the vitamins and minerals that may be lacking in plant foods. B12 and B2, as well as vitamin D, are found readily in animal foods, so you may be concerned about getting enough in a vegan diet. Iron, calcium and zinc are minerals that may, at first glance, be harder to get from vegan foods. There are excellent plant sources of these natural minerals, and even some ways to help your body utilize them better. The final section in this chapter also addresses whether vegans need to use supplements and if so, what types to try.

The bottom line for proper nutrition is that natural food is your best bet for all-around health. Separating nutrients and vitamins into stand-alone sources of nutrition can lead to overdose or an inadvertent depletion of another necessary vitamin or mineral.

"B"-ing Healthy with B12 and B2

B vitamins often are referred to as a *complex* — this doesn't mean that they're difficult to understand and have a lot of emotional issues; it just means that they all need to be present in order for the body to use them properly. While most of the B vitamins can be found easily in plant foods, vegans need to be aware that two very important B vitamins — B12 and B2 — are a little harder to find in plant foods. So be sure to include in your diet foods that have been fortified.

B12 is the most important of all the B vitamins when you're a vegan. Necessary for building blood and cell division, B12 isn't made by any plants or animals — it's actually made by bacteria. Humans used to get their B12 by eating foods contaminated with bacteria that had produced the B12. However, because our food is so clean and sterilized these days, we don't get a reliable source of B12 from bacteria. The other main source of bacteria-produced B12 is animal flesh. Food animals still eat bacteria, which accumulates the B12 in their flesh and muscles. Research also shows that the bacteria in the human body make small amounts of B12. But, because the body may not absorb and use it, you're still better off using fortified foods or B complexes.

B12 deficiency isn't common, but can be serious, leading to nerve damage and anemia. The body also uses B12 to protect nerve fibers and metabolize and use carbohydrates, fat, and protein. The most common sign of B12 deficiency is fatigue, which can be avoided with a well-planned diet that includes B12-rich foods or regular supplementation.

B2, also known as riboflavin, is easier to find in plant foods than B12, but it's still important to be aware of the vegan sources you can get it from. Important for overall skin and eye health, B2 is also necessary for cellular energy production. Deficiencies of B2 can lead to mouth and lip sores, a swollen tongue, and dermatitis.

I give you the lowdown on vitamins B2 and B12 in the following sections, including where to find them and how much to consume.

Finding B12 and B2 in vegan foods

These days B12 is often added to a variety of vegan foods, so be sure to have these items on your weekly shopping list:

- Fortified cereals
- Nutritional yeast flakes, like Red Star
- Fortified soy, rice, and hemp milks
- Fortified fake meats made from wheat gluten and soy

Note: Some fermented soy foods like miso, natto, and tempeh, as well as some sea vegetables, have been reported to contain vitamin B12. The amounts found in these foods are too small to make them reliable sources.

B2 is a bit easier to find in natural vegetables. The following items are easy sources to work into your menu on a regular basis:

✔ Almonds	✔ Asparagus
✔ Bananas	✔ Broccoli
✔ Brussels sprouts	✔ Mushrooms
✔ Nutritional yeast	✔ Peas
✔ Soybeans	✔ Soymilk, fortified
✔ Spinach	✔ Whole grains
✔ Wheat germ	✔ Wild rice

Getting enough of the right kind

Even though many foods are fortified with B12, vegans can still be deficient. This deficiency isn't due to the amount they consume; instead it's due to the fact that their body isn't absorbing the B12 from the intestines well. In this case, a probiotic, to improve the health and ability of the digestive system to absorb nutrients properly, and a B-complex vitamin would be useful. You also may try other measures to ensure that the intestines are healthy and working properly. A daily probiotic can help ensure that the good bacteria are present to help digest and absorb nutrients in the gut. A high-fiber diet, which isn't difficult to achieve as a vegan, helps keep the digestive system clean and clear.

Luckily, the human body doesn't need a huge amount of B12; however, it does need a little bit on a regular basis. The current RDA for B12 is 2.4 micrograms a day. About 2 tablespoons of nutritional yeast fortified with B12 can provide your daily dose. Sprinkle nutritional yeast on air-popped popcorn, salads, and pasta; stir it into soups; or use one of the many vegan recipes that use nutritional yeast to imitate cheese. Try the Hungry Man Tofu Scramble or the Tempeh Hash recipes in Part IV with Red Star Nutritional Yeast — it's fortified with B12.

Counting on Calcium for Strong Bones

Have you ever seen a cow or elephant up close? These enormous animals carry around their hefty weight on strong bones, much like ours. Where do you think these gigantic animals get the calcium to create their bones? Do they drink cow's milk as the USDA recommends? Of course not. They eat plants.

While humans and animals certainly don't build their bodies in the same way — or even digest food in exactly the same way — humans, like animals, can get the required calcium needed to build bones from plant foods. Our bones hold the largest store of the calcium in our bodies; when they're healthy, bones are firm and rigid. The body doesn't just use calcium to build bones, however; it also needs the mineral to clot blood and for many muscle and nerve functions.

Plant foods, like leafy green vegetables, have a better bioavailability of calcium than dairy products. This means that our bodies can better absorb and use the calcium present in these greens as compared to dairy foods. While dairy foods are rich in calcium, they are also rich in protein, which inhibits the body's ability to absorb calcium. A vegan diet rich in greens and calcium-enriched foods will ensure the recommended intake of 1,000-1,200 milligrams a day is met.

In this section, I help you understand your calcium requirements, and I tell you how, as a vegan, you can successfully meet those requirements. I round out the section by discussing calcium's role in the important acid-alkaline ratio in the body.

Boning up on calcium requirements

Most nutrition guidelines recommend getting between 800 to 1,500 milligrams of calcium a day, mostly from dairy products. The United States Department of Agriculture (USDA) guidelines state that to avoid osteoporosis and grow healthy bones, these levels must be reached. However, according to the Physicians Committee for Responsible Medicine, healthy bones can be maintained with a daily consumption of 600 milligrams a day. And the World Health Organization (WHO) recommends between 400 and 500 milligrams daily, which is half of the U.S. recommended dietary allowance.

When paired with a healthy nonsmoking lifestyle, regular weight-bearing exercise, and healthy levels of vitamins D and K, the body can build and maintain healthy bones on a sensible vegan diet.

Never heard of vitamin K? That's because it's so easy to get all you need from natural foods that people rarely worry about it. Vitamin K helps blood to clot, protects bones, and prevents cell damage from oxidation. If you find yourself bruising and bleeding easily or having liver, gallbladder, or digestive system problems, you may need more vitamin K. Good sources are spinach, Brussels sprouts, carrots, green beans, peas, broccoli, kale, and asparagus.

The truth about dairy products

The dairy industry has a lot of money and has been influencing the government, the American public, and health organizations to believe that their products are necessary for good health for decades. But the story doesn't hold up. If we eat more dairy products than most countries on the planet, why do we have some of the highest osteoporosis rates? There's clearly more to the story. To truly build strong, healthy bones and avoid other major health problems, green leafy veggies, which are often lacking in the average American's diet, are better sources of calcium than dairy products.

To prove my point, consider the Harvard Nurses' Health Study that was published in 2003. This study followed more than 72,000 women for 18 years and found no link between increased milk consumption and risk of fractures. On a similar note, in his groundbreaking research project, *The China Study,* Dr. T. Colin Campbell showed that the vast majority of the population of China consumes no dairy products. Instead, these people get their calcium from mostly plant-based sources, including green leafy vegetables.

American women have one of the highest rates of hip fracture in the world. The only other countries with higher rates — a few Northern European countries as well as Australia and New Zealand — actually eat more dairy than we do. On the other hand, Chinese women have much lower osteoporosis and hip fracture rates, and they eat no dairy. Instead, these women get their calcium from leafy green veggies, tofu, and other natural foods like nuts and seeds.

Seeking out calcium in vegan foods

Since you won't be consuming dairy products to reach your daily calcium requirements, you may be wondering what foods you should eat. Don't worry. You have tons of wonderful, natural vegan foods available to you that will ensure you have enough calcium in your diet. Just be sure to eat a variety of the foods in Table 4-1 on a regular basis.

Spinach, amaranth, rhubarb, chard, and beet greens, which may seem like good sources of calcium, all contain *oxalic acid,* which can bind with calcium and reduce its absorption. These foods are healthy in general, but they shouldn't be considered good sources of calcium because they can cause the body to lose as much calcium as it gains. Other greens like kale, broccoli, mustard greens, and bok choy are better calcium choices.

Table 4-1	Vegan Sources of Calcium	
Food	**Amount**	**Calcium (mg)**
Vegetables		
Collard greens	1 cup	350
Turnip greens	1 cup	250
Kale	1 cup	180
Okra	1 cup	170
Bok choy	1 cup	160
Arame (sea vegetable)	½ cup	100
Broccoli	1 cup	90
Wakame (sea vegetable)	⅓ cup	77
Kelp	⅓ cup	66
Fruits		
Currants, zante, dried	1 cup	86
Prunes	1 cup	75–95
Orange	1 large	74
Apricots, dried	1 cup	73
Currants, black, fresh	1 cup	62
Blackberries	1 cup	42
Fig, fresh	1 fig	18
Beans and Grains		
Cornmeal, self-rising	1 cup	483
Wheat flour, enriched	1 cup	423
White beans, cooked	1 cup	130
Quinoa	1 cup	102
Oats	1 cup	84
Chickpeas	1 cup	80
Rye flour, dark	1 cup	72
Buckwheat flour	1 cup	49
Bulgur	1 cup	49
Nuts and Seeds		
Almonds	¼ cup	89
Sesame seeds, whole	1 Tbsp.	88
Walnuts, black	1 cup	76
Pecans	1 cup	70

Food	Amount	Calcium (mg)
Tahini	2 Tbsp.	64–154
Brazil nuts	1 oz.	45
Hazelnuts	1 oz.	42
Almond butter	1 Tbsp.	40
Flaxseeds	1 Tbsp.	26
Sunflower seeds	1 oz.	25
Soy Foods		
Tofu (made with calcium sulfate)	4 oz.	200–325
Edamame (soybeans)	½ cup	197
Soy yogurt	8 oz.	150–350
Soymilk	8 oz.	80-300
Other		
Enriched orange juice	1 cup	300
Blackstrap molasses	2 tsp.	80–120 mg

Source: From the USDA and manufacturer information

Avoiding foods that leach calcium

The WHO recommends half the daily calcium intake that the United States National Academy of Sciences recommends. So, if the rest of the world is consuming less calcium than we are, why do we have more osteoporosis? (I discuss this question in the nearby sidebar, "The truth about dairy products.") The secret part of the calcium story is that calcium isn't the only player in the bone health game. Excess acids, protein, and alcohol cause the body to leach calcium out of the bones, setting them up for fractures and osteoporosis.

For example, several well-publicized studies have shown that soda drinkers of all ages have higher rates of broken bones and fractures than people who don't drink soda. Most sodas, both regular and diet, contain phosphorus or citric acid. The phosphorus and citric acid in these drinks create too much acidity in the body. And your body is so smart that it can balance the acid-alkaline ratio by drawing calcium (an alkaline material) out of the bones.

The human body likes to stay in a narrow range on the acid-alkaline scale. Calcium is the most plentiful mineral in the human body and it is alkaline, as opposed to acidic. A diet high in acidic foods like dairy, meat, and refined sugars, can lead to fatigue, stiffness, and canker sores. When the body gets too acidic, calcium is drawn out of the bones for an alkalinizing effect, therefore evening out the balance, but weakening the bones.

Like acids, excessive amounts of protein also affect bone health. A diet high in animal protein is high in sulfur, because amino acids contain sulfur. These sulfur-based amino acids negatively affect the body's pH balance, causing the bones to release calcium stores so the body can become more alkaline. Protein from plants have less sulfur-based amino acids, so they're already more alkaline and less likely to cause calcium leaching. So, if you want healthy bones, you should avoid meat and eat more green leafy veggies!

Pumping Up Your Iron Intake

Big guys in weight rooms may be the ultimate icons of strong bodies and human health, but vegans can pump some iron too with natural foods for supreme health. It's true that iron is vitally important for energy, but it's also a needed component of *hemoglobin* — the part of our blood that carries oxygen. *Anemia,* dangerous iron deficiency, is a major health problem all over the world that's all too common in young women and kids.

Our bodies can take in two forms of iron — heme or nonheme — but vegans need to think about only one: nonheme iron. *Heme iron* is found in animal flesh foods like meat and fish. *Nonheme iron* is found in plant foods like vegetables, fruits, nuts, seeds, grains, and beans. Vegan diets, of course, rely on nonheme iron, which isn't absorbed by the body as well. So vegans need to be aware of their iron intake more than the average person. Good thing we're not average!

To get you on track with your iron intake, the following sections provide info on how much to consume and what sources to rely on. I also tell you what other foods you need to consume in order for your body to best absorb the iron efficiently.

Understanding how much you need

The standard recommendation for iron intake is 8 milligrams a day for men between the ages of 9 and 13 and 19+, and 11 milligrams a day for men between the ages of 14 and 18 years and for postmenopausal women. Premenopausal women between the ages of 14 and 18 (who lose more iron due to their menstrual cycles) need 15 milligrams per day, while women 19 to 50 need 18 milligrams a day. Pregnant vegans are encouraged to talk with their midwives or doctors about taking a prenatal iron supplement and eating iron-rich foods. (You can read more on pregnant vegans in Chapter 20 and vegan kids in Chapter 22.)

The preceding recommendations are a little confusing for vegans; they're lower and meant for meat eaters. Because the nonheme iron we eat isn't absorbed as well as the heme iron found in a meat eater's diet, vegans should safeguard against iron deficiency by eating more iron-rich foods.

Luckily, it's not difficult to get sufficient iron from vegan foods. Anemia is no more common in vegans than in the rest of the population. If you understand how much you need, take a look at the iron-rich foods available to vegans, and plan to eat them regularly, you'll have no trouble with anemia.

Obtaining your iron in vegan foods

A diet full of various whole foods and vegetables will easily meet your iron requirements. Take a look at Table 4-2 to start adding up your needs.

Using iron to the best of your body's ability

Iron doesn't work alone — just like a man, iron is no island in the bloodstream. It needs the help of another nutrient to do its work efficiently. Luckily, a well-rounded vegan diet provides this nutrient in abundant quantities.

Vegans are thought to equal the iron capacity of nonvegans because their diets are rich in vitamin C. When vitamin C is present with nonheme iron, the body can absorb it up to six times better. And it just so happens that many vegan sources of nonheme iron are naturally high in vitamin C as well. Most leafy greens like broccoli and bok choy, are great for both iron and vitamin C (and calcium), so the iron is easily absorbed by the body. It's a win-win-win situation!

Table 4-2	Vegan Sources of Iron	
Food	*Amount*	*Iron (mg)*
Beans and Grains		
Soybeans	1 cup	8.8
Lentils	1 cup	6.5
Quinoa	1 cup	6.3
Tempeh	1 cup	4.8
Black beans	1 cup	3.6
Pinto beans	1 cup	3.5
Chickpeas	1 cup	3.2
Bulgur	1 cup	1.7
Vegetables		
Spinach, cooked	1 cup	6.4
Swiss chard, cooked	1 cup	4.0
Potato	1 medium	3.2
Kelp	⅓ cup	3.0
Peas	1 cup	2.5
Wakame (sea vegetable)	½ cup	2.0
Brussels sprouts	1 cup	1.9
Broccoli	1 cup	1.1
Nuts, Seeds, and Fruits		
Prune juice	8 oz.	3.0
Tahini	2 Tbsp.	2.7
Dried apricots	8	2.1
Dried figs	8	2.1
Cashews	¼ cup	2.0
Raisins	½ cup	1.6
Almonds	¼ cup	1.5
Other		
Blackstrap molasses	2 tsp.	2.4
Veggie burgers	1 patty	2.0–3.5
Tofu hot dogs	1	1.5–2.5

Source: From the USDA and manufacturer information

Coax out the iron with cast-iron cooking

According to a 1986 study in the Journal of the American Dietetic Association, cooking food in a cast-iron skillet is a good way to add iron to your diet. Researchers found that foods, especially acidic ones, increased their iron content when cooked in these pots and pans. The acidity in foods like tomatoes reacted with the metal and absorbed more of the iron. Spaghetti sauce that originally contained less than 1 milligram per serving increased its iron content to almost 6 milligrams. Applesauce cooked in cast iron went from less than 1 milligram per serving to more than 7 milligrams! Older, more seasoned cast-iron pans may have less iron to offer after years of use, but they're still an excellent way to easily increase your iron intake.

Think of all the iron-rich foods you already eat, and then consider the foods you eat with them. You'll probably find that you're already eating iron and vitamin C together, which is why vegans can do so well nutritionally. Tofu, broccoli, and brown rice dishes, beans and salsa, and spinach salad with bell peppers and tomatoes are great iron and vitamin C combinations.

As you can see, vegans should have no problem getting the iron they need. You should be aware of the signs of iron deficiency, however, just in case you let your healthier eating habits slide. Iron anemia is more common in the general population than most folks realize, so be aware of your body and any symptoms.

Feeling fatigued or lethargic can be a sign of iron deficiency. If your blood iron levels are low, your capacity to work can be reduced, and you may get tired easily from normal physical exertion or exercise. The body needs iron to maintain a healthy immune system, so low iron stores can decrease your body's ability to fight infections. Pale skin, breathlessness, feeling tired, lightheadedness, weakness, a sore or inflamed tongue, headaches, nausea, and abdominal pain are all associated with anemia.

Staying away from iron blockers

Vitamin C helps your body absorb iron, but other foods and risk factors can lead to poor absorption. One of the main foods to avoid is cow's milk — thank goodness you're vegan now! The American Academy of Pediatrics has made a recommendation that children under the age of 1 year not be given any cow's milk or milk products. A dairy-rich diet is more likely to cause iron deficiency, as cow's milk has very little iron itself. Because calcium can interfere with iron absorption, eating a lot of dairy can lead to anemia.

The tannins and caffeine found in tea and coffee also can block iron absorption, so try drinking herbal or decaf teas and coffees instead if your iron levels are a concern. Because caffeine also affects calcium levels in the bones, it's best to avoid drinking it regularly.

Phytates are naturally found in most plant foods, including soy and other beans, nuts, seeds, and grains. Phytates can bind with minerals like iron, making it more difficult for the body to absorb them. Luckily, cooking, sprouting, and soaking can help to disable phytates.

Unhealthy behaviors like smoking and excessive alcohol consumption also can block your body's ability to absorb and properly use iron.

Vitamin D: The Sunlight Vitamin

Did you know that you, as a human being, are kind of like a sunflower? Most plants create their food and energy from *photosynthesis,* the process by which they turn sunlight into *chlorophyll* (the green stuff in their leaves). Chlorophyll is basically trapped sunlight! The human body also uses the sun to create vital nutrients for energy use. One of these vitamins is vitamin D.

Proper vitamin D intake is essential for bone health and can reduce or prevent the onset of the bone disease *osteoporosis.* Vitamin D promotes bone formation by helping the body use calcium and phosphorus. Recent studies have shown that proper supplementation with vitamin D reduces and reverses bone loss, so there's great hope for osteoporosis sufferers.

As an ex–milk drinker, you probably remember seeing cow's milk cartons exclaiming that the product was "Vitamin D fortified!" This supplementation was necessary to stave off the rampant spread of *rickets,* a vitamin D deficiency, across the United States in the early 20th century. Because of this (and the "Got milk?" campaigns), most of us strongly link bone health with cow's milk.

Vitamin D also is essential for a healthy immune system and for improved cardiovascular, skin, and prostate health. Vitamin D is a fat-soluble vitamin that's stored in the liver, and it can be used by the body during the dark winter. (Just don't beat up your liver with alcohol; otherwise it can't properly dispense the D you need.)

Elevating your vitamin D intake naturally

Vitamin D is created in your body after your skin is exposed to sunlight or UVB and UVA rays. Without these rays, your body can't naturally produce this essential nutrient. But never fear! The body only needs about 15 to 30 minutes in the sun to create all the D it needs. Fair-skinned people need 10–20 minutes a day, while people with naturally dark skin need between 15 to 30 minutes a day in the sun to create adequate D.

Avoid using sunblock for those times each day that you're restoring your body's vitamin D. The rays that are blocked are necessary for vitamin formation. Keep the sunblock handy for later in the day, or just apply it to your face. Try giving your arms and legs totally unrestricted access to Helios, the sun god, for just a few minutes. Sun — it does a body good!

Adding food or supplements to get your Vitamin D

If we could all live our lives naked near the equator, vitamin D deficiency would never be a problem. However, most of us wear clothes on a daily basis and live far away from the constant sunny skies of the equatorial countries.

So, if you live in any northern location where you rarely see the sun all winter, or if you cover every square inch of your body with clothing when outside, you must get vitamin D from food or supplements.

Not all Vitamin D is equal. It comes in two forms: D2 and D3. The D3, cholecalciferol, is not vegan as it is derived from lanolin in sheep. D2, ergocalciferol, is derived from a yeast, and is vegan. Many studies suggest that D2 is as effective as D3 in raising blood serum levels of vitamin D, when taken in large enough amounts. Getting your blood levels tested is needed to determine how much vitamin D supplementation, if any, is needed.

Fortified soy, rice, and hemp milk, as well as many fortified boxed cereals, orange juices, and breads, are some of the products available for getting your daily dose of vitamin D. These foods aren't difficult to find, but, if you prefer, you also can get vitamin D from most daily vitamin supplements. If you take calcium supplements, you're likely getting vitamin D from it as well, but check the label to make sure.

Don't Forget Zinc!

Zinc is another important mineral that many people — vegan and nonvegan — seem to be lacking. However, vegans can get enough from their diet, and it's pretty easy to ensure that your food supplies the amount of zinc that you need. Vegan women, in particular, must remember to focus on eating enough calories from zinc-rich foods and ensure that their zinc requirements are met.

Dangerous zinc deficiency isn't common in vegans, but it's good to be aware of what it looks like: Impaired immunity, loss of appetite, hair loss, and growth retardation are all signs of zinc deficiency. Zinc deficiency also exacerbates acne and diabetes and makes it difficult for the body to produce insulin, eliminate toxins, and keep the entire immune system strong.

Men need a bit more zinc than most women to ensure healthy reproduction. Sperm is high in zinc, and so a deficiency should be considered strongly if you have any fertility concerns. Males and females ages 9 to 13 should get 8 milligrams daily, while males 14 and older should consume 11 milligrams a day. Women ages 14 to 18 need 9 milligrams a day, while women 19 and older need 8 milligrams daily. (Pregnancy and breastfeeding require more zinc, which I cover in Chapter 20).

Picking up zinc from vegan foods

Fortified foods are always going to help you get the nutrition you need, but unadulterated, natural foods are a fantastic source of whole nutrition. Not only will these natural foods provide you with the zinc that you need, but they also will provide you with other healthy benefits as well, such as fiber and healthy fats. Table 4-3 lists some great sources of zinc.

Table 4-3	Vegan Sources of Zinc	
Food	*Amount*	*Zinc (mg)*
Red Star Nutritional Yeast	2 Tbsp.	3.2
Breakfast cereals	¾ cup	3.0–4.0
Peanuts	¼ cup	3
Brazil nuts	½ cup	2.2
Baked beans, canned	½ cup	1.6
Cashews, dry roasted	¼ cup	1.6
Tahini	1 Tbsp.	1.5
Almonds	¼ cup	1.3
Chickpeas	½ cup	1.3
Kidney beans	½ cup	0.9

Source: Compiled from the National Institutes of Health and manufacturer information

Making sure your body absorbs it

Certain aspects of food can hinder your zinc absorption. Too much calcium in your diet, for example, can impede your body's ability to absorb zinc. Some calcium supplements now come with added zinc to offset this disparity.

Found in the outer layers of seeds, beans, grains, nuts, peas, and legumes, *phytic acid* can keep your body from absorbing zinc properly. Luckily, simply soaking and rinsing these foods in water will remove much of the phytic acid. Similarly, soymilk contains large amounts of the old foe (and clearly you can't rinse it away!). So make sure that you're getting plenty of zinc from other healthy foods and don't drink gallons of soymilk — moderation, of course, is key.

Wildwood Organics now makes soy foods like tofu from soaked and sprouted soybeans. Sprouting and soaking the beans removes much of the naturally occurring phytic acid.

A Little Help from Our Friends: Giving Supplements a Try

Take a good look at the food you're eating on a regular basis. Are you hitting those markers for protein, B12, vitamin D, iron, calcium, and zinc? If not, can you add any whole and supplemented foods that will improve your intake? If so, this is my first recommendation toward reaching your daily requirements. (Refer to the earlier sections on each of these nutrients for more information.)

The second best way to ensure that you're getting all the nutrients you need is to take a supplement or multivitamin. If you tend to eat poorly several days a week or really aren't sure about your nutrition, a properly chosen daily supplement can help. You have many vegan multivitamins to choose from, and several of them derive their ingredients from plants and whole foods. Supplements made from whole foods as opposed to isolated chemicals are widely believed to be more easily absorbed by your body. You also can purchase liquid supplements that allow your body to more quickly absorb the nutrients.

The number one supplement that most people benefit from is a good probiotic. *Probiotics* are supplements of living dietary bacteria, such as *acidophilus* and yeasts, that help the human digestive system work properly. Choose a refrigerated probiotic that's dairy free. If your digestion is working well, you don't need a probiotic because you'll be able to absorb the nutrients you need from your food and other supplements.

Regarding the B vitamins, it's best to take them as a complex. That's because there are eight B vitamins, and they all need to be in proportional quantities to work well. If you have concerns about B12 specifically, ask your doctor to check your levels before starting a separate B12 supplement.

Make sure that any supplement containing vitamin D is vegan. Vitamins D2 and D3 are different, and D3 pills aren't vegan. Supplementing with D2 has been shown to be a valid way of improving your body's ability to create healthy bones.

Many supplement companies make quality vegan products. Deva, VegLife, New Chapter, Rainbow Light, and Country Life are a few companies to look into. Several Web sites, such as www.veganessentials.com and www.cosmosveganshoppe.com, sell only vegan products and offer a wide range of supplements to choose from.

If you feel you have some sort of nutrient deficiency, talk to your doctor about getting some simple blood tests that can pinpoint any specific areas to address. However, be assured that eating a well-planned vegan diet can give you everything you need.

Water, water everywhere

In your quest for optimum nutrition, don't forget about water! Eight 8-ounce glasses daily is the general guideline. Need help remembering to drink enough water? When you're spending time at home or at work, give yourself a visual reminder to drink your daily ration. Fill a pretty, eye-grabbing pitcher with the amount of water you want to drink in a day. Set it somewhere you'll see it often, such as on a kitchen counter, at the corner of your desk, or on a little tea table next to the TV. Put a nice glass next to the pitcher so you have no excuse not to drink up!

Avoiding plastic bottles, which can leach petro-chemicals, hormone disrupters, and plasticizers into your drinking water, is a great step toward detoxifying your body and saving a landfill from unnecessary waste. Plus, because bottled water isn't regulated like public water supplies, you'll probably have a better quality of water straight out of your tap. If you don't like the taste or quality of your tap water, you can get great home water filters that will remove heavy metals, pesticides, chlorine, and bacteria. If you want to take water with you in the car or to your workouts, buy a stainless steel, reusable water bottle. Plastic ones are risky because, again, they can leach nasty chemicals into your water.

Chapter 5

Protein Protocols

· ·

· ·

*I*magine you're at a party about to meet some new people. As you're introduced around, it might come up in conversation that you're a vegan —
perhaps you politely declined the passed shrimp hors d'oeuvres (or as I like
to call them, "fingers of flesh"). You can be certain that one of the first questions will be "Where do you get your protein?"

Don't be alarmed — take a deep breath and get ready to charm the pants
off of those well-meaning yet ill-informed meat eaters. The basics of protein
are simple, and vegans can and do get plenty. The average American has too
much protein in her diet, mainly because she eats so many animal foods,
including meat, eggs, and dairy. (According to USDA predictions for annual
meat consumption, by 2007 each person in the United States consumed
roughly 221 pounds of animal meat a year.) Yes, those foods are sources of
protein. But they aren't the only sources; nor are they necessarily the healthiest or cheapest!

In this chapter, you find out how protein works in the body and how much
different people need on a daily basis. New vegans can get confused about
the types and quality of plant sources of protein, so I've provided detailed
charts and lists to help you plan your healthy diet successfully.

What You Need to Know about Protein

The difference between a *source* of protein and the protein itself is a matter of
molecules. Good vegan sources of protein, for example, are tofu and nuts. But
when you look at those foods, can you see the protein? Of course not. The
protein is a part of the structure of the food, but it's not the food itself.

Proteins are large, complex molecules that perform important functions in your body. They do most of the work in cells and are used by your body to regulate water in tissues and organs, perform functions like repairing cells and building new ones, and create the structure of the bones, blood, hormones, muscles, and everything else in the body. Every cell in the body contains protein, and protein is a large part of the muscles, organs, and skin.

Proteins are composed of many thousands of smaller units called *amino acids.* To form a complete protein, all 22 of the different amino acids must be present. Your body does create some of these amino acids by itself, but it must receive nine of the amino acids it needs from food, called *essential amino acids* — meaning it's essential that you eat foods containing them! These essential amino acids can all be found in plant foods, so as long as your diet is varied and provides you with enough calories, you don't need to worry about getting enough of these building blocks.

Your body creates the specific forms of protein it needs from the dietary protein you eat. When you eat a bunch of nuts, beans, or soy, your body *macerates,* or breaks down that food with saliva and chewing. Then the food gets digested by the stomach. The original food source of protein begins to break down into the different amino acids, which your body can absorb and form into new proteins that it can use to perform whatever function it needs. Isn't the human body amazing?

How Much Protein Do You Need?

The National Institute of Health recommends that the average man eat between 30 to 60 grams of protein a day; it says women need between 25 to 50 grams a day. Most Americans are getting closer to 100 to 120 grams a day, which is leading to a host of health problems. While protein is necessary and good for the body, too much can be dangerous over time. And remember that the source of your protein can matter just as much as the quantity you're consuming. (I talk more about the difference in protein sources in the later section "Why Vegan Protein Is Better Than Animal Protein.")

Protein needs for all ages and stages

The recommended daily allowance (RDA) for protein intake is based on a simple calculation used by the National Institute of Health. The basic formula is this:

1. **Weight in pounds ÷ 2.2 = weight in kilograms.**

2. **Weight in kilograms × 0.8 = grams of protein a day.**

So, for a 125-pound woman who gets moderate to light exercise, the RDA would be about 46 grams of protein a day. If you exercise more vigorously, are pregnant, lactating, or are a growing kid or teenager, you may need to increase your protein. Table 5-1 shows the average recommended dietary allowances for protein. If you notice you are getting most of your protein from unrefined grains, beans, and produce, and very little from tofu, tempeh or soy-based meats, it's recommended that you increase the calculation to 0.9 for Step 2.

Table 5-1	Recommended Daily Allowances for Protein
Group	*Recommended Allowance*
Boys and girls ages 0 to 6 months	9.1 grams
Boys and girls ages 7 months to 1 year	11 grams
Boys and girls ages 1 to 3 years	13 grams
Boys and girls ages 4 to 8 years	19 grams
Boys and girls ages 9 to 13 years	34 grams
Males ages 14 to 18 years	52 grams
Males ages 19+ years	56 grams
Females ages 14+ years	46 grams
Pregnant and lactating women	71 grams

Source: 2002 National Academy of Sciences

As you can see, protein needs and requirements can change over the course of one's lifetime; they're especially important for growth in childhood, the teen years, the elderly, and for pregnant and lactating women. Athletes and body builders (yes, vegans can be body builders too!) also have different protein needs than the average, healthy, and moderately active person. (Check out Part VI for info on vegan dietary needs for all walks of life.)

Plant proteins aren't as easy for the human body to access during digestion as animal proteins, and all but a few plant foods are lacking some of the essential amino acids to create a complete protein. Because of these factors, the healthy vegan should consider consuming a slightly higher amount of protein to ensure adequate intake. However, remember that ensuring a proper intake shouldn't be a problem! The average American eats considerably more protein than is needed, and adequate protein is available in the healthy plant foods discussed in this chapter. As long as you eat a variety of *whole foods,* unrefined foods with all the edible parts intact like brown rice and potatoes and apples with the skin on, throughout the day — and eat enough of them to meet your caloric needs — you'll easily hit your protein target.

Protein problems: Why too much of a good thing is a bad thing

As a hot-button topic among vegans and the people who love them, protein comes up often and causes heated discussions. Many omnivores and well-meaning parents are under the impression that animal-derived foods are the only quality sources of protein. True, meat and eggs are complete proteins. However, the quality of plant-based protein is excellent and even superior when you consider the dangers associated with meat consumption.

The high fat content, acidity, and toxins found in animal products cause numerous health problems if consumed excessively (and most Americans do fall into this category of excessive consumers). The major health problems associated with meat consumption are heart disease, certain cancers, strokes, obesity, and osteoporosis. A staggering majority of meat produced in this country is very high in fat and cholesterol, which is an unsavory side dish to the protein that people really need.

The acidic nature of animal foods causes your alkaline-loving body to try to balance itself. The quickest way for the human body to get more alkaline is to draw calcium out of the bones (calcium is an alkaline substance). So diets rich in animal foods lead to constant losses of calcium through the kidneys, leaching the bones of that essential mineral. It now makes sense that the countries with high meat and dairy consumption also have high osteoporosis rates.

Excessive intake of protein leads to other concerns besides brittle bones, however. Other damaging effects are high cholesterol, kidney stones and renal failure, overstressed liver and kidneys, and a risk of gout, which is also known as "the disease of kings." *Gout* is described as painful, recurring attacks of joint inflammation that are brought on by high levels of uric acid in the body. Gout is often a hereditary disease, but this acidic condition also can be brought on by a diet that includes excessive amounts of animal foods. About 200 years ago, gout was associated with the upper classes because they could afford to eat more meat and assume a more leisurely life.

Not enough protein? Symptoms to look out for

The scourge of too much protein is a concern in developed, Western cultures, but health concerns also (though rarely) arise from diets lacking adequate protein. Some of these health concerns should be of special interest to vegans, because when left unchecked, these problems can lead to serious damage over time.

Here are some indications that you may need to focus your diet on more high-quality proteins:

- ✔ Feeling constantly lightheaded, unmotivated, and overtired
- ✔ Constant sugar and carbohydrate cravings (when your body is lacking sufficient protein and nutrients to power itself, it craves sugar to get the quick energy it so desperately needs)
- ✔ Hair loss
- ✔ Growth retardation in babies and toddlers
- ✔ Increased susceptibility to infection
- ✔ Weight loss
- ✔ Muscle wasting
- ✔ Weakness and fatigue

While these deficiencies are seen more often in underdeveloped nations, especially during times of famine, vegans who eat a variety of whole, unprocessed foods will easily meet their protein requirements. Just be sure to consume a healthy variety of vegan protein ingredients throughout your day.

Thinking about high-protein diets

Once a decade a "new" diet fad gets dusted off and presented as the best way to lose weight and control blood sugar issues. The high-protein, low-carbohydrate diet has had many names, including the Atkins diet, Scarsdale diet, Carbohydrate Addict's diet, and the Endocrine Control Diet. These diets are all variations on the theme of eating foods that are high in protein and low in carbs; and they all have well-known side effects: the risk of bone loss, kidney failure, kidney stones, digestive problems, constipation and sluggish elimination, gas, and bad breath.

The proponents who endorse a high-protein diet believe that eating carbohydrates leads to blood sugar issues and diabetes as well as weight gain and obesity. By eliminating most carbohydrates from their diet, high-protein advocates are successful, usually in the short term, in losing weight and ending their out-of-control carbohydrate cravings.

Ultimately, these diets are unsuccessful for many people. Focusing on a diet mostly devoid of fruit, sweet vegetables, and whole grains, these followers are forced to use fiber supplements to ensure regular bowel movements. Even with daily doses of fiber, the huge amount of meat and dairy consumed leads to digestive problems and constipation since animal proteins take longer to eliminate due to their utter lack of natural fiber. Because most animal proteins are cooked, except for sushi (which is often still thawed from frozen fish), they're lacking enzymes and never contain any of the powerfully healing aspects of plant foods. Chlorophyll from green plants, phytonutrients, vitamins, and fiber are sorely lacking in these diet plans, leading to a lack of vitality over time.

Why Vegan Protein Is Better Than Animal Protein

The standard American diet, or SAD (it is pretty sad, isn't it?), relies heavily on animal foods as the main source of protein. At the same time, health experts and doctors have been warning that the current avalanche of diseases and the growing obesity problem are direct results of our diet. These same experts plead with us to eat more fiber and fresh fruits and vegetables as a way to avoid and heal these illnesses. And it's true; one of the easiest ways to recover from a lifetime of the SAD state of affairs is to rely on plant-based proteins.

Plant sources of protein are a wise choice, especially because so many Americans aren't getting enough fiber in their diets. Beans, nuts, whole grains, and seeds are rich in fiber and plant-based *phytochemicals,* which are plant chemicals that have protective or disease preventive properties that help lower the risk of cancers and heart disease. The positive effect of plant sources of protein is twofold:

- ✔ While ensuring your body has enough plant-based protein, you're also taking the burden of digesting a diet full of cholesterol-filled meat and difficult-to-assimilate fats off your liver and digestive system.
- ✔ You also get the powerful protection of the natural health benefits found in these whole foods.

A diet high in plant proteins can extend more benefits than just protecting your heart and bones. The Nurses' Health Study, a long-term study involving 18,000 women, showed that infertility in women can be greatly affected by the type of protein they consume. Women who ate more plant sources of protein were much less likely to have infertility issues than women with few plant protein sources in their diet. Amazingly, infertility was 39 percent more likely in women who ate the most animal protein.

In T. Collin Campbell's incredible book *The China Study,* the link between cancer growth and protein is drawn out. Several studies cited in this book show that a diet including animal proteins can lead to cancer cell proliferation. The vegetable sources of protein have not shown the same link with cancer growth, so a vegan diet can be considered much safer for overall cancer avoidance.

Animal-based foods provide certain other important nutrients besides protein, but perfectly wonderful plant sources can provide these minerals and vitamins as well. Zinc, iron, vitamin B12, and calcium can be found in the plant kingdom (the sources and considerations are covered in Chapter 4).

One sign that the human body is designed to absorb protein and other nutrients from plant foods is the length of our digestive tracts. A carnivore's digestive tract is several times shorter than a purely vegetarian animal's. So when the meat eater eats its dinner, probably a freshly caught wildebeest, it's finished digesting the meat within a few hours. A plant-eating animal has a much longer set of intestines, so the body can spend more time absorbing the nutrients available in plant foods. The human body has intestines that are ten times the length of the body. How's that for a pretty clear indication that we were meant to be plant eaters?

Finding Protein in Vegan Foods

After you've done the math and understand how many grams of protein you need per day (see the earlier section "Protein needs for all ages and stages"), you need to plan to eat foods that will give you that amount every day. In this section, you find a helpful list of healthy vegan protein-rich foods to help you plan a delicious diet full of variety.

The best way to ensure that your body can use the vegetable-based protein that's abundant in a vegan diet is to chew your food properly. Human saliva is the first step of the digestive process. Saliva, which contains *salivary amylase,* and chewing help your body begin to break down carbohydrates and starches. Because a majority of vegan protein sources are rich in carbohydrates (think grains and beans), you need to break down your food well before swallowing it. After the food gets through your stomach and into your intestines, your body can't do much more to break down the fibers. And if your food is still in larger chunks, your body won't be able to access all that nutrition you have worked so hard to get on your plate.

Protein-rich vegan favorites

Once you look at the following list of vegan foods in Table 5-2 and their protein contents, you'll feel much more comfortable creating healthy menus for yourself and your family. Get out your slide rule, or an old fashioned pen and paper, and figure out how much protein you need according to the formula listed earlier in this chapter. Put together a few days worth of menus that include the foods included on this list that also reach your daily needs for protein.

Table 5-2	Protein Values of Popular Vegan Foods	
Food	*Quantity*	*Grams of Protein*
Almonds, raw	¼ cup	8
Amaranth	1 cup	28
Beans, black	1 cup	15
Beans, chickpeas	1 cup	11
Bread, whole-grain	2 slices	5–8
Broccoli, cooked	1 cup	4
Cashews, raw	¼ cup	5
Hemp seeds	1 oz.	9
Lentils	1 cup	18
Nutritional yeast	1½ Tbsp.	8
Pasta, whole-grain, cooked	1 cup	8–10
Peanut butter	2 Tbsp.	7
Quinoa	1 cup	9
Rice, brown	1 cup	5
Seitan	3 oz.	31
Sesame seeds	1 oz.	5
Soymilk (enriched)	1 cup	8–11
Spinach, cooked	1 cup	5
Sunflower seeds	¼ cup	6
Tahini	2 Tbsp.	5.8
Tempeh	1 cup	41
Tofu	4 oz.	11
Veggie burger	1 patty	8–22

Sources: USDA Nutrient Database for Standard Reference, Release 18, 2005, and manufacturers' information.

Including fermented foods for easy protein digestion

Some folks have problems digesting vegan sources of protein when they first make changes to their diet. If you haven't eaten a lot of beans or soy foods in the past, you may experience some "musical" meals. Your intestines can do a better job digesting certain plant proteins if fermented proteins are used more often.

Pickled foods will also help your body adjust its digestion of certain proteins. In addition, Asian cultures believe that adding pickled vegetables to meals with fried foods will help you digest those fats better.

Fine fermented proteins

A realm of vegan proteins that brings up a fascinating topic is fermented foods. *Fermentation* is the process in which a food is exposed to a bacteria or culture. These living organisms, such as *lactobacillus,* which is found in yogurt, start living on and consuming the original food. These little critters actually break down the difficult-to-digest parts of foods, such as sugars and proteins, thereby making the nutrition easier for our bodies to absorb.

Fermented proteins, such as the soy foods tempeh, miso, and shoyu or tamari (the naturally brewed soy sauces), generally are easier for your body to digest. Fermented protein is digested more easily because it's predigested by the healthy bacteria; your body is then better able to assimilate the nutrients, leading to better nutrition.

Tempeh is a great choice for people who have difficulty digesting plant-based proteins like beans or lightly processed soy foods such as tofu. Found in the refrigerator section of the grocery store, this bean product originated in Indonesia. Tempeh, which is made from whole soybeans that have been diced and exposed to a nontoxic mold called *Rhizopus,* is more of a whole food than tofu because it's barely processed. Because tempeh is a fermented soy product, its enzymes are partially broken down, making it easier to metabolize. It's a complete protein and doesn't produce the uncomfortable gas, stomach pain, and bloating that some other plant-based proteins do. Besides being a terrific cholesterol-free, easy-to-digest meat alternative, it's also ideal for people on low-sodium diets. A great substitute for recipes that call for fish, poultry, or meat, this meaty bean product also can be crumbled to make pasta sauces just like Mom used to make. Try the Mushroom Sloppy Tempeh Joes recipe in Chapter 14 or the Tempeh Hash breakfast recipe in Chapter 12 for delicious fermented protein meals.

Pickles for better protein digestion

Pickled foods can help you digest other proteins. The bacteria found in the unpasteurized versions also increase vitamin levels of the pickled foods and help to promote a healthy digestive tract. Rather than using the pasteurized pickles found on grocery store shelves, which no longer contain the beneficial bacteria, try the fresh pickles from the refrigerated section or Asian markets.

You can also make your own at home using the Homemade Pickled Vegetables recipe in Chapter 13.

Combination, shmombination!

The seminal book *Diet for a Small Planet* by Frances Moore Lappe detailed the political, environmental, and moral impact of a meat-based diet for a fledgling vegetarian movement in the early 1970s. Her book also made popular the idea that protein foods needed to be combined properly so that all the amino acids were present at each meal to form complete proteins. She created entire lists of combined foods, such as different whole grains with certain beans as well as a type of nut and a certain vegetable. Many vegetarians stuck to eating from these lists to ensure they were getting the proper protein. This rather arduous style of vegetarianism has since been proven unnecessary, however. By eating a varied vegan diet every day, including whole grains, beans, soy foods, and fresh fruits and veggies, you get all the protein you need. Lappe has recanted her own theory of food combination as inaccurate and has since written more books that offer valuable lessons about the food justice movements as well as global food scarcity.

Traditionally, these pickled or fermented foods are eaten with or after a heavy, fatty, or protein-rich meal to help aid digestion. It's remarkable that this incredible knowledge has been used the world over by many cultures without anyone ever using the Internet or sharing a recipe. It has been simultaneously used around the world in various cultures because people knew the natural fermentation helped them digest their food better. Vegetable foods like sauerkraut from Eastern and Northern Europe, cucumber pickles, kimchee from Korea, yogurt and lemon pickles from India, and umeboshi plums from Japan are all examples of pickled foods that are traditionally eaten with protein-rich meals to help the digestion process.

Soy, oh boy! The controversy and confusion

If you pay any attention to health and nutrition in the news, things can get a little confusing, especially when it comes to the topic of soy. One week soy foods and tofu are applauded in the media as a way to avoid heart disease and cancer, and the next week they're vilified as the cause of other diseases and cancers. What's the deal here? Consider the following contradictory statements:

- Soy is good and protects against breast cancer and should be eaten by healthy women and breast cancer patients.

  Soy is dangerous for women with estrogen-positive breast cancer or with a family history of breast cancer.

✔ A study of Alzheimer's patients found that rates were slightly higher in Hawaiian citizens who had eaten a lot of tofu over the course of their lives.

Studies in Asia, where soy intake is generally high, show lower rates of Alzheimer's.

✔ Contradictory studies from Harvard show that regular soy consumption raised or lowered sperm count in men.

Unfortunately, scientists don't have enough evidence on either side to declare a winner.

A healthy vegan diet includes a wide variety of beans and legumes, and it shouldn't rely on one food for a majority of its calories. Adding some *edamame* (whole soybeans), tofu, tempeh, soy sauce, and miso to your diet isn't dangerous. Unprocessed soy foods or lightly processed soy foods like tofu, soymilk, and miso can be used regularly without creating health concerns. However, relying on highly processed foods like soy hot dogs, soy ice cream, soy cheese, and soy burgers for your daily protein is a cause for concern. These foods often contain *isolated soy protein* (a highly refined powder made from defatted soy flour), abundant salt, preservatives, and other food additives that aren't part of a healthy diet. (Check out the nearby sidebar "Isolated soy proteins: Whole foods or manufactured protein?" for more on how these proteins are created.)

Keep in mind that 99 percent of soybeans produced in the United States are *genetically modified.* These manufactured organisms don't appear naturally in the world, and little to no testing has been performed to discover the possible health side effects these foods can cause. The only way to ensure you're eating truly healthy soy products is to only buy organic soy.

The key to healthy vegan eating is to keep consuming a diet of mostly unprocessed, whole foods to maintain high nutrient-per-calorie levels.

Isolated soy proteins: Whole foods or manufactured protein?

Isolated soy protein isn't something you can make at home. It's made in industrial factories where mashed soybeans are mixed with alternating alkaline and acid washes to remove the fiber and separate the usable parts. The resulting curds are then spray-dried at high temperatures to create a powder that's high in protein. Then the powder can be processed again with more high-temperature, high-pressure extrusions to make *textured vegetable protein,* or TVP. You wouldn't call this a whole food.

Chapter 6

Transforming Food into Health-Supportive Meals

. . . .

In This Chapter

▶ Paying attention to food quality instead of quantity

▶ Choosing healthy, nutrient-dense foods from the key food groups

. . . .

*W*hether you're converting to veganism straight from the standard American diet heavy with meat, dairy, and refined processed foods, or you've been a vegetarian for years, you can bolster your health-sustaining vegan diet with a little knowledge and planning. You don't need to keep a food log or start making charts of percentages and proportions to ensure that your diet is truly whole and nutritious. Transforming your diet to include healthy ingredients and simple methods of preparation ensures that you won't feel limited or deprived!

My love of food started in my mother's garden when I was just a wee lass. I was given free range to gobble up ripe raspberries and pick all the sweet peas I could eat, so healthy food is ingrained in my brain as joyous and natural. Nothing tastes better than food from your own garden, freshly picked and perfectly ripe. This kind of energy can be re-created through every season in any region of the world.

Nourishing your body with vegan food is a great start — but focusing on health-supportive recipes and ingredients can affect every aspect of your mind, body, and mood. If you want real health, great energy, and long-lasting stamina, choose foods wisely. In this chapter, I show you how natural, plant-based foods do more than just stop the rumbling in your tummy. I explain how the quality of your food is even more important than the quantity, and I help you begin to get in touch with your body's cravings and deepest needs.

Focusing on Quality over Quantity

When clients ask me about serving sizes and portion control, I usually give them an answer that makes them look at me like I'm crazy. I don't recommend servings and portions.

Those numbers, weights, and percentages get in the way of truly balanced eating, because every person has a unique body and lifestyle as well as a specific schedule. Quantity *and* quality are important subjects to consider while moving forward into a vegan lifestyle.

The proportions of your portions

Every vegan's body and metabolism are different. Some people feel better eating three regular meals a day, while others do better with five or six smaller, more frequent meals. If you sit in a chair all day, you may digest food slower and feel fine with three regular meals. If you have a more physical job, you can benefit from more frequent, smaller meals that will replenish your blood sugar and help you avoid an overly-full feeling. Give yourself a chance to experiment with both eating styles to see which method works best for you and your lifestyle. Pay attention to the total quantity of foods you consume with three meals a day versus more frequent, smaller meals.

Gauge your energy levels throughout the day and notice if you feel better with a small snack before or after lunch. Try a protein-rich snack of nuts or hummus with carrots in the morning and fresh fruit in the afternoon. If your body doesn't respond well to those foods at those times of day, switch them around.

Choosing a variety of plant-based foods provides you with all the nutrition you need! Make sure you're choosing protein, complex carbohydrates, and mineral-rich ingredients for each meal. This variety of whole and fresh food will protect your long-term health.

Quality is key

Rather than focusing on specific serving sizes, choose your meals from a wide variety of truly healthy and whole foods throughout the day. Nutritional experts' understanding of food has led to a better understanding on a scientific level of what real food includes. It's simply much more difficult to eat 500 calories of brown rice than 500 calories of cheese. When you eat a huge bowl of fresh vegetable salad with some cooked garbanzo beans, slivered almonds, shredded carrots, avocado, cherry tomatoes, lemon juice, and olive oil, you're giving your body the recommended daily servings of vegetables, but you're also getting a whopping dose of fiber, antioxidants, vitamin C, protein, healthy fat, and phytochemicals that support your body in countless ways.

A healthy vegan diet is mainly comprised of proteins, complex carbohydrates, healthy fats, and unrefined sugars. Choose a variety of proteins from the lists and suggestions in Chapter 5, and foods that offer consistent iron, calcium, B12, and other nutrients from the lists in Chapter 4. Planning your menus on paper using the charts in Chapter 9 for the first few months of your vegan life will help you put together delicious meals that are truly supportive of your health.

Picking and Choosing: Healthy Vegan Food Groups

Your body needs to consume amino acids and protein, carbohydrates, minerals, vitamins, and water to survive. Choosing vegan foods that provide all these essential dietary players isn't difficult. Plant foods offer everything you need in terms of nutrition; they also offer a variety of colors, complex flavors, textures, cooking techniques, and preparation methods.

The most important qualities to remember when choosing foods are *variety* and *vitality.* Choose foods that are fresh and nutrient rich, not overly processed and packaged. Get to know the food groups in the following sections and begin to experiment with different ways to get several servings of each into your diet on a regular basis. You also can use Figure 6-1 as a guide.

Complex carbohydrates

Most healthy eating guides and gurus recommend getting most of your calories from complex carbohydrates. Complex carbohydrates are the main source of fuel for human activity and productivity. The old USDA food pyramid recommended 6 to 11 servings of grain-based foods a day — that seems like a lot, especially when there was no talk of quality! Nowadays, nutritional experts know better, and they recognize the division between processed, refined carbohydrates and whole, complex carbohydrates. White bread and bagels, white sugar, and high-fructose corn syrup are common refined carbohydrates found in American homes. When you look at the true nature of foods that contain complex carbohydrates, such as beans, whole grains, and vegetables, getting most of your calories from this group doesn't seem hard or unhealthy at all.

You find complex carbohydrates in brown rice, millet, quinoa, barley, yams, potatoes, beans, legumes, and whole-grain flour products like crackers, bread, pasta, and seeds. When you look at this wider variety of sources, then yes, getting most of your calories from complex, carb-rich food makes sense. You're not just getting the carbs; you're also getting minerals, protein, vitamins, and good fiber. These complex carbohydrate foods are *nutrient-dense,* meaning you get more nutrition per serving than a refined carbohydrate offers.

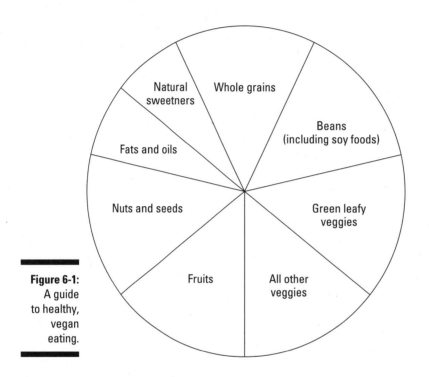

Figure 6-1:
A guide
to healthy,
vegan
eating.

Seasonal veggies

In the last 100 years, modern technology has created a seasonless supermarket. Global transportation systems and long growing seasons in places like California and Florida have created a situation where you can get pretty much any kind of food you want at any time. But is this style of eating healthy?

By choosing to eat local and seasonal fruits and vegetables for most of your needs instead of produce that was grown in another hemisphere and shipped halfway around the world to your table, you accomplish several goals at once. Not only are you supporting local economies and farmers, you're actually getting better nutrition. As soon as most fruits or vegetables are harvested, they start losing nutrients. The fresher the better — and an apple grown in New Zealand takes at least a few days to get to the United States!

Eating seasonally also keeps your body in tune with the natural variations in temperature that occur throughout the year. Eating raw fruits and vegetables in the summer makes sense as it keeps your body cool and allows you to take advantage of local produce. Choose heartier fall and winter produce during the colder months. The foods growing near you in these darker days are recommended in the Ayurvedic and Macrobiotic culinary and medical traditions to keep your body healthy through the cold and flu seasons.

Eating some frozen blueberries or canned tomatoes in the winter won't immediately cause you to catch a cold. Still, focusing on local, seasonal produce will fortify you with nutrients and energy needed at certain times of year. Let the seasons help guide your choices:

- ✔ In spring, focus on leafy vegetables that really embody the new energy of the season, including green chard, spinach, lettuces, and herbs like basil and parsley.

- ✔ Summer is abundant with natural cooling foods from Ayurveda and Traditional Chinese Medicine, such as berries, summer squash, zucchini, watermelon, corn, pears, cilantro, and peppermint.

- ✔ The harvest of fall and winter vegetables, such as carrots, onions, sweet potatoes, pumpkins, squashes, and warming spices (cayenne pepper, cinnamon, nutmeg, and curry powder), brings more warming energy to the human body.

Sea vegetables

When I think nutrient-dense food, I think sea vegetables. These gems of the ocean are incredibly valuable for vegans and anyone who wants to be truly healthy and vibrant. While the American palate may not be used to the taste of sea vegetables, or seaweed, cultures like Japan, Iceland, Ireland, China, and many others have been using native sea vegetables for centuries.

Sea vegetables provide the widest variety of minerals available of any food group, including all the minerals that are found in human blood and, not coincidentally, the ocean. A great source of iron, calcium, vitamin K, iodine, and B vitamins, several sea veggies also are good sources of magnesium and cancer-fighting *lignans*. Lignans are phytoestrogens that have antioxidant activity and have been shown to protect the body from certain cancers, osteoporosis, and cardiovascular disease. Used for inflammatory conditions, cancer treatment and prevention, and to boost the immune systems, sea vegetables also are a source of plant protein.

Hundreds of types of sea vegetables are edible, and because of their recent uptick in popularity, they're becoming easier to find in grocery stores, health food stores, and ethnic markets. Just a small amount, about 2 to 3 tablespoons, every day of the following is beneficial:

- **Nori:** Popular because of its role in making sushi rolls. You can buy this dark, green-black paper in page-sized sheets. It's easy to carry around for snacks and lunch — just snip a sheet with kitchen scissors to add to your meal. No other preparation is needed.

- **Arame:** These little black wires are mild tasting compared to other sea veggies. Wash arame well, soak for 5 minutes, and drain before cooking. Good in soups and combined with tofu dishes, arame doubles in volume when cooked.

- **Dulse:** You can find this reddish-brown sea veggie in flattened, chewy ribbons or flakes. The flakes need no preparation, and you can sprinkle them directly on food. The ribbons are soft enough that you only need to rinse them before adding them to a recipe, unless otherwise directed.

- **Hijiki:** Easy to prepare, these little, wiry, spaghetti-like strands have a strong flavor. Simply rinse and soak for 5 minutes before adding to a recipe, or eat raw tossed into a salad.

- **Kelp:** Kelp is sold in flakes, powder, or flat ribbons, and you can add it to soups and stews after rinsing it off.

- **Kombu:** Kombu's secret power is that it helps you digest beans and prevents gas. Add a 2- or 3-inch piece of rinsed, dark kombu to a pot of cooking beans or soup. To add it to a recipe, simply soak in warm water for 10 to 15 minutes and chop.

- **Wakame:** If you've ever ordered miso soup, you've eaten wakame. This soft, green, silky sea vegetable is mild tasting and easy to cook. Rinse the wakame and then soak in warm water for 5 to 7 minutes. Rinse again, chop, and add to your recipe.

Want to try some easy techniques for cooking sea veggies? Hijiki is a nice addition to salads. Just toss one or two tablespoons with chopped lettuce and your favorite dressing. Prepare dulse, kombu, or wakame according to package directions and add a small handful to soup. You can even buy small shaker containers of sea vegetable flakes to keep on your table. Just shake a little on top of your meal, sandwich, soup, or salad!

Unless you're going with an expert, don't try collecting your own sea vegetables in the wild. Certain coastal areas are polluted with toxins, and other sea beds may harbor bacteria that you don't want to consume with your miso soup.

Finding good fruits

I've heard health experts complain that Americans eat the same five or six fruits their entire lives. I've seen similar eating habits with my clients, and I do think that everyone could benefit from a wider variety of fruity foods in their diets. *Fruits* are defined as the ripened reproductive body of a seed plant, which means that any plant you eat that contains seeds is a fruit. Officially, this means that tomatoes, eggplants, and cucumbers are fruit. That scientific fact doesn't matter much to me — I just want to encourage people to eat more fruits and vegetables, period.

Eating fresh fruit regularly has been shown to reduce the risk of developing diabetes, heart disease, Alzheimer's, and certain cancers. Fruits also fortify the body with the nutrients it needs to fight infection and repair cells.

Fruits are generally easier for people to increase in their diet than vegetables because they're sweet, they don't need a lot of preparation, and you can take them to school or work as a quick, healthy snack. So which fruits are most beneficial to your health? Well, it's difficult to pick a few specific superfruits, but here's a list of fruit-related tips to keep in mind:

- ✔ **Try to eat two to three pieces of fresh fruit every day.** An easy way to do this is to make a smoothie for breakfast. You can include a banana and two other fruits as the base and kick-start your day quickly.

- ✔ **Choose some of these super fruits for your daily menus:**
    - **Berries,** including blueberries, blackberries, raspberries, and strawberries, are high in vitamin C, folate, and phytochemicals.
    - **Pomegranate seeds** are very high in antioxidants, and the juice is used to help inflammatory conditions.
    - **Acai berries** also are high in antioxidants and are a good source of essential oils. They're believed to help the body slow the aging process as well.

- ✔ **Buy seasonal fruit from your farmer's market.** Not only is the fruit super fresh and at its optimum taste, but it also has more nutrients.

- ✔ **If you drink fruit juice, try to drink fresh-squeezed, unsweetened juice.** Investing in a juicer gives you the option of drinking many servings of fruit in one glass.

- ✔ **Fresh fruits are best, but frozen fruit and berries are good, too.** Canned fruit is a very distant third choice.

- ✔ **If you consume tropical fruits and their products, such as acai berries, mangosteen, noni juice, and goji berries or goji juice, make sure they're naturally sweetened.** These products have been in the news lately because of their purported anti-cancer and weight-loss action.

Color me healthy: The rainbow color code

Eating a rainbow of colorful fruits and vegetables on a regular basis will flood your body and bloodstream with powerful chemicals.

- **Red:** Strawberries, tomatoes, red bell peppers, beets, pomegranates, red apples, cayenne pepper, dulse, and watermelon contain *lycopene,* which the body uses to fight cancer and cardiovascular disease.

- **Orange/yellow:** Oranges, carrots, winter squash, orange bell peppers, peaches, mangos, pineapple, papayas, nectarines, and hot peppers offer *alpha* and *beta carotene,* antioxidants used to protect eye health and some skin diseases. The citrus fruits also provide folate, which help to reduce the risk of birth defects.

- **Green:** Leafy green vegetables, edible algae, lettuce, and sprouts all teem with chlorophyll. This powerful green aspect of plants is believed to protect the body from cancers, increases stores of red blood cells, binds with and removes heavy metals from the blood, is anti-inflammatory, and even prevents bad breath.

- **Blue/purple:** Blueberries are very high in vitamin C and offer a good dose of manganese. As antioxidant powerhouses, these little blue nuggets of nutrition will increase the power of any breakfast. High in cancer-preventing flavonoids *proanthocyanidins,* purple foods include eggplant, peppers, purple cabbage, plums, prunes, and grapes.

- **White:** Bananas, cauliflower, garlic, ginger, jicama, mushrooms, onions, parsnips, potatoes, and turnips contain *anthoxanthins,* which help to lower cholesterol and blood pressure, helping lower the risk of heart disease.

Proper proteins: Beans and legumes

Beans and legumes are great sources of nutrition, no matter which one you choose. Higher in protein and fat than whole grains, beans and legumes, when combined with grains, give you all the amino acids to form a complete protein. Completely cholesterol-free, beans are a good source of iron, calcium, phosphorus, vitamin E, and thiamin. Beans are useful in fighting several diseases because of their high fiber content. Bean dishes provide a slow drip of energy, fortify the body and blood, and are truly satisfying.

When buying beans and legumes, quality is important. Several studies have shown that organic foods, including beans, offer your body more nutrition because they're grown in healthier soil.

A multiyear study by the European Union declared that organic foods offer higher nutrition than conventionally raised foods, and often have higher levels of cancer-fighting antioxidants.

Canned beans are convenient and relatively inexpensive, so keeping several types in your cupboard makes financial sense. Bulk dry beans are even cheaper and are very simple to cook. Just look for uniformly sized beans that are smooth and free of wrinkles, cracks, and pits. Store each type of dry bean in an airtight glass jar, away from light and heat.

Aw, nuts! (And seeds)

Rich in protein, healthy monounsaturated fats, fiber, vitamins, and minerals, nuts and seeds are wonderful additions to a vegan diet. Just because they're high in fat doesn't mean they'll make you fat! Eaten in moderation, nuts and seeds help you feel full faster, which can help you to eat less overall.

To make them even more nutritious and easy to digest, you can soak nuts and seeds overnight in cool water. This starts the germination process and activates certain enzymes that pre-digest some of the proteins and fats, increasing certain nutrients, and make it easier for the body to break down the fats and protein. Store your raw nuts in the refrigerator or freezer to preserve their natural oils.

Either raw or soaked, nuts and seeds are easy to carry with you, so grab a container or baggie and fill up on some of these little, nutrition-rich nuggets:

- **Almonds:** A good source of protein, vitamin E, manganese, magnesium, copper, vitamin B2 (riboflavin), and phosphorus, almonds help lower bad cholesterol, reduce the risk of heart disease, and provide protection against cardiovascular disease. Eating raw almonds with the skin still on provides the most heart-healthy benefits.

- **Cashews:** Cashews are lower in fats and higher in antioxidants than most nuts. A good source of monounsaturated fats, copper, and magnesium, cashews promote good cardiovascular health, even for diabetics.

- **Flaxseeds:** Flaxseeds, also known as linseeds, are a great source of omega-3 fatty acids. Flaxseeds offer anti-inflammatory benefits and protect against heart disease, breast cancer, high cholesterol, and diabetes. Flaxseeds are rich in fiber and manganese and also are a good source of folate, vitamin B6 (pyridoxine), magnesium, phosphorous, copper, and lignan phytonutrients.

To get the most nutrition and benefits from flaxseeds, grind them fresh with a blender or spice grinder. You also can buy ground flax meal; just be sure to store it in the freezer between uses to protect the delicate fats from breaking down in heat and light. Use ground flaxseeds in homemade smoothies, oatmeal, soup, or on top of salads and grain dishes.

- **Peanuts:** Officially a legume, heart-healthy peanuts are a good source of monounsaturated fat, antioxidants, phytosterols, phytic acid (inositol hexaphosphate), and folic acid. Peanuts also are a good source of vitamin B3 (niacin), folate, copper, manganese, and protein, and they're a significant source of resveratrol, which is being studied for its anti-aging effects. Peanuts and peanut butter also may help prevent gallstones and protect against Alzheimer's disease. Always store your raw peanuts and peanut butter in the freezer or refrigerator, respectively, to prevent mold.

- **Pepitas/pumpkin seeds:** Pumpkin seeds are a good source of the essential fatty acids, copper, iron, potassium, phosphorous, magnesium, manganese, zinc, protein, and vitamin K. These little green seeds may promote prostate and bone health and offer anti-inflammatory benefits.

- **Sesame seeds:** Sesame seeds and tahini, or sesame butter, are rich in beneficial minerals. Tahini is a good source of manganese, copper, and calcium. Good for lowering cholesterol, sesame seeds also are recommended for rheumatoid arthritis.

To really gain access to sesame seeds' benefits, it's best to grind or smash them before eating. Tahini already is ground into a paste, and therefore, it's an easy way to eat sesame's goodness.

- **Sunflower seeds:** Offering anti-inflammatory and cardiovascular benefits, sunflower seeds lower cholesterol and help to prevent cancer. A good source of vitamin E, sunflower seeds also provide linoleic acid (an essential fatty acid), fiber, protein, and minerals such as magnesium and selenium.

- **Walnuts:** Walnuts are an excellent source of omega-3 essential fatty acids, manganese, and copper. Good for cardiovascular health and lowering cholesterol, walnuts also help brain function.

Healthy fats

Good fats are healthy for you — look at any healthy, glowing raw foodist or vegan who scarfs down handfuls of nuts and bowls of avocados regularly to see what I mean. Diets that include the monounsaturated fats from nuts and seeds, olives, avocados, and unrefined vegetable oils like olive and canola oil lower the risk of heart disease, still the leading cause of death in the United States.

Fat is a source of energy for the body, supplying 9 calories per gram, which is more than carbohydrates and protein supply. Fat is necessary for many bodily functions like protecting and cushioning internal organs and helping the body absorb vitamins like A, E, D, and K.

Omega-3 fatty acids, found in good amounts in flax and hemp seeds, are important for treating conditions such as allergies, arthritis, eczema, inflammatory diseases, learning problems, and depression. Good sources of omega-6 fats are most of the vegan cooking oils like olive, safflower, soybean, and sesame. Nuts and seeds also contain omega-6 fatty acids. Many health experts believe that the balanced consumption of omega-6 to omega-3 fatty acids should ideally be three to one. Because vegetable oils are more common for cooking, it's important to include the omega-3 rich foods often to ensure the proper balance.

Supportive sweets

I've loved to bake since childhood, but my relationship with sugar has changed greatly over the years. Long gone are the days of slurping down Super Big Gulps and munching candy bars between classes. But I still love a good cookie! A healthy vegan diet can include sweets and baked goods, but they must be consumed thoughtfully. You can find several sweeteners that are healthier than refined white sugar.

Sugar is not the devil — the human brain is just hard-wired to crave it, and it has never been easier to get your hands on the stuff. Back when humans were foraging and hunting for food, sugar was hard to come by. Naturally sweet fruits, vegetables, and honey were hard to find and were limited by season and geography. Today, you can have sugar for every meal of the day, and many people often do!

So rather than load up on the refined white stuff, use these natural, mellower sweeteners. They won't hit your bloodstream like lightning the way white sugar does, but you can still use these sweeteners moderately to create lovely treats and desserts:

- **Agave:** A natural syrup derived from the same plant that's used to make tequila, agave has a low glycemic level when used a teaspoon at a time. The darker the syrup, the more minerals it has, so the richer the taste. Because agave is sweeter than sugar, you can use less in your baking recipes for cupcakes, cookies, puddings, sweet sauces, quick breads, and scones. It's also a wonderful sweetener for hot and iced teas and coffee. Agave can be found at health food stores and gourmet grocery stores.

- **Blackstrap molasses:** A byproduct of the sugar-refining process, molasses comes from sugar cane. The thick black syrup is full of minerals. A good source of iron, blackstrap molasses provides a good amount of calcium, copper, manganese, potassium, and magnesium. Switching from refined, nutrient-poor white sugar, corn syrup, or artificial sweeteners to blackstrap molasses is a sweet idea. Excellent for baked goods like muffins, ginger cookies, and banana bread, blackstrap molasses can be found in your local health food store and in many grocery stores.

✔ **Brown rice syrup:** This gooey syrup is made from cooked rice. Light and mild tasting, and about half as sweet as sugar, it's good for cakes, pastries, and puddings. You also can stir it into tea and coffee. This polysaccharide is a more complex sugar than agave, so it releases more slowly into the bloodstream.

✔ **Date sugar:** This granular sweetener is made from dried, pulverized dates. Because these little flecks don't melt like regular cane sugar, and because they're very sweet, I suggest that you use two-thirds of the recommended amount of sugar when using date sugar in recipes for cookies, pies, cakes, and scones.

✔ **Maple syrup:** Fifty gallons of maple water are required to boil down to one gallon of maple syrup. This syrup concentrate is an excellent source of manganese and a good source of zinc. Grade B syrup is darker than Grade A, and because it offers a more pronounced taste than sugar, Grade B syrup is good for baking sweet breads, scones, cookies, puddings, mousses, and savory marinades. Be sure to keep maple syrup in the refrigerator after you open it. Found at health food stores and gourmet grocery stores, some states like New York don't allow Grade B to be sold to the public in stores.

✔ **Stevia:** Found in either powder or liquid form, this super concentrated sweetener is derived from the leaves of a South American plant. Because stevia is 100 times sweeter than sugar, you must use it in tiny amounts if you buy it in a concentrated form. Stevia has no carbohydrates, so it doesn't affect blood sugar at all, making it a good alternative for diabetics and people with other sugar problems.

✔ **Xylitol:** Made most often from birch trees, this natural sweetener is a sugar alcohol and is actually good for preventing cavities and reversing tooth decay. You can find xylitol in crystalline form in health food stores, and though it's expensive, it's a good, healthy sweetener option for baking.

Xylitol has been known to cause diarrhea or loose stools for some, so use caution.

Part III
Sticking to Your Guns: Staying Vegan

The 5th Wave   By Rich Tennant

"I substitute tofu for eye of newt in all my recipes now. It has twice the protein and doesn't wriggle around the cauldron."

In this part . . .

After you're on board with all the reasons that a vegan diet is the right choice for you and how it can provide you with everything you need nutritionally, making this healthy and ethical diet a reality requires planning, strategy, and know-how.

The chapters in this part detail how to shop in a new world of health food stores, farmer's markets, and unexplored aisles at your old supermarket. You determine what you need to plan for when creating your new vegan kitchen, menus, and home. Even old family recipes can be enjoyed with some tweaks and experimentation. Finally, understanding how to live with nonvegans is an important part of this journey, so commit to memory the tips on cooking and living with your fellow meat eaters.

Chapter 7

Cooking and Shopping Like a Vegan

· ·

In This Chapter

▶ Gathering the basic cooking supplies you need to maximize your success

▶ Stocking the pantry with all the good stuff, and storing it properly

▶ Becoming a savvy vegan shopper

· ·

*T*wo of the most challenging aspects of adopting a vegan diet are figuring out what to eat and how to cook in a new style. Setting up your vegan kitchen requires some thought, and you need to analyze your past and future ideas about cooking in order to use your culinary skills and create healthy, delicious food in this new vegan style. This chapter helps you figure out the tools you need and how to get started. You also get the lowdown on stocking your pantry with quality vegan basics and supplies while weeding out old, animal-derived goods. This chapter also helps you understand which ingredients on food labels are hidden traps for vegans.

Feeling confident in your kitchen and knowing that you have foundational vegan ingredients and supplies on hand will empower you to create healthy, delicious meals for your fast-moving, vegan-rific lifestyle.

Gearing Up with Basic Cooking Equipment

To eat is human, to cook, *divine*. Living a vegan lifestyle without cooking for yourself is possible, but doing so can be expensive and arduous. Besides, cooking for yourself is a basic life skill that allows you to practice the powerful tool of self-healing with your own conscious energy.

Choosing and using the appropriate kitchen gear enables you to consistently cook up healthy, plant-based fare. If you aren't already comfortable in the kitchen, don't worry about purchasing the fancy one-job gadgets yet. Instead, focus on the items in this section that do double duty. Doing so allows you to reduce the amount of money you need to spend to get started. If you already cook somewhat regularly, you probably own many of these items.

Pots, pans, and bakeware

A few good-quality pots and pans will take you far in your cooking. How can you tell if these items are good quality? Look for terms like "good heat conductor" and "heavy gauge." You're safest with stainless steel, cast iron, or enamel, because these types of pans won't react with most foods. Teflon and most nonstick pans can chip over time, allowing chemicals to leach into your food. Plain aluminum pots and pans can react to foods that are acidic, like tomato-based recipes, which can make the foods taste metallic. The following list can help you build your collection of pots, pans, and bakeware. As you build your collection, you can add more as you need. Here are some of the essentials you should consider buying:

- ✔ **A 10- to 12-inch high-sided stainless-steel sauté pan with a lid** for frying, braising vegetables, sautéing, and making sauces, rice pilafs, and risottos

- ✔ **A 3-quart saucepan** for steaming vegetables and cooking grains and pastas

- ✔ **A 5-quart saucepan** for cooking soups, stews, and chilies

- ✔ **A 10-inch cast-iron skillet,** which will become more nonstick as it's used and seasoned (without the harmful and toxic chemicals that Teflon or other nonstick pans often contain)

  Cooking in cast-iron pans actually increases the amount of iron in your food, a fact that's good for nonmeat eaters to know! After all, adequate dietary intake of iron is important for healthy blood production.

- ✔ **One or two cookie sheets** for baking cookies, biscuits, scones, and roasting vegetables

- ✔ **A 13-x-9-inch glass baking pan** for making casseroles, lasagna, and other entrees

- ✔ **A 9-x-5-inch metal bread loaf pan** for sweet and savory breads

- ✔ **A 9-inch-diameter round cake pan** to bake layer cakes

- ✔ **An 8-inch square cake pan** for brownies and other cakes

- ✔ **A 9-inch pie pan** to wow your family with fresh pies

Cooking utensils

The right tool for the job streamlines your cooking. I prefer tools that serve more than one function so my kitchen isn't stuffed with single-job items. Saving space leaves more room for better organization. You can accomplish just about any basic vegan cooking task with the following cooking implements:

- **Three nesting mixing bowls:** Stainless steel bowls are lightweight and easy to clean. However, heavier glass bowls stay put as you stir.

- **One set of dry measuring cups:** I recommend getting these cups in 1 cup, ½ cup, ⅓ cup, and ¼ cup sizes. These cups can be used to measure dry ingredients like whole grains, flour, or chopped nuts.

- **One set of measuring spoons:** Spoons in 1 tablespoon, 1 teaspoon, ½ teaspoon, ¼ teaspoon, and ⅛ teaspoon sizes work well. Plastic or metal spoons are good options.

- **A 2- or 4-cup liquid measuring cup:** I love the new ones where you can pour liquid in and look down (instead of leaning over and looking to the side) to read the measurement — brilliant!

- **A vegetable peeler:** A Y-shaped peeler is best because you can use it for potatoes, apples, and harder squashes, too. The ceramic blades won't rust as easily as the metal peelers.

- **A fine mesh, bowl-shaped strainer:** This tool can be used for washing grains and straining tea or infusions.

- **A colander:** Use your colander for rinsing veggies and fruit as well as for draining pasta and cooked vegetables.

- **A wooden cutting board:** A board of at least 12 x 14 inches works well for most of your cooking needs.

    To keep your cutting board from slipping and sliding while you chop up your veggies, place a couple of slightly damp kitchen or paper towels underneath it for traction.

    Avoid plastic cutting boards so you don't ingest microscopic bits of plastic that chip off over time.

- **A rolling pin:** You have three types to choose from these days: a long, smooth wooden cylinder with tapered ends for your hands, a traditional pin with handles, and now *silpat* pins that are nonstick and work great for delicate pie crusts. I love the silpat and wooden cylinders because they're both easy to clean.

- **A rubber spatula:** A traditional rubber spatula is great, but you may prefer a "spoonula," which has more of a scoop to it.

✔ **Kitchen tongs:** These tongs are great for lifting hot tempeh bacon and other items out of a pan, tossing a salad with dressing, scooping vegetables from boiling water, and placing hot food on composed plates. They're also invaluable for germ-a-phobes who don't want someone else's hands touching their food.

✔ **A wire or bamboo steaming basket:** These baskets are wonderful for steaming veggies.

✔ **A timer:** Timing is everything in cooking, so be sure to invest in a timer to avoid overcooking your dishes. You also can use it to limit the amount of time you spend on Facebook — I'm allowed 20 minutes a day.

✔ **A wire whisk:** Whisking allows for the proper combining of liquids such as homemade salad dressings or the adding of wet ingredients into dry.

✔ **A few wooden spoons:** Wooden spoons are indispensible in the kitchen; they're easy to grab and they clean up in a snap.

✔ **A slotted spoon:** Wooden or stainless steel work well for scooping veggies, pasta, beans, or other bits out of water.

✔ **A microplane:** This type of grater, which is sometimes called a "ginger grater" or "micro-zester," is great for zesting citrus fruits and grating ginger or nutmeg.

✔ **A metal spatula:** Perfect for the vegan grill-master in charge of flipping veggie burgers. A metal spatula also is useful for turning pancakes or sautéed tofu in a skillet.

Knives

You can remove that huge butcher block of knives cluttering your counter; vegans don't need all those steak and boning knives! However, a few good knives are essential for any chef — vegan or otherwise. I use the following knives most often (see Figure 7-1):

✔ A serrated bread knife that's at least 10 inches long (this knife is great for bread but also perfect for thinly slicing tomatoes)

✔ An 8- to 10-inch chef's knife for chopping vegetables

✔ A paring knife, used for peeling fruit and broccoli stems, coring apples and pears, and several other basic kitchen tasks

You also want to get a sharpening steel that you can use to sharpen your knives at home. High-carbon steel knives are easier to sharpen at home.

Is my old cookware considered vegan?

A common concern among new vegans is whether their old cooking equipment, which once cooked and prepared animal foods, is considered vegan. For example, a baking dish that was used to broil meat can still be used to roast cauliflower, but is it still vegan? The answer lies with you and your personal comfort level. In my opinion, we already consume more than our fair share of material goods, so I choose to allow my family and friends to use my kitchen tools for their nonvegan cooking. Doing so is more earth friendly and takes up less space in my cramped cabinets. For me, these values are more important.

If you feel terribly uncomfortable with using old dishes and utensils that once touched meat and can afford to do so, consider donating or selling your used kitchen tools and buy new, unused items. Vegans are obliged to consider their consumption based on several levels: environmental friendliness, personal health, and animal safety. If you share a kitchen with nonvegans, discuss your wishes with your housemates if you prefer to keep cooking tools separate. For more in-depth discussion on living in harmony with meat eaters, see Chapter 8.

Note: If sharing gadgets doesn't bother you, be sure to make the necessity of extreme cleanliness clear when it comes to preparing animal foods. Cross-contamination of food-borne illnesses can easily occur in a mixed diet kitchen.

Figure 7-1: The basic knives that any cook should have.

chef's knife

paring knife

serrated knife

Go to a home or kitchen store and hold several brands and styles of knives to get a feel for which ones you like best. Consider how heavy the knife feels, how easy the grip feels, and whether you like the balance of the weight as you rock it back and forth across a cutting surface.

Sharp knives are safe knives! Have your knives professionally sharpened one or two times per year, and then use your steel at home regularly. The sharper the knife, the less pressure you need to cut, which prevents spastic flailing of knives in the kitchen.

Special equipment to consider

The preceding sections cover the basics, but in this section I want to introduce you to a few more fun and useful kitchen items that can add a lot of power to your recipe repertoire. These items allow you the versatility to save time and dish washing and increase your success when attempting more complicated dishes and party menus. These specialized tools include the following:

- An immersion or "stick" blender for blending soups in the pot and creating smooth, creamy sauces without using the extra dishes that a counter top blender does

- An electric rice cooker for cooking all kinds of grains and saving space on the stove

- A toaster oven for quick reheats and toasting without having to use the whole oven or the microwave (whose safety and healthfulness is questionable; see the nearby sidebar, "Rethinking the microwave")

- A food processor for chopping, grating, and mixing larger quantities quickly

- Washable kitchen scissors for cutting herbs, opening packaging, and trimming veggies

- A mortar and pestle, sometimes called a *suribachi,* for grinding herbs, spices, mixtures, and pastes

- A silicon or nylon pastry brush (the new silicon brushes are much easier to clean and can be used for both sweet and savory applications)

- A funnel for pouring homemade sauces, purees, and other liquids into smaller receptacles

---

Rethinking the microwave

A microwave may seem like a kitchen must-have, but as you turn the corner and start down the path of a healthier way of eating and living, I encourage you to reconsider the microwave's role in your kitchen. According to many doctors and nutrition experts, microwave ovens create carcinogenic compounds in food and destroy much of the nutrition found in natural foods. Apart from these health concerns, microwave cooking tends to encourage reliance on frozen and processed meals. Cooking or reheating natural foods on your stove top or in a toaster oven takes a tiny bit more time, but it tends to be healthier and tastier!

Filling Your Kitchen with Wholesome Whole Foods

It's simply smart (and easy!) to stock up on a variety of *whole foods,* those foods that have all their original, edible parts intact (see the nearby sidebar "The skinny on whole foods" for more info). Fresh, packaged, canned, and frozen whole foods allow flexibility for your personal tastes and nutritional needs.

Fresh foods are definitely more healthful, but it's unrealistic to think that everyone can rely completely on fresh food. So stock your cupboard with the basics listed in this section to provide yourself with a variety of menu options. Rely on these packaged, canned, and frozen foods to round out your on-hand options. Whole grains and other cereal products, legumes such as beans, peas, and lentils, as well as herbs, spices, seasonings, and canned and frozen goods are inexpensive and smart pantry essentials.

To ensure your success, prepare your pantry in steps with a clear goal of where you want to go. Compile lists of foods you want to accrue over time, choose a handful of beginning recipes, and cut yourself some slack: This transition *will* be bumpy for a while. With a little practice and continued education, your new vegan lifestyle will work out nicely!

Great grains

Whole grains and other cereal products provide excellent complex carbohydrates, minerals, and energy in the form of protein and healthy fats. These nutritional must-haves are so versatile that they're an excellent choice for every meal: breakfast porridge, side dish, or entree for lunch and dinner. You can even bake them into breads and desserts! Eating grains in whole, stone-ground, sprouted, split, or cracked varieties ensures that you're getting great nutrition.

When buying cereal and grain products like pasta, bread, crackers, and boxed cereal, check the ingredients for natural sweeteners like agave, molasses, and brown rice syrup. These sweeteners are more healthful than the more refined options like high-fructose corn syrup and white sugar.

Multigrain and *sprouted grain* products are easier to find these days. Products labeled "multigrain" offer more nutrition and amino acids (read: complete protein!) from a variety of grains. Sprouted grain breads and cereals are made using soaked and sprouted grains that are mashed together and baked into a loaf. The sprouting activates the grain's enzymes, which create more protein, vitamins, and minerals and often create a product with higher protein and fiber. The nutty, rich flavor of these products is wonderful.

The skinny on whole foods

The most common reasons for choosing a vegan lifestyle are to improve your health and reduce your impact on the environment — and whole foods help you on both fronts. Eating whole foods ensures your body's access to unadulterated nutrition that it can use while creating true vitality. Whole foods also require less energy to produce and package than highly processed foods. So consuming whole foods reduces your *carbon footprint,* the amount of pollution your actions and purchases contribute to the environment via plastic, fuel for transportation, and energy for production.

An apple with the skin on is a whole food. A peeled apple is not. Whole foods contain more nutrition and health benefits. For instance, an unpeeled apple contains more fiber and heart disease–preventing flavonoids. Similarly, brown rice is a whole grain and a whole food, while white rice is a processed or refined grain (it isn't in its original state, and it isn't a whole food). Brown rice still has its outer layers, the germ and bran, attached, which gives it more energy and nutrition. White rice has been processed to remove the germ, bran, and natural fats. This removal extends the shelf life of the rice, but leaves it devoid of its original nutrition and energy.

Whole grains are *unpolished,* meaning the outer layers haven't been polished away; the intact outer layers help maintain the foods' health-supportive fats. But these fats are more likely to oxidize and turn rancid, so proper storage is an important factor. Check out the later "Storing Your Goods to Ensure Freshness" section for more information on proper food storage.

Including a variety of whole foods is necessary to ensure a healthy vegan diet. The best way to start cooking with whole foods is to take it easy on yourself: Master a few whole food recipes and techniques and repeat them until you get really comfortable. Simple menus with fresh, quality ingredients taste great and improve your health. Slowly transitioning your cooking style will ensure your success. After these recipes and techniques become second nature, you can expand your repertoire and get creative. Flip to Part IV for some recipes to get you started.

Whole grains and whole-grain products bring balanced energy and fantastic nutrition to your everyday diet — and using them couldn't be easier! Consider a variety of grains, such as the following, to ensure good options for taste and texture:

- ✔ Bulk whole grains like brown rice (short grain, long grain, jasmine, and basmati), millet, quinoa, amaranth, barley, spelt, oat groats, kamut, teff, and rye
- ✔ Whole-grain pastas in various shapes and flavors
- ✔ Whole-grain baking and pancake mixes
- ✔ Cornmeal polenta that's premade, dry in a box, or in bulk

- ✔ Frozen whole-grain pancakes, waffles, premade pizza crusts, vegan tortellini, and ravioli in various flavors
- ✔ Breads (sliced or fresh, locally made whole-grain loaves), pita bread, tortillas, English muffins, bagels, and rolls
- ✔ Whole-grain breakfast cereals and hot porridges

Luscious legumes

Filling, cheap, nutritious, and delicious — legumes have it all! Useful for meals of any ethnic bent, these versatile bundles of energy are easy to find, store, and prepare. This food group is a large plant family made up of beans, lentils, peanuts, and peas.

Beans are tiny powerhouses of protein, complex carbohydrates, fiber, calcium, iron, potassium, and B-vitamins. When you get the inevitable question, "Where do you get your protein and iron from?" your answer is simply: "Beans!"

Beans are good for you and easy to find. Even if your local supermarket only carries a few varieties of dry beans and lentils, you can stock up on countless varieties from any ethnic market. Indian, Chinese, Japanese, Hispanic, and even specialty European grocers often carry many kinds of beans whether they're dried, canned, or frozen.

Common frozen varieties are soybeans (also referred to as edamame), green beans, and peas. Canned beans are convenient because they're already cooked, and you can choose from countless types. The most common canned beans are chickpeas (also called garbanzo beans), kidney, black, adzuki, navy, and pinto. You also can find cans of soups and chili mixes containing black beans, kidney beans, pinto beans, lentils, and peas. The available choices for dried beans are too numerous to list here, and because they're so cheap, you can feel confident when picking out a few types of beans with exotic-sounding names.

Beans and peas often lurk in premade products in the supermarket deli or freezer section. Lentil and pea soups made with vegetable stock may be found on the hot deli counter. Check out the packaged veggie burgers made with mashed beans, falafel, and hummus mixes made from chickpeas. You can find the hummus mixes freshly made in the deli or dried in packages. Dried bean flakes can be a time-saver as well. Simply add water to create a cheap, yummy, protein-packed side dish or burrito filling.

Digesting beans and legumes more easily

Some people have difficulty digesting beans and other legumes, and in turn develop gas, bloating, and other intestinal problems. If you have these issues, here are a few tips for alleviating them when cooking and eating legumes:

✔ Chew beans thoroughly and eat smaller amounts.

✔ Choose smaller beans, such as adzuki, lentils, mung beans, and peas, because they're usually easier to digest. Larger beans like pinto, kidney, navy, black-eyed peas, soybeans, garbanzo, lima, and black beans are harder to digest and should be eaten in smaller amounts and less often. Luckily, soy products such as tofu, soymilk, tempeh, and miso are easier for most people to digest.

✔ Season beans with vinegar, salt, miso, or soy sauce near the end of cooking. If these seasonings are added at the beginning, the salt interferes with the cooking process and the bean won't cook completely. Plus, adding vinegar toward the end of cooking helps break down the indigestible sugars in beans, making them easier to digest.

✔ Cooking with herbs and spices such as fennel, epazote, or cumin helps your body digest beans more easily.

✔ Place 1 to 2 inches of kombu or kelp seaweed in your pot of beans to aid in digestion, add nutrients, and soften the beans.

✔ Soak your beans for eight hours in clean, cold water. Drain the soaking water and rinse the soaked beans to remove any released *oligosaccharides*, or sugars, released by the soaking process. Cook the soaked, drained beans in fresh water as directed.

Combined with whole grains, vegetables, or mock meats, beans are a fabulous savior to the harried, healthy home chef. Stock up on some of the following products:

✔ Dried, bulk, fresh, canned, or frozen beans and peas

✔ Brown, green, red, black, white, or yellow lentils

✔ Several of these types of beans: lima, pinto, navy, mung, soy, great northern, cranberry, chickpeas, white cannellini, black-eyed peas, adzuki, anasazi, black, or kidney

Babies under 18 months shouldn't eat beans because they can't digest them properly. However, maturing digestive tracts can usually tolerate lightly processed soy-based foods like tofu and soymilk, steamed green beans, and peas. Head to Chapter 21 for more on baby vegan diets.

Fruits and veggies

Buying and eating more produce is on everyone's New Year's resolution list, but it can be tough to decide which items you should buy fresh, frozen, or canned. All three are valid choices, but certain methods are better for certain types of produce. Use the general guidelines in this section when making your produce purchases.

Foods to buy fresh

Most fruits and vegetables taste better when purchased fresh rather than frozen or canned. I find that salad greens, especially leafy greens like kale, collard, and bok choy, should always be purchased fresh.

Don't rely on the implied cleanliness and safety of produce that has been pre-wrapped or precut. It isn't as fresh as the real thing and may not have been washed properly. Even those convenient organic baby-sized carrots should be given a proper rinse before eating, because they may have been dipped in a bleaching agent to prevent discoloration.

Frozen for convenience

While fresh is generally considered the healthiest form of fruits and vegetables, you may not have access to quality items year-round. So you may need to purchase frozen veggies from time to time.

Flash-freezing technology has come a long way: Fresh produce is often frozen within a few hours of harvest these days. You can now find apples, beans, berries, broccoli, collards, corn, okra, peaches, peas, and even precut winter squash in the freezer aisle of the grocery store. Keeping several of these options on hand, along with the obvious veggie burgers and vegan ice cream, helps your freezer help you.

Canned goods . . . good?

You may ask: If fresh is best, why would I ever buy canned foods? The short answer is convenience. Canning used to be a home-based enterprise where people preserved their extra harvests in cans and jars for consumption during the long winter months. But now, because fewer people grow their own food, companies have perfected factory canning to bridge the gap.

Automated factory canning is now the norm, and the industrialization of canning has brought with it a few important considerations:

- ✔ Canned food can be high in sodium, which is directly associated with high blood pressure and heart disease.

- ✔ The high-heat processing needed to ensure a safely canned product also destroys many of the nutrients found in fruits and vegetables.

- ✔ Fruit from cans and jars is often packed in sugary syrups, so it shouldn't be counted as part of your daily recommended intake of fresh produce.

Preserving the goods you find on sale

When your local farmer's market is offering organic blueberries at $2 per pint, stock up! You can easily save those goldmines at home, along with many other fresh items. Simply pour the berries onto a large plate in batches and pick through to remove any leaves, stems, or moldy berries. Rinse the berries, pat dry, and freeze in plastic freezer bags or other freezer-safe containers.

You can do the same with fresh tomatoes that you've cooked down (cool to room temperature before pouring into containers, of course), cleaned and chopped leafy greens, shucked corn kernels (or whole, fresh cobs), peas, and green beans. To freeze potatoes, peel them, cut them into chunks, and then blanch them for about 2 minutes in boiling water. After blanching, immerse the chunks in a bowl of ice water to stop the cooking. Drain and cool them and then freeze in freezer bags. Properly stored produce can keep for up to six months in the freezer.

However, if you're stuck buying canned veggies, don't worry. It's still better to eat canned veggies than no veggies at all. In fact, canned beans, vegetables, and soups can be used healthfully in a vegan diet. Just be sure to read the label and buy low-sodium cooked beans, vegetables, and vegan soups. And only buy canned fruits that are sugar free. To further reduce the sodium of canned beans, be sure to rinse before cooking.

My cupboard is always stocked with several kinds of canned beans, tomatoes, and vegetable bean soups for vegan eating on the fly. The convenience of canned foods lies in the fact that you can stock up to ensure you always have access to healthy food choices at home.

If possible, skip the canned corn and peas; these vegetables are better-tasting and better for you when frozen.

Spices, seasonings, and handy condiments

Round out your pantry with the following flavoring basics, and you'll never be at a loss for a fully satisfying, health-supportive meal:

- ✔ **Sweeteners:** Barley malt, maple syrup, agave syrup, and brown rice syrup
- ✔ **Herbs and spices:** Ground ginger, chili powder, curry powder, ground cumin, onion flakes, garlic powder, thyme, oregano, marjoram, rosemary, bay leaf, and cinnamon

✔ **Baking ingredients:** Vanilla extract; baking powder; baking soda; whole-wheat pastry flour for baking cookies, cakes, muffins, and breads; cornmeal; flaxseeds; and kuzu, a powdered starch made from the root plant that's used as a thickener and that's great for strengthening the digestive tract

✔ **Oils and vinegars:** Balsamic, brown rice, red wine, and ume vinegars; canola oil; extra-virgin olive oil; and toasted sesame oil

✔ **Sea vegetables:** Nori paper, dulse flakes, hijiki, and kombu (kelp)

✔ **Condiments:** Fruit juice-sweetened ketchup; stone-ground or American-style yellow mustards; *ume paste,* a pureed paste made from pickled plums; *shoyu* or *tamari,* naturally fermented soy sauces; sesame tahini paste; miso paste; mirin cooking wine; canned unsweetened coconut milk; olives; sea salt; fresh black peppercorns in a grinder; and vegetable stock, either in cubes or in aseptic boxes.

Storing Your Goods to Ensure Freshness

Proper storage of whole foods, seasonings, and herbs is important to ensure that they stay fresh as long as possible. After all, transforming and bulking up your kitchen with vegan products can be expensive — you don't want to lose any ingredients to moisture, pests, damaging light, or heat. Instead of leaving open bags of food in your cupboard, which can invite pests and moisture-causing mold, store packages in sealable bags or airtight containers. This section provides you with an overview of how to store your new vegan ingredients appropriately.

How to store your food depends on the type of food it is. Consider the following guidelines:

✔ **Dry grains and legumes** should be kept in a cool, dark, and dry place. Dried beans can keep for more than 20 years when stored properly! Keep beans and grains in well-sealed containers away from light and heat. A dark basement is an excellent storage place. Just be sure to keep all food containers at least a few inches off the ground to prevent moisture and rodent problems.

✔ **Shelled nuts and seeds** keep for up to a year if stored in well-sealed containers in the freezer.

✔ **Whole-grain products** such as breads and crackers come without suspicious preservatives and shelf-stabilizing additives (see the later section "Decoding food label lingo" for more information). However, that means they're more likely to mold. Storing these products in the refrigerator or freezer helps them last longer.

I especially like to keep my Ezekiel sprouted, whole-grain, and multigrain breads in the freezer. Then when I need a piece of toast or a "cheese" sandwich, I simply pop them in the toaster and they're good to go.

✔ **Most fresh fruits and vegetables** fare best in the crisper drawer of your fridge. Exceptions are bananas, stone fruits like peaches, and tomatoes, which lose flavor in the fridge. Strawberries keep longer when refrigerated, but they taste better when allowed to warm up to room temperature before you eat them. To ripen avocados, leave them on the counter. But after you mash them into guacamole, press plastic wrap or a glass bowl onto the surface of the guac to prevent browning and refrigerate. Store apples in the fridge to keep them cold and make them taste sweeter.

✔ **Potatoes, onions, ginger, and garlic** are fickle, but when stored properly, they stay fresh for a long time. Store garlic heads in a cool, dark place to prevent sprouting. I keep mine in the silverware drawer. Potatoes and onions should be kept separate from each other in a cool, dark place to reduce contact spoiling, and don't leave them in the plastic bags they come in. Also, don't eat potatoes that have "gone green" under the skin. Fresh ginger keeps best in the butter section of your fridge.

✔ **Dry seasonings** like herbs and spices typically keep for six months after opening, so buy them in small quantities. Store them in sealed containers in a dark cabinet or drawer away from the heat and moisture of the stove. You often can buy dry seasonings more cheaply, and in whatever quantity you like, in bulk from health food stores.

Keep a permanent marker in your spice cabinet and write the date on the jar whenever you open a new spice.

✔ **Fresh herbs** should be stored in plastic storage bags or other sealable containers in a 40- to 45-degree crisper. Don't wash them until you're ready to use them, because moisture promotes spoilage. Several varieties can be kept in separate bags or wrapped in dry, clean cloths or paper towels. When it's time to use them, wash the herbs and dry them completely; they're much easier to chop when dry.

Shopping Savvy

Shopping for your healthy vegan foods will be a little different from your old grocery routine. You have many sources to explore, and you'll be surprised at how many good options you have available to you. Even your old supermarket will offer great choices; you just need to find out how to read labels with a new set of eyes. So, in this section, I show you the best places to search out your vegan food, and I give you the lowdown on reading those food labels. (Chapter 11 deals with shopping for vegan nonfood items.)

Vegan-friendly places to shop for food

To find all the amazing, health-supportive vegan foods that you want to start including in your menus, you may need to broaden your shopping trips in variety and geography. But don't worry: Even the corner deli can offer surprising proteins and a diverse array of snacks to tide you over between trips to the health food store. With planning and practice, your vegan-oriented grocery shopping will become second nature and will bring you into contact with a more diverse population of food lovers. Check out the following places to start stocking your new vegan kitchen:

- **Co-ops:** These are cooperative operations that usually are run by members or the people who shop there. Most co-ops are akin to health food stores, but they offer a substantial discount to members who work a few hours a month or pay a yearly membership fee.

- **Delis and convenience stores:** These places aren't known for their variety of healthy food options, but even truck stops often carry raw nuts, seeds, and fruit. Some delis offer a fully stocked, meat-filled case of food that you wouldn't touch in your current vegan life, but they also may provide bean and veggie salads, vegan soups, bread, fruits, nuts, and bottled water to get you to the next health food store.

- **Ethnic markets:** These markets may seem mysterious, with their foreign aromas and alphabets and exotic displays, but they hold wonderful ingredients and surprises for vegans. Most ethnic cuisines base a large proportion of their meals on grains, beans, and vegetables — just like vegans!

  Indian markets, for example, offer dahl or lentils, herbs and spices (often in bulk for less expensive prices), curry mixes, fresh produce, and whole grains. Chinese and Japanese markets offer huge varieties of leafy green veggies, ginger, spices, soy foods and tofu, teas, grains, and beans. Middle Eastern markets offer hummus, beans, stuffed grape leaves, and rice dishes.

- **Farmer's markets:** These fresh markets can be found in every state, and the numbers are growing every year. Most of the markets offer a variety of fruits and vegetables, ethnic prepared dishes, vegan baked goods and condiments, and sometimes soy products.

  Farmer's markets can be indoors or outdoors, and they offer a wonderful opportunity to connect to your food on a deeper level. Talking to the farmer who grew your fresh, local produce, for example, can be a profound experience that makes every bite taste a little better. Plus 100 percent of your dollar goes directly to the small farmer rather than being divided between grocery brokers and manufacturers. Farmer's markets also give you a better understanding of what's growing seasonally in your area. Eating seasonal, local produce offers better nutrition and leads to less pollution because the food had a shorter distance to travel.

✔ **Grocery stores:** The average grocery stores today offer more and more vegan-friendly products as well as organic produce sections and bulk and ethnic aisles. My trips to see family in West Virginia have become easier to pack for over the years because the local grocery chain has expanded its health food section to include organic nut butters and frozen vegan burgers.

Don't be afraid to talk to your local grocery store manager to request that they start carrying certain items. If you bring a list of products and brands that you will buy, they may just start carrying them! You'll have even more success if you encourage your vegan friends to do the same!

✔ **Health food or natural food stores:** These stores offer a safe haven for vegans. You'll get to know staff members there who are familiar with the foods that are truly vegan, you'll find loads of soy-based proteins, and you can even purchase organic, vegan versions of your favorite treats. Even health food stores that seem to carry 90 percent supplements and vitamins and 10 percent whole foods can offer good products when you're in a pinch.

Stores that have a lot of high-quality, fresh produce and high product turnover are best, especially when buying bulk. Many of these stores offer deli counters with premade vegan options as well as fresh juice and smoothie bars. These stores also are good places to connect with other vegan-minded locals, find a book on alternative health, buy cruelty-free health and beauty products, and even sit down for a cup of organic tea if the stores have cafes.

✔ **Warehouse and membership stores:** These stores can offer great deals on certain bulk purchases, such as grains, beans, herbs, spices, soy foods, and even organic produce.

If you don't already belong to one of these stores, find out whether any of them offer special sneak-previews for nonmembers. These sneak-previews allow you to explore the aisles to look for items that you would buy, which in turn helps you to decide whether the membership is worth the price.

Decoding food label lingo

Discovering how to read the ingredients on a food label is as important as learning to balance your checkbook or drive a car — it's a basic skill in this modern age. So, if you're in the dark, here's what you need to know: The first ingredient on the label is the largest ingredient in the package, by volume, followed by the next largest, down to the smallest. If a bottle of pasta sauce lists tomatoes first, for instance, that bottle contains mostly tomatoes. If the second ingredient is high-fructose corn syrup, however, put the bottle back! Even though this sweetener is vegan, it's difficult for your body to process and shouldn't be considered part of a healthy diet.

You can determine the quality of a product by its ingredient list. In general, a healthier product has fewer ingredients on the label. Lean toward products that contain whole-grain flours or whole grains, recognizable ingredients, and natural sweeteners (see Chapter 6 for more on natural sweeteners). Don't buy products that contain artificial flavors, colors, or preservatives, because they can be neurotoxic, lead to mood swings, and interfere with good health.

Labels can be difficult to read, especially when it comes to *trans fats* — the unhealthy, harmful-to-your-heart fats that can be included in many packaged, frozen, and fried foods. If you see *hydrogenated* or *partially hydrogenated oils* anywhere on the ingredient list, that means there are trans fats in the food. Manufacturers can state "0 grams trans fats" on the labels if the product contains less than .50 grams of trans fats. Only labels that read "trans fat free" are truly devoid of this cholesterol-raising fat. Even though you can eat vegan sources of trans fats, I recommend staying away from these foods completely.

Don't be shy about asking health food store employees if they know about a certain product. If you're unsure of the source of a product's ingredients and don't get the answers you need from store employees, contact the manufacturer by calling the 800 number listed on the food. Or go to the brand Web site to find out more. Companies are happy to give you this information, especially if it leads to more sales because their products are appealing to other segments of the population.

Foods with the USDA Organic label on the front (see Figure 7-2) are made from at least 95 percent organic ingredients, and products with the Vegan label are 100 percent certified vegan (see Chapter 11 to find out what this label looks like and for more about it). These labels are important for you as a vegan to recognize because one of the reasons you probably chose to become vegan was to live healthier and lighter on the earth. Even though you don't have to eat organic foods to be vegan, eating organic foods is healthier and better for the planet and your body.

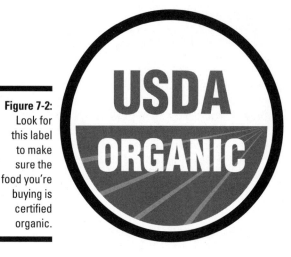

Figure 7-2:
Look for
this label
to make
sure the
food you're
buying is
certified
organic.

Surprisingly vegan supermarket sneaks

Though I don't encourage people to eat these foods often, it's surprising and fun to discover that an old "bad" treat is actually vegan! These foods were compiled from PETA's Web site as well as information from the manufacturers:

- Charms Blow Pops and Lollipops
- Cracker Jack
- Dot candies
- Dum Dum Pops
- Famous Amos Sandwich Cookies (Vanilla)
- Fritos Original corn chips
- Hot Tamales
- Hubba Bubba bubble gum
- Jolly Rancher hard candies
- Jujubes
- Lemonhead candies
- Mike and Ike candies
- Now and Later candy
- PEZ Candy
- Sour Patch Kids candy
- Starburst candy
- Swedish Fish
- Sweet Tarts candy
- Twizzlers
- Wheat Thins (Original, Multigrain, and Reduced Fat)

Eco-vegan shopping tips

Keeping your vegan head on straight may seem like a big enough challenge without worrying about the health of the planet — but isn't that one of the reasons veganism sounded like a good idea in the first place? There are countless ways to reduce, reuse, and recycle your way to vegan heaven (like keeping those broccoli rubber bands for organizing long extension cords!). Here are some ideas to get you started:

✔ **Buy food in bulk.** *Buying in bulk* can mean one of two things: Either you buy the large packages and quantities of food at once or you buy unpackaged foods from large bulk bins that don't require individual packaging and labeling. Each option is less expensive than buying one package at a time. Buying unpackaged bulk foods like loose beans, grains, flours, teas, coffees, herbs and spices, nut butters, and oils requires less packaging, and, therefore, less plastic and cardboard is used to deliver the goods.

   This method is ideal because it offers big discounts on those foods, and you can even reuse your old plastic bags and containers to refill with food again and again. If you choose to use clean glass jars to refill at the store, be sure to weigh them first so you can subtract the weight of the container from the total cost at check-out.

✔ **Use cloth bags to carry your groceries home.** They're nicer looking, and they make eco-sense! You also can consider reusing the plastic shopping bags that you already have stuffed in the closet.

✔ **Lather up with bar soaps (instead of liquid) when washing your hands and dishes and even when cleaning around the house.** Bar soaps are cheaper, lighter, and require less fuel to transport. Many liquid soaps contain animal-derived ingredients, and all are packaged in unsustainable plastic bottles. To use bar soap when cleaning the dishes, your hands, or your house, simply shave or grate some soap into a spray bottle and fill with water, shake, spray, and clean!

✔ **Buy your food in easier-to-recycle containers like cardboard or paper instead of plastic bags or tubs.** Some vegan margarines come in cardboard boxes wrapped in paper and others come in plastic tubs. Try the paper one first. You also can buy great healthy pastas in boxes instead of plastic bags.

✔ **Grow your own herbs, fruit, and veggies.** Growing your own food is inexpensive, good for the environment, and better for you because you have access to fresh food that isn't treated with herbicides and pesticides. Setting up a little container garden of herbs in your window is easy and inexpensive, and it looks great with any décor.

Chapter 8

Coexisting with the Meat Eaters in Your Home

In This Chapter

▶ Living happily with nonvegans

▶ Understanding the food and comfort needs of everyone in your household

▶ Teaching children valuable cooking and meal planning skills

*A*t some point in your vegan life, you'll most likely live with a nonvegan. You may find one on craigslist as a roommate, marry one, give birth to one, or marry into a family populated by meat and dairy lovers. All these carnivores will eye your tempeh and nutritional yeast flakes suspiciously at first. Considering vegans comprise less than 5 percent of the population, it's no surprise that you need to get comfortable with mixed company.

Living with nonvegans presents interesting and unique challenges. Some households are able to find a middle road that works for everyone relatively easily and quickly. Others find it difficult to accommodate everyone's culinary and ethical desires in the same kitchen and dining room.

This chapter helps you figure out a way to work with most mixed living situations. Every home is comprised of unique individuals, so unless you're all holding hands and happily skipping toward vegan utopia, you'll encounter some bumps in the road. But not to worry. Every kitchen has room for upgrades that can facilitate a calm and civil co-cooking environment. Discovering how to offer a gracious dining experience for nonvegan guests is another topic of concern that I cover here.

Any children in the household can learn valuable lifelong habits about healthy eating and cooking when the topics of menu planning, shopping, ingredient selection, and cooking together are discussed openly and honestly.

Cementing a relationship with the 4 C's

Every relationship, including marriages, roommate partnerships, and child-parent relationships, requires a bit of work and attention. However, relationships that involve a battle of diets require even more effective effort to achieve success. Remember the 4 C's when building your household partnerships: clear, consistent, compassionate communication. You may come to an agreement about how to shop, cook, and eat together, but your cohabitants may evolve their diets or get frustrated with previously agreed-to boundaries. The vegan in the house must take it upon herself to generate positive, productive conversations about everyone's satisfaction with the meals and cooking routines. Don't let bad moods fester; otherwise they result in blow-up fights, bigger problems, and a tense living environment. Remember that everyone needs to feel respected and valued. You can always find a way to compromise and find options that work for the group as a whole.

Kitchen Etiquette for Mixed Households

Many vegan activists recommend that we be *vegangelical* with our loved ones and friends, taking every opportunity to point out why their flesh food is hurting their health, the planet, and the animals who unwillingly give it up. However, keep in mind that as you like to have your choices respected, so do they.

Some meat eaters are willing to avoid eating and cooking nonvegan foods around their vegan partners. Others are happy to eat vegan food at home while feeling relaxed enough to order anything outside the home. You just have to figure out what works best for you and those who live under the roof with you. In the illustrious words of Tim Gunn, you can find a way to "make it work."

If you can't tolerate living with someone who continues to eat meat or dairy, it's best to look for people who share your view.

Who's in a mixed household?

Mixed households can include all sorts of combinations of vegans and nonvegans, including the following:

- Multigenerational splits (mom and dad are nonvegan and the two kids are vegan, or vice versa)
- Several lifetime vegans
- A 50-50 split of 2 meat eaters and 2 vegans

✔ A whole family that has agreed to venture into the vegan lifestyle together

✔ A lone vegan amongst a crowd of omnivores, which is the most common instance

Luckily, no matter what your situation, you can live by your principles for a peaceful, cruelty-free life and still share your kitchen with someone who eats meat and dairy products. It isn't always easy, so you have to be strong. Every relationship is about giving and receiving, and sharing food is one of the most intimate things we do with the people we love and live with.

Staying sane in a mixed household

Long-time couples who have been happily living and eating together for years may suddenly have major problems when one person decides to change his diet for health, spiritual, or other reasons. When the other person gets angry about the changes or rules required for a vegan diet, it's important to remind her that you still care about and respect her and her choices. Be honest and tell that person that your dietary changes don't mean you're going to judge her or love her any differently.

If your current cohabitant doesn't fully embrace the vegan lifestyle and he only changes for *you,* it may result in unexpressed anger or discomfort in the house. If you live with someone who refuses to stop bringing meat or dairy into the house after you have asked him nicely and explained why you desire it, you can take the following steps to make the kitchen easier for everyone to use:

✔ **Keep a separate set of cutting boards for nonvegan use.** Color-coding is easiest, because no one will be able to claim confusion as to which board is used for cutting chicken. Use red cutting boards for meat and green cutting boards for vegan foods. Alternatively, you can keep wooden cutting boards and write the words "vegan" or "veggie" on some and "meat," "fish," or "dairy" on others in the corner with permanent ink.

✔ **Label vegan-only areas of the refrigerator so that meat isn't placed next to the vegetables.** This reduces the risk of crossover contamination from flesh-borne bacteria and illnesses.

✔ **Reserve a special glass in your cupboard for the cow's milk drinker** if you dislike the idea of sipping your hemp milk from the same cup.

✔ **Label chef's knives for different purposes.** You can use a similar process that you do for the cutting boards. Or you can buy one good-quality chef's knife just for the vegan and ask that it not be used to cut meat, poultry, fish, or dairy products.

✔ **Consider buying mixed sets of Fiesta dishes with two colors.** One color can be used for the vegans and the other color for the meat eaters. These colorful sets are nice because you can mix and match to go with whatever color scheme you have chosen for your kitchen or dining room.

  ✔ **Work out rules for the stove and for the pots and pans.** If sharing the stove top becomes too contentious, or if you don't have the space to keep or the money to buy an extra set of pots and pans just for meat preparation, ask the meat eater to prepare his flesh foods outside on a meat-only grill. This compromise keeps the meat smell out of the kitchen and provides a safe haven for their cooking.

Use nonconfrontational humor to deflect minor issues at home. Rather than turning every slight refrigerator indiscretion into World War III, tell your friend, husband, wife, or child to "Mooooooove your cow's milk over to the dairy side of the fridge, please!" or "EGGs-cuse me! There are eggs on top of my tofu salad." Respect the fact that your humor and grace will lead to widening acceptance for your dietary choices — after all, no one wants to convert to a militant, humorless lifestyle.

Many families and roommates are able to "agree to disagree" and try to keep the dinner duels out of the house completely. The meat eater or cheese lover agrees to keep those foods out of the house and live vegan with their friend or loved one. When they eat outside the home, however, all bets are off and they can order whatever they want. This plan works pretty well for most people. The whole family can be vegan at home, and the omnivore can eat whatever he desires at work, school, or out for dinner. Just remember to keep the lines of communication open — the last thing loved ones need is to stress each other out about food.

To get some support and ask questions of other vegans who have gone down this mixed-household path before, join `www.veggieboards.com`, which is a huge online community that allows you to post questions and read experiences from others.

Keeping Everyone Healthy and Happy

In a majority of households in the United States, the woman does the cooking . . . and the cleaning and the windows and the childcare, but that's another book (*Feminism in the 21st Century For Dummies,* anyone?). If the goddess in your kitchen has gone vegan, and no one else has bought a ticket for that bus ride yet, it may be up to her to organize the menus, choose healthy ingredients, plan the cooking schedule, and ensure a wide variety of satisfying meals that keep everyone happy.

The vegan and the carnivore: Eating out on date night

For obvious reasons, when a mixed, vegan-carnivore couple goes out to eat, they may have trouble choosing a menu that suits both people's desires. Consider making a pact to visit a dedicated vegan restaurant every other outing.

Certainly the meat eater can find something he likes on a vegan menu, just as the vegan can find some combination of side dishes at a steak house.

This amount of work can be too much for one person to handle, no matter how much of a superwoman (or superman) the vegan at home may be. For a family that contains more than one eating style, making sure that nutritious ingredients are used and available takes planning — and the whole crew must get in on the act. Using a weekly menu planner, like the one in Chapter 9 can help you make sure that no one goes hungry. The last thing you need on a Wednesday night is for the vegan in your house to be left with brown rice and old carrots while the rest of the family chows down on frozen chicken wings.

Variety for vegans and nonvegans alike

If meat is on the menu (and hopefully the omnivore will be cooking it outside away from the open kitchen window), provide many vegan side dishes. Offering a variety of side dishes ensures that the nonvegan gets enough fiber, minerals, and vitamins. If you're making mixed steamed vegetables, quinoa pilaf, and baked tofu, make extra of each to share with the meat eater (and anyone else who would like to partake of them).

Here are some vegan side dish ideas that everyone can rejoice over (especially because they take less than 5 minutes to prepare):

- Artichoke hearts, hearts of palm, caper berries, and pickles
- Baked tortilla chips, vegan refried beans, salsa, and guacamole
- Brown rice tossed with a favorite salad dressing
- Carrot sticks, celery sticks, and red pepper spears with Tofu Sour Cream for dipping (see Chapter 13 for the recipe)
- Chickpeas tossed with olive oil, lemon juice, and sea salt and then sprinkled with fresh parsley

✔ Cucumber and radish slices sprinkled with sea salt

✔ Fresh, whole-grain bread dipped in warm vegan spaghetti sauce

✔ Hummus, rice crackers, and olives

✔ Steamed broccoli and carrots drizzled with olive oil

Vegan meals everyone can love

Shopping for two separate meals for one family or group of people can get expensive. It's usually much healthier for your bottom line to all go in on vegan ingredients together. If the nonvegans in your home will agree to it, you can all save money by eating vegan at home and focusing your food dollars on organic produce instead of the more expensive organically raised animal products. Choose the best quality ingredients no matter what your meals contain. Avoiding high-fructose corn syrup, genetically modified organisms, and antibiotic-laced dairy and meat products is the healthiest way to eat.

Plus, making several vegan meals for the whole family on a weekly basis can cut down on grumpy attitudes and extra cooking for the house chef. The vegans in the house will appreciate the effort, and it will introduce new foods to the rest of the family. If the normal chef isn't vegan, perhaps the new herbivore can take responsibility for cooking these meals, giving the overworked kitchen slave a night off.

Use some of these ideas for your "vegan night" family meals that everyone can enjoy:

✔ **Greek garden picnic:** steamed whole-wheat pitas, hummus, kalamata olives, stuffed grape leaves, carrot sticks, sliced avocado, and tofu cubes marinated in olive oil, salt, pepper, and lemon juice (or try marinating Tofu Cheese cubes; find the recipe in Chapter 13)

✔ **Italian night:** spinach lasagna with shredded vegan mozzarella, whole-wheat garlic bread, and green salad with oil and vinegar

✔ **Mexican burrito bar:** steamed whole-wheat tortillas, vegan refried beans, black beans, pinto beans, brown rice, tofu sour cream, shredded lettuce, diced tomato, sliced black olives, minced green onions, guacamole, and fresh salsa (or whip up the Seitan Burrito recipe in Chapter 14)

✔ **Moroccan night:** blended carrot soup, couscous, and cucumber salad with marinated tofu cubes

✔ **Pizza party:** premade frozen vegan pizza crusts (or homemade ones) topped with tomato sauce, vegan pepperoni or sautéed tempeh, sautéed mushrooms, and any other toppings your family likes

> ✔ **Soup night:** white bean minestrone made with vegetable stock, creamed broccoli soup, and hearty lentil stew alongside fresh, crusty bread (a great Sunday dinner — makes great leftovers for days!)

> ✔ **Sushi night:** white and brown rice, slivers of carrots, avocado slices, and baked and marinated tofu or tempeh for a make-your-own sushi bar, which you can serve alongside dishes of pickled ginger and wasabi paste

Supporting the family vegan nutritionally and emotionally

No one is perfect, even an ethical vegan striving for food nirvana. In fact, some of us vegans are still called by the siren song of the cheese counter or dairy cooler. If you're having a difficult time quitting eggs, turkey, or cheese, you'll be relying on your willpower a lot, even if your logical brain constantly reminds you of all the reasons why you should be vegan. Do your best, do what you can, and resolve to feel good about what you *are* doing. And most important, seek out support from the family and friends you're living with.

When one family member is vegan, and the rest aren't, work together to ensure that the "odd man out" gets proper nutrition and emotional support. Even though parents or kids may decide to continue eating dairy or meat, they can still take care of the vegan's needs.

Here are some ways to support the vegan nutritionally:

> ✔ Let your newly vegan teenager have some say over what foods he will eat. He may even want to prepare his own meals when the rest of the family is dining on eggs, meat, or fish.

> ✔ If you feel that the vegan's food choices aren't nutritionally sound, speak up and offer alternative ingredients to help bolster the quality of the meal.

> ✔ Ensure that the kitchen is always stocked with healthy vegan snacks, such as a bowl of fresh fruit on the counter, dishes of nuts, seeds, and dried fruit in the pantry, and chopped veggies in the refrigerator.

> ✔ Stock up on quality vegan dinner options like vegan burger patties, frozen edamame, whole-grain pasta, and vegan canned soups. This way the vegan always has a standby option for a wholesome supper.

As you support your vegan loved one nutritionally, be sure to support him emotionally as well. Vegans don't make the choice to change their diets and lifestyles lightly. They have often researched a lot of information, and they're usually inspired by their knowledge to make positive changes in their lives. Supporting a new vegan in their efforts is important for nonvegans who love them. And to the vegan that support means the difference between success and struggle or even failure.

Rather than taunting, teasing, or even sabotaging your vegan family member, ask what you can do to help him. Perhaps visiting a health food store once a week for special ingredients would be useful. You also may be able to help by looking up new vegan recipes and offering to help cook with him. If you see that your loved one is having a difficult time eliminating meat or dairy, be a cheerleader and tell him that you respect his decision to go vegan even if he can't do it 100 percent at first. These words and deeds will give your loved one the strength he needs to be healthy and happy.

Getting Your Kids Involved in Making Healthy Meals (Vegan or Otherwise)

Just because both parents are committed to providing a vegan diet at home doesn't mean the kids will be on board for changing the family feasts. Because there are several stubborn stages of childhood, kids of any age may refuse to board the broccoli bandwagon. If your child or teen goes against the family grain and doesn't want to go vegan with everyone else, offering him healthy vegan side dishes alongside an agreed upon nonvegan portion can help integrate the teen into meal times.

It's always a good idea to use a transition period (rather than going cold Tofurky) when the whole family isn't 100 percent behind the idea of changing the household diet. If every person has a say and an opportunity to take ownership of the process, it's more likely that the plan will be successful.

I recommend having a family powwow, where everyone sits down together and chats about the changes family members may soon see. The parents present the information behind their choices and the reasons for the upcoming dietary changes. The kids can ask questions, talk about their concerns, and have a chance to present their arguments as well. Each person can talk about their concerns and everyone can present ideas on how to eliminate those concerns. Once the meeting is over, agree that family members can stick to their diets at the end of this meeting. Children may decide to continue eating meat or dairy, but the quantity and quality can be improved and changes agreed to. Each family will find their own way; just be respectful of every person's feelings and health concerns.

In order to create some excitement for the next phase of your family's dietary shift, try some of these methods for getting your kids involved in the process:

- ✔ **Give each person a cookbook budget.** Every member in the house can spend a set amount of money on new vegan-friendly cookbooks to bring new ideas into the kitchen. Don't edit their choices, however. If your young one wants to buy *Vegan Cupcakes Take Over the World,* so be it! The recipes will come in handy when trying to soothe a cranky sweet tooth, and they'll inspire culinary curiosity.

- ✔ **Hold a vegan milk taste test.** Buy one box each of plain soymilk, vanilla soymilk, plain rice milk, vanilla rice milk, plain hemp milk, and vanilla hemp milk. You also can get a box each of the chocolate versions of soy, rice, and hemp milk. Give everyone a scorecard and use a scoring system of 0–10 to grade each milk. This taste test can help the family decide which milks they like to drink plain, use over cereal, and add to their tea or coffee. Bonus round: Make your own nut milks like almond and cashew and hold a separate competition for those.

- ✔ **Let each person plan at least one meal a week and bulk it up with healthy, vegan ingredients.** Say that your oldest son chooses Thursday's dinner and wants a spaghetti dish with garlic bread. Talk to him about using whole-grain pasta and adding olives, crumbled tempeh, mushrooms, or other favorite vegan ingredients to the sauce. The garlic bread can be whole grain as well. Plan ahead to use the best quality ingredients as well as healthy side dishes like steamed broccoli, green salads, and baked sweet potato fries.

- ✔ **Involve your children in the cooking process as often as possible.** Kids as young as 2 years old can help out in the kitchen with pouring premeasured ingredients, mixing, or just playing with cooking spoons. Older kids can measure, chop, mix, and pour with a responsible sibling or a parent. And because most kids like projects that involve getting ready (assembling the ingredients, preheating the oven), making messy fun, transforming ingredients, and seeing the finished results of their labors on the dinner table, it pays to dedicate a little time every day to their culinary education. If you do, they'll be more likely to eat the healthy ingredients you desire. To help instill the important life skills of basic human meal preparation, invite (or require) their help a few times a week or even nightly. Stock up on kid-friendly cooking tools like smaller aprons, animal-themed spatulas and measuring spoons, and brightly colored, shatter-resistant mixing bowls.

To help smaller vegans get involved in the kitchen, consider purchasing a Learning Tower. This adjustable step stool with safety railings ensures that your little one can help mix, stir, and pour at the counter without falling. Visit www.learningtower.info for more information.

Planning, shopping for, and preparing healthy meals are invaluable life skills. All children, whether they're vegan or not, should be coached on the following abilities before they leave home:

- ✔ Planning a menu, writing a shopping list, formulating a food budget, and shopping for good-quality ingredients

- ✔ Washing produce, mixing ingredients, using a timer, sifting, baking, sautéing, and roasting

- ✔ Using knives and stoves safely

- ✔ Using appliances properly (All children will reach the age when they can use blenders, ovens, food processors, and toasters without adult supervision, but until that age, make sure they only use them with an adult.)

- ✔ Practicing proper hygiene in the kitchen, including washing hands thoroughly and regularly, cleaning up as they go, and properly handling and storing food

Chapter 9

Planning Your Meals to Stay on Track

*L*iving vegan means becoming a skilled food detective. Navigating the grocery store can be like picking your way through a field of land mines — but only in the first couple of weeks. You'll quickly pick up on the ingredients to avoid and discover new favorite products to fill up your cupboard.

This chapter can help you plan a healthy week of meals to get you started in la vida vegan. Shopping from lists of staple supplies, planning well-rounded meals, and stocking up on snacks all ensure that your best vegan intentions are successful. So grab your magnifying glass, your shopping list, a quick swig of hemp milk from your hip flask, and then head out the door to your local health food store. And don't forget to bring your reusable shopping bags for extra eco-vegan street-cred.

Building a Plan for Vegan-rific Success

Looking at lists of possible vegan staples can help you understand what's necessary to round out your kitchen supply. After all, creating your own lists and planning out meals is your key to success and really owning this process. As many coaches have said, "If you fail to plan, you're planning to fail."

As you begin planning, first think about what types of foods you want to eat on a regular basis and begin amassing recipes that you can go to time and again. Then use the lists provided later in this section to plan your own shopping trips.

As you're making the transition to a vegan lifestyle, you can start with a clean slate and dump every nonvegan item in your cupboard (giving the items away to someone who will use them, of course). Or, to make the switch a little more sane, you can begin by planning to eat one or two vegan meals each day. Doing so allows you to keep some of your old food habits while transforming your shopping, cooking, and eating habits slowly.

Gathering easy and appealing recipes for meal planning

Begin your vegan adventure by looking through recipes and choosing several that fit your taste preferences and cooking abilities. Selecting simple foods and recipes that don't require too many sophisticated cooking tools or techniques can help you transition in the beginning. Also, starting your cooking projects on the weekend will allow you more time and flexibility. Running to the store for a missing ingredient will be less stressful on a Saturday afternoon compared to a Tuesday night.

Include complex carbohydrates, protein, and healthy fat sources throughout your day. And don't rely too heavily on processed "fake" vegan foods like soy hot dogs and deli meats. These foods are fine every once in a while, but you can easily fall into the habit of using them every day instead of cooking with fresh food. These soy foods aren't inherently unhealthy, but they aren't whole, vital foods like vegetables and whole grains either.

Make sure you have a healthy breakfast every day so you don't get stuck starving out in the wilds of your office or in the car on the way to school. Keep a variety of snack options stocked at home so you can take a couple with you to help you through the day.

Here are some smart and simple menu planning tips to help you succeed:

- ✔ **Provide variety and choice.** Start with foods you know that you and/or your family enjoy and offer several healthy options that they can pick and choose from.

- ✔ **Offer a variety of textures, tastes, and temperatures.** A variety of textures, tastes, and temperatures, including smooth, creamy, crunchy, chewy, cold, spicy, hot, sweet, salty, bitter, and sour, can make mealtimes more interesting.

- ✔ **Appeal to the senses with colors, smells, and presentation.** Food should be visually appealing and fragrant as well as tasty. Choose foods of different colors and arrange them with some care and attention to make the dish look nice and appetizing. Include herbs, spices, garlic, and onions to fill the air with delicious smells to stimulate your appetite.

Shopping smarter with vegan shopping lists

If you become a wiser shopper, you'll find it much easier to stick to your vegan lifestyle. Shop smarter by doing the following:

- ✔ Take a list and hit the right stores at the right times. To avoid long lines and crowded aisles, try shopping during off-peak hours like weekend evenings or early in the morning.

- ✔ Don't shop when you're starving — you're more likely to fill your cart with junk food. Eat a small, healthy snack before you leave the house.

- ✔ Choose a grocery store that offers you most, if not all, of the items on your list. Store hopping to find everything you need will only become a chore and cause you to resent your new diet.

- ✔ Get to know a few stores to help you find better priced items, and you'll learn the lay of the land, making for a faster shopping experience.

Get ready, get set, shop! The following sections provide you with lists of basic vegan foods that you can begin accumulating to ensure healthy, delicious vegan cooking. You certainly don't need to buy these items all at once (you likely already have some of them); start with what you think you'll use most often or with what's on sale and work from there.

Staples and dry goods

You'll be able to whip up any number of yummy vegan meals and treats with these items:

- ✔ **Baking ingredients:** baking powder, baking soda, dry active yeast

- ✔ **Dried beans:** black beans, chickpeas, kidney beans, lentils, pintos, white beans

- ✔ **Dried mushrooms:** morels, porcini, shiitake

- ✔ **Egg replacements:** Ener-G Egg Replacer, ground flax meal, whole flax-seeds

- ✔ **Flavorings:** carob or cocoa powder, kosher salt, sea salt, vanilla extract, vegetable broth cubes, wasabi powder

- ✔ **Flours:** buckwheat flour, cornmeal, oat flour, spelt, unbleached white flour, whole-wheat flour

- ✔ **Herbs and spices:** allspice, basil, bay leaves, chili powder, cinnamon, cloves, cumin, curry powder, five spice powder, garlic powder, ground ginger, ground mustard, marjoram, onion flakes, oregano, paprika, red pepper flakes, rosemary, sage, thyme, turmeric, whole black peppercorns, whole nutmeg

As a general rule when cooking with herbs, 1 teaspoon of dried herb may be substituted for 1 tablespoon of chopped fresh herb. Store your herbs and spices away from heat and light sources. Similarly, don't store them over the oven or in the window because heat and light cause them to lose their flavor faster. Replace herbs and spices that are older than 1 year.

- **Milks:** boxes of almond, carob, hemp, oat, plain chocolate or vanilla, rice, or soymilks

- **Natural sweeteners:** agave, blackstrap molasses, brown rice syrup, maple syrup, rapadura

- **Nuts and seeds:** almonds, cashews, pecans, popcorn kernels, pumpkin seeds, sesame seeds, shelled sunflower seeds, walnuts

- **Pasta and noodles (whole-grain flour):** buckwheat soba noodles, couscous, elbow noodles, spaghetti, lasagna noodles, rice

- **Sea vegetables:** arama, dulse, hijiki, kombu, nori paper, wakame

- **Organic soy products:** silken tofu in aseptic packages, frozen edamame beans

- **Teas:** black, green, herbal

- **Thickeners:** agar, arrowroot, cornstarch, kudzu

- **Unsweetened dried fruit:** banana chips, dried apples, Medjool dates, raisins

- **Whole grains:** barley, brown rice, bulgur, corn grits, millet, oat groats, quinoa

- **Whole-grain products:** cereals, bagels, multigrain bread, pita, wraps

Canned goods and condiments

The following pantry items will last for months or even years, so stock up when they're on sale:

- Canned tomatoes in diced, crushed, paste, or whole form

- Capers

- Hearts of palm

- Jams and fruit butters, including strawberry, blackberry, marmalade, apple butter, and pumpkin butter

- Marinated artichoke hearts

- Mustards such as yellow, Dijon-style, and spicy

- Naturally brewed soy sauce like Bragg's Liquid Aminos, shoyu, and tamari (wheat free)

- Naturally sweetened ketchup (the regular stuff is vegan, but full of high-fructose corn syrup, which isn't healthy)

- Nut and seed butters like almond, peanut, cashew, and tahini

✔ Oils, including extra-virgin olive, flaxseed, coconut, canola, and toasted sesame

✔ Pasta sauce

✔ Salad dressing (vegan varieties, of course)

✔ Salsa

✔ Unsweetened coconut milk

✔ Vegan mayonnaise

✔ Vegetable broths in different varieties, including salted, unsalted, mushroom flavored, and onion flavored (buy cans or aseptic boxes)

✔ Vinegars such as Balsamic, red wine, unpasteurized apple cider, umeboshi, and white

Refrigerated products

You'll be buying these products more often, but still be on the lookout for sales. Just make sure you don't buy more than you'll actually eat before the expiration date:

✔ Fresh ginger

✔ Hummus in all kinds of flavors, including plain, garlic, roasted red pepper, green onion, and kalamata olive

✔ Leafy green vegetables such as broccoli, kale, bok choy, cabbage, lettuce, and spinach

✔ Mushrooms in varieties like portabella, button, shiitake

✔ Olives and pickles

✔ Seitan

✔ Soy-based margarines like Earth Balance

✔ Soy foods, including chickpea miso, barley miso, tofu, tempeh, hot dogs, veggie sausages, and deli meats

✔ Tofu cream cheese and sour cream

✔ Yogurt, including soy or coconut milk-based, plain, unsweetened, and vanilla

Freezer items

Having some convenience food and treats on hand is a great way to stay on track with your vegan meals. Stock your freezer with the following essentials:

✔ Frozen vegan meals or pizzas

✔ Fruits like berries, pitted cherries, and peaches

✔ Juices such as apple, cranberry, and orange

  ✔ Nondairy ice cream

  ✔ Tofu- or vegetable-stuffed ravioli

  ✔ Vegan potstickers and spring rolls

  ✔ Vegetables, including broccoli, corn, edamame, mixed stir-fry vegetables, peas, and spinach

  ✔ Veggie burgers

Fresh produce

Fresh produce is delicious and relatively inexpensive. Whenever possible, buy local and go for organic varieties. The following items are versatile enough to work in numerous vegan recipes:

  ✔ Avocados

  ✔ Bell peppers

  ✔ Fresh fruit of all kinds, including bananas, apples, pears, kiwi, grapes, cherries, pineapple, and melon

  ✔ Garlic

  ✔ Lemons and limes

  ✔ Onions, including yellow, white, Vidalia, and red

  ✔ Sweet potatoes

  ✔ Tomatoes

  ✔ White potatoes

  ✔ Winter squash varieties like butternut, acorn, and kabocha

Starting Your Meal Planning with the Best Breakfast for You

Your doctor and your mom were both right: Breakfast *is* the most important meal of the day. Many of my clients have seen dramatic decreases in sugar and caffeine cravings when they finally commit to daily breakfast plans. If you have a cup of coffee and chocolate for breakfast, you'll most likely fall headlong into a sugar crash by late morning. This type of eating — loading up on caffeine and sugar in the early morning hours — is all too common. Cravings for more sugar and caffeine are more likely in the afternoon if you rely on them in the morning.

Breakfast is the most important part of your meal planning because preparing a healthy breakfast that includes the most supportive foods for you and your body type ensures that your energy is more stable throughout the day. If your energy is stable and your nutrition needs are met, you'll be less likely to go off track with junk food or other less-than-desirable choices.

Try this unique, half-week breakfast test to find out which foods set you up for a day of solid energy, and which foods lead to energy crashes or sugar cravings later in the day. Eat as much of each food as you want, but choose only one food each day. Here are your options:

> **Saturday:** steel cut oats, brown rice, or quinoa (no sweetener)
>
> **Sunday:** orange juice, green tea, black tea or coffee (added sweetener is okay)
>
> **Monday:** steamed vegetables
>
> **Tuesday:** nuts and seeds, vegan cheese, or steamed tofu
>
> **Wednesday:** quick oats, toast, or bagel (no sweetener, soy margarine, or nut butter)

Immediately after you eat each of the foods, note how you feel. Do you feel full? Bloated? Content? Then note how you feel a few hours later. Were you hungry for more food within an hour or so? Did you eat a smaller lunch or a bigger one? Were your food cravings throughout the day worse or diminished?

After you try this evaluation of different foods, you'll have a better idea how your food choices affect your energy. This knowledge helps you plan your menus better. If you have a presentation at work or school, for instance, you can choose the breakfast you know works better to create the steady, focused energy you need.

Exploring Some Menu Ideas to Get You Started

Leafing through cookbooks can be intimidating for some new vegans. You may feel that you need to whip up complicated, multicourse menus right out of the gate.

No need to fret — start your first couple of weeks by using the menu ideas I list in the following sections. These options offer you simple cooking ideas that pair up all the foods your body needs. Protein, complex carbs, and healthy fats should appear regularly throughout your day.

Also be sure to check out Part IV in this book for loads of tasty and easy recipes for every meal.

Easy breakfast options

After you understand your reactions to different breakfast foods, you can put together several options for healthy morning munchies that give you the energy you need. Vegan breakfast options abound and the recipes in Chapter 12 can help you develop a grand repertoire. This list offers suggestions for delicious yet simple vegan breakfast foods:

- Leftover beans warmed up and wrapped in a tortilla with salsa.

- Leftover brown rice reheated with steamed broccoli, cubed tofu, and carrot coins.

- Leftover whole grain reheated with soy, rice, hemp, or coconut milk. Add a pinch of cinnamon, ¼ cup chopped nuts, and a handful of raisins.

- Sautéed tofu slices on whole-grain toast drizzled with flax oil, salt, and pepper.

- Smoothie with bananas, berries, or cherries, ½ cup raw nuts, and 1 or 2 tablespoons flaxseeds. Add enough hemp, rice, or soymilk to liquefy.

- Soy or coconut milk–based yogurt mixed with 1 tablespoon flaxseed oil, berries, and sunflower seeds.

- Whole-grain bread spread with Earth Balance, nut butter, and apple butter. Add a glass of hemp, soy, rice, or almond milk.

- Whole-grain cereal with vegan milk, banana slices or berries, and slivered almonds.

Quick lunch list

Lunch can be a fly-by or a drive-through, but it also can be healthy and vegan. Use this list to stock up your kitchen with easy, fortifying midday meal options:

- Carrot sticks dipped in hummus with a side of olives

- Leftover grain rolled into nori paper with cucumber spears

- Leftover rice and beans folded in a tortilla with salsa

- Leftover whole grain heated up with a can of soup and 1 tablespoon of nutritional yeast flakes

- Mashed avocado and hummus spread on top of rye crackers

- Peanut butter and jelly sandwich with a glass of almond or rice milk

- Pita bread with baba ghanouj, avocado slices, and cucumber slices

- Soy hot dogs smothered with vegan chili and chopped onions

- Tomato soup sprinkled with nutritional yeast flakes and drizzled with flax oil

- Whole-grain toast spread with hummus and fresh tomato slices

Seven days of dinner

Dinnertime is a hectic affair in many households. With evening activities, household chores, traffic jams, and homework filling up our nights, fixing a healthy meal can seem overwhelming.

Use the following wholesome vegan dinner plans to get a new, positive rhythm into your evening agenda. These dishes can all be scaled up or down depending on the size of your appetite:

- ✔ **Very vegan dinner 1:** 1 to 2 cups quinoa cooked in vegetable broth served with 1 to 2 cups steamed broccoli drizzled with olive or flaxseed oil and sprinkled with slivered almonds or sesame seeds

- ✔ **Very vegan dinner 2:** A bed of lettuce covered with 1 to 2 cups brown rice, 1 to 2 cups cooked pinto beans, a scoop of salsa, tofu sour cream and sliced avocado

- ✔ **Very vegan dinner 3:** Veggie burger on whole-grain bread served with a pickle, baked sweet potato fries, and quick sautéed bok choy

- ✔ **Very vegan dinner 4:** Hummus, baba ghanouj, rye crackers, kalamata olives, avocado slices, carrot sticks, cherry tomatoes, and 1 to 2 cups bulgur wheat tabbouleh

- ✔ **Very vegan dinner 5:** Hot vegetarian baked beans on top of steamed broccoli and baked Yukon Gold potatoes

- ✔ **Very vegan dinner 6:** Bean soup with steamed corn served alongside a green salad with olive oil and lemon juice

- ✔ **Very vegan dinner 7:** Roasted root vegetables (cubed beets, sweet potatoes, onions, and carrots) with curried red lentils simmered in coconut milk served over jasmine rice

Cook a double portion of any of these menu items at dinner and have leftovers for an easy, cheap lunch the next day.

Using menu charts

Planning a week of menus can really take the guesswork and stress out of shopping trips. If you already know what you're having for dinner on Thursday, you don't need to worry about running by the crowded grocery store on the way home from work. And you won't be tempted to order takeout or veggie pizza again either. Use the menu chart in Figure 9-1 to help guide your shopping trips.

Monday   **Date:**

Breakfast:

Lunch:

Dinner:

Tuesday   **Date:**

Breakfast:

Lunch:

Dinner:

Wednesday   **Date:**

Breakfast:

Lunch:

Dinner:

Thursday   **Date:**

Breakfast:

Lunch:

Dinner:

Friday   **Date:**

Breakfast:

Lunch:

Dinner:

Saturday   **Date:**

Breakfast:

Lunch:

Dinner:

Sunday   **Date:**

Breakfast:

Lunch:

Dinner:

Notes

Grocery List

☐ _____

☐ _____

☐ _____

☐ _____

☐ _____

☐ _____

☐ _____

☐ _____

☐ _____

☐ _____

☐ _____

☐ _____

☐ _____

☐ _____

☐ _____

Figure 9-1:
Sample
menu chart.

Making Sure You Have Healthy Snacks On Hand

Between tweeting your every move and posting your new vegan recipe demonstrations on YouTube, a busy vegan doesn't always have time for a sit-down meal. Don't worry new vegans — healthy snacking isn't difficult and options abound! You probably won't find many vending machines with healthy vegan choices, but you can find vegan snacks in almost every grocery store, deli, or convenience store.

Plan for your day by thinking ahead — will you be near a health food store in between meals? Do you have access to a refrigerator at school or work where you can store perishable snacks? Many nonperishable snacks are easy to just slip into your purse, backpack, messenger bag, or briefcase.

Staving off hunger with a well-timed nibble can prevent overeating at mealtimes. In fact, some people do better with several small meals a day rather than three squares. Any of the healthy snacks listed in the following sections can be expanded to create a substantial picnic plate of variety.

If you need to eat your snack on the run or won't have access to water for washing up, choose simple, cleaner foods. Bananas, mixed nuts, or an individual box of soymilk are easy to consume quickly without fuss or muss. On the other hand, if you can sit down on a "coffee break" in your staff room, you may be able to snack on something slightly more elegant like a soy yogurt with berries, or some carrot sticks with a small container of hummus.

Use the lists in the following sections to choose a variety of healthy snacks that will satisfy any kind of food craving you may have.

Sweet treats

To satisfy your sweet tooth, try the following:

- Carrot sticks
- Coconut date rolls
- Dried fruit like banana chips, mango slices, or apple slices
- Edy's Fruit Bars or Edy's No-Sugar Bars
- Frozen grapes
- Fruit salad
- Homemade apple juice popsicles
- Homemade oatmeal cookies with a glass of hemp, soy, or rice milk

- ✔ Lärabars

- ✔ Leftover cornbread muffin spread with apple butter

- ✔ Mixed melon cubes

- ✔ Raisins and sliced almonds

- ✔ Soy yogurt mixed with 100 percent fruit jam or jelly

- ✔ Soy yogurt with blueberries and crushed pineapple

- ✔ Stretch Island Fruit Company Original Fruit Leather

- ✔ Trail mix made of vegan chocolate chips, raisins, and raw almonds

- ✔ Whole-grain bagel spread with almond butter and jelly

- ✔ Whole-grain tortillas spread with vegan margarine and sprinkled with cinnamon and agave or brown rice syrup

Heretofore nonvegan treats like marshmallows were a luxury of the past. No longer! The good ladies from Sweet and Sara have now concocted several lovely flavors of marshmallows that hold up to roasting over a fire and mixing into veganized Rice Krispies Treats recipes. Find their mallow goodness online at www.sweetandsara.com. For other professional-quality sweet treats like truffles, brownies, cookies, and fudge, check out Allison's Gourmet online at www.alisonsgourmet.com. You also can flip to Chapter 15 to experiment with some tasty vegan dessert recipes, such as Fruit Kanten and Chocolate Peanut Butter Bombs.

Salty and savory snacks

When sweet just won't do, try these snacks instead:

- ✔ Dried, seasoned peas

- ✔ Grape leaves stuffed with spiced rice (also known as dolmas)

- ✔ Pickles and olives

- ✔ Rice Balls with Sesame Salt (see Chapter 13)

- ✔ Roasted, salted nuts

- ✔ Tamari-baked pumpkin seeds

Crunchy morsels

For whatever reason, a bit of something crunchy can really hit the spot. Here are some ideas to try:

- Air-popped popcorn drizzled with olive oil, salt, and nutritional yeast
- Blue, white, yellow, or red corn tortilla chips dipped in fresh salsa or bean dip
- Carrot and celery sticks or red bell pepper spears
- Celery sticks filled with almond or peanut butter
- Celery sticks filled with tofu cream cheese and raisins
- Kale Chips (recipe shown in Chapter 13)
- Mixed raw nuts
- Nabisco Saltine Crackers
- Original Triscuit Crackers
- Original Wheat Thins Crackers
- Raw sunflower and pumpkin seeds
- Rye crackers
- Sesame Melba Toast
- Soy crisps

Chapter 10

Comfort Foods: Veganizing Meat, Dairy, and Other Old Favorites

In This Chapter

▶ Creating vegan-friendly meals based on old favorite recipes

▶ Getting the scoop on vegan substitutions for meat, dairy, and eggs

*F*ood is often an important part of family history. Certain dishes make an appearance at holiday tables year after year, and they often have a story or fond memory stirred in with the ingredients. *Veganizing,* or re-creating a recipe with vegan ingredients, can be a nice way to keep an old family recipe in the fold of your new vegan lifestyle. Your tweaks will add a layer of family lore to Grandma's apple pie so that the original stories attached to it can continue to be shared at the table.

In this chapter, you find new ways to use vegan ingredients for creating menus that remind you of your old favorites. If you're a baker looking to transform some old recipes, you'll enjoy the tips for cooking without eggs, dairy, or butter. Later tips can help you thicken, gel, and bulk up recipes with cruelty-free ingredients for delicious vegan meals.

Taking Comfort in Your Vegan Food: Why Veganizing Is Helpful and Fun

Stepping into a new style of eating can feel uncomfortable at first. Your normal daily routines get shaken up. Going to the grocery store involves more planning than ever before. Favorite meals that you relied on contain ingredients that you want to avoid — but they were delicious and you miss them. Thankfully, you can veganize recipes so they don't include dairy, meat, fish, or eggs but still taste and look a lot like the dishes Mom or Dad used to make.

Researching recipes and browsing through vegan cookbooks to find veg-anized recipes can help you get your footing. *Vegan with a Vengeance* by Isa Chandra Moskowitz (Da Capo Press), *Cooking the Whole Foods Way* by Christina Pirello (HP Trade), and *The Garden of Vegan* by Tanya Barnard and Sarah Kramer (Arsenal Pulp Press) are excellent resources for tested vegan recipes. If you're trying to change a chicken potpie recipe, for example, look for existing vegan potpie recipes and compare them. Eventually you'll start trusting your instincts when deciding which substitutions work well in your recipes. Cooking regularly helps you understand what textures and flavors you're looking for and how to create them.

When converting any recipe with new ingredients, it's important to give your-self at least a couple test runs to try out your new ideas. In other words, don't plan on taking the very first batch to a potluck or family gathering. The results may need more refining.

Here's a basic checklist you can use to begin veganizing recipes:

- ✔ **Look through your recipes and choose a favorite that you know how to cook already.** Familiarity with a recipe gives you a mental image of what to aim for. If you know what the finished product is supposed to look and taste like, you'll find it easier to adjust your recipe as you work your way through it.

- ✔ **Circle all the ingredients that aren't vegan: dairy, eggs, gelatin, meat, fish, and so on.** Start substituting the ingredients with the appropriate amount of your chosen vegan substitute, as detailed throughout this chapter. Not every vegan ingredient is substituted one for one.

- ✔ **Try to use the same techniques, steps, times, and temperatures that are used in the original recipe.** Doing so gives you a good platform from which to make future changes.

- ✔ **Take notes as you cook.** You're basically writing your own new recipe, so you want to be sure and have a detailed record of how you did it for the future. Write down how much of each ingredient you used, and whether you did anything different than the description in the original recipe.

Some traditional egg or dairy recipes have a yellow coloring or certain savory flavor to them. To re-create that color use a pinch of turmeric or a little pre-pared mustard. For the missing flavor, try adding a little nutritional yeast or instant vegan broth powder.

Taking Advantage of Mock Meats

Some vegans miss the mouth feel of animal protein. It's human to enjoy a variety of textures, so including chewy, dense foods is a good way to ensure that your diet stays interesting. Luckily, protein alternatives offer an incredible array of textures and tastes on which to build new recipes. These fake meats can be like a blank canvas; most have naturally mild tastes, so you can create almost any flavor profile you want with herbs, spices, and seasoning.

Hundreds of vegan foods that mimic the animal foods you may be missing are available. Consider these wonderful alternatives:

- Vegan jerky made from soy, wheat gluten, and mushroom bases
- "Sausages" in many different varieties, including Italian, spicy Mexican chipotle, and apple sage
- Deli "meat" slices that come in turkey, bologna, and ham flavors
- Premade roast loaves for Thanksgiving
- Meatballs and great pizza toppings like vegan pepperoni and Canadian bacon
- Animal-free hot dogs and burger patties, which may be made with a soybean base or with nuts, vegetables, grains, and beans

Other vegans don't want anything with a fleshy texture in their mouths — hence, part of the reason they became vegan! Still, if you're in this camp, you'll find it easy to turn vegetables into the hearty portion of your meal. Here are some ideas:

- Try cutting vegetables like carrots, zucchini, and celery into larger chunks in your next stew. Doing so gives you those big bites of veggie flavor to crunch through.
- Mushrooms offer a wonderful savory taste and texture that can lend a new layer of flavor to stir-fry, sandwiches, pasta sauces, or soups.
- If you want a brunch recipe for vegan sausages, but the fake-meat versions taste a little too much like pork for your comfort, you can choose from many excellent recipes to make your own sausage "links" or "patties" out of beans, grains, and vegetables.

Soybeans as protein

The incredible soybean isn't much to look at in its natural state. It looks like any other bean. Yet this incredible vegetable has become the base for countless meatless meals. Two vegan power foods, tofu and tempeh, are derived from the soybean and can play a part in your daily menu planning. I give you the lowdown on these power players in the following sections.

Tofu

Tofu, sometimes called *bean curd* on Chinese restaurant menus, is basically soy cheese. A coagulant, such as naturally occurring calcium sulfate, gypsum, or magnesium chloride, is added to soymilk to curdle the liquid. The curds are separated and formed into cakes of tofu and then packaged. Some tofu is packaged in aseptic, vacuum-packed containers that are stocked in the Asian or health food aisle. Other types are refrigerated in water.

Tofu comes in several textures, which can be used for different types of dishes. *Silken* and *soft* tofu can be used to make mousse-like creations, desserts, and scrambles. *Firm* and *extra-firm* tofu are often used for more savory dishes, because they can be shredded or cut into chunks, cubes, or strips.

Firm and extra-firm tofu also are strong enough to be made into more meaty textures through freezing or pressing. Freezing and then thawing an unopened package of firm or extra-firm tofu gives it a spongy, meaty texture. You can then marinate and grill, broil, fry, or sauté it with ease. Freezing tofu removes excess moisture once it thaws and makes the texture spongier than pressed tofu. Freezing also keeps tofu fresh longer, so you won't have to worry about the expiration date. Just take it out of the freezer to thaw in the refrigerator at least 8 hours before you want to cook with it.

Pressing is a technique for pushing the excess water out of firm or extra-firm tofu. Pressed tofu absorbs more marinade flavor and won't release as much moisture into your recipe. To press your tofu, follow these simple steps and refer to Figure 10-1:

1. **Layer one or two clean kitchen towels on a cutting board near the kitchen sink. Set one edge of the cutting board on another folded towel to create a slight incline.**

   The incline allows excess moisture to drain away from the tofu.

2. **Place the block of firm or extra-firm tofu on the towels, and then lay another clean towel on top of the tofu.**

3. **Carefully place a plate or small cutting board on top of the tofu.**

4. **Balance a small weight, like a can of beans or tomatoes, on top of the plate.**

Let the tofu sit for at least 15 minutes. To remove even more water, change the towels around the tofu and allow the tofu to sit for another 10 minutes.

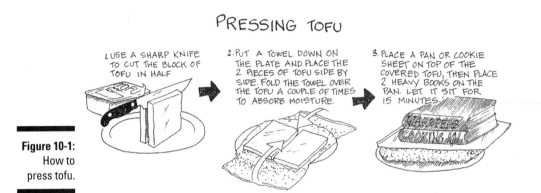

Figure 10-1:
How to
press tofu.

Tofu has little taste of its own. This mild taste is what makes it one of the best ingredients for veganizing recipes. Tofu absorbs any flavors, sweet or savory, so by using marinades, syrups, sweeteners, sauces, oils, vinegar, lemon juice, soy sauce, herbs, and spices, you can make tofu taste like practically anything!

Here's a basic preparation for tofu that has been pressed or frozen and thawed:

1. **Cut the tofu into four long, equal slabs, or dice it into cubes.**
2. **Marinate the tofu in a mixture of soy sauce, toasted sesame oil, minced ginger, garlic, maple syrup, and a pinch of cayenne pepper.**

   Refrigerate the marinating tofu for at least an hour, turning once after 30 minutes.
3. **Fry, sauté, or bake it at 350 degrees for about 15 minutes.**

The resulting tofu is great in a sandwich with your favorite fillings, or tossed on a green salad with your favorite dressing.

Tempeh

Tempeh is a less-refined version of tofu that originated in Indonesia. Whole, cooked soybeans are diced up into small bits and then mixed with an edible mold to start a fermentation process (much like the process through which some cheeses are produced). This fermentation creates enzymes, which make the soy protein more digestible and higher in B vitamins. The mold can look like veins of black, white, or gray running through the beans. The result is a dense, mashed cake of soybeans. These cakes of tempeh can be found in the refrigerator section at health food stores.

Tempeh has a denser texture than tofu, but like tofu, it can be baked, fried, sautéed, crumbled into casseroles or sauces, sliced into slabs and used for sandwich filling, or cubed and tossed into salads instead of croutons. Sticking with the "flavor sponge" theme, tempeh can be marinated in any mixture you like because it will soak up the flavors nicely. For a nice meaty recipe, try the Mushroom Sloppy Tempeh Joes in Chapter 14.

Wheat meat (a.k.a. seitan)

Seitan (say-tahn), also known as *wheat gluten,* is a great source of protein and is very low in fat. Even though it's made from wheat flour, seitan takes the place of the protein on your veganized menu. Because it's made by kneading and washing the bran and starch out of wheat flour, seitan is totally bland. However, to add flavor, you simmer it in a marinating broth. Chinese vegetarian restaurants commonly use seitan to make mock chicken, beef, or pork dishes.

Premade seitan can be found in tubs or vacuum packages in the refrigerator section at your local health or natural foods store. You can find seitan in many different forms, such as precut fajita strips, cutlets, or loaves. The texture of seitan is close to chicken, so it's especially good for replacing poultry in recipes. Dense, chewy, and often very tender, seitan can be a real crowd pleaser for dinner parties and celebrations that include meat eaters. Seitan is even tough enough to stand up to grilling and broiling, and it works nicely in stews and rich pasta sauces.

Making traditional seitan at home takes a little time, but it's pretty simple. The kneading process can be a meditation to enjoy and can easily be shared with family and friends. To make traditional seitan at home, follow the recipe in Chapter 13.

If you want a shortcut for making your own seitan at home, try purchasing one of the mixes available at your health food store. Harvest Direct's Seitan Quick Mix is a premade dry mix that shortens the cooking time and that is cheaper than premade seitan at the store. Make sure you follow the directions on the box exactly until you feel confident with the end result. After you're comfortable, you can move on to making your own from scratch.

Mushrooms

Mushrooms make frequent appearances on vegan menus due to their rich tastes and dense and chewy textures. Dried and fresh mushrooms add depth and earthy flavor to savory meals while adding medicinal benefits to your menus. Because mushrooms contain *glutamic acid,* the natural version of monosodium glutamate (MSG), they really liven up the flavors in dishes.

Shiitake, portabella, button, chanterelle, morel, and many other varieties can easily be added to soups, stir-fry, pasta, bean and grain dishes, stews, gravies, and sauces. Fresh mushrooms are wonderful to add to different kinds of dishes, and keeping a few varieties of dried mushrooms expands the variety of last-minute dinner options you have at home. Simply soak dried mushrooms in water until tender, about 15 to 20 minutes, before cooking. Some top *mycologists* (mushroom scientists) recommend cooking button mushrooms to break down cancer-causing toxins in this variety.

To replace meat in a casserole or chili, chopped portabellas can be sautéed with a little olive oil, garlic, and salt and then added in the meat step. Sautéed mushrooms also can be pulverized in a food processor to mimic the texture of ground beef in tacos or burritos. Grill or broil large, marinated portabellas and serve them between burger buns for a meat-like treat. Most Italian-style pasta sauces work well with sliced, diced, or whole mushroom caps cooked into them.

Textured vegetable protein (TVP)

Textured vegetable protein, or TVP, is a cost-saving, soy-derived product. Made from defatted soy flour, TVP is cooked under high pressure and then dried into flakes, granules, or chunks. An excellent source of protein and fiber, TVP is an inexpensive way for large institutions to feed huge numbers of people when meat is too costly. TVP also is a decent source of potassium, magnesium, and calcium.

TVP can be bought in bulk or in smaller packages and is a great substitute for ground meat in recipes like chili, tacos, and meatloaf. TVP keeps well in a cool cupboard in a sealed container for at least a year. This feature makes it a good option when stocking your vegan cupboards.

TVP absorbs liquid from sauces and marinades really quickly, so it's a nice fast-cooking protein source. Because TVP is such a great sponge, you may need to add extra liquid when converting traditional recipes. Add about 1 cup of TVP and an extra cup of liquid to your dish, and then combine well and cook according to the recipe. Dishes with TVP tend to freeze and defrost well, so they're good for time-saving, cook-ahead menus.

You may already be eating TVP and just haven't realized it. Did you know that you can buy TVP Bacon Bits? These vegan nibbles aren't wholesome enough to consume regularly (partially hydrogenated soybean oil, anyone?), but they can be a fun, occasional treat — especially for the aspiring vegan who struggles with giving up meat.

Bean and grain mash-ups

Countless cultures around the globe use native varieties of beans and whole grains as dietary staples. In the southwest United States and Central America, beans and corn have always been a part of the culinary tradition. Eastern European and Russian cultures include rye, spelt, and barley along with local beans to create hearty meals and complete proteins. Indian, Japanese, Chinese, Korean, and other Asian cultures have used many varieties of rice along with soybeans, lentils, and adzuki beans as the base for diets that many experts believe to be among the healthiest in the world.

Mixing different grains and beans together can be a wholesome technique for creating hearty meals. As you experiment with different combinations, you'll discover the wide world of bean and grain mash-ups. The possibilities are only limited by your imagination. Here are some ideas to get you started:

- Cooked kidney beans and brown rice can be mashed together with onions, celery, sunflower seeds, and herbs to create tasty veggie patties for burgers or to serve alongside breakfast.

- Lentils and quinoa can be mixed with mushrooms and sage for morning "sausages" to be baked or lightly fried.

- Refried beans and corn can be mixed with chilies and other vegetables to create delicious chili stews or layered dips.

- Any combination of grain and bean can be combined to form a loaf with whole-grain breadcrumbs, chopped nuts, and sautéed vegetables and mushrooms to bake a veggie loaf. Drizzle some naturally sweetened ketchup on top and bake for an old-fashioned presentation that will remind you of Grandma's meatloaf!

Egg-cellent Egg-Free Cooking and Baking

When nonvegans bite into my egg-free cookies and cakes, their eyes light up with delight, but they inevitably ask, "How did you make this without eggs?" Luckily, there are many ways to bake delicious creations without cracking eggs.

Traditional recipes for baked goods rely on eggs for specific functions. In these recipes, eggs

- Act as a binder to keep the ingredients and flour all working together in harmony

- Contain specific chemicals that react with other ingredients to create the *leavening,* or lifting, that happens during baking

- Thicken recipes

All three of these results can be obtained without eggs; you just need to understand what effect the recipe needs the egg for. If you're making a muffin recipe, the eggs would have been used as a binder. Mashed banana or flax-seeds will work well in that case. If you need to thicken a custard or quiche recipe, tofu will work well. Leavening is often created with baking powder or baking soda instead of eggs.

Tofu as ovo

Tofu comes to the rescue again; this time, instead of standing in for meat (as described earlier in the chapter), it becomes an egg replacer. Not only does tofu work well as a binder in baked recipes, but it also can actually look like eggs in other recipes. Full of protein without the cholesterol or bad karma of eating a baby chicken, tofu eggs are easy to prepare and delicious.

If you're looking for some ways to use tofu as a stand-in for eggs, try these tasty options:

- Crumble drained soft or silken tofu to make a scramble. To spice up your scramble, mix the tofu with sautéed onions, garlic, a pinch of tur-meric, and a little nutritional yeast. The flavors and colors all combine to create a very real-looking breakfast dish.

- Slabs of pressed tofu can be cut into rounds with a biscuit cutter and sautéed in olive oil, garlic and onion powders, and salt and pepper to make fake fried eggs. These "eggs" work nicely on toasted English muf-fins with Tofu Sour Cream for a nice brunch dish. (See the recipe for Tofu Sour Cream in Chapter 13.)

- Tofu can stand in the place of eggs for any quiche recipe. Buy a premade vegan pie crust or make your own, fill with mixed tofu filling, and bake for a glorious presentation.

Opting for vegan gelatin

Gelatin is an ingredient that's used to turn liquid into a solid or semi-solid. (Think Jell-O.) Gelatin is often used to thicken desserts, candy, ice cream, marshmallows, and low-fat yogurt. It also is used to make vitamin capsules, cosmetics, and photographic film, and to filter some alcohol, beer, and wines. Believe it or not, gelatin is made from the collagen found in animal bones, horns, hooves, skins, tendons, and other miscellaneous body parts. Commercial gelatin is a byproduct of the meat and veal calf production industry — so it's definitely not vegan.

Luckily, we vegans can avoid gelatin and still create dishes that need binding or gelling. You can now purchase packaged vegan gelatins in some natural food and grocery stores and online. Another excellent natural gelling agent is *agar,* or Kanten. (See the recipe for Fruit Kanten in Chapter 15.) This sea vegetable can be found in flakes, bars, and powders. Especially good for gelling aspics and terrines and creating creamy fillings for cakes and mousse, agar can be found in natural food stores and Asian grocery stores.

Binding without eggs

Certain recipes, such as casseroles, sauces, veggie patties, and simple cookie and muffin recipes, need a binder to keep all the ingredients together. To create the binding effect of one egg, use any of the following options:

- **A flour and water mixture:** Use 1 tablespoon plus 1 teaspoon soy, garbanzo, or whole-wheat flour mixed with 2 tablespoons of water to bind a muffin recipe or thicken a sauce or gravy.

- **Applesauce:** For sweet baked goods, such as cookies, cakes, muffins, and scones, ⅓ cup applesauce works well. Add ¼ teaspoon extra baking powder to the recipe to help with rising or leavening.

- **Ground flaxseeds:** Simmer 2 tablespoons of ground flaxseeds in a small saucepan with 3 tablespoons of water until thickened. Allow to cool before adding to recipes for baked goods in place of the egg.

    Flaxseeds are a great source of omega-3 oils, which means they can spoil quickly. Grind them fresh for each recipe, and store whole flaxseeds in the freezer in an opaque, air-tight container to prevent spoilage from light and heat.

- **Mashed fruits and vegetables:** For example, ⅓ cup mashed very ripe banana works well in sweet baked goods. Other substitutes include ⅓ cup of either mashed white or sweet potatoes or mashed or blended cooked vegetables.

✔ **Nut or seed butters:** You can use ¼ to ⅓ cup almond, cashew, or peanut butter. Or try the same amount of tahini or sunflower butter to bind a muffin or quick bread recipe. The same amount, or smaller, can be used to add richness and thickness to a sauce recipe.

✔ **Oats:** You can use ¼ cup quick oats as a binder, mixed with the liquid ingredients, in muffin or quick bread recipes. Oats also can act as a thickener in sauces and soups.

✔ **Powdered egg replacer:** You can find this egg substitute in health food stores. This product lasts indefinitely if properly stored in a cool, dry place. Best used in baking to bind recipes.

✔ **Tofu:** Use ¼ cup mashed or blended silken or soft tofu to help bind muffin, scone, and quick bread recipes. Add ¼ teaspoon extra baking powder to the recipe to help with rising or leavening.

✔ **Yogurt:** Try ⅓ cup soy yogurt to bind a muffin, pancake, or cookie recipe. Use unsweetened yogurt for thickening savory dishes like soups or sauces.

The New Dairy: Substituting with Vegan Milks, Butters, and Cheeses

Bessie the cow can have her retirement party now — the vegan dairy cooler is stocked full with cow's milk replacements that work really well in recipes. With all these great nondairy milks, butter substitutes, and cheese stand-ins, vegans can indulge in every food craving and texture possible.

Products can be made from grains, nuts, soy, or a combination of these. Vegan milks are easy to use in traditional recipes, because they generally replace the same amount of cow's milk. Baking, basting, grilling, and spreading are all still possible with your new favorite foods.

Got other milks?

Baking and cooking without cow's milk couldn't be easier these days. It's rare to enter a grocery store that doesn't carry at least soymilk. (And most stores even carry different varieties, such as unsweetened, sweetened, unsweetened vanilla, sweetened vanilla, chocolate, carob, and eggnog). You can even purchase soy cream and little individual juice-box sizes for kids. Many varieties of rice milk, hemp milk, and almond milk are available for people who want or need to avoid soy products. (Because soy is one of the top ten food allergies, it may make sense for you to try a non-soy version.)

Converting cow's milk in recipes is easy: If the recipe calls for 1 cup of cow's milk, use 1 cup of soy, rice, hemp, or nut milk. It couldn't get any easier than that!

A delicious way to get a larger variety of milks into your diet or baking is to make your own nut milks at home. Simply blend 2 cups of raw nuts with 3 to 4 cups of water for at least 2 minutes. Strain the resulting liquid through a fine mesh strainer lined with cheesecloth and you have delicious, homemade nut milk! This recipe works well with almonds or cashews.

Baking recipes sometimes call for buttermilk, which is a fermented product made from cow's milk. Buttermilk is great for leavening and is used in baking because it reacts with the baking soda to form more bubbles in the batter. To make your own vegan buttermilk, simply stir 1½ teaspoons apple cider vinegar into 1 cup of soymilk and allow to curdle at room temperature for at least 5 minutes before adding to your recipe. This makes 1 cup of buttermilk.

When converting a recipe by using vegan buttermilk, cut the amount of baking powder in half and use ¼ teaspoon of baking soda for each cup of buttermilk used. Use a one-to-one ratio when replacing milk with vegan buttermilk. This technique works really well in quick breads, scones, muffins, and biscuits.

Baking with "butter"

Butter or shortening is used in baking to add fat and flavor while also creating pockets of air within dough to give pastry a light and flaky texture. Butter also is used in recipes to create a golden brown crust in baked goods and gives a moist and rich mouth feel. Because butter is now off your menu, you need to use other products to create delicious baked goods.

Traditional shortening is technically vegan and can be used in place of butter in recipes, but it's so unhealthy and full of heart disease–inducing hydrogenated fats that I don't recommend it.

An alternative to shortening or butter in baking recipes is to use ¾ of the amount in an oil, such as canola or liquid unrefined coconut oil. You also can use vegan margarine for baking without much difference in the final product. Earth Balance is an excellent brand of vegan margarine; it cooks up nicely in cookies, cakes, and pie crusts.

Unrefined coconut oil, a healthy saturated fat, also can be used to replicate butter. Freeze the appropriate amount of unrefined coconut oil in a small bowl until it's hardened. Remove the bowl from the freezer and sit it in another bowl with warm water to loosen the chunk of coconut oil. Grate the frozen oil on a cheese grater and add the pieces to the flour in a pie crust recipe to mimic the little "pebbles" of butter fat that make a light, flaky pie crust.

Cheese options: Nutritional yeast, miso, and mochi

I've often heard aspiring vegans lament about their fondness for cheese and how much they miss it. The flavor and texture of cheese are sometimes difficult to duplicate, but you have more wonderful options to try every day.

Soy-, nut-, and rice-based "cheeses" can be found in any natural food store, and they're becoming more common in regular grocery stores as well. You can buy American-style, individually wrapped squares as well as blocks of cheddar-, mozzarella-, and Monterey Jack–flavored varieties. Some of the most amazingly rich-tasting nut cheeses come from the raw foods world. Using old-world cheese-making techniques, these raw food culinary geniuses are making spreadable, savory cheeses that can be found online and in select natural food stores that carry raw vegan foods.

Look online or ask your natural food store manager for the following varieties of cheese: Dr. Cow's Tree Nut Cheese, Follow Your Heart cheese, Galaxy's Vegan Rice slices, and Teese Vegan Cheese.

Remember to read the label on "fake" cheeses carefully. If a cheese contains *casein,* a protein found in cow's milk, it may be lactose free, but it isn't vegan.

A cheesy flavor and texture can be created without the processed "fake" cheeses that you find on store shelves. The ingredients in the following sections can either add a rich, savory flavor, like with nutritional yeast and miso, or a gooey texture to dishes like with mochi. These ingredients appeal to people who prefer to use less processed foods, and they each also offer their own special nutritional benefits.

Nutritional yeast

Nutritional yeast is a marvelous addition to converted recipes as well as an excellent condiment for your kitchen table. Made from inactive dry yeast, Red Star vegan nutritional yeast is loaded with protein and B vitamins, including B12. These savory, cheesy flakes can be sprinkled liberally on pasta, steamed veggies, salads, and soups instead of Parmesan cheese. Great for creating a cheesy, rich flavor, nutritional yeast is common in vegan cooking for converting recipes like macaroni and cheese and creamy sauces. (You can find a recipe for Mac n' TeaseCheese in Chapter 14.)

Miso

Another excellent soy food is *miso.* A fermented soybean paste rich in protein and digestive enzymes, miso can help add a savory, cheese-like taste to soups, salad dressings, and marinades. It also can be used in place of Worcestershire sauce, salt, and soy sauce. The Tofu Cheese recipe in Chapter 13 is made with miso paste.

Miso paste is considered one of the most powerful soy foods in terms of its medicinal properties. Miso has been used to diminish the effects of smoking, air pollution, and radiation.

Miso soup is familiar to a lot of people because of the growing popularity of sushi restaurants. This rich vegetable and tofu broth is flavored with miso paste. Be careful, though: Most sushi restaurants also use *bonito,* or dried fish flakes, in their miso soups. You can easily make your own at home by simply adding a slurry of whisked miso paste and water into cooked vegetable soup. Because the soybean enzymes are delicate and can taste bitter when boiled, miso shouldn't be boiled. Instead, you should stir it into the soup at the end of cooking.

Mochi

Sometimes vegans miss the creamy, gooey, and sticky nature of cheese. These textures aren't always easy to find in the fruit and vegetable world. Enter *mochi.* A traditional Japanese food made from pounded glutinous rice that's formed into cakes, mochi is a favorite New Year's food in Japan and a year-round snack in Hawaii.

While mochi can be made at home, it takes a lot of time and a lot of muscle. The pounding process can take a few hours. Luckily, cakes of plain, naturally sweetened, and savory flavored mochi can be found in the refrigerator section of your natural food store.

Mochi can be used in the following ways:

- **Grated or chopped very finely and sprinkled on steaming vegetables:** The mochi will melt on the vegetables like cheese.

- **Grated and added to sauces for pizza or pasta:** Again, the mochi will melt and become creamy.

- **Cubed into 1-inch squares and then baked at 450 degrees for 10 minutes or until the squares puff up and brown slightly:** Top the mochi with nut butter and jam; dip in a mixture of soy sauce, agave, and grated ginger; or slather with vegan butter and maple syrup.

- **Made into mochi cheese:** Dice 8 ounces of mochi and simmer it in a small saucepan with just enough water to cover. Stir regularly until the mochi melts. Season with a little soy sauce, umeboshi vinegar, and a variety of herbs suited for your recipe. Use a combination of thyme, rosemary, and oregano to create mochi cheese suitable for Italian pizza or lasagna. For a Thanksgiving cream sauce, try mixing up the seasoning by adding sage, thyme, and freshly ground black pepper into the melted mochi.

Chapter 11

Beyond Food: Embracing the Whole Vegan Lifestyle

In This Chapter

▶ Finding vegan clothes and shoes

▶ Making sure your health and beauty products are animal-free

▶ Veganizing your home

Some vegans say they make a difference three times a day — by eating vegan at breakfast, lunch, and dinner. But being vegan isn't just about food — it's a whole lifestyle. Living as a vegan requires a deeper examination of your entire life, from your shirt and shampoo to your furniture and laundry detergent. Everything you do, use, and buy is another chance to practice your vegan ethics in a very real way.

The basic premise of being vegan is that it's a lifestyle that doesn't abuse or use animals in any way. This means that using animals as food, clothing, furniture, or ingredients is a no-no. Vegans aspire to avoid using animal products of any kind — period.

You don't have to explain yourself to anyone, but vegan living isn't the norm, and it generally requires more thought than nonvegan living when it comes to just about every aspect of your life. At first it may seem overwhelming, and you may feel like you have to do everything at once and change every bit of your daily experience. No worries! This is a big transition, and no one expects you to do everything right, or right now.

This chapter leads you through the other areas of vegan living that may be less familiar than what you're going to eat for lunch. You need to develop a new vocabulary regarding ingredients and materials. As you discover and explore different areas, you'll become an expert in choosing products that fit the spirit of being vegan.

Fashionably Compassionate: Animal-Free Clothing and Footwear

Animal products and skins are very common in clothing manufacturing — you'd be surprised at how many of these items you probably already own. Leather, down, suede, fur, feathers, sheep's wool, silk, shells, angora rabbit fur, and other animal skins are all produced by killing or confining animals, and these materials aren't considered vegan. (Because leather and fur require the killing of an animal outright, they shouldn't even be considered vegetarian.)

Clothing made from animal materials comes at a high price to other living creatures, whether you buy it at a discount mall or a high-priced designer boutique. Vegan fashions have evolved quickly over the last decade, and designers now create current looks in cruelty-free fabrics and materials. Some are even at the forefront of the fashion trends, and these products are getting easier to find every year.

Where to buy the latest looks

Vegan fashionistas can rejoice in this modern age of clothing design and accessibility. Buying vegan clothing is much easier these days thanks to the Internet, forward-thinking designers, and those old standbys — discount stores. Whether you're looking for daily wear, shoes, bags, belts, formal wear, party clothes, wallets, accessories, coats, or faux apparel, you should have no trouble finding a variety of animal-friendly, cruelty-free options:

- **Athletic shoes:** You can find vegan-friendly athletic shoes by searching the stores and Web sites of Zappos and New Balance for running and walking shoes, Airwalk and Burton for snowboard boots, and Vans for skateboard shoes. You can order vegan ballet shoes from Cynthia King Dance Studio in Brooklyn, New York. Your vegan shoes can be a walking billboard for cruelty-free ethics!

- **Daily wear/casual clothing:** You can put together vegan outfits on the cheap and on the fly by shopping at discount clothing stores like Target, Wal-Mart, and Payless Shoes, which offer shoes, bags, and belts created from man-made materials — usually plastic, hemp, canvas, or "pleather." The online store Alloy has current bag, belt, and shoe designs for teens and women.

Because living "green" is often synonymous with living vegan, you may want to avoid shopping at Wal-Mart and other large chains. These corporations often have a history of mistreating their employees or involving themselves in other irresponsible business practices.

✔ **Designer fashions:** Cutting-edge shoe designs are available from Mink Shoes, based in Los Angeles. You can purchase trendy handbags online from Matt and Nat and in large department stores like Bloomingdales. And Stella McCartney's clothing designs can be seen on the catwalk at fashion shows around the world. These are just a few examples of how vegan clothing has finally reached the highest levels of the fashion world.

✔ **Outdoor apparel:** Synthetic down and fleece jackets offer fantastic protection from the elements, so true down coats are no longer necessary. Several outfitters nationwide — notably REI, Pangea, and Patagonia — sell hiking, snow, and camping gear in synthetic and canvas materials. And nonleather saddlebags are available for motorcycle and scooter riders from such companies as Cycleport and Motoliberty.

✔ **Sporting equipment:** Don't throw in the towel yet — order a vegan baseball glove from Rawlings or Heartland Products, Ltd. Rawlings and Spalding offer vegan versions of balls for most sports, including volleyball, soccer, and baseball.

To find vegan clothing online, try searching for "vegan clothing." To get more specific, search for "leather-free shoes" or "non-leather shoes." You also can sign up for vegan glamazon Chloe Jo Berman's fabulous weekly e-zine at www. girliegirlarmy.com for the latest in stylish fashion and other vegan topics.

If you happen to find yourself in Portland, Oregon, you should know that it boasts the only 100 percent vegan mini-mall! Including a vegan grocery store, tattoo parlor, the offices of vegan publication Herbivore, and a bakery, the Vegan Mini-Mall offers a haven of vegan goodness in the Great Northwest. You can check out the mall's location at www.veganminimall.com.

Flying away from feathers and skirting silks

Two popular materials used for clothing and housewares are very un-vegan: feathers and silk. You can find feathers on countless articles of clothing and tchotchkes, including hair accessories, boas, cat toys, and earrings. You should avoid purchasing products made with feathers. Birds of all kinds use their feathers to insulate themselves from water and weather, and some birds use certain feathers to control their movements while in flight. Birds even use found feathers in constructing their nests, so reconsider picking feathers up from the ground. Many species of gloriously colored birds have been hunted to near extinction because their feathers, so bright to attract mating partners, are desired by humans for their hats and clothing. Many birds, like peacocks, are kept alive in order to be painfully plucked periodically for their tail feathers.

Silk is shiny, but also cruel. After about a month of life, silkworms work for three to four days to spin a glorious cocoon out of over a thousand yards of a single silk strand. The cocoons are kept warm for just over a week and then steamed to kill the developing moth inside. The silk is then woven into a delicate thread and made into clothing, sheets, and various other products for human consumption. Up to 30,000 worms are killed to produce 12 pounds of raw silk.

What about wearing those old, nonvegan items?

Choosing to buy new items in vegan-only materials is the logical next step for someone eating a plant-based, animal-free diet. But what about all those leather shoes still populating your closet floor? Are you really a vegan if you still use your leather purse? Is it bad to keep wearing your animal-based clothing?

These decisions must be made by the individual. Some vegans believe that using, wearing, or consuming any animal products is not living a truly vegan lifestyle. For them, wearing old or used nonvegan clothing is unacceptable. Leather shoes are made from a dead animal, and because the animal dies in the process of producing the shoes, some vegans believe that you shouldn't wear the shoes at all — even if you owned them long before you adopted the vegan lifestyle.

Other vegans have no problem continuing to wear the leather, wool, or feathered items they already own. Their attitude is more "waste not, want not." Very few vegans will begrudge you your decades-old leather belt, or a pair of vintage shoes passed down from a grandparent.

If you want to stop wearing your animal-based clothing, consider donating it. Often, when people adopt a vegan lifestyle, they donate all their leather things, including belts, briefcases, cellphone cases, and guitar straps. By giving these items to others, the products are used rather than thrown away, and so the animal didn't die in vain. Most people never think about the impact their purchases and consumption have on the world around them, so even slow or minor changes are an indication of your caring and empathy.

If you're looking to get rid of old fur coats, stoles, or sheepskin jackets, a compassionate option is to donate them to Coats for Cubs. This program is run by the Humane Society of the United States, which collects fur items and distributes them to wildlife rehabilitation centers around the country. These centers use the coats as bedding to warm and comfort injured or orphaned wildlife. Some younger animals make imaginary friends out of their new fur blanket, playing and wrestling with the item as if it were a sibling. Your donation is tax-deductible and provides an amazing end to the coat of shame hanging in your closet. For information, see www.hsus.org/furfree/campaigns/c4c.

Don't be concerned with the attitude that other people may hold about your clothing — if you cared what other people thought, you probably wouldn't have become vegan in the first place!

Vegan Beauty Aids and Health Products

Beauty aids have been around almost as long as people. Ancient Egyptians used fly dung and animal fat to create dark eye paints for both men and women. Nowadays, some people are content to let their natural beauty shine through with no adornment, but many modern men and women still like to jazz things up a little with makeup and perfume. Modern beauty products are hiding an ugly secret, however. Sadly, most of these products come at a high price, as countless animals are killed every year to create and test cosmetics for humans to use.

Vitamins and supplements are a $20 billion business in the United States alone. While these products can be used to protect and heal your body from illness, many are nonvegan because they contain animal ingredients. For a full list of nonvegan ingredients to look out for, check the PETA Web site for their comprehensive animal ingredients list.

Fortunately, finding vegan beauty aids and health products has become easier in the last few years, because vegan certification labels have become more popular and traditional companies have begun to formulate vegan product lines. Many companies use no animal products at all and don't test their products on animals, so they can be considered entirely vegan companies.

Waking up to your makeup

Educating yourself about the origins of the ingredients in your makeup is another step toward an integrated vegan lifestyle. You should consider two issues with beauty products:

✔ Do they contain animal byproducts or ingredients derived from an animal source?

✔ Were they tested on animals?

Many products advertise that they weren't tested on animals, but they may still contain animal-based ingredients.

The term *cruelty-free* is used a lot when it comes to vegan products. It means that no animals were harmed in the testing or production of the ingredients used in a product. Any product with this kind of label is 100 percent free of all animal ingredients. In other parts of the world, including England, the term *animal-free* is more commonly used because cruelty-free labels were abused by companies that still included ingredients from animals even though they no longer tested the products on animals.

It would be difficult, to say the least, to remember all the animal and insect ingredients used in cosmetics. Rather than take a list with you to the store, it's easier to buy makeup from companies that have been through a certification process and are labeled vegan. Some of the great vegan companies producing top-quality beauty products are Urban Decay, Ecco Bella, Zia, BWC, and Gabriel Cosmetics. This takes all the guesswork out of it — now you just have to find the right shade of blush!

Checking labels and seals of approval

A few different certification organizations deem a product or company to be vegan and cruelty-free. The Coalition for Consumer Information on Cosmetics (CCIC) gives a leaping bunny symbol to companies that don't use any new animal testing in developing their products, either by the company, its suppliers, or laboratories (see Figure 11-1). The products covered by this label can be cosmetics, personal health and beauty, or household products. The CCIC has a list of certified companies on its Web site, www.leapingbunny.org.

Because this designation only covers the testing aspect of a product and not its ingredients, you need to check the list of ingredients for any animal byproducts.

Another seal to look for is the "Certified Vegan" logo used by Vegan Action (www.vegan.org). This logo, shown in Figure 11-2, is used on products that haven't been tested on animals and don't contain any animal or insect ingredients or byproducts.

Figure 11-1:
This logo indicates that a product hasn't been tested on animals.

Figure 11-2:
This logo indicates a product that contains no animal ingredients and wasn't tested on animals.

Certifed Vegan Logo – Trademarked

These logos make identifying vegan products easier and can help you shop without carrying around an ingredient list in your bag. Buying these products is another way to show companies that the vegan market is growing, and such purchases make the ideals of vegan living more visible to mainstream consumers. Note that not every vegan product is certified by these organizations, so if you like a product but don't see a label, do a little investigating, because the company may be in the certification process.

Beauty Without Cruelty was the first cosmetics and beauty brand formed specifically to offer an alternative to products that use animal testing and ingredients. Founded in England in 1963, this brand has grown worldwide and is a true vegan success story.

The animal rights activism group PETA, People for the Ethical Treatment of Animals, also has devised a labeling campaign to help guide your purchases of beauty, healthcare, and cleaning products. The companies that make the products certified with the "Caring Consumer" bunny logo (see Figure 11-3 and `www.caringconsumer.com`) have either signed a statement of assurance to PETA or verified a statement that they don't perform animal testing and promise not to do any in the future.

None of these labels are legally binding, and the companies could theoretically perform testing anyway, but it would be a public relations nightmare for them if the public found out they were secretly using animal ingredients or testing.

Many companies carry both cruelty-free products and products that contain animal byproducts or may still be tested on cats, dogs, and rabbits. These companies take the liberty of presenting the image of a caring, concerned organization on a certain product while continuing to use and abuse animals for other gains. If you feel strongly about not supporting a company that harms animals in any way for any of its products, don't buy any of its cruelty-free products either.

Figure 11-3: This logo indicates that a product has been approved by PETA.

Scrutinizing ingredient lists

The U.S. Food and Drug Administration hasn't set forth a law or mandate that requires companies to test products for safety. That's right: The government doesn't test cosmetics and personal care products for safety, because the industry is supposed to police itself. That can lead to problems for consumers, because many beauty products contain toxic components, including known carcinogens, phthalates, and hormone disrupters.

Because no oversight committee exists to make sure that companies are truly living up to their supposed code of ethics, it's wise to get acquainted with well-known vegan companies and common ingredients used in products. The more you look at labels, the more you become aware of which words are code for "cruelly obtained ingredient."

One example is *carmine,* a dye found in many lipsticks and blushes, which is made from crushed red beetles. *Lactose* and *casein* are ingredients used in many skin care products that are derived from cow's milk. You can always contact a manufacturer directly if you have any questions about its products.

The nonprofit Environmental Working Group has compiled a safety guide, titled "Skin Deep," that provides toxicity information on personal care products and cosmetics. This independent research is the best available information with which to make safer purchasing decisions. Check out your favorite products at www.cosmeticsdatabase.com. You can also go to www.peta.org to find a list of ingredients to watch for and avoid.

Being careful with medicines and flu shots

One of the most common reasons that people cite for becoming vegan is that they want to be healthy. A sound vegan diet is better for protecting your body from the main causes of disease and death in the United States than any other way of eating. But what happens when you do get sick?

Medicinal drugs are certainly a miracle of modern science, and going to the emergency room for a broken leg is certainly more advisable than wrapping tofu around your compound fracture. However, lurking in those medicines, flu shots, and vaccines are many ingredients that don't jive with the vegan ethics of cruelty-free living.

Boxes and bottles of over-the-counter medications are rarely vegan. That's usually because of the coating or capsules, which often contain gelatin. Because these drugs also are tested on animals, they aren't vegan even if they are void of animal ingredients. Seek out alternatives of the medicine in a liquid form that doesn't contain gelatin.

Similarly, many forms of prescribed medicines and drugs are tested on animals and may contain actual animal byproducts. For example, Premarin, used to treat menopausal women for hormonal issues, is derived from the urine of a pregnant mare, hence the name. Flu shots are routinely tested on animals and contain animal byproducts and tissues. Vaccines are produced using animal tissues to grow the viruses. Chick embryos, gelatin, and cells from calf fetuses are common ingredients and growing media. Some vaccines also use human tissues like liver albumin.

Weigh your beliefs about whether these drugs are effective in keeping you healthy and whether they violate your vegan ethics. You may be able to find alternatives, so talk with your healthcare provider. Perhaps you can find a version of a pill that doesn't come in a gelatin capsule, or perhaps you can see a homeopathic doctor or naturopath that can offer more natural, vegan options and medicines. *Compounding pharmacies* can make some prescriptions to order and may have vegan ingredients available to create the right dosage and combinations. However, call ahead and ask about the specific medication you're looking for. If you can't find a vegan medication, don't be a martyr — protect your health and that of your family.

The Physicians Committee for Responsible Medicine (www.pcrm.org) is steadily gaining ground in encouraging medication that isn't tested on animals. Find out as much as you can, and maintain a healthy lifestyle so you don't need as many medications in the long run. If you discover a vegan alternative, great. If not, ensure that your health isn't endangered.

Because babies are given vaccines within the first few hours of life, it's wise for expecting vegan parents to understand the issues and ingredients before making their choices on how best to protect their children. Because the vaccine ingredients aren't vegan, parents must weigh the possible consequences of not vaccinating their children. It's understandable to want to go forward with vaccinating your kids if you believe that doing so will protect them from serious illnesses later on, regardless of the nonvegan nature of these drugs. I strongly encourage you to become familiar with the health issues surrounding vaccinations and flu shots in order to make the most informed choices possible.

The following groups offer resources and information that question the safety of vaccines: The National Vaccine Information Center (www.nvic.org), Dr. Joseph Mercola (www.mercola.com), and Gary Null (www.garynull.com). The Centers for Disease Control and Prevention (www.cdc.gov) offers information on the other side of the issue and encourages parents to vaccinate based on their documentation.

Keeping a Truly Vegan Home

Your home should be a safe, comfortable place, filled with good energy and products that make you happy. Filling your home environment with vegan products is another step toward fully realizing this lifestyle. Every new purchase for your home can add to the solid foundation of your dedication to vegan living.

Spotting and replacing hidden nonvegan home items

Take a look around your home and begin to notice what materials are used to create the items you own. You often can find vegan alternatives for everything from candles to comforters. Activities you may enjoy at home, like gardening or playing music, may have relied on animal byproducts in the past, but not anymore. Staying vegan goes hand in hand with nontoxic living as well, and you can start making stronger connections between cruelty-free purchases and eco-friendly living.

Busy bees: That's a lot of work!

The process through which bees create their wax is extraordinary. Young worker bees use special wax-producing glands in their abdomens. They eat enormous amounts of honey, and the glands transform the sugar into wax, which the bees then excrete through these glands. The bees chew up the bits of wax from their abdomens and plaster the wax to the walls of the hive to construct the honeycomb. This amazing structure is built to maintain the hive's temperature at around 95 degrees Fahrenheit, which is just right for bees to be happy and go about their business.

Honeybees fly vast distances every day to gather nectar from flowers. They collect nectar from 100 to 1,500 flowers before their second "honey stomach" is full enough to return to the hive. The honeybees then pass on the gathered nectar to worker bees in the hive. The worker bees chew the nectar with special enzymes and distribute it among the little holes in the honeycomb. The hive's internal air circulation evaporates the excess water, turning the nectar into honey. A colony of bees requires between 120 and 200 pounds of honey a year to survive, and this amount of honey production requires an incredible amount of work.

Be gentle with yourself. No one is perfect, and you're already doing more than most people by even thinking about these things.

Leaving honey and beeswax for the bees

The vast majority of vegans don't consider beeswax candles — or any product derived from beeswax or honey — to be vegan. A beehive is created with countless hours of effort by the bees in each colony (see the nearby sidebar, "Busy bees: That's a lot of work!"). Flying vast distances to gather the necessary ingredients for honey and wax, bees defend their hives and the queen with their very lives if they perceive attack.

Any product that's taken from another species isn't vegan. Some bees may be hurt or killed inadvertently by beekeepers, and bees aren't programmed to gather honey for human uses — they use it to raise their young.

Luckily, countless products are available that are natural and nontoxic alternatives to beeswax and honey products. You can easily substitute for honey in cooking by using agave, maple syrup, or brown rice syrup. Soy candles are an excellent alternative to beeswax and are preferable to standard paraffin candles, which are a petroleum product. The more natural soy candles also refrain from using toxic metals in the wick, and paraffin candles can pollute your indoor air with wisps of black smoke.

Turning down fleece and down in favor of synthetics

Grandma's feather bed may have been comfortable and warm for the cold winter months, but her comfort came at the expense of a lot of geese. Birds aren't protected by the humane slaughter laws, and they're often kept in terrible conditions before they're killed for food. Because their feathers, or down, are then used to make comforters and coats, these products aren't vegan. Even more disturbing is that some ducks and geese are plucked repeatedly during their lives to produce down, all without any pain relief.

But you can now find wonderful, animal-free, synthetic down pillows, comforters, and coats. Some of these products are even made from recycled plastic bottles. Fleece jackets and blankets are excellent at holding warmth and wicking away moisture for bedding. The Patagonia outdoor equipment company has been using this excellent recycled plastic fleece since 1993 and is saving tons of plastic from ending up in landfills.

Getting rid of pesticides in the garden

When you think of gardening, you may envision digging happily in the earth or harvesting fresh lettuce from your backyard. These activities can be wonderful and in line with vegan living — or not. Using pesticides at home to poison and kill pests and rodents in the garden isn't a vegan way of doing business. These chemicals only end up hurting us in the long run as well. Using organic gardening methods helps you deter pests in the yard without resorting to the toxic chemicals used to hurt other species. Check out *Organic Gardening For Dummies,* 2nd Edition, by Ann Whitman and Suzanne DeJohn (Wiley).

Making beautiful vegan music

Drumming, strumming, and fiddling around with instruments at home and with friends is a wonderful way to build community and express your creativity. But many instruments are made using animal products, so be aware when buying new ones.

Many stringed instruments like violins, violas, and cellos are made with glue made from animals or varnishes made with insects. And while the term "catgut" may sound familiar if you ever played viola in elementary school, strings for these instruments were never made from felines. They were, and still are, made from sheep's intestines. Most modern musicians prefer to use synthetic strings, but some still use the gut strings made from sheep. If you have an older stringed instrument, you can take it to your local instrument shop and have it restrung with synthetic strings.

You now can purchase drums with synthetic coverings rather than the old animal skin hides. And even though guitar straps are often made of leather, many vegan brands are now made of synthetics, plastics, hemp, and other fabrics.

A quick Internet search can help you find a good used instrument. You'll be saving money and the environment — and that's music to this vegan's ears!

Cleaning up your cleaning products

Cleaning products can be cruelty-free and nontoxic, which is a win-win for any vegan household! Choose your nontoxic cleaning products from companies that have taken a cruelty-free pledge. Biopack, Biokleen, Seventh Generation, Shaklee, Dr. Bronner's, Citra Solv, and Green Forest are just a few vegan, cruelty-free companies that offer good cleaning products.

You also can make your own inexpensive, natural cleaning products at home using a few simple ingredients, including lemon juice, salt, and vinegar.

Here are some ways to use fresh lemon juice:

- ✔ Mix a paste of lemon juice and baking soda and rub onto chrome or copper. Rinse off with water and then buff with a soft cloth.

- ✔ Mix 1 cup of fresh lemon juice with ½ cup borax for a powerful toilet cleaner that will leave a clean, natural lemon scent.

- ✔ Get rid of lime scale on faucets and taps by rubbing with a cut lemon and then rinsing well with water.

- ✔ To naturally bleach linens and whites, add ½ cup of strained lemon juice to the rinse cycle and hang clothes outside in the sun to dry.

- ✔ Reduce bad odors in your fridge by storing half a lemon in it.

- ✔ Freshen up a smelly garbage disposal by running the blades with fresh lemon rinds and water.

Here's how to clean with salt:

- ✔ To clean your cast-iron pan, sprinkle it with salt and wipe clean. Doing so helps protect the seasoned surface and ensures a more nonstick surface.

- ✔ Sprinkle salt on fresh wine stains to absorb most of the color. Wipe clean with a cloth and dab with white vinegar before washing.

- ✔ Dabbing salt on mosquito bites takes away the itchiness. Just wet the place of the bite and rub some salt in.

Here are some home uses for vinegar:

- ✔ To deodorize and unblock partially clogged drains, mix together ½ cup baking soda with ½ cup salt. Pour this mixture into the drain and then pour in 1 cup of white vinegar. A foam will bubble up. After an hour, flush the drain with hot water.

- Remove onion or garlic odor from your hands by wiping them with vinegar.

- To remove the odor of smoke, paint, vomit, or alcohol, place a bowl of vinegar in the room.

- Remove odors from older cars by leaving 2 cups of vinegar in the car overnight. Yes, you have to keep the windows rolled up. Remove the bowl before driving, and repeat as often as necessary.

The Internet has countless "recipes" for making your own cleaning and beauty products from natural ingredients. Annie B. Bond's classic book *Better Basics for the Home* (Three Rivers Press) is an encyclopedia of knowledge in these areas and is invaluable for anyone who wants to explore making their own products.

Keeping pests away in a gentle way

Now that you're beginning to clean out your coat closet of animal products, it's time to move on to the hall closet. Embracing the vegan lifestyle means holding respect in your heart for all living creatures, even bugs and mice. Rather than using toxic cleaning supplies and bug sprays to keep little critters away, try using these alternatives at home:

- Trace an ant column back to the ants' point of entry. Set any of the following items at the entry area in a small line, which ants will not cross: cayenne pepper, citrus oil (soaked into a piece of string), lemon juice, cinnamon, or coffee grounds.

- Purchase clove-, orange-, and mint oil-based repellents from health food stores. Spray these oils at the bugs' point of entry into your house.

- Clean up your kitchen and living areas. Sweep and mop frequently, especially where you prepare and eat food.

- Don't leave any food on the counters.

- Block or build out rodents and bugs by sealing any holes and cracks in baseboards, doors, and windows.

- Rub topical garlic oil on pets' ears, paws, and the base of the tail to deter fleas. Add raw or cooked garlic or garlic oil to pet food.

Part IV
Tasting Is Believing: Vegan Recipes

The 5th Wave   By Rich Tennant

©RICHTENNANT

"Do I like arugula? I _love_ arugula!! Some of
the best beaches in the world are there."

In this part . . .

*E*ating great food is part of the joy of living a vegan life! New tastes, techniques, and ingredients are waiting to be enjoyed.

These chapters offer a treasure trove of delicious, healthy meals for vegans — and their friends — to enjoy. Everything you need is here: Breakfast recipes for slow, late morning brunches or for get-out-the-door-quick school and workday mornings; lunches for a crowd or for one; and dinner recipes for parties, celebrations, and quiet evenings for two. I introduce a range of cooking methods as well as several gotta-have-'em vegan ingredients.

Chapter 12

Breakfasts of Vegan Champions

In This Chapter

▶ Grabbing a fast vegan breakfast

▶ Preparing savory morning starters

▶ Fixing quick breads for a sweet breakfast

*B*reakfast truly is the most important meal of the day. Starting your day with sugary, caffeine-filled fuel dooms you to a day full of roller coaster cravings and energy crashes. Eating no breakfast at all sets you up to feeling totally starved by lunch, which causes you to eat a huge meal and feel tired and bloated in the afternoon. Now you know why a coffee at 3 p.m. is necessary to get you through your day!

You say you don't have time for breakfast? Well, no sweat. I offer several nourishing ideas in this chapter to help you plan for success. Baking some dense muffins on the weekend enables you to grab a healthy morsel on your way out the door for the early, hectic part of the week. Simple, fast smoothies loaded with nutritional extras make the end of the week easier to finish.

The beauty of vegan breakfasts is that you can make them in any array of flavors you choose, free of guilt. Enjoy starting your day cruelty- and cholesterol-free with some of my favorite breakfast recipes.

Quick Fixes for Vegan Breakfasts

Easy breakfasts can be so much more nourishing than a bowl of processed cereal or a piece of toast. In one easy meal, you can get complex carbohydrates, protein, healthy fats (also important for longer satiety/fullness), and a variety of flavors to start your day right. The quick and healthy breakfast options I share in this section can be tweaked to your liking too.

Smoothies, for instance, are a cheap, fast meal, and they're perfect for breakfast. These blended beverages enable you to consume a variety of healthy foods easily in the morning. Proteins like nuts, seeds, and soy yogurt or milk can be supplemented with natural, unprocessed hemp seed powder. Blending several fruits into one drink gets you halfway to the recommended daily intake as set forth by the USDA.

Another fantastic way to make breakfast a quick, healthy meal is to use those leftover grains that are sitting in your refrigerator. Any cooked grain can be made into "oatmeal" with a few simple steps. Thinking ahead to the next morning by ensuring your grains are ready to go is a nice method for eating more complex carbohydrates in the morning. Getting creative with leftover grains offers you a whole new set of breakfast choices. For even easier breakfast options, look at the list in Chapter 9 for some more ideas.

Wake-Me-Up-Before-You-Go-Go Breakfast Smoothie

What's the easiest way to take your supplements? Buy food-based versions and add them to your morning ritual! This smoothie is a real blast of energy that keeps you full until lunch and provides everything a growing vegan could need. Because this recipe makes a lot, you can easily drink one filling glass and leave the rest in an airtight container for the next morning, thereby reducing calories. The added vitamin C helps preserve the smoothie overnight.

Preparation time: 5 minutes

Yield: 1 large serving or 2 small servings

1 banana, peeled

1 apple, unpeeled, cored

½ cup frozen blueberries or cherries

½ teaspoon ground cinnamon

1 tablespoon flaxseeds

⅓ cup raw almonds or cashews

⅓ cup soy yogurt

1 tablespoon flaxseed oil or Udo's 3-6-9 Oil

1 teaspoon unflavored vitamin C crystals

1 tablespoon liquid chlorophyll, spirulina, or blue-green algae powder or liquid

2½ cups plain or vanilla soy, rice, or hemp milk

Add all the ingredients to a blender and blend until smooth. Enjoy!

Tip: Using water or a nondairy milk instead of fruit juice reduces the amount of sugars contained in smoothie recipes. Too much sugar in the morning can lead to energy lows or cravings for more sugar later in the day.

Per serving: Calories 937 (From Fat 497); Fat 55g (Saturated 5g); Cholesterol 0mg; Sodium 103mg; Carbohydrate 95g; Dietary Fiber 26g; Protein 33g.

Groggy Grain Breakfast Porridge

This porridge is good for those bleary mornings when you can't put sentences together, let alone complete a recipe! Make the lightly sweetened version if you're heading out for a long hike, or try the savory option if you want to create a longer-lasting stable energy for a day at the office.

Preparation/cooking time: 5 minutes

Yield: 1 serving

Lightly sweetened porridge

1 cup leftover grain (brown rice, quinoa, or whatever you have)

⅓ cup vanilla soy, rice, or hemp milk

½ teaspoon ground cinnamon

¼ cup nuts or seeds

2 teaspoons agave or maple syrup

Combine all the ingredients in a medium saucepan. Cook slowly over medium heat for about 10 minutes, stirring occasionally.

Vary It! *Feel free to add naturally sweetened dried fruit or diced fresh fruit to this recipe. Fresh apple chunks, banana slices, berries, dried cranberries, and raisins are all great additions.*

Per serving: Calories 309 (From Fat 25); Fat 3g (Saturated 0g); Cholesterol 0mg; Sodium 40mg; Carbohydrate 64g; Dietary Fiber 5g; Protein 7g.

Savory porridge

1 cup leftover grain

¼ cup water

¼ cup cashews, sunflower seeds, or pumpkin seeds

1 cup thinly sliced bok choy

1 teaspoon naturally brewed soy sauce (tamari, shoyu, or Bragg's Liquid Aminos)

1 Combine the grain and water in a medium saucepan. Whisk to break up the grain and bring to a low simmer over medium heat.

2 Add the nuts, bok choy, and soy sauce. Cover and simmer for 2 minutes.

Per serving: Calories 425 (From Fat 160); Fat 18g (Saturated 4g); Cholesterol 0mg; Sodium 345mg; Carbohydrate 57g; Dietary Fiber 6g; Protein 12g.

Overnight Muesli

Scandinavians have the right idea — make breakfast before bed and save time in the morning. The oats and flax in this recipe gives you a nice dose of fiber, and you can mix up the other ingredients to your liking.

Preparation time: *5 minutes*

Chilling Time: *8 hours or overnight*

Yield: *1 serving*

1 cup rolled oats	2 tablespoons chopped almonds
1 cup soy, rice, or hemp milk	2 tablespoons agave syrup
¼ apple juice	⅛ teaspoon salt
¼ cup dried apples or fruit juice-sweetened cranberries	¼ teaspoon ground cinnamon
	1 tablespoon ground flaxseeds or flaxseed meal
¼ cup Medjool dates, pitted and chopped (see Figure 12-1 for instruction)	

1 Combine all the ingredients except the flaxseeds in a medium mixing bowl. Cover with plastic wrap or a clean kitchen towel.

2 Chill the mixture in the refrigerator at least 8 hours or overnight.

3 Sprinkle with flaxseeds and serve cold or at room temperature.

Per serving: Calories 831 (From Fat 177); Fat 20g (Saturated 2g); Cholesterol 0mg; Sodium 345mg; Carbohydrate 150g; Dietary Fiber 23g; Protein 25g.

HOW TO PIT AND CHOP DATES

USE A SHARP KNIFE TO CUT DATES IN HALF. REMOVE THE PITS.

THEN, CHOP THE DATE INTO SMALL PIECES. YOU CAN DIP YOUR KNIFE IN WARM WATER IF IT GETS TOO STICKY.

Figure 12-1:
Pitting and chopping dates is a simple process.

Savory Starters Vegan Style

Choosing a breakfast that tastes more like dinner is often a good idea if you have blood-sugar issues, feel lightheaded in the morning, or just need to be more grounded for a busy morning at work. Sugary cereals or overly caffeinated beverages don't support the kind of stable energy you need long term. The savory recipes in this section also are useful for those of you who may have had one too many drinks last night — heavier, slightly salted breakfasts can do wonders for a hangover.

Playing with old favorites, the rich breakfasts here are a nice choice for someone who lives in a mixed house where the other eaters may normally opt for eggs or bacon. Feel free to use soy sauce, miso, salsa, avocados, or other denser ingredients like seitan, tempeh, or beans.

Starting your day with a protein-rich breakfast can offer sustained energy and can help you feel full longer. People need something different for breakfast depending on their health, body type, and plans for the day. Start experimenting with more protein-rich meals in the morning to determine whether that type of food changes your energy over the course of the day. Refer to Chapter 5 for more on sneaking vegan proteins into your diet.

Hungry Man (or Woman) Tofu Scramble

This filling scramble is a necessary recipe for any vegan. It's delicious, nutritious, and will help you convince friends and family members that vegan protein ain't that hard to come by!

Preparation/cooking time: *12 minutes*

Yield: *4 servings*

1 pound firm (not silken) tofu, drained and patted dry

1 teaspoon onion powder

¼ teaspoon turmeric

½ teaspoon mustard powder

¼ teaspoon salt

½ teaspoon freshly ground black pepper

2 tablespoons extra-virgin olive oil

¼ cup diced red onion

1 clove garlic, minced

1 cup sliced link soy sausage, ¼-inch rounds

½ cup shiitake mushroom caps, thinly sliced

1 tablespoon nutritional yeast flakes

2 teaspoons naturally brewed soy sauce (tamari, shoyu, or Bragg's Liquid Aminos)

1 Crumble the tofu into a mixing bowl and sprinkle with onion powder, turmeric, mustard, and salt and pepper. Set aside.

2 Heat a large cast-iron skillet over medium heat and add the olive oil. Add the onion and garlic, sprinkle with a pinch of salt, and sauté for 2 to 3 minutes. Use a metal spatula to help scrape up bits of tofu that may stick to the pan.

3 Add the sausage rounds and mushrooms to the skillet and sprinkle with the nutritional yeast. Cook for 5 minutes, stirring often.

4 Add the tofu mixture to the skillet and stir well. Drizzle with soy sauce and continue to cook for 4 minutes, stirring often, or until the tofu is dry and slightly brown.

Tip: *Nonstick pans that are coated with chemicals can emit toxic fumes, so they're best avoided. Instead, cook with a cast-iron pan that can become more nonstick as it seasons over time.*

Per serving: *Calories 330 (From Fat 205); Fat 23g (Saturated 3g); Cholesterol 0mg; Sodium 633mg; Carbohydrate 13g; Dietary Fiber 6g; Protein 25g.*

Tempeh Hash

Ready for the hearty, veganized version of hash, the traditional breakfast favorite? Where omnivorous versions of this recipe often have chunks of ham or ground beef mixed in, this incarnation offers savory slabs of tempeh for nutty protein power. Serve this dish with biscuits and hot tea for a warming winter brunch.

Preparation time: *15 minutes*

Cooking time: *25 to 30 minutes*

Yield: *4 servings*

2 tablespoons naturally brewed soy sauce (tamari, shoyu, or Bragg's Liquid Aminos)

¼ cup extra-virgin olive oil

1 tablespoon apple cider vinegar

1 teaspoon freshly ground black pepper

1 teaspoon paprika

1 teaspoon onion powder

1 teaspoon mustard powder

½ cup diced red onion

2 garlic cloves, minced

½ cup chopped kale

1 medium red bell pepper, seeded and diced

1 cup grated Yukon Gold potatoes

¼ cup raw pumpkin seeds

¼ cup nutritional yeast flakes

16 ounces tempeh, crumbled

3 tablespoons chopped parsley, as garnish

1 Preheat the oven to 350 degrees.

2 Cover a large cookie sheet with parchment paper or aluminum foil. Set aside.

3 In a large mixing bowl, combine soy sauce, olive oil, vinegar, pepper, paprika, onion powder, and mustard powder. Whisk well to combine.

4 Add the onion, garlic, kale, bell pepper, potatoes, pumpkin seeds, yeast flakes, and tempeh. Toss well to coat evenly.

5 Spread the mixture evenly over the prepared cookie sheet.

6 Bake for 35 to 40 minutes. Sprinkle with parsley before serving.

Per serving: Calories 472 (From Fat 275); Fat 31g (Saturated 5g); Cholesterol 0mg; Sodium 481mg; Carbohydrate 27g; Dietary Fiber 10g; Protein 30g.

Savory Breakfast Polenta Pizza with Spinach

Inspired by an article on savory breakfast fare by Mark Bittman in the New York Times, this veganized breakfast pizza offers hearty flavors and a nice alternative to sweeter morning dishes.

Preparation/cooking time: *1 hour*

Chilling time: *1 hour*

Yield: *4 to 6 servings*

¼ cup plus 1 tablespoon extra-virgin olive oil	½ cup diced onion
1½ cups unsweetened soymilk	½ cup diced seitan
1½ cups water	1 clove garlic, minced
½ teaspoon salt	1 pound spinach, washed, stemmed, and dried
1 cup cornmeal	1 cup Tofu Cheese (see recipe in Chapter 13)

1 Preheat the oven to 425 degrees. Lightly oil a springform or 9-inch cake or pie pan with 1 tablespoon of the olive oil and line with a precut circle of parchment paper, set aside.

2 Prepare the polenta by combining the soymilk, water, and ½ teaspoon of salt in a medium saucepan. Bring the mixture to a simmer over medium-high heat. Pour the cornmeal in a steady stream into the pot, whisking constantly to prevent lumps. Turn the heat to low and simmer, whisking often, for 6 minutes, so the polenta is thick yet still pourable.

3 Stir 1 tablespoon of the olive oil into the cooked polenta, and then pour the polenta into the prepared springform pan. Spread to an even thickness and sprinkle with a pinch of salt and freshly ground pepper. Cover with a clean kitchen towel (not touching the polenta) and cool in the refrigerator until firm, at least 1 hour.

4 Remove the polenta from the refrigerator and bake, uncovered, for 30 minutes.

5 While the polenta is baking, heat 2 tablespoons of the olive oil over medium heat in a large skillet or pot. Add the onion, seitan, garlic, and a pinch of salt. Cook, stirring occasionally until the onion is soft, about 8 minutes.

6 Add the spinach to the skillet and stir until the leaves are well wilted. Sprinkle with salt and pepper to taste.

7 Remove the polenta crust from the oven, sprinkle with the Tofu Cheese, and then spread the seitan and spinach mixture evenly on top. Drizzle with another tablespoon of the olive oil and return to the oven for 3 minutes.

8 Cut into slices and serve hot or at room temperature.

Tip: *Prepare the recipe up through Step 3 and chill overnight to save time in the morning.*

Per serving: Calories 474 (From Fat 204); Fat 23g (Saturated 3g); Cholesterol 0mg; Sodium 628mg; Carbohydrate 44g; Dietary Fiber 8g; Protein 27g.

Better-Than-British Beans on Toast

Old school beans on toast often comes with ham-flavored beans, a side of sausage, and sometimes a slice of cheese melted on top. This new take on the old favorite offers tofu and vegetarian beans for a hearty start to a busy day. Serve with fresh tomato slices and Earl Grey tea with agave and soymilk.

Preparation/cooking time: *20 minutes*

Yield: *2 servings*

1 pound extra-firm tofu, drained, patted dry, and cut into 8 slices

1 tablespoon naturally brewed soy sauce (tamari, shoyu, or Bragg's Liquid Aminos)

One 15-ounce can vegetarian baked beans

4 slices crusty whole-wheat bread

1 Preheat the broiler.

2 Lightly oil a cookie sheet. Lay the tofu slices on the pan and drizzle evenly with the soy sauce.

3 Broil the tofu until golden, about 7 minutes. Flip slices over and broil for another 7 minutes. Remove from the pan and set aside to cool.

4 Meanwhile, heat the baked beans over medium heat in a small saucepan until warmed through.

5 Toast the bread and set 2 slices each on 2 plates. Layer 2 slices of tofu on each piece of toast and scoop the heated beans onto the tofu in even amounts.

Per serving: Calories 233 (From Fat 35); Fat 4g (Saturated 1g); Cholesterol 0mg; Sodium 872mg; Carbohydrate 37g; Dietary Fiber 7g; Protein 17g.

Quick Breads for a Fast Breakfast

Baking is therapy. It's calming and comforting. In fact, baking the vegan *quick breads* (baked goods that don't need yeast) that I introduce in this section is a pleasure. Fragrant and easy, quick breads can be sweet or savory and simple or complex in flavor.

Baking bread on your day off is a smart idea for preparing for your week ahead. These breads keep well for a few days, which can give you a few extra minutes of rest on work or school mornings. Simply bake on Sunday, enjoy a few pieces, and then store the remaining goodies in airtight containers or bags.

To save yourself time in the future, consider baking a double batch of these quick breads and freezing them. Muffins and scones can be frozen together in a freezer bag after they've cooled to room temperature. Breads such as banana bread can be cooled, sliced, and frozen as well. Simply remove individual muffins, scones, and slices and warm or toast when you're ready to snack on them again.

Sharing these breads with friends and family is a sneaky and lovely way to introduce people to great vegan food. These breads also can be made to offer extra doses of nutritional support. Using whole-grain flour, ground flaxseeds, fruit puree, dried fruit, and sautéed vegetables is easy to do in loaves, scones, and muffins.

Cornbread Muffins

These muffins are delicious with vegan, trans fat–free margarine and blackberry jam — just ask my 2-year-old! The flaxseeds make the muffins rich in fiber, and the added soy, rice, or hemp milk can add extra nutrients and protein as well.

Preparation/cooking time: *30 minutes*

Cooling time: *10 minutes*

Yield: *About 12 muffins*

6 tablespoons water

2 tablespoons ground flaxseeds or flaxseed meal

½ cup whole-wheat flour

½ cup unbleached white flour

1 cup corn flour or finely ground cornmeal

¼ cup rapadura sugar, Sucanat, Turbinado sugar, or maple crystals

4 teaspoons baking powder

1 cup unsweetened vanilla soy, rice, or hemp milk

¼ cup canola oil, plus extra for oiling pan

¾ teaspoon salt

1 Preheat the oven to 425 degrees.

2 Prepare a muffin tin by lightly oiling each cup or placing an unbleached cupcake wrapper in each cup.

3 Bring the water to a simmer in a small saucepan over medium-high heat. Add the ground flaxseeds and whisk to dissolve any lumps. Simmer for 2 minutes and set aside.

4 Sift the flours, sugar, and baking powder into a large mixing bowl.

5 In a small mixing bowl, whisk the milk, oil, and salt until the salt is dissolved.

6 Whisk the flax mixture into the milk mixture until well combined. Add this wet mixture to the dry, flour mixture. Stir until just smooth, and then add the batter into the prepared cups until ¾ full.

7 Bake for 15 minutes, or until a toothpick inserted in the center of a muffin comes out clean. Remove from muffin pan and allow to cool for 10 minutes before serving.

Vary It! *Mix up the taste and texture of these muffins by adding ⅓ cup shredded zucchini, ⅓ cup corn kernels, or ¼ cup shredded apple.*

Per serving: Calories 142 (From Fat 50); Fat 6g (Saturated 0g); Cholesterol 0mg; Sodium 272mg; Carbohydrate 21g; Dietary Fiber 2g; Protein 3g.

Chocolate Chip Banana Bread

Don't we all need a little dessert for breakfast sometimes? This tasty bread is a great brunch crowd pleaser. Try serving the slices with vegan, trans fat–free margarine and hot mint tea. Be sure to use the ripest bananas you can find. The riper they are, the sweeter and mushier they'll be.

Preparation time: *15 minutes*

Cooking time: *40 to 45 minutes*

Cooling time: *15 minutes*

Yield: *1 loaf (12 slices)*

2 large overripe bananas	1 cup whole-wheat or spelt flour
6 tablespoons soy, rice, or hemp milk	1 cup unbleached white, wheat, or spelt flour
⅔ cup agave syrup	1 teaspoon baking powder
⅓ cup canola oil	1 teaspoon baking soda
1 teaspoon vanilla extract	¼ teaspoon ground cinnamon
¾ teaspoon salt	¼ teaspoon ground nutmeg
½ cup vegan chocolate chips	

1 Preheat the oven to 350 degrees.

2 Lightly oil a 9-inch loaf pan.

3 In a medium mixing bowl, mash together the bananas, milk, agave, oil, vanilla, and salt. Stir in the chocolate chips.

4 In a large mixing bowl, sift the flours, baking powder, baking soda, cinnamon, and nutmeg.

5 Pour the banana and chocolate chip mixture into the flour mixture and stir with a spatula until just blended.

6 Pour the batter into the prepared loaf pan and bake for 40 to 45 minutes, or until a toothpick inserted in the middle comes out clean.

7 Cool for 15 minutes before removing from the pan and serving.

Per serving: *Calories 203 (From Fat 74); Fat 8g (Saturated 1g); Cholesterol 0mg; Sodium 282mg; Carbohydrate 33g; Dietary Fiber 2g; Protein 2g.*

SOD Scones (Sun-dried Tomatoes, Onion, and Dill)

These savory scones are mouthwatering and great for a savory breakfast or served alongside soup for lunch or dinner.

Preparation time: *30 minutes*

Cooking time: *15 minutes*

Cooling time: *10 to 15 minutes*

Yield: *8 scones*

1 medium yellow onion, diced	⅓ cup unsweetened, plain soy, rice, or hemp milk
¼ cup extra-virgin olive oil	½ cup water
1 cup whole-wheat or spelt flour	½ teaspoon salt
1 cup unbleached white flour	¼ cup canola oil
1 tablespoon baking powder	1 teaspoon apple cider vinegar
½ teaspoon freshly ground black pepper	¼ cup oil-cured sun-dried tomatoes, drained and chopped
1 tablespoon plus 1 teaspoon dried dill	

1 Preheat the oven to 400 degrees, and prepare a large cookie sheet by covering the bottom with parchment paper.

2 Heat a cast-iron skillet over medium heat. Add the olive oil and sauté the onion until mostly brown, about 10 minutes. Set aside.

3 In a large mixing bowl, combine the flours, baking powder, pepper, and dill. In a separate medium mixing bowl, whisk together the milk, water, salt, canola oil, and apple cider vinegar.

4 Add the sautéed onions and sun-dried tomatoes to the milk mixture. Then add the milk mixture to the flour mixture. Stir until just combined (the dough should barely be holding together).

5 Gently pour the dough onto the prepared cookie sheet. Using your hands, lightly knead the dough to form an even, round loaf about 8 inches across.

6 Using a large knife, cut the dough into eighths, but don't fully separate the slices. (Cutting the dough in this way makes the scones easier to cut completely once they're baked.)

7 Bake for 15 minutes. Cool for 10 to 15 minutes before serving.

Per serving: *Calories 245 (From Fat 134); Fat 15g (Saturated 2g); Cholesterol 0mg; Sodium 299mg; Carbohydrate 25g; Dietary Fiber 3g; Protein 4g.*

Chapter 13

Sides and Lighter Meals

*T*hinking and cooking small can make a big difference for your vegan kitchen. For instance, you can make your meals more exciting by mastering a few homemade condiments. Tofu Sour Cream, Homemade Pickled Vegetables, and fresh salad dressings, like Carrot Ginger Dressing, can take a simple plate of beans and whole grains in a totally new direction. Find all three of these recipes in this chapter.

Side dishes can make or break a meal as well; I know I've chosen certain meals from a menu just for the side dish! While a bunch of steamed veggies is nice, wouldn't that homemade vegan lasagna be a little more exciting if it came with some creamy broccoli soup? Discovering a wide variety of healthy, tasty side dishes and lighter meals is simple and helps you feel like a budding gourmet.

After you discover the joys of creating your own condiments and side dishes, you can progress up the culinary ladder and start making simple, one-dish meals. Soups and salads, for example, can easily make a meal by themselves, and they also offer an opportunity for you to get creative: You can add almost anything to a salad, and soup can be made out of various bits and pieces from your refrigerator and cupboard. These dishes are healthy and delicious, and they're easy to take to school or work.

Concocting Your Own Condiments

Making your own condiments, such as dips, cheeses, pickles, dressings, and spreads, allows you to create flavor combinations specific to your tastes. Vegan cheeses are available in many health food stores, but making your own gives you the ability to make it spicy, strong, or mellow tasting. All the condiments in this section have versatile uses and come in handy if you keep a nice selection in your refrigerator.

Dairy alternatives are easy to make at home, and the following recipes for Tofu Cheese and Tofu Sour Cream use simple techniques to get you started. And for you pickle lovers out there, rejoice! Did you know you can pickle almost any veggie or fruit? Use the Homemade Pickled Vegetables recipe to get your feet in the brine, and then branch out and start adding new spices or vinegars to explore the possibilities. You can impress your friends and family with a platter of homemade pickles at your next gathering.

Tofu Cheese

Cheese is often missed by new vegans; luckily the void can be filled with this recipe. This tofu dish is simple and tasty, and it comes with none of the negative attributes of cow's milk. Spread this cheese on toasted bread or crackers, or crumble it on top of salads like you would feta cheese.

Preparation time: 5 minutes

Chilling time: At least 8 hours

Yield: 4 servings

1 pound extra-firm tofu, drained	1½ cups any color or flavor miso paste

1 Gently wrap the drained tofu in a clean kitchen towel and lightly squeeze out some of the remaining moisture.

2 Spread a ¼-inch-thick layer of the miso on a dinner plate and place the tofu on top of it; be sure to make the layer large enough to accommodate the entire block of tofu. Spread the rest of the miso all over the tofu completely. Don't leave any tofu visible, because it will spoil if left uncovered.

3 Cover the tofu with a clean kitchen towel or cheesecloth, place in a sealable container, and set in the refrigerator for at least 8 hours and up to 3 days. The longer the tofu sits, the stronger the miso flavor will become.

4 When the tofu is ready, scrape off the miso. The tofu cheese can be crumbled on salads or vegan pizza, or sliced and eaten on crackers or toast. You can save the leftover miso for another use, such as for soup or dressings.

5 Gently rinse the tofu in cold water. Store any unused cheese in an airtight container for up to 2 days.

Per serving: Calories 180 (From Fat 82); Fat 9g (Saturated 1g); Cholesterol 0mg; Sodium 1,265mg; Carbohydrate 12g; Dietary Fiber 2g; Protein 16g.

Tofu Sour Cream

This sour cream substitute is excellent for dipping chips and carrots or drizzling over burritos and chili — and the best part is that it's guilt free!

Preparation time: 10 minutes

Chilling time: 1 hour

Yield: 1½ cups

One 12.3-ounce package of silken tofu, drained	1 teaspoon agave syrup
1 tablespoon extra-virgin olive oil	½ teaspoon miso paste
1 tablespoon fresh lemon juice	1 clove garlic, minced
3 teaspoons ume vinegar or apple cider vinegar	

1 Place all the ingredients in a blender or food processor and process several minutes, or until very smooth and creamy. You can serve the sour cream immediately, but it tastes best when refrigerated for at least 1 hour before serving. The sour cream keeps for 2 days if refrigerated in a well-sealed glass container.

Per serving: Calories 17 (From Fat 10); Fat 2g (Saturated 0g); Cholesterol 0mg; Sodium 6mg; Carbohydrate 1g; Dietary Fiber 0g; Protein 1g.

Homemade Pickled Vegetables

Naturally fermented foods, including pickles, can help the body to digest heavy, fatty meals — and they're delicious! Used in most ethnic cuisines, pickles add zest and texture variety to your menus.

Preparation time: *15 minutes*

Chilling time: *12 hours or overnight*

Yield: *3 cups*

2 cups water

2 tablespoons umeboshi vinegar

1 tablespoon brown rice vinegar

1 tablespoon salt

1 clove garlic, minced

4 cups mixed vegetables (choose from red cabbage, radishes, red onion, string beans, cucumber, cauliflower, carrots, or celery)

1 Combine the water, vinegars, salt, and garlic in a large saucepan. Bring to a boil over high heat and then remove from the heat.

2 Place the vegetables in a glass jar just large enough to hold them.

3 Cool the liquid mixture, or "brine," and then pour it into the jar with the vegetables. Cover with a tight-fitting lid or plastic wrap held on tightly with a rubber band around the mouth of the jar. Refrigerate overnight, or for at least 12 hours.

4 These pickles will keep for up to 3 weeks in the refrigerator.

Per serving: Calories 25 (From Fat 1); Fat 0g (Saturated 0g); Cholesterol 0mg; Sodium 1,163mg; Carbohydrate 6g; Dietary Fiber 2g; Protein 1g.

Carrot Ginger Dressing

This dressing has a spicy kick paired with the natural sweetness of fresh carrots. Drizzle it on a simple green salad, or dress up your steamed veggies or cooked grains with a nice dollop. The dressing will keep fresh in your refrigerator for up to a week.

Preparation time: *10 minutes*

Yield: *8 servings*

½ pound carrots (about 3 medium carrots), grated

¼ cup water

¼ cup white rice vinegar

3 tablespoons peeled and minced fresh ginger

1 tablespoon naturally brewed soy sauce (tamari, shoyu, or Bragg's Liquid Aminos)

1 tablespoon toasted sesame oil

1 shallot, chopped

1 tablespoon mirin (rice wine)

½ cup extra-virgin olive oil

1 In a blender, combine the carrot, water, vinegar, ginger, soy sauce, sesame oil, shallot, and mirin, and then puree.

2 While the blender is running, drizzle in the oil until incorporated. Store in the refrigerator until ready to use.

Per serving: *Calories 156 (From Fat 137); Fat 15g (Saturated 2g); Cholesterol 0mg; Sodium 131mg; Carbohydrate 4g; Dietary Fiber 1g; Protein 1g.*

Filling Up with Some Sensational Sides

The side dishes in this section are so good that you may just want to make a meal of several of them. They're versatile and pair well with countless main dishes. The seitan is an incredible base for numerous recipes, but it also can stand alone as a simple protein for making sandwiches or reheating for a quick snack. The rice balls can be eaten alone for a midday snack or laid on the table alongside homemade soups and casseroles. Kale chips serve as a lovely and healthy stand-in for the deep-fried potato version found in stores. Keep in mind that because you cook all these side dishes yourself, you can control the quality of the ingredients and the cooking techniques.

Homemade "Wheat Meat"

Seitan is a protein-rich, easy-to-flavor ingredient used in many vegan dishes. Making seitan at home saves you money and reduces plastic packaging waste. This useful ingredient can be bought at the store, but once you start making it at home, you'll feel empowered and prepared for many different dishes like soup, stew, sauces, and stir-fry. The kneading process can be fun and satisfying. It hearkens back to the days when our great-great-grandparents churned butter and made their bread from scratch. You can easily double this recipe — just use a really big bowl and pot!

Preparation time: *30 minutes*

Cooking time: *1½ to 2½ hours*

Yield: *4 servings*

Seitan

3 cups vital wheat gluten flour

½ cup nutritional yeast flakes

2 cups cold water

½ cup naturally brewed soy sauce (tamari, shoyu, or Bragg's Liquid Aminos)

1 Place the vital wheat gluten flour and nutritional yeast flakes in a large mixing bowl and stir well with a whisk to combine.

2 While stirring with a wooden spoon, gradually pour the cold water and soy sauce into the flour to form a stiff, but not too sticky, dough that can be kneaded.

3 Knead the dough for about 5 minutes to develop the gluten. The dough will become elastic. (See Figure 13-1 for instructions on kneading dough.)

4 When the dough is finished, set it aside and prepare the simmering stock (as shown in the following recipe).

Simmering stock

8 cups water

1 cup naturally brewed soy sauce (tamari, shoyu, or Bragg's Liquid Aminos)

5 quarter-sized slices of ginger

5 garlic cloves, roughly chopped

1 bay leaf

5 inches kombu

1 In a large pot, combine the water, soy sauce, ginger, garlic, bay leaf, and kombu.

2 Pull pieces of the seitan dough (see preceding recipe) into small billiard-size balls. Drop the pieces into the cold liquid, one at a time, stirring occasionally to prevent sticking.

3 Bring the stock to a boil, lower to a simmer, and then cover and cook for 1 to 1½ hours, depending on the size of the pieces.

4 Allow the seitan to cool to room temperature in the broth and store it in the refrigerator in an airtight container, submerged in the broth.

Tip: You can buy your own seitan at most health food stores in the refrigerator section near the tofu. Some are teriyaki flavored or cut into strips for immediate stir-fry use.

Vary It! Seitan can be flavored to your liking. Instead of the traditional ginger and garlic marinade, try premade, vegan "no-chicken" broth. An Italian blend of herbs can include garlic, red wine, onion flakes, rosemary, marjoram, fennel seeds, and red pepper flakes.

Per serving: Calories 804 (From Fat 28); Fat 3g (Saturated 1g); Cholesterol 0mg; Sodium 3,705mg; Carbohydrate 162g; Dietary Fiber 16g; Protein 34g.

Kale Chips

Crunchy, salty, and satisfying, these chips replace the deep-fried potato version in many vegan homes. Eating a leafy green vegetable while getting your chip fix is a pretty amazing feat. Kids and adults alike love these little crunchy morsels, so you may need to buy a few heads of kale each week. Never thought you'd do that, did you?

Preparation time: 10 minutes

Cooking time: 7 to 11 minutes

Yield: 4 servings

2 tablespoons extra-virgin olive oil

2 teaspoons apple cider vinegar

1 teaspoon kosher salt

1 bunch of curly kale, washed, dried, destemmed, and torn into 2-inch pieces

2 teaspoons nutritional yeast flakes

1 Preheat the oven to 425 degrees.

2 Mix the olive oil, vinegar, and salt together in a large mixing bowl. Toss the kale in the liquid mixture.

3 Put the kale on a baking sheet, sprinkle with nutritional yeast. Bake for 5 to 8 minutes, or until the kale starts to brown. Keep an eye on the kale, because it can burn quickly.

4 After the one side starts to brown, toss the kale with tongs on the baking sheet and bake with the other side up for another 2 to 3 minutes. Remove the chips from the baking sheet and enjoy!

Tip: Nutritional yeast adds a rich, cheesy taste and protein to dishes. Enriched flakes also add vitamin B12 and zinc! Find it in shakers in the condiment aisle or in the bulk bins at your health food store.

Per serving: Calories 99 (From Fat 66); Fat 7g (Saturated 1g); Cholesterol 0mg; Sodium 606mg; Carbohydrate 8g; Dietary Fiber 2g; Protein 3g.

Figure 13-1: Kneading dough.

'Mazing Mashed Potatoes with Mushroom Gravy

The name says it all: Share this dish with the carnivores in your life for Thanksgiving and wait for the applause. The flavors are rich and savory, providing everything you love about gravy, without the guilt. Many a carnivore has asked for this recipe, which says a lot! It's also good over roasted tempeh or served with vegan biscuits.

Preparation/cooking time: *45 minutes*

Yield: *4 servings*

Mashed Potatoes

1½ pounds quartered Yukon Gold potatoes (peeled or unpeeled)

½ teaspoon salt

¼ cup unsweetened plain soymilk

2 bay leaves

2 tablespoons Earth Balance spread or organic olive oil

1 Put the potatoes and salt in a large saucepan. Add enough cold water until the potatoes are covered by ¼ inch of liquid. Bring to a boil, and then reduce heat to a simmer. Cover and cook for 15 minutes, or until fork tender.

2 As the potatoes cook, warm the soymilk over low heat with the bay leaves. Heat until the milk just comes to a simmer, and then remove from the heat and set aside.

3 After the potatoes are cooked, reserve a cup of the cooking water in case you need to moisten the mashed potatoes. Drain the remaining water.

4 Place the cooked potatoes in a large mixing bowl. Remove the bay leaves from the soymilk and pour over the potatoes. Add the Earth Balance spread or olive oil. Mash the mixture with a potato masher or large fork until well mashed. Serve with Mushroom Gravy (see the following recipe).

Mushroom Gravy

12 shiitake mushrooms, rinsed, patted dry, stems removed, and thinly sliced (see Figure 13-2 for instruction or use 12 rehydrated dried shiitakes; soak according to package directions)

1 teaspoon extra-virgin olive oil

½ teaspoon salt

1 garlic clove, minced (see Figure 13-3 for instruction)

3 cups low-sodium vegetable stock

¼ cup extra-virgin olive oil

⅓ cup brown rice flour

¼ cup naturally brewed soy sauce (tamari, shoyu, or Bragg's Liquid Aminos)

1 Preheat the oven to 400 degrees.

2 Toss the sliced mushrooms with the teaspoon olive oil, salt, and garlic in a small bowl. Spread the mushrooms on a baking sheet in a single layer and roast for 15 minutes.

3 Heat the vegetable stock in a small saucepan until simmering, and then remove from the heat.

4 Heat the ¼ cup of extra-virgin olive oil in a medium saucepan over low heat. Whisk in the brown rice flour and stir constantly for 4 to 6 minutes, or until the mixture begins to brown.

5 Whisk in the hot vegetable stock slowly, stirring constantly to avoid lumps. Add the soy sauce and whisk until smooth. Add the mushrooms and stir well to combine. Cook for another 10 minutes over low heat. Serve the hot gravy over mashed potatoes (see preceding recipe).

Vary It! Mix up the flavor of the gravy with different broths like no-chicken, no-beef, or onion stock.

Per serving: Calories 390 (From Fat 186); Fat 21g (Saturated 3g); Cholesterol 0mg; Sodium 2,019mg; Carbohydrate 44g; Dietary Fiber 4g; Protein 8g.

How to Trim and Slice Mushrooms

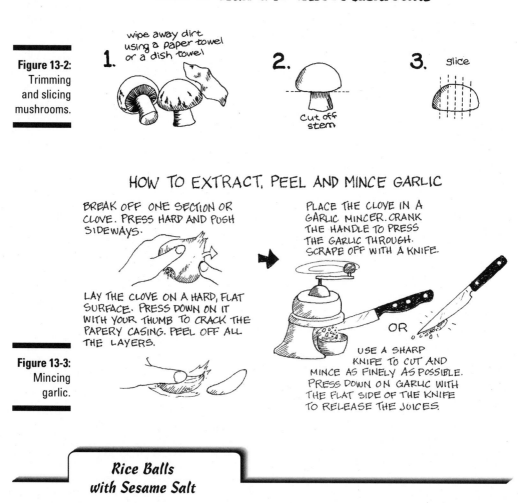

Figure 13-2:
Trimming and slicing mushrooms.

1. wipe away dirt using a paper towel or a dish towel

2. Cut off stem

3. slice

HOW TO EXTRACT, PEEL AND MINCE GARLIC

BREAK OFF ONE SECTION OR CLOVE. PRESS HARD AND PUSH SIDEWAYS.

LAY THE CLOVE ON A HARD, FLAT SURFACE. PRESS DOWN ON IT WITH YOUR THUMB TO CRACK THE PAPERY CASING. PEEL OFF ALL THE LAYERS.

PLACE THE CLOVE IN A GARLIC MINCER. CRANK THE HANDLE TO PRESS THE GARLIC THROUGH. SCRAPE OFF WITH A KNIFE.

OR

USE A SHARP KNIFE TO CUT AND MINCE AS FINELY AS POSSIBLE. PRESS DOWN ON GARLIC WITH THE FLAT SIDE OF THE KNIFE TO RELEASE THE JUICES.

Figure 13-3:
Mincing garlic.

Rice Balls with Sesame Salt

Easy to make and fun to roll, these little whole-grain gems are great snack food; they have protein, complex carbohydrates, and a bit of healthy fat as well. Kids love to help make these balls in the kitchen — even a 2-year-old can roll the rice ball around in the salted sesame seeds. Sesame salt, which is also called gomasio, is a staple in macrobiotic food. Make an extra batch and keep it in a salt shaker at the table. When you sprinkle sesame salt on food instead of regular salt, you get the added benefit of a little more protein and calcium from the seeds.

Preparation/cooking time: 2 hours

Yield: 12 to 15 rice balls / 1 cup sesame salt

Rice Balls

¾ cup short-grain brown rice	2 cups water
¼ cup white rice	½ teaspoon salt

1 In a medium saucepan, mix together the water and brown and white rice. Add ½ teaspoon salt and bring to a boil over medium-high heat. Cover, and then lower the heat to a simmer.

2 Cook the rice until all the water evaporates, about 50 minutes. Do not stir the rice until the water has evaporated.

3 Allow the rice to cool to room temperature before making rice balls.

4 Scoop about ⅓ cup of the cooked rice into water-moistened hands and pack it into a small ball.

5 Roll the ball in Sesame Salt (see the following recipe), covering all sides. Keep rolling balls until you're out of rice. Rice balls keep refrigerated in a well-sealed container for 3 days. Try serving on top of tossed salad greens.

Sesame Salt

1 cup unhulled brown sesame seeds	1 teaspoon salt

1 Rinse the sesame seeds and drain through a fine strainer. Place the seeds in a skillet over medium heat. Toast the seeds, stirring often, until they begin to give off a toasty aroma, about 3 or 4 minutes.

2 Place the toasted seeds and salt in a mortar and pestle or spice grinder and grind until well combined and the seeds are starting to break down. This condiment can be refrigerated in a sealed container for a week and used in place of salt on salads, soup, and air-popped popcorn.

Tip: *If you're short on time, try using precooked rice, which cuts the time in half.*

Per serving: Calories 120 (From Fat 62); Fat 7g (Saturated 1g); Cholesterol 0mg; Sodium 390mg; Carbohydrate 14g; Dietary Fiber 2g; Protein 4g.

Whipping Up Soup and Salad Sensations

Soups and salads offer opportunities to combine all the best flavor profiles together. Soups run the gamut: Thick, thin, chunky, or smooth and creamy. Soups can help you use up all the leftover grains, beans, and veggies that are hanging around your fridge, or they can allow you to combine just a few choice ingredients to suit your tastes. Similarly, one salad can contain crunchy, raw, roasted, sweet, and peppery veggies and be topped with a creamy and savory dressing. In this section, I help get your taste buds moving with a creamy soup recipe and a tangy, protein-filled salad recipe.

Greek Lentil Salad

This veggie and lentil salad is fresh and protein-rich. The crumbled Tofu Cheese (see the recipe earlier in this chapter) adds a nice tangy, creamy bite. Because this salad tastes so good the next day, it can be made a day ahead and chilled for a picnic or summer dinner party.

Preparation/cooking time: *55 minutes*

Yield: *4 to 6 servings*

1 cup green lentils

¼ cup extra-virgin olive oil

3 tablespoons fresh lemon juice

1½ teaspoons salt

½ teaspoon freshly ground black pepper

2 tablespoons finely chopped red onion

1 medium tomato, seeded and diced (see Figure 13-4 for instruction)

½ cup seeded and diced cucumber (see Figure 13-5 for instruction)

¼ cup finely chopped flat-leaf parsley

1 tablespoon finely chopped fresh oregano

1 recipe Tofu Cheese (recipe included earlier in this chapter)

1 Pour the lentils on a white plate, pale counter top, or cutting board. Remove any broken lentils, pebbles, or twigs. Rinse in two changes of water and drain.

2 Place the lentils in a medium saucepan with 2½ cups of water and bring to a boil over medium-high heat.

3 Lower the heat to a simmer and cover. Cook for 35 to 40 minutes or until the lentils are tender. Pour into a large bowl and allow to cool to room temperature.

4 In a medium mixing bowl, combine the olive oil, lemon juice, salt, and pepper. Whisk well. Add the remaining ingredients, except the Tofu Cheese, and toss. Add to the cooked lentils and toss well.

5 Crumble the Tofu Cheese with your hands over the lentil salad and gently toss.

6 Allow the flavors to marry in the refrigerator for at least 2 hours. The salad can be refrigerated for up to 2 days.

Per serving: *Calories 475 (From Fat 207); Fat 23g (Saturated 3g); Cholesterol 0mg; Sodium 2,123mg; Carbohydrate 45g; Dietary Fiber 10g; Protein 28g.*

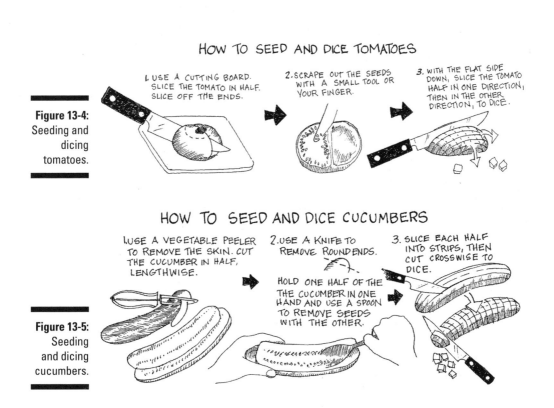

HOW TO SEED AND DICE TOMATOES

1. USE A CUTTING BOARD. SLICE THE TOMATO IN HALF. SLICE OFF THE ENDS.

2. SCRAPE OUT THE SEEDS WITH A SMALL TOOL OR YOUR FINGER.

3. WITH THE FLAT SIDE DOWN, SLICE THE TOMATO HALF IN ONE DIRECTION, THEN IN THE OTHER DIRECTION, TO DICE.

Figure 13-4: Seeding and dicing tomatoes.

HOW TO SEED AND DICE CUCUMBERS

1. USE A VEGETABLE PEELER TO REMOVE THE SKIN. CUT THE CUCUMBER IN HALF, LENGTHWISE.

2. USE A KNIFE TO REMOVE ROUND ENDS.

HOLD ONE HALF OF THE THE CUCUMBER IN ONE HAND AND USE A SPOON TO REMOVE SEEDS WITH THE OTHER.

3. SLICE EACH HALF INTO STRIPS, THEN CUT CROSSWISE TO DICE.

Figure 13-5: Seeding and dicing cucumbers.

Creamy Broccoli (or Spinach) Soup

People are always asking me how they can give up dairy without missing that creamy, satisfying taste and texture. Believe it or not, you can still indulge in creamy textured foods — you just have to do it the vegan way. This recipe, for example, is smooth, full of veggie goodness, and easy and delicious.

Preparation/cooking time: *30 minutes*

Yield: *6 servings*

8 cups low-sodium vegetable stock

1 tablespoon extra-virgin olive oil

3 ribs celery, diced

1 medium yellow onion, diced

3 heads of broccoli or 3 bunches of spinach, cut into small pieces

3 cups plain, unsweetened soymilk

1 container soft or silken tofu, drained

½ teaspoon cayenne powder

1 teaspoon freshly ground black pepper

Salt to taste

1 Add the vegetable stock to a large saucepan and bring to a boil over high heat.

2 Meanwhile, add the oil to a skillet heated over medium-high heat. Add the celery and onion and sauté with a pinch of salt until they start to turn a bit translucent, about 5 minutes.

3 When the vegetable stock comes to a boil, add the broccoli and cook for 3 to 4 minutes, or until it turns bright green.

4 Add the celery and onion mixture to the pot of broccoli. Turn off the heat and add the soymilk.

5 Place the tofu in a medium mixing bowl. Mush the tofu through your fingers to break it up. Add the tofu, cayenne pepper, and black pepper to the pot with the broccoli.

6 Blend the soup using either an immersion blender or a countertop blender. If using a standing blender, blend the soup in small batches, 2 cups at a time. Cover the blender lid with a kitchen towel to prevent any hot liquid from flying out. After each batch is blended, pour it into a separate mixing bowl until the entire pot is empty. Return the soup to the saucepan.

7 Taste the soup and add more seasoning, if desired, but be sure to blend again or stir really well to combine if you do season further.

Per serving: *Calories 183 (From Fat 63); Fat 7g (Saturated 1g); Cholesterol 0mg; Sodium 1,075mg; Carbohydrate 22g; Dietary Fiber 6g; Protein 11g.*

Chapter 14

Main Course Recipes

In This Chapter

▶ Enjoying vegan burgers and burritos

▶ Making easy and healthy pasta and noodle dishes

▶ Experimenting with a variety of ethnic cuisines

▶ Filling up on meals made with beans and rice

The average American is accustomed to eating in restaurants that serve huge portions of bread, fried potatoes, and heavy dairy cream sauces alongside hefty doses of high-fructose corn syrup and processed chemicals. You aren't the average American, however, and your body will thank you for your healthier diet in the coming years.

Instead of dining out, you can dine in and eat rich, sustaining meals of whole grains, beans, and vegetables in countless combinations that will satisfy any craving. Vegan food is delicious and fortifying. Building your meals around main dishes that offer a balance of healthy cooking techniques and high-quality ingredients is a good first step on the path of a long and vigorous life.

The main course recipes in this chapter offer something for every palate. Ethnic spice combinations can take the same basic bean and grain ingredients around the world. You can bake, sauté, blend, boil, or combine vegetables and tofu with pasta to fill the gap left when you decided to leave dairy and meat behind.

Use your mealtimes wisely to choose the kind of energy you want to create in your life. You are what you eat: Your food goes into your stomach and becomes the building blocks of your tissues, muscles, bones, and thoughts. Rest easy knowing that you can choose delicious, nourishing recipes that help you create an amazing life. Did you know that food could do so much for you? It's part of the reason that many of us become vegan: We know that what we eat matters!

Oh Boy! Burgers and Burritos

Putting protein between two pieces of bread or wrapping it in a tortilla can be wonderfully satisfying. The recipes for the hand-held foods in this section offer an easy, one-dish way to create a sensible meal. With protein, complex carbohydrates from grains and whole-grain bread, veggies, and spices, burgers and burritos can be a healthy lunch or dinner. You can easily make larger batches of these recipes for gatherings, or you can scale down the amounts for solo eating. Kids will be thrilled about a fun food that their parents are happy to serve.

Seitan Burritos

These filling burritos are easy to make, and they're handy for casual gatherings. Providing lots of quality protein and veggie goodness, this dish can fortify a bunch of vegans on Super Bowl Sunday or before a big hike. For an even easier preparation, set out a variety of toppings on the counter and let your guests make their own burritos.

Preparation/cooking time: *30 minutes*

Yield: *10 servings*

3 tablespoons olive oil

1 small onion, chopped

2 green onions, chopped (use both green and white parts)

1 clove garlic, minced

1 red bell pepper, seeded and diced (see Figure 14-1 for instruction)

½ teaspoon naturally brewed soy sauce (tamari, shoyu, or Bragg's Liquid Aminos)

Ten 10-inch vegan flour tortillas

8-ounce package seitan, drained and cut into 1-inch cubes or strips

One 15-ounce can black beans, rinsed and drained

½ cup diced tomato

3 cups cooked brown or white rice

3 tablespoons chopped fresh cilantro

½ cup salsa

Mashed avocado (optional; see Figure 14-2)

1 recipe Tofu Sour Cream (optional; see Chapter 13)

1 Preheat the oven to 350 degrees.

2 Heat the olive oil in a large skillet over medium-high heat. Sauté the chopped small onion for 2 minutes until it just begins to brown. Add the green onions, garlic, bell pepper, and soy sauce to the skillet. Continue to stir regularly and sauté for 5 minutes.

3 Wrap the tortillas in a damp paper towel, and then wrap the entire bundle in foil. Place in the heated oven to warm through.

4 Add the seitan to the vegetable mixture in the skillet and sauté for another 5 minutes. Add the black beans and tomatoes. Heat through for 2 more minutes.

5 In a medium mixing bowl, combine the cooked rice with the seitan mixture. Toss with a wooden spoon to combine. Add the cilantro and salsa and stir well to combine.

6 Remove the tortillas from the oven and unwrap. Fill each tortilla with ¾ cup of the filling and roll up burrito style (Figure 14-3 shows you how to wrap a burrito). Top each burrito with mashed avocados and homemade Tofu Sour Cream, if desired.

Tip: *Using brown rice adds extra nutrition points to this dish.*

Per serving: *Calories 405 (From Fat 93); Fat 10g (Saturated 2g); Cholesterol 0mg; Sodium 559mg; Carbohydrate 62g; Dietary Fiber 6g; Protein 15g.*

How to Core and Seed a Pepper

1. cut out stem  twist and pull out

2. cut in ½ remove membranes

3. 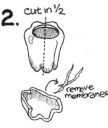 Cut into lengthwise strips

4. 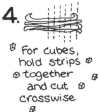 For cubes, hold strips together and cut crosswise

Figure 14-1: Coring and seeding a pepper.

Baked Black Bean Burgers

Burgers are good — and vegan bean burgers are the best! You can serve them alongside traditional burger toppings to your loved ones for a fun Friday night dinner or a summer outdoor get-together. You also can make a double batch and freeze the individual patties before baking them. Simply thaw the individual patties in the fridge overnight and bake them fresh later.

Preparation/cooking time: *25 minutes*

Chilling time: *1 hour*

Yield: *12 patties*

1 tablespoon organic olive oil	*Salt and pepper to taste*
¼ cup diced yellow onion	*1 teaspoon hot sauce*
¼ cup diced green pepper	*2 tablespoons chopped fresh parsley*
1 celery rib, diced	*2 tablespoons flour*
One 15-ounce can black beans, rinsed and drained	*12 whole-grain hamburger buns*
1 teaspoon thyme	*Traditional burger toppings, such as lettuce, onion slices, tomato slices, and pickles (optional)*
1 teaspoon paprika	
Pinch of cayenne pepper	

1 Heat oil in a frying pan over medium heat. Sauté the onion, green pepper, and celery for 5 to 7 minutes, or until softened. Remove from heat.

2 Place the beans in a food processor along with the onion mixture. Pulse the mixture 8 times, being sure to chop the beans well. However, don't process the mixture too smooth.

3 Place the bean mixture in a bowl and add spices, hot sauce, and parsley. Mix well and add salt and pepper to taste. Add flour and mix well. Cover the bowl and refrigerate for at least 1 hour.

4 While the mixture chills in the refrigerator, preheat the oven to 350 degrees.

5 Form the chilled mixture into 12 evenly sized patties with slightly wet hands. The patties are delicate, so move them around with a spatula. Bake on a cookie sheet lined with parchment paper for 15 minutes.

6 Remove from the oven with a spatula and allow to cool slightly before removing from cookie sheet. Serve on whole-grain buns, and, if desired, top with lettuce, onion slices, tomato slices, and pickles.

Per serving: *Calories 37 (From Fat 12); Fat 1g (Saturated 0g); Cholesterol 0mg; Sodium 115mg; Carbohydrate 6g; Dietary Fiber 2g; Protein 2g.*

Mushroom Sloppy Tempeh Joes

These aren't the sloppy Joes you remember from the middle-school cafeteria. Tempeh and other quality ingredients make this dish a healthy vegan treat that's perfect for a mixed crowd of vegans and meat eaters. Add a sweet side dish like steamed corn on the cob or baked sweet potato fries to round out the savory flavors.

Preparation/cooking time: *20 minutes*

Yield: *4 servings*

3 tablespoons organic olive oil

½ cup diced yellow onion

1 cup thinly sliced button mushrooms

1 clove garlic, minced

½ cup diced green bell pepper

2 teaspoons naturally brewed soy sauce (tamari, shoyu, or Bragg's Liquid Aminos), divided

8-ounce package tempeh, crumbled into small pieces

⅔ cup naturally sweetened ketchup

1 tablespoon stone-ground or yellow mustard

1 tablespoon apple cider vinegar

¼ teaspoon ground cloves

⅛ teaspoon cayenne powder

4 whole-wheat hamburger buns or 8 pieces of whole-grain toast

Sliced pickles for garnish

1 Add the olive oil to a large skillet over medium heat. Add the onion and mushrooms and sauté for 3 minutes. Add the garlic, bell pepper, and 1 teaspoon of soy sauce. Sauté for 8 more minutes.

2 Add the tempeh to the onion mixture, stir well, and drizzle with remaining soy sauce. Cook for another 8 minutes, or until the tempeh begins to brown.

3 In a small mixing bowl, whisk together the ketchup, mustard, vinegar, cloves, and cayenne powder. Pour over the tempeh mixture and stir well to combine.

4 Reduce the heat to low and cook uncovered for another 5 minutes. Spoon the mixture onto the buns or over the toasted bread. Garnish with sliced pickles.

Per serving: *Calories 391 (From Fat 166); Fat 18g (Saturated 3g); Cholesterol 0mg; Sodium 1,019mg; Carbohydrate 42g; Dietary Fiber 7g; Protein 16g.*

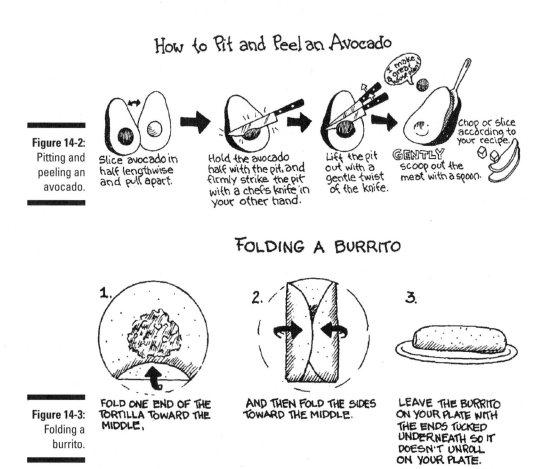

How to Pit and Peel an Avocado

Figure 14-2: Pitting and peeling an avocado.

Slice avocado in half lengthwise and pull apart.

Hold the avocado half with the pit, and firmly strike the pit with a chef's knife in your other hand.

Lift the pit out with a gentle twist of the knife.

I make a great guacamole!

GENTLY scoop out the meat with a spoon.

Chop or slice according to your recipe.

FOLDING A BURRITO

Figure 14-3: Folding a burrito.

1. FOLD ONE END OF THE TORTILLA TOWARD THE MIDDLE.

2. AND THEN FOLD THE SIDES TOWARD THE MIDDLE.

3. LEAVE THE BURRITO ON YOUR PLATE WITH THE ENDS TUCKED UNDERNEATH SO IT DOESN'T UNROLL ON YOUR PLATE.

Comforting Noodles and Pasta

Noodles and pasta have gotten a bad reputation in recent years. The popularity of high-protein diets have pushed these dishes aside and labeled them as unhealthy. In reality, however, countless varieties of healthy noodles offer complex carbohydrates, fiber, and protein, while still being a cheap and tasty menu item.

You have countless types of pasta and noodles to choose from, including rice, gluten-free, whole-wheat, spelt, mung bean, and even Jerusalem artichoke flour noodles. Pasta lends itself well to any combination of sautéed vegetables, simple olives and olive oil, chopped herbs, or rich sauces.

Keeping several types of pasta on hand ensures that you can save money and time by cooking fresh, quick meals at home instead of ordering in or taking out. Store pasta in airtight containers away from light and heat in a cupboard or pantry.

Check the ingredients when buying pasta. Some types are made with eggs, and some frozen varieties like stuffed ravioli often contain cheese. You can find good vegan versions in many health food stores.

Pasta and noodles are the ultimate comfort food for many of us. You don't have to give up those yummy, easy-to-prepare dishes after you go vegan, however. Even gluten-intolerant vegans can enjoy pasta and lasagna with the great rice-based noodles now available. The following recipes cover a variety of flavors and work well for large or small groups. They make great leftovers, too.

Tofu Pad Thai

Pad Thai is normally served with scrambled eggs and sometimes chicken, shrimp, or pork. This recipe uses only tofu, which gives the dish a nice protein profile, and brings it close to the original while still being vegan. This spicy noodle dish has lots of veggies and the flavors enliven your palette and warm you up quickly. While great fresh out of the pot, Tofu Pad Thai is also tasty served cold for picnics or as a party salad.

Preparation/cooking time: *25 minutes*

Yield: *4 servings*

Fried Tofu

1 package extra-firm tofu, cut into 1-inch cubes

6 tablespoons unrefined coconut oil

2 tablespoons agave or brown rice syrup

2 tablespoons naturally brewed soy sauce (tamari, shoyu, or Bragg's Liquid Aminos)

1 teaspoon cayenne powder

1 Remove the excess moisture from the tofu by laying the tofu cubes between two clean kitchen towels and gently pressing down.

2 Whisk the oil, syrup, soy sauce, and cayenne powder together in a small mixing bowl. Heat a large skillet over medium heat and add the oil mixture. Allow to heat for 1 minute.

3 Fry the tofu slices in the hot oil for about 2 minutes on one side, and then turn over and fry for 1 minute more. Be aware that the tofu may splatter in the oil even if it's patted dry. Transfer to a plate lined with clean paper towels to drain and set aside.

Noodles

8 ounces dry mung bean or very thin rice noodles, sometimes called "glass noodles"

1 tablespoon unrefined coconut oil

2 cloves garlic, thinly sliced

1 red bell pepper, seeded and thinly sliced

2 large tomatoes, thinly sliced into half-moons

1 cup sugar snap peas or snow peas

1 tablespoon naturally brewed soy sauce (tamari, shoyu, or Bragg's Liquid Aminos)

½ teaspoon chili powder

¼ teaspoon cayenne powder

1 tablespoon fresh lime juice

1 tablespoon toasted sesame oil

¼ cup finely minced fresh cilantro

½ cup raw peanuts

3 green onions, thinly sliced (green parts only)

1 Cook the noodles according to the package directions. Drain and set aside.

2 Heat a wok or large skillet over medium heat and add the oil. Allow the oil to heat for 1 minute.

3 Sauté the garlic and bell peppers in the hot oil for 2 minutes. Stir in the tomatoes, peas, and tofu. Drizzle the soy sauce over the mixture and stir. Sauté for another 2 minutes and add the chili and cayenne powders and fresh lime juice. Turn the heat to low and cook for another 4 minutes and remove from heat.

4 Pour the drained noodles into the vegetable mixture, add the sesame oil and cilantro, and then stir well. Spoon the pad Thai into bowls and sprinkle with peanuts and green onions. Drizzle each serving with a little more soy sauce and lime juice.

Per serving: Calories 741 (From Fat 396); Fat 44g (Saturated 23g); Cholesterol 0mg; Sodium 729mg; Carbohydrate 74g; Dietary Fiber 6g; Protein 21g.

Mac N' TeaseCheese

This is vegan comfort food at its best. Now when you're going through a break-up, feeling under the weather, or feeling homesick, you can coast through the rough spot with vegan ease. Because of the nutritional yeast, you get a nice dose of vitamin B12, which is great for soothing your frazzled nerves.

Preparation/cooking time: *38 minutes*

Yield: *4 main course servings*

3 cups dry elbow macaroni

1¾ cups unsweetened, plain rice milk or soymilk

1 teaspoon fresh rosemary leaves, minced

2 tablespoons canola oil

⅓ cup plus 1 tablespoon unbleached white flour

1 teaspoon yellow, stone-ground, or Dijon-style mustard

½ cup nutritional yeast flakes

1 teaspoon salt

½ teaspoon black pepper

1 cup frozen peas, thawed

1 Cook the macaroni according to the package directions. Drain and set aside.

2 Heat the milk and rosemary in a small saucepan until it just starts to simmer. Remove from heat and set aside.

3 Heat a large saucepan over medium heat and add the canola oil. Whisk in the flour, mustard, and nutritional yeast flakes, stirring constantly to make sure there are no lumps.

4 Slowly whisk the warmed milk into the flour and mustard mixture, whisking constantly to make sure no lumps form.

5 Continue to cook the sauce, uncovered, until it becomes thick and creamy, up to 5 minutes more.

6 Season the sauce with salt and pepper and then stir in the cooked macaroni. Stir well to coat the noodles. Add the thawed peas and stir once more.

Per serving: Calories 427 (From Fat 102); Fat 11g (Saturated 1g); Cholesterol 0mg; Sodium 663mg; Carbohydrate 63g; Dietary Fiber 10g; Protein 22g.

Noodles with Seitan and Shiitake Mushrooms

This lovely noodle dish tastes fancy, but it's surprisingly easy to prepare. The shiitake mushrooms and seitan provide a very meaty texture (for those who crave nonvegan meats) while the mirin gives a sophisticated aroma and taste.

Preparation/cooking time: *30 minutes*

Yield: *4 servings*

8 ounces dry elbow-style pasta

1 tablespoon extra-virgin olive oil

¼ cup minced shallots (about 3 shallots)

16 shiitake mushrooms, stemmed and thinly sliced

1 teaspoon naturally brewed soy sauce (tamari, shoyu, or Bragg's Liquid Aminos)

8 ounces seitan, thinly sliced

1 teaspoon dried thyme

¼ cup mirin cooking wine or other white wine

1 Cook the pasta according to the package directions. Drain and set aside.

2 Heat the olive oil in a skillet over medium heat. Sauté the shallots and mushrooms with the soy sauce for 5 to 7 minutes, or until the mushrooms start to give up their moisture.

3 Add the seitan and thyme to the mushroom mixture in the skillet and stir well. Cook for another 6 to 8 minutes, or until the seitan is warmed through.

4 Stir in the wine and cook for 2 to 3 more minutes. Then add the drained, cooked pasta to the mushroom mixture and stir well to combine.

Per serving: *Calories 398 (From Fat 48); Fat 5g (Saturated 1g); Cholesterol 0mg; Sodium 244mg; Carbohydrate 64g; Dietary Fiber 4g; Protein 22g.*

World Cuisine: Trying Some Ethnic Staples

Every culture has a few staple dishes that people rely on, and every family has its own special version. After all, there must be thousands of curry powders in India alone! Culturally inspired recipes bring in new flavors and health benefits with different herbs and spices and introduce new vegetables. Curries have been studied for their anti-inflammatory ingredients, and the fermented soy in miso has been used to help treat radiation sickness.

The recipes in this section provide you with a few ethnic dishes you can master. Both recipes can include any number of ingredient combinations, so feel free to start mixing up the vegetables or beans depending on what you have in your refrigerator or cupboard.

Miso Stew

Miso soup is usually a simple broth made with sea veggies and tofu, but this Miso Stew is much heartier and can be a full meal. Plus this amazing one-pot meal is healing. You could call it the Japanese vegan version of Mom's American chicken soup: Take 2 bowls and call me in the morning.

Preparation/cooking time: *25 minutes*

Yield: *4 to 6 servings*

1 tablespoon extra-virgin olive oil

1 medium yellow onion, diced

2 cloves garlic, minced

1 carrot, cut into ¼-inch half moons

1 celery rib, cut into ½-inch half moons

1 package firm tofu, drained and cut into ½-inch cubes

½ cup hijiki seaweed, soaked according to the package directions

2 cups vegetable stock

2 cups filtered water

2 cups cooked brown rice or other whole grain

2 teaspoons naturally brewed soy sauce (tamari, shoyu, or Bragg's Liquid Aminos)

3 tablespoons any flavor miso paste

1 teaspoon freshly grated ginger

2 green onions, sliced, for garnish

1 Heat a large saucepan or soup pot over medium heat. Add the oil and onion and sauté for 5 minutes, or until the onion begins to turn translucent.

2 Add the garlic, carrot, celery, tofu, and hijiki. Pour in the stock and water and bring to a simmer. Add the rice and soy sauce. Cover and cook for 5 minutes.

3 Meanwhile, add the miso paste to a few tablespoons of water in a small mixing bowl. Whisk to combine, and then add just enough water that the miso is smooth and pourable.

4 Move the soup off the heat and stir in the ginger. After the simmering has stopped, add the miso and stir well. Sprinkle with the green onions. (Never boil miso soup after the miso is added. Doing so will destroy the healing benefits of the living enzymes.)

Tip: *When ordering miso soup or stew in restaurants, be sure to ask whether it's vegetarian — most sushi and Japanese restaurants add bonito dried fish flakes.*

Per serving: *Calories 273 (From Fat 88); Fat 10g (Saturated 1g); Cholesterol 0mg; Sodium 609mg; Carbohydrate 34g; Dietary Fiber 4g; Protein 14g.*

Cauliflower Chickpea Curry

This curry has so much flavor, so much protein, and so many veggies — and it's so great for leftovers. What's not to love? Don't let the list of ingredients scare you. You'll use the spices over and over again, so they're a good investment.

Preparation/cooking time: *40 minutes*

Yield: *6 servings*

3 tablespoons unrefined coconut or canola oil

2 teaspoons whole mustard seeds

1 large yellow onion, diced

3 cloves garlic, minced

1 teaspoon plus ½ teaspoon salt

2 tablespoons plus 1 teaspoon ginger, grated or minced

3 teaspoons curry powder

½ teaspoon garlic powder

3 teaspoons cumin seeds

1 teaspoon ground coriander

⅛ teaspoon ground cloves

½ teaspoon ground cinnamon

¼ teaspoon asafetida (sometimes called "hing")

2 green cardamom pods

One 24-ounce can diced tomatoes, undrained

8 cups rinsed, stemmed, and lightly chopped fresh spinach

2 cups cooked and drained chickpeas or a 15-ounce can, drained

2 cups cauliflower, chopped into small florets

1 Preheat a large saucepan or soup pot over medium heat. Pour in the oil, and then add the mustard seeds. Stir and heat until the seeds start popping.

2 Add the onion and sauté for 8 minutes, or until the onion begins to brown. Add the garlic, 1 teaspoon of salt, and the ginger. Stir well to combine and cook for another 3 minutes.

3 Add the curry powder, garlic powder, cumin seeds, coriander, cloves, cinnamon, asafetida, and cardamom pods. Stir in the whole can of tomatoes and juice, and then bring the mixture to a simmer.

4 Add the spinach in large handfuls and stir into the mixture until the leaves begin to wilt down. Add more as space allows, if desired. When all the spinach is wilted down, add the chickpeas and cauliflower to the pot. Add the remaining ½ teaspoon of salt and stir well.

5 Cover and cook for another 20 minutes over low heat. Remove the cardamom pods and serve hot with rice or warmed pitas.

Per serving: Calories 354 (From Fat 103); Fat 11g (Saturated 6g); Cholesterol 0mg; Sodium 772mg; Carbohydrate 51g; Dietary Fiber 16g; Protein 16g.

Beans and Rice Are Nice

Living on minimum wage for an episode of FX Network's series *30 Days* reminded me of the numerous benefits of bean and grain combinations. First, they're cheap. Even organic rice and beans, when bought dry in bulk, cost pennies per serving. Second, they're versatile. You can take lentils and millet and make them into diverse ethnic dishes with a few herb and spice tricks. Consider the following combinations:

✔ **Indian lentils and millet:** Add curry powder and a can of coconut milk.

✔ **Italian lentils and millet:** Combine the lentils and millet with canned tomatoes, rosemary, and oregano.

✔ **Mexican lentils and millet:** Mix the millet with a scoop of salsa, toss the lentils with cilantro and lime juice, and dice up some avocado for the top.

Last, but not least, beans and whole grains offer superior nutrition, with protein, complex carbohydrates, minerals, and fiber.

The following recipes are instant classics because they're easy to make, delicious, and come in handy for lunch the next day. Stocked with veggies, these hearty bean dishes can be served alone or with a simple side salad. You can use these dishes to warm your bones in the winter or give you the energy you need for big days in the active summer months.

Southern Style Red Beans and Rice

Rich and savory, this one-pot meal sticks to your ribs and offers the flavors of a traditional meat dish. The beans and rice offer protein and complex carbohydrates while soaking up the spices. Not only is this a simple meal to prepare, but this hearty dish also freezes well to save you time in the future. Simply eat dinner tonight, and then freeze individual portions for later use in glass jars from pickles, jams, or nut butters.

Soaking time for beans: *At least 8 hours or overnight*

Soaking time for rice: *1 hour*

Preparation/cooking time: *2 hours*

Yield: *10 servings*

2 cups dried red beans, sorted, rinsed, and drained	2 roasted red bell peppers, diced
6 cups water or low-sodium vegetable stock	1½ cups brown rice, rinsed and drained
2 bay leaves	¼ teaspoon cayenne powder
¼ cup extra-virgin olive oil	¼ teaspoon red pepper flakes
1 large red onion, diced	2 teaspoons salt
2 celery ribs, diced	1 teaspoon black pepper
1 carrot, diced	1 teaspoon hot sauce
5 cloves garlic, sliced	1 recipe Tofu Sour Cream (see Chapter 13)
1 teaspoon naturally brewed soy sauce (tamari, shoyu, or Bragg's Liquid Aminos)	

1 Place the beans in a large bowl and add enough water to cover them by 2 inches. Let the beans soak overnight or for at least 8 hours.

2 Drain and rinse the soaked beans and add to a large heavy pot with the 6 cups of water or stock and the bay leaves. Bring to a boil, lower heat to a simmer, and continue to cook partially covered.

3 While the beans are cooking, heat a cast-iron skillet or other large, heavy skillet over medium heat and add the oil. Sauté the onion, celery, carrot, and garlic with the soy sauce until the vegetables begin to soften, about 5 minutes. Add the roasted bell peppers, cayenne, and red pepper flakes to the onion mixture, stir, and cook for another 5 minutes.

4 Add the onion mixture to the cooking beans. Bring the beans back up to a boil, reduce to a simmer, and cover. Cook for 1 hour, or until beans are soft. While the beans are cooking, soak the rice in water for 1 hour and then drain.

5 Add the salt, pepper, hot sauce, and drained brown rice to the beans. Add another 1 to 2 cups of water or stock to ensure that you have enough cooking liquid.

6 Bring the whole pot back to a boil, reduce to a simmer, and cook, covered, for another 45 minutes. Check the pot a few times to ensure you have enough cooking liquid. Add more water or stock as necessary until the rice is cooked through. Serve hot with Tofu Sour Cream.

Per serving: *Calories 278 (From Fat 58); Fat 6g (Saturated 1g); Cholesterol 0mg; Sodium 521mg; Carbohydrate 45g; Dietary Fiber 10g; Protein 11g.*

Beanie Broccoli over Polenta

My 2-year-old son was the first to test this dish. He loves it, and so as a mom, I'm thrilled! After all, what could be better than to feed your family something that's filling, simple, and versatile? The dish can be modified in a number of ways. Try using a variety of beans, greens, and whole grains to mix it up.

Preparation/cooking time: *45 minutes*

Yield: *6 to 8 servings*

4 tablespoons extra-virgin olive oil, divided

5 cups filtered water

1 teaspoon salt, divided

1 cup organic yellow corn grits

½ cup diced red onion

2 cloves garlic, minced

1 teaspoon red pepper flakes

2 cups cooked and drained pinto beans, or a 15-ounce can, drained and rinsed

4 cups broccoli florets

1 cup low-sodium vegetable stock

1 Lightly oil a 13- x 9-inch baking dish with 2 tablespoons of the olive oil and set aside.

2 Set a large saucepan over medium heat. Add the water and then whisk ½ teaspoon of the salt, 1 tablespoon of the olive oil, and the corn grits together. Whisk constantly to avoid lumps, cooking until it comes to a rolling boil.

3 Reduce heat to low and cook, stirring often, for 30 minutes.

4 Remove the cooked polenta from the heat and pour it into the oiled baking dish. Cover with a kitchen towel and set aside while you prepare the vegetables.

5 Heat a large skillet over medium-high heat. Add the remaining tablespoon of olive oil to the skillet and sauté the onion for 2 minutes. Add the garlic and the remaining ½ teaspoon of the salt and sauté for 1 minute more.

6 Add the red pepper flakes and stir well. Then add the beans and broccoli and stir well to combine. Pour the vegetable stock into the skillet and cook covered for 5 minutes. Remove the lid and cook until the liquid has evaporated, about 2 minutes more.

7 To serve, spoon the polenta into individual bowls and cover with large scoops of beans and broccoli. Serve hot.

Per serving: *Calories 231 (From Fat 88); Fat 10g (Saturated 1g); Cholesterol 0mg; Sodium 556mg; Carbohydrate 30g; Dietary Fiber 6g; Protein 6g.*

Chapter 15

Just Desserts

1've been saving the best for last: Here's the scoop on vegan desserts — they're amazing! Entire cookbooks have been devoted to decadent, sweet, yummy vegan treats, so this chapter offers just a sampling of what's possible. You don't have to leave the realm of healthy food to enjoy desserts; you can combine great taste and good nutrition. Fruits, nuts, seeds, healthier sweeteners, and quality ingredients are important to the taste and nutrition of these dishes. Make dessert a healthy indulgence by discovering how to create creamy, rich, dense, or flaky concoctions without eggs or dairy.

A good dessert offers a variety of flavors and notes to liven up your taste buds. A little salt can make the flavors pop in either a fruit or chocolate dessert. For moist textures in cakes and pastries, fat must be used. So without the conventional aid of eggs, cream, or butter, you need to use vegan margarine or vegetable oils, such as olive, canola, or unrefined coconut, to create these vegan desserts.

When choosing flour for your baked desserts, try whole-wheat pastry flour. It's finely ground and bakes into a light, soft texture while still offering more nutrition than white flour. You also can use unbleached white flour instead of conventional bleached white flour. The bleaching process uses harsh chemicals and removes the nutrition from the flour.

I've had great success working out new, vegan recipes by removing the eggs, butter, and milk from traditional recipes. If you have an old recipe for cake or cookies that you love, try your hand at veganizing it by replacing the dairy products with vegan ingredients. See Chapter 10 for information about vegan substitutions that will keep Mom's apple pie on the vegan table.

Whipping Up Some Vegan Cookies, Brownies, and Bars

Nothing is more satisfying than baking a dense and moist dessert and eating it with your hands. That's why cookies and bars appeal to the kid inside all of us; using your fingers instead of forks to eat dessert brings it to another level of intimacy and basic enjoyment.

Even though they're loaded with chocolate, these recipes offer greater nutrition than more conventional recipes. The techniques are likely familiar to anyone who has baked cookies before, so take pleasure in a no-fail, sure-to-please cooking adventure.

Pepper Chip Cookies

This recipe is a nice spin on the old favorite: chocolate chip cookies. These morsels offer a savory hint of black pepper and soy sauce — in a good way! If you take these cookies to a party, everyone who tries them will have a new perspective on what a vegan eats and will want to try more.

Preparation time: *20 minutes*

Baking time: *10 minutes*

Yield: *2 dozen cookies*

2 cups flour (unbleached white, wheat, or spelt)

1 teaspoon baking soda

¼ teaspoon naturally brewed soy sauce (tamari, shoyu, or Bragg's Liquid Aminos)

1¼ cup rapadura sugar

¾ cup vegan margarine, softened

1 teaspoon pure vanilla extract

⅓ cup soft tofu

¾ teaspoon freshly ground black pepper

1 cup vegan chocolate chips

1 Preheat the oven to 375 degrees.

2 In a large mixing bowl, sift together the flour and baking soda, and then set aside.

3 Using a food processor, blend together the soy sauce, sugar, margarine, vanilla extract, tofu, and black pepper until smooth.

4 Add the soy sauce mixture and the chocolate chips to the flour mixture and stir until combined.

5 Drop tablespoons of dough onto a parchment paper–lined cookie sheet and bake for 10 minutes.

6 Allow to cool slightly before removing from the cookie sheet.

Per serving: Calories 162 (From Fat 65); Fat 7g (Saturated 2g); Cholesterol 0mg; Sodium 123mg; Carbohydrate 23g; Dietary Fiber 0g; Protein 2g.

Chocolate Chick Blondies

These gluten-free bars are dense and full of nutrition. The chickpeas (also known as garbanzo beans) offer substantial protein and replace the flour normally found in dessert bars. After you cut them, these squares can be individually wrapped and frozen for quick snacking later. Make a double batch and freeze half for a road trip, picnic, or upcoming potluck.

Preparation time: *5 minutes*

Baking time: *25 minutes*

Chilling time: *30 minutes*

Yield: *6 to 8 servings*

Canola, sunflower, or unrefined coconut oil (for oiling pan)

One 15-ounce can chickpeas, drained and rinsed

½ cup agave syrup, rapadura sugar, or brown rice syrup

½ cup applesauce

¼ cup almond or peanut butter (crunchy is best)

2 teaspoons vanilla extract

⅓ cup ground flaxseeds or flaxseed meal

2 tablespoons brown rice flour

½ teaspoon baking powder

½ cup vegan chocolate chips

1 Preheat the oven to 350 degrees.

2 Lightly coat an 8-inch square baking pan with oil.

3 Combine the remaining ingredients, except the chocolate chips, in a food processor. Process until smooth, scraping the sides a few times.

4 Pour the batter into the pan and stir in the chocolate chips.

5 Bake for 25 minutes.

6 Cool to room temperature, and then refrigerate for at least 30 minutes before slicing into 8 squares.

Per serving: Calories 343 (From Fat 130); Fat 14g (Saturated 2g); Cholesterol 0mg; Sodium 158mg; Carbohydrate 50g; Dietary Fiber 5g; Protein 7g.

Double Chocolate Brownies

Thank heaven that chocolate is vegan! These rich brownies are indistinguishable from their dairy- and egg-heavy relatives. These brownies are cholesterol-free, and each bite gives your body a little healthy bonus from the fiber-rich flaxseeds.

Preparation time: *25 minutes*

Baking time: *25 to 30 minutes*

Yield: *9 servings*

¼ cup canola or unrefined coconut oil (melted), plus extra for oiling pan

6 tablespoons water

2 tablespoons ground flaxseeds or flaxseed meal

¼ cup applesauce

1 cup agave, brown rice, or maple syrup

1 teaspoon pure vanilla extract

1 cup whole-wheat pastry flour

¾ cup cocoa powder

¼ teaspoon salt

½ teaspoon baking soda

1 cup vegan chocolate chips

1 Preheat the oven to 350 degrees.

2 Grease a 9-inch square baking pan with a little oil and set aside.

3 In a small saucepan, heat the water over medium heat until just simmering. Add the ground flaxseeds and whisk to combine. Cook for 1 minute and remove from the heat. Set aside.

4 In a medium-sized mixing bowl, combine the ¼ oil, applesauce, agave, heated flax mixture, and vanilla. Whisk together well to completely combine.

5 In another mixing bowl, combine the flour, cocoa powder, salt, and baking powder. Whisk together well to completely combine.

6 Add the wet ingredients to the dry ingredients and stir well until combined. Then stir in the chocolate chips.

7 Pour the batter into the prepared pan and bake for 25 to 30 minutes, until a toothpick inserted in the center comes out clean. Allow to cool completely before cutting into 9 equal squares.

Per serving: *Calories 349 (From Fat 105); Fat 12g (Saturated 3g); Cholesterol 0mg; Sodium 217mg; Carbohydrate 63g; Dietary Fiber 4g; Protein 5g.*

Tasting the Vegan Fruit

Fruit-based desserts can be delicate and light or sophisticated and full of complex flavors. Something as simple as a bowl of fresh berries with a scoop of vegan ice cream can end a fantastic summer meal. Winter fruits lend their heavily spiced sweetness to long baking techniques, which make them fortifying, cozy desserts that are appropriate for the darker months. This seasonality should be relished when choosing fruit desserts. Try using peaches at the height of their ripeness from the farmer's market for a cobbler, or pick something fresh from your garden to add to a fruit pudding.

Lime in the Coconut Ice

Beat the heat with this fruit ice! It won't be green unless you add food coloring (and because some food dyes are derived from insects, I say skip 'em!). Despite its lack of color, however, it's amazingly refreshing and deliciously limey — perfect for an ending to a summer meal or as a palate cleanser between courses of a fancier, sit-down meal.

Preparation time: *8 minutes*

Chilling time: *2 hours*

Freezing time: *20 minutes*

Yield: *6 servings*

1½ cups agave or brown rice syrup	1 teaspoon grated lime peel
1 cup freshly squeezed lime juice	1 teaspoon grated lemon peel
4 cups unsweetened coconut milk	

1 Slowly heat the agave and lime juice in a medium saucepan over low heat. Whisk often to combine.

2 In a large mixing bowl, combine the agave-lime mixture with the remaining ingredients and stir well.

3 Cover and allow to cool in the refrigerator for at least 2 hours.

4 Freeze in an ice cream maker according to the manufacturer's directions for a sorbet recipe, approximately 20 minutes.

Per serving: Calories 653 (From Fat 295); Fat 33g (Saturated 29g); Cholesterol 0mg; Sodium 202mg; Carbohydrate 92g; Dietary Fiber 2g; Protein 4g.

Fruit Kanten

What the heck is Kanten, you may ask? Well, it's actually a pudding made from *agar*. What the heck is agar? Well, agar is a sea vegetable and Mother Nature's gift to vegans. This natural plant food is a vegan's answer to gelatin. These clear flakes are used as a gelling agent in culture media (remember your experiments in biology and chemistry class?) and delicious desserts. Find more info about vegan gelatin alternatives in Chapter 10.

Try seasonal combinations of juice and fruit to use your farmer's market or backyard bounty. Apple juice and chunks of pear, pear juice with cherries, or peach juice with melon balls are winning combinations. This type of dessert will look a little cloudy, not clear like old-school Jell-O, but it will be delicious!

Preparation/cooking time: *15 minutes*

Chilling time: *1½ hours*

Yield: *4 to 6 servings*

4 cups fruit juice (apple, grape, cherry, or a combination of any 2)

5 tablespoons agar flakes

¼ teaspoon salt

1 cup diced fruit (apples, grapes, blueberries, cherries, or a combination)

1 Place all the ingredients in a medium saucepan and bring the mixture to a boil, uncovered.

2 Reduce the heat to medium-low and simmer for 5 to 7 minutes, stirring occasionally, until the agar flakes have dissolved.

3 Pour the mixture into individual bowls, wine glasses, or a shallow serving dish and refrigerate until gelled, about 1½ hours. Spoon out or slice to serve.

Tip: *Agar is also a great natural laxative, so if you're feeling "stuck," make some Kanten. Cherry or apple Kanten gives you a double whammy!*

Per serving: *Calories 149 (From Fat 5); Fat 1g (Saturated 0g); Cholesterol 0mg; Sodium 153mg; Carbohydrate 37g; Dietary Fiber 1g; Protein 1g.*

Summer Smoothie-sicles

Kids and adults alike love popsicles. So why not make them a little healthier and more substantial than what the ice cream truck guy has to offer? You can take this simple recipe and add all kinds of healthy secrets: liquid chlorophyll, dehydrated greens powders, or even ground nuts and flaxseeds. Go crazy! One caveat: Don't try to use citrus juices in this recipe — they don't work well.

Preparation time: *10 minutes*

Freezing time: *6 hours*

Yield: *6 to 10 servings, depending on the size of your popsicle molds*

2 cups fruit juice (except citrus juices)

1 cup soy yogurt

2 tablespoons agave syrup or brown rice syrup

¼ cup fresh green juice from kale or broccoli (optional)

1 Blend all the ingredients together, including green juice, if desired, until creamy and smooth.

2 Pour into popsicle molds.

3 Freeze for at least 6 hours and then serve.

Tip: *Run the mold under cool water once the popsicles are completely frozen. This will help loosen your treats and make them easier to remove.*

Vary It! *If you have any leftover mashed sweet potatoes, dregs of almond butter in a jar, or a handful of cashews waiting to be eaten, throw them in when blending the ingredients together too!*

Per serving: *Calories 88 (From Fat 5); Fat 1g (Saturated 0g); Cholesterol 0mg; Sodium 23mg; Carbohydrate 20g; Dietary Fiber 0g; Protein 1g.*

Everything Old Is New Again

The recipes in this section are my vegan takes on old favorites. These recipes provide a good learning opportunity for anyone who's worried about converting their old dairy and meat recipes to vegan ones. Candy, cakes, shakes, and baked goods can be made vegan and still taste delicious.

Baking and candy making require more precision than other types of cooking, because they involve more chemistry than average cooking. So, when learning how to bake, freeze, and cook vegan desserts, be patient with the process and with yourself. Use vegan recipes to get acquainted with the techniques and ingredients; and if a recipe doesn't work out as planned, just let it roll off your back. Nine times out of ten it still tastes good, even if it doesn't look like the picture in your mind.

Chocolate Peanut Butter Bombs

A simple take on the old favorite chocolate peanut butter cups from childhood, these delicious morsels will win over any crowd. They also can be made using almond or cashew butter, if desired.

Preparation time: *20 minutes*

Chilling time: *4 hours*

Yield: *12 to 15 servings*

1 cup vegan chocolate chips	*½ teaspoon pure vanilla extract*
½ cup chunky peanut butter	*¼ teaspoon salt*
⅓ cup agave or brown rice syrup	

1 Combine all the ingredients in a small saucepan. Cook over low heat, stirring constantly with a heat-safe spatula until completely smooth and melted.

2 Set 12 to 15 mini paper and foil muffin cups on a cookie sheet.

3 Pour the mixture in small spoonfuls into the muffin cups, filling them to the brim.

4 Refrigerate the filled cups for at least 4 hours, or until completely set and firm.

Tip: To help the muffin cups retain their shape, you can set the empty cups in a mini-muffin tin and then fill them. Set the entire tin in the refrigerator to set.

Per serving: Calories 159 (From Fat 71); Fat 8g (Saturated 2g); Cholesterol 0mg; Sodium 120mg; Carbohydrate 22g; Dietary Fiber 1g; Protein 3g.

Apple Crumble

Share this simple dish with friends and family for a holiday feast. Try using local, heirloom apples to explore the different flavors available. Try sweet apples like Baldwin, Gala, Honeycrisp, or Pippin, combined with tart apples like Fuji, Winesap, or Mutsu. You can substitute pears for all or some of the apples. You can even try using sweet potatoes or sweet winter squashes for another color or taste.

Preparation/cooking time: *10 minutes*

Baking time: *30 minutes*

Yield: *8 servings*

Filling:

3 tart apples, cored and sliced thinly (see Figure 15-1 for instruction)

3 sweet apples, cored and sliced thinly

½ cup fresh or frozen (thawed overnight in the refrigerator) cranberries

1 teaspoon cinnamon

¼ teaspoon nutmeg

⅛ teaspoon ground cloves

½ teaspoon salt

3 tablespoons whole-wheat pastry flour

2 tablespoons agave, brown rice, or maple syrup

1 cup apple cider

1 teaspoon orange peel

2 tablespoons vegan margarine

Crumble topping:

1 cup raw nuts (almonds, cashews, walnuts, pecans, or a mixture)

1 cup rolled oats

½ cup unsweetened coconut flakes

2 tablespoons whole-wheat pastry flour

½ teaspoon salt

½ teaspoon cinnamon

1 Preheat oven to 350 degrees.

2 Combine all the filling ingredients, except the margarine, in a saucepan. Stir well and cook over medium-high heat for about 5 minutes.

3 Pour the mixture into a greased baking dish and dot the top with the margarine. Set aside.

4 Combine all the topping ingredients in a food processor and pulse 10 to 12 times to chop well. Spread the topping mixture evenly across the top of the apples.

5 Bake for 30 minutes. Remove from oven and allow to rest for 5 minutes before serving hot. Serve with vegan ice cream for an a la mode creation.

Per serving: *Calories 342 (From Fat 170); Fat 19g (Saturated 7g); Cholesterol 0mg; Sodium 345mg; Carbohydrate 41g; Dietary Fiber 8g; Protein 7g.*

HOW TO CORE AND SLICE AN APPLE

CUT THE APPLE IN HALF. USE A MELON BALLER TO SCRAPE OUT THE CORE AND SEEDS. CUT THE STEM OFF AT BOTH ENDS.

PLACE A HALF ON A CUTTING BOARD, FLAT SIDE DOWN. USE A SHARP KNIFE TO CUT SLICES.

Figure 15-1:
Coring and slicing an apple.

Glazed Carrot Pineapple Cake

This cake is simple, yet very moist and aromatic. A lovely compliment to a brunch, tea party, or as a simple dessert for any occasion. Traditional glazed pineapple cakes can be heavy with syrup. Lightly sweetened and full of healthy ingredients, this delicate cake can be made a day ahead and covered and refrigerated overnight.

Preparation time: 15 minutes

Baking time: 40 to 45 minutes

Yield: 8 to 10 servings

Cake

2 ¾ cups white, unbleached flour

2 teaspoons baking soda

2 teaspoons cinnamon

½ teaspoon nutmeg

1 teaspoon baking powder

1 teaspoon salt

1 cup agave, maple, or brown rice syrup

3 egg equivalent in Ener-G egg substitute

1 teaspoon pure vanilla extract

1 teaspoon lemon peel

1 teaspoon orange peel

1 cup canola or melted unrefined coconut oil, plus extra for oiling the baking dish

2 cups finely grated carrots

One 14-ounce can crushed pineapple, drained

1 cup unsweetened coconut flakes

1 Preheat the oven to 350 degrees.

2 Grease a 13-x-9-inch baking dish with a little canola oil or vegan margarine. Set aside.

3 In a medium bowl, combine the flour, baking soda, cinnamon, nutmeg, baking powder, and salt. Whisk well to combine.

4 In a large bowl, mix agave and egg substitute with a hand mixer until creamy. Add vanilla, zests, and canola oil to the agave and egg substitute mixture.

5 Mix the wet and dry ingredients together and stir in the carrots, pineapple, and coconut. Pour the batter evenly into the prepared pan.

6 Bake for 40 to 45 minutes, or until a toothpick inserted into the center comes out clean.

7 Allow the cake to cool completely before glazing.

Glaze

½ cup apple juice

½ cup orange juice

2 teaspoons arrowroot

1 tablespoon agave, maple, or brown rice syrup

Pinch of salt

1 Combine all the ingredients in a small saucepan. Whisk well before heating.

2 Cook over low heat, stirring constantly, until the glaze begins to thicken, about 6 minutes.

3 Allow the glaze to cool for a few minutes before pouring over the carrot cake while it is still warm.

Tip: *Don't be alarmed that the batter is very wet when being poured into the pan. It bakes up just fine and is nice and moist.*

Per serving: *Calories 691 (From Fat 301); Fat 34g (Saturated 6g); Cholesterol 0mg; Sodium 819mg; Carbohydrate 91g; Dietary Fiber 3g; Protein 7g.*

Silk Shake

Shakes are hard to beat when you're looking for a rich, smooth, and easy dessert. The frozen banana is a key ingredient — room-temperature fruit just won't create the same creamy texture. When summer arrives, I like to keep several peeled bananas waiting in the freezer at all times for when the mood strikes for this tasty treat.

Preparation time: *10 minutes*

Yield: *2 servings*

1 cup cashews	*¾ cup vanilla rice, soy, or hemp milk*
1 banana, peel removed and frozen	*1 tablespoon agave, maple, or brown rice syrup*
3 tablespoons unsweetened cocoa powder	*Pinch of salt*
3 Medjool dates, pits removed and chopped	*2 cups ice*

1 Combine all the ingredients except the ice in a sturdy blender. Blend until the whole mixture is smooth and well combined.

2 Add the ice and continue blending until smooth. Pour into tall glasses and serve.

Vary It!: *To vary this shake, you can skip the cocoa powder and add more nutritional power by throwing in ½ cup frozen raspberries or pitted cherries. You also can add ¼ cup peanut butter or almond butter to the original recipe for a rich treat.*

Per serving: *Calories 592 (From Fat 306); Fat 34g (Saturated 7g); Cholesterol 0mg; Sodium 357mg; Carbohydrate 71g; Dietary Fiber 7g; Protein 13g.*

Part V
Living Vegan in the Real World

The 5th Wave   By Rich Tennant

"No, I don't mean the shoes are the color of eggplant, I mean they're eggplant shoes."

In this part . . .

*E*ating vegan meals at home is easy once you get the hang of some new recipes. Venturing outside the house to eat can be more of a challenge, however. It's important to stick to your convictions, but you also want to be a gracious guest and not alienate those who haven't seen the vegan light yet.

The chapters in this part offer practical tips on how to have a social life in a nonvegan world. Whether you're going to a wedding, cocktail party, or conference, traveling abroad, or driving across the country, you can make any situation work for you and your vegan lifestyle.

Chapter 16

Walking the Vegan Walk (without Being Preachy!)

Some people become vegan because their health problems can be healed with a plant-based diet. Others focus on veganism as a path to spiritual health and enlightenment. Still other vegans love and respect the lives of nonhuman animals and refuse to participate in their enslavement and deaths, or they just don't like the taste and texture of animal foods. People have so many reasons for living a vegan life, and the resulting benefits to your health and well-being are positive.

You may feel the temptation to start talking about your own vegan experience with the people around you, especially when you have been profoundly affected by specific vegan-related knowledge that has changed your own life. Veganism becomes religion. You have seen the light! Sharing yourself authentically with people is important, but you don't want to alienate loved ones or live too single-mindedly.

A big part of this new lifestyle is incorporating different ingredients and creating a fresh perspective that includes like-minded people and your current friends and family. If, like me, you find that your new vegan diet and lifestyle are exciting and easy, you'll always be looking for ways to widen your food experiences. Sometimes, however, new and old vegans alike can get stuck in a rut of the same old food choices. They may have lost the zest for vegan living or feel tired of explaining their choice in diet to nonvegans. But don't worry; this chapter can help focus your intentions for a whole, vegan life and offer you support in speaking and living in the world with gentle love for everyone — including meat eaters!

Encouraging and Enjoying Variety in Your Diet

Some experts estimate that most Americans eat the same ten fruits and vegetables for most of their lives (and that's if they eat fruits and vegetables at all). Think of it this way: A narrow diet can lead to limited energy and life experiences. If you want a full life, enriched by a wide array of adventures, your diet must include a diversity of flavors, colors, and textures. Include a variety of seasonal and local plant foods in your menus, and share these new discoveries with your loved ones. Doing so ensures that you don't get bored with vegan meals — and you'll get better nutrition to boot. When family and friends taste your locally inspired dishes and see how flavorful they can be, your reasons for going vegan will be easier for them to understand.

Imagine eating the same ten foods for the rest of your life. Even if those foods were carefully chosen, you would probably still be missing some important nutrients — and you would certainly get bored. A healthy diet is a diet full of variety. Getting your nutrition from many different sources ensures that your body is taking in all the benefits foods can offer, while also ensuring happy taste buds.

As a Certified Holistic Health Counselor, I meet with Americans from every walk of life and background. Their health concerns usually stem from being overfed and undernourished. They get plenty of calories and plenty of carbohydrates, protein, and fats, but their diets are totally lacking in simple, energizing, living foods also known as "functional foods." Don't make that same mistake. As you begin planning your vegan menus, be sure to include a variety of fruits, vegetables, whole grains, nuts, seeds, and legumes. These whole foods will collectively contribute the nutrients necessary for a healthy body. Also be sure to share delicious, healthy foods on a regular basis to ensure that your friends and family enjoy the vegan bounty and see how wonderful vegan eating can be.

The best ways to encourage a varied diet of fruits and vegetables are very simple: Maintain your vegan diet and stay away from junk food. Eating a vegan diet automatically increases your intake of plant foods, and serving simply prepared veggies and raw fruit at home is a delicious alternative to labor-intensive menus. Who doesn't love some simple carrot sticks, steamed broccoli, lightly dressed salad greens, or baked sweet potatoes? Well, many people. But as you share more fresh fruits and vegetables with the people you love, their taste buds will start to love them. The less junk food you eat, the more you appreciate natural foods. And avoiding the fast-food and processed chemical-filled junk food is easy, because most of it isn't vegan. Keeping the junk out of the house and only offering fresh, whole foods will ensure consumption of a wider variety of healthy foods.

When healthy food is the only option

My client D.G. decided to stop offering junk food to her teenaged son's friends when they came over to play video games. Instead she put a big bowl of apples, bananas, and oranges on the table. When the boys said they were hungry, she simply said: "Eat an apple." They did. All of them! When she saw how well that was working, she decided to go one step further. When the boys decided to stay over for dinner, she made a big pot of pasta, simple tomato sauce, whole-grain garlic toast, and a huge plate of steamed broccoli. They ate it all. Copy this example of sharing simple, vegan foods with friends and family in a non-confrontational manner, and everyone will benefit.

Here are some great ways to ensure variety in your diet and spread the vegan love:

✔ **Get away from boring (and boiled) vegetables and fruits:** To get out of the rut, try the following alternatives: Eat green salads with fruit; leave bowls of dried fruit around the house instead of candy; and serve raw veggies with Tofu Sour Cream (see Chapter 13) or your favorite vegan salad dressing. Offering healthy, delicious snacks to people will help them understand why you love this diet.

✔ **Roast 'em if you got 'em:** Roasted veggies taste delicious and keep well for a few days. Try tossing 1-inch cubes of carrots, sweet potatoes, beets, parsnips, sweet winter squashes, and halved Brussels sprouts with just enough organic olive oil to coat and a pinch of salt. Place the veggies in a glass baking dish or on a cookie sheet in a 375 degree oven and roast for 30–45 minutes, stirring once. These roasted veggies make a great side dish for leftovers and lunches.

✔ **Visit your local farmer's market:** Pick up a new fruit or veggie each week to expand your repertoire. Ask the farmer for an easy recipe or for his favorite way to cook this new produce. Though keep in mind that seasonal produce is picked at the peak of its flavor, so often it doesn't need much preparation to taste good. Take your family or roommates with you to the market — they'll enjoy the experience and can help find delicious new produce to try.

✔ **Join a CSA:** A Community Supportive Agriculture program, or CSA, is a system where small farmers offer seasonal shares in their crops. Individuals and families can pay in advance for a weekly box of fresh, seasonal food to be delivered to a local drop-off point. This system encourages the shareholder (that would be you) to eat a more diverse selection of produce because you already have a box of nice food that you may not normally purchase. Many CSAs also provide recipes that use their seasonal produce.

✔ **Shake it up:** Smoothie chains, which are everywhere these days, offer the opportunity to get several servings of fruit and veggies into your menu plan. Bring a bunch of vegan smoothies to your next meeting or group gathering to share the goodness with co-workers and friends.

Smoothie shops often have soy yogurt and soymilk or rice milk, so be sure to ask if you don't see what you're looking for on the menu. If you can't find a yogurt or nondairy milk for your smoothie, ask for fruit, juice, nuts, or seeds to be blended together. Be sure to ask for unsweetened fruit. Employees at these establishments are familiar with personalized blends and will be accommodating if asked nicely.

✔ **Get juicy:** Get a juicer or high-quality blender and make a fresh juice with several fruits and veggies daily. You can make juices with countless combinations; in fact, entire books are dedicated to juice recipes that focus on taste themes and specific health concerns.

✔ **Be like the French and shop often:** It's normal in many European cultures for families to shop every two or three days for fresh produce. Shopping this often may be easier in Paris or Milan where every neighborhood has a fresh street market several times a week, but you can still make a quick trip into the grocery store for salad greens and fruit to ensure healthy snacking.

✔ **Don't turn a cold shoulder on the freezer:** Keeping frozen fruits and veggies on hand enables you to have a quick, healthy side dish for every meal. Even vegan chefs need a quick bag of frozen green beans or edamame to round out a meal sometimes.

✔ **Plan ahead:** Use a menu plan and weekly shopping list to make sure you're ready to prepare a healthy meal or snack at a moments notice. Scrambling for dinner ideas at 5 p.m. will lead to drive-through cravings and old junk-food habits. Head to Chapter 9 for more details on planning meals.

Displaying Kindness and Understanding with Your Nonvegan Friends and Family

You can (and should!) set kind and loving intentions for yourself that your life's actions will be harmless and bring positive change to the world. These thoughts probably aren't new to you. After all, if you're on the path toward vegan living, you've clearly begun to see and understand the consequences of your actions. Life is fragile, and eating a plant-based diet makes real your understanding that all life-forms deserve respect.

In this section, I show you the best ways to defend your vegan lifestyle without burning bridges, and I also help you understand why you can't always force others to see your point of view or take your life's path.

Defending yourself without hurting others' feelings

Food is an emotional, cultural, and personal issue for most of us. It evokes memories, acts as the glue at community and family bonding ceremonies, and becomes who we are. You are what you eat, and as a vegan, you have thought about what you eat on a much deeper and more profound level than most of the people around you.

After your decision to become vegan is made, it can bring joy and sorrow to you and the people who love you. You may feel challenged by other's desires for you to conform to cultural norms. So be prepared to calmly defend yourself to the people you love. Know your facts and read about the benefits of the lifestyle you have chosen. Project loving kindness toward anyone who gently, or crudely, asks "Why are you a vegan?" Chapter 26 provides you with responses to the most common questions you're likely to encounter.

Avoiding the temptation to encourage others to follow your path

While every choice in your day may seem weighty as a vegan — from what to order for brunch to what shoes to buy — you may notice that the people you love aren't so concerned with the impacts of their choices. It can be tempting to start encouraging people to make different choices and to explain why they're doing something harmful. I remember saying things like "Did you know that your ham sandwich once had a mother?" or "That lady's fur coat probably looked a lot better on the fox that first owned it." These types of comments are not appreciated.

Instead, I discovered that most people don't like being told what to do, and they really don't like being told that their lifestyle is all wrong. Take note of how you feel when people discover how you eat and start making fun of you — does it make you want to stop being vegan and go back to what you were eating before? Certainly not! That's why we need to be compassionate with our nonvegan friends and family. You need to have just as much compassion for them as for the animals you're trying to save. Be passionate and steadfast, but also try to be gentle with others and yourself.

For example, instead of getting angry because your mother bought a new leather purse, take a moment and think about what she's truly looking for in her choices. Be compassionate with her. Is your mother trying to update her style or make herself feel better about herself by purchasing new things? Try complimenting the style or color of her new purchase instead of insulting her because she bought leather. You could go online and print out pictures of other vegan purses and share them with her. Doing so could lead to a conversation where you not only get to share her love of fashion, but you also get the chance to delve deeper and ask whether she's happy with how her life is going. Perhaps what she really needed was someone to compliment her on how nice she looks, or recognize how hard she has been trying to lose weight. Compassion means having love and understanding for another being. Loving your mom means offering her support. If you gently show her other ways to fulfill her desires to look more attractive, she may be more interested in how fashionable vegan clothes are or how a vegan diet could help her lose even more weight.

Determining your way of being compassionate

There are many ways to be compassionate and kind in this life. Living a vegan life is a tremendous step away from a life that's based on cruelty toward animals and the earth. You may decide to simply live a quiet vegan life for the rest of your days. You won't offer information about your lifestyle unless you're asked about it. And even then, you'll project kindness no matter what. You could also feel so strongly about the injustices caused by the meat-and-dairy-based diet you abandoned that you feel compelled to speak up and encourage others to make similar changes.

Choose the way that's right for you. We each have strengths that can lead to positive transformations in the world. You may write a best-selling book or make a movie that causes thousands of people to change their lives. You may cook healthy vegan food for your friends, which in turn may cause a few people to eat less meat and dairy. You may raise your children to be lifelong vegans. Each path is a good one. Be kind to others who have chosen their own paths.

The Whole Enchilada: Yoking Your Mind, Body, and Spirit with the Earth

We live in a highly mechanized, isolating culture of technical communication and fewer and fewer authentic human interactions. So becoming vegan is often a natural response that people have to feeling that they want to connect with something good in the world. Becoming vegan also can be the first step toward living a fully integrated life where you see the connections between your career, lifestyle, diet, and the state of the world.

Meeting other vegans and participating in gatherings centered on food or a love for animals brings new friends into your life. Offering lovingly prepared plant-based meals to your family is a wonderful way to show them how much you care about them. Cooking becomes a form of meditation and an act of loving kindness. Keeping good thoughts in mind and blessing the food as you prepare a meal brings each dish a spirit of respect for the earth, animals, and your loved ones.

The growing trend among environmentalists, animal-rights advocates, and foodies alike is to eat as locally and seasonally as possible. The *Slow Food* movement was started in Italy in 1986 by a small group of people who wanted to be more conscientious about their food choices. The ideals of recognizing and honoring the connections among the food on their dinner plates, the people who produce that food, animal welfare, and the environmental health of the planet are the mission of this movement.

Freshness is an important part of a healthy diet. Once a plant is picked, it retains its energy, nutrients, and, in essence, it's life force for only a short period of time. The fresher your food, the more energy you'll receive from it. The more energy you receive from your food, the healthier you'll be. Local foods are freshest because they were in the ground, growing and storing energy from the sun, rain, and earth, until just hours or days before entering your home.

Perform a simple experiment at home to really see my point here. Try a local, living food test with a friend or family member who isn't yet vegan. For two days eat only fresh, locally prepared and produced foods. Go to your farmer's market and buy fruits and veggies that were grown within 100 miles of your home. Eat these simple foods and take notes on how you feel. Then try eating only canned, packaged, and processed foods for two days. All these foods will have been made in a factory somewhere with ingredients that were sourced from distant locations. After the four days, compare the two different styles of eating. How did your body respond to each style? How did your energy levels fluctuate with each type of food?

Even with your best intentions spurring you to eat more local and organic foods, you may find that you just want strawberries for Valentine's Day. Your local farmers may not supply that food in winter, but you can still buy these off-season items organically. Buying organic food will still ensure that you're feeding yourself nutritious, nontoxic food. You may be increasing your carbon footprint a little, because those strawberries were probably trucked from California or Florida, but you're still voting with your dollars for a more sustainable food supply.

Eating mostly organic, locally produced foods can be expensive. Your priorities to eat this way may require sacrifices of other luxuries. For some, that's a happy decision and feels worthy.

No one is perfect, and it's out of reach for most of us to eat local, organically produced food for every meal. Cut yourself a little slack and remember that you're working hard to eat and live in a way that does as little damage as possible to others, yourself, and the earth.

Coming home to eat

In his fascinating autobiography *Coming Home to Eat: The Pleasures and Politics of Local Food* (W. W. Norton & Co.), Gary Paul Nabhan decided to explore the realities and challenges of eating closer to home. Nabhan performed a one-year eating experiment where he only ate foods that could be grown or found naturally within his watershed. His tale brings to light the amazing impact our food choices can have. The book helps the reader discover the why's and how's of eating locally, and how to work with and support local farmers and food producers.

To find inspiration for your own food odyssey, read Nabhan's book as well as these others:

- ✔ *Animal, Vegetable, Miracle* by Barbara Kingsolver, Steven Hopp, and Camille Kingsolver (Harper Perennial)

- ✔ *Slow Food Nation: Why Our Food Should Be Good, Clean, And Fair* by Carlo Petrini and Alice Waters (Rizzoli Ex Libris)

- ✔ *The Omnivore's Dilemma: A Natural History of Four Meals,* by Michael Pollan (Penguin)

Chapter 17

Vegans on the Move: Travel and Hotel Issues

*P*icking a date for your vacation is important, but planning your eating strategy while you're away is just as significant for a successful vegan adventure. You may be set in your eating and shopping routine at home, but going on the road in this meat-minded world is another story. You'll have less control over when you eat, where you can shop, and what choices you have.

The danger lies in the easy temptation to rely on junky, nonnutritious food that can lead to health problems during your trip or after you get home. Changing your dietary routines also can wreak havoc on your digestive system, especially while traveling. Vacation food can be loaded with sugar, unhealthy fats, and sodium. The food also may be of questionable origins — who knows where that salad was made? And how was it washed? Was it even washed at all? Don't be lured in by the standard away-from-home-mindset of "All rules are off! I'm not home!" Eating poorly can lead to a regrettable vacation experience.

Several fast-food chains are now serving vegan veggie burgers, and you may even find a vegan hot dog. You also can get by on a baked potato topped with veggies and a little salt, so be sure to get creative with the server behind the counter. Whether going overnight to grandma's, flying away for the weekend, shipping out on your reunion cruise, or touring Southeast Asia for a month, you need to prepare yourself with options, strategies, and vocabulary to travel smart and stay true to your vegan commitment.

The world of vegan-friendly travel options is expanding every year. Are there more vegans or just more people who want to walk on the wild side? I can't say, but this bodes well for the adventurous tofu eater. Search online or talk with a travel agent about packages geared toward vegans. There are bike trips, tour groups, cruises, private yachting trips with private chefs, and yoga retreats around the world that can provide all the rest and relaxation you need — all while providing you lovely, vegan food.

Mapping Your Meals on the Road

Thinking through your entire road trip before you set foot out the door is the first step to successful travel — especially when your eating habits are different than most people you'll come in contact with. Not spontaneous enough for you? Don't worry. You'll find plenty of opportunities on every journey to explore unplanned sites and meet new people. But as a traveling vegan, you need to remember that proper sustenance is as important as your traveler's checks. You can still find great surprises and the best soy latte you ever had, but you need an outline of where to get something substantial to eat, too.

Thanks to the Internet and a little contraption called a cooler, you'll never be at a loss for healthy, delicious food when traveling by car or by train. Mapping your route well in advance allows you time to explore and plan your pit stops before you leave home. Just follow these steps:

1. **Get out your map and draw a red line along your planned route.**

2. **Circle a sizeable town or city every 50 to 100 miles along your journey.**

3. **Search the Internet for health food stores, grocery stores, and vegan and ethnic restaurants at each location.**

   Try searching the well-organized vegan restaurant finders like www.happycow.net and www.vegdining.com to look for vegan-friendly restaurants and grocery stores.

4. **Put together a list with addresses, maps, and basic directions from the freeway. Also include business hours and a phone number for each stop you'd like to make.**

You also want to put together a snack list and perishable meal list. Nonperishable snacks, such as crackers and pretzels, can be stored in the car or overhead storage on a train in bags or boxes and won't go bad if unrefrigerated. Perishable items can be kept in a cooler with refreezable ice packs or ice cubes.

If using ice cubes, plan on replenishing with new ice every two to three days on your trip. Gas stations, liquor stores, and grocery stores all usually sell bags of ice. If you bring ice packs with you, ask your hotel or train porter if you can refreeze them in an onsite freezer overnight. If driving in a car, use the hotel ice bucket to bury the packs in free hotel ice in your room overnight.

Consider the following list of healthy, easy, cheap, and yummy meals and snacks to keep stashed in your cooler. Many of these items can be replenished along your route if you get your list of health food stores together:

- ✔ Carrot and celery sticks, sliced cucumbers, and red bell pepper spears
- ✔ Individual bottles of water
- ✔ Individual instant soup containers, which can be mixed with hot water from gas station tea machines, hotel bars, or diners
- ✔ Individual juice boxes and soy or rice milk boxes with straws
- ✔ Nut butter sandwiches made with whole-grain bread and naturally sweetened jam or apple butter
- ✔ Road-worthy fruits like apples, oranges, and bananas
- ✔ Seeds, nuts, dried fruit, and vegan chocolate chips mixed into your own trail mix
- ✔ Tea bags or individual coffee pouches, salt and pepper packets from fast-food joints, and a squeeze bottle of agave or brown rice syrup
- ✔ Tofu Sour Cream or Tofu Cheese to spread on veggies (check out Chapter 13 for these recipes)
- ✔ Vegan snack bars like Lara, Vega, Raw Revolution, Pro Bars, and Oskri Coconut Bars
- ✔ Wraps made with tortillas, hummus, beans and rice, or vegan veggie tofu cream cheese

Don't forget to bring a few trash bags, napkins, and some washable spoons, forks, knives, and plates. Travel mugs are handy for refilling your tea and coffee on the road.

Consider stocking up on takeout orders if you find a great vegan-friendly restaurant while driving to your destination. These leftovers can be kept in the cooler for a couple of days.

Think "picnic in a car" when planning out your travel menu. Your road and train meals can be as fancy as you want, with slabs of marinated tofu on slices of fresh tomato and bread. They also can be as simple as gorp ("good old raisins and peanuts") and a bottle of water. Try something new!

Being a vegan in someone else's home

You may find it hard to believe, but many people really don't understand what being vegan means. Many times they incorrectly assume that you're vegetarian and will load you up with mashed potatoes with butter. My sweetheart of a mother-in-law made green beans for me on my first visit to her home. She happily announced that she "took the bacon out" just before serving it to me. When you're traveling to someone's home, you get your chance, not to preach, but to inform your family and friends about veganism.

So, how can you be a polite houseguest while still getting the foods you need? Before you arrive, let your hosts know of your special dietary needs. Explain what it means to be vegan and do the following:

✔ **Give some meal suggestions for when you first arrive.** Many hosts will want to have some foods on hand that you will enjoy, so help them create this list.

✔ **Offer to lead a shopping trip.** Doing so enables you to pick up foods that you want and helps you educate your hosts.

✔ **Make meals and snacks.** Offer to be in charge of preparing some vegan foods, including main meals, side dishes, desserts, and snacks. Make it a truly vegan experience for your hosts.

✔ **Research restaurants and grocery stores online before your travels.** Many nonvegan hosts may not know where to take you out to eat or where to go shopping. In order to take the pressure off your hosts, come armed with ideas that you have researched.

Bring some food items with you in your luggage to ensure that you'll have something on hand for the first several hours in case the first dietary conversation is misunderstood. A box of Mori-Nu tofu and a can of pinto beans don't need to be refrigerated, so you can keep them in your checked baggage or backseat of the car.

Flying with Skill: Vegans in the Air and at the Airport

You've bought your airplane tickets, and your itinerary is set. Eating or snacking on your long flight is easy, right? And after you arrive at your destination, you can merrily skip away from the airport into exotic vegan paradise — or can you? Planning ahead for air travel requires a new set of skills, but isn't impossible — consider it an exciting part of your journey! I provide plenty of pointers in the following sections.

Requesting a vegan meal (and making sure you get it)

Airline food isn't known for its diversity and vegan-friendly bent. Even the peanuts you may receive on the plane (if they're even serving those anymore) can be roasted with honey, a vegan no-no. Most airlines have cut back considerably on their meal service, so you may only get water or $2 cans of reconstituted orange juice.

If your flight does offer food, make sure your needs are known. As soon as you book your flight, whether it's through a travel agent or online, be sure to contact the airline directly using its customer service line to ask specifically for a *dairy- and egg-free, vegetarian or vegan* meal. You may click corresponding boxes on the airline Web site or tell your travel agent, but you still want to be sure that the airline gets the message more than once. Often, the vegan meal is much better than the regular options, and you'll often get served first! Bonus! International flights often offer an ethnic version of the vegan meal; the "Asian vegetarian" option is your best bet. Be sure to explain that you want to avoid both dairy and eggs.

Double-check with the agent when you check in that your special meal request has been noted on the flight plan. You may not be able to get a vegan meal on board if the request didn't go through, but at least you'll know to pick something up in the airport before getting on the plane. Also try to alert the flight attendants of your special request when you're sitting down before takeoff. Doing so helps them keep you in mind and show them where you are so your meal doesn't end up on someone else's tray table. Remember that politeness and a smile go a long way for these hardworking men and women.

If, for some reason, your special meal didn't make it on the plane, ask if any suitable first- or business-class meals are left. The attendants usually help to remedy the situation with extra fruit, bread, or appropriate snacks if your meal was mislaid.

Carrying on your own food

It used to be that you could carry on just about anything when traveling by airplane, and that made it easier for us vegans to snack on flight. However, security has tightened severely since September 11th, 2001, restricting carry-on approved foods. Not to worry, though; you can still carry on some foods to hold you over. Here are items you can safely bring with you for your airport picnic:

✔ Plastic spoon, fork, and knife. Smaller regional airports may not have these available.

✔ Beverages and soups in 3-ounce or smaller containers. Be careful, however, because these may spill en route to the airport or on the plane. Good soup options that can be eaten cold are lentil and gazpacho.

✔ Homemade sandwiches, leftovers (nonliquid, unless in 3-ounce or smaller containers), fruit, beans, and whole grains. Because taking small coolers on your flight will be problematic, just take a bag of food that doesn't need refrigeration.

✔ Food bars and dry snacks, such as crackers, pretzels, and so on.

Stashing food in your carry-on will get you through your travel plans — unless something unplanned occurs. Weather delays, missed connections, and bizarre computer glitches can leave you stranded for longer than your apple and nuts will sustain you. So try to carry at least one vegan snack bar (see the snack list in the earlier section "Mapping Your Meals on the Road" for some suitable varieties) to get you through a missed meal. Also, eating a substantial meal before leaving for the airport ensures that you aren't starving by the time you get through security.

Finding vegan food in any airport

Say you didn't have time to eat before your 6 a.m. flight, and you were out of vegan food bars to stash in your backpack or suitcase before getting into the taxi. You've made it through security, your flight leaves in 45 minutes, and you're starving — now what?

Depending on how large the airport is, your choices will vary greatly. Smaller, out-of-the-way airports may only have a newsstand while huge regional hubs will have food courts with ethnic joints, fast food, lounges, and restaurants. Here are some ideas of where to look for vegan food to tide you over until you reach your destination:

✔ **Newsstands:** At these stands you often can find water, trail mix, fruit, nuts, pretzels, and crackers.

✔ **Fast-food joints:** If you're forced to choose something from a fast-food restaurant, try a baked potato. Ask for an ingredient list if the restaurant offers veggie burgers or bagels to ensure there are no hidden animal ingredients.

✔ **Delis and food stands:** If you come across a deli, see if it sells peanut butter and jelly sandwiches, veggie wraps (though check for cheese and mayo), nuts, fruit, pretzels, crackers, veggie sushi, bagels, or packets of peanut butter.

✔ **Restaurants:** Some restaurants provide a vegan-friendly selection. Look for ethnic dishes like stir-fried rice and vegetables, vegetarian burritos and tacos (hold the cheese), bagels, salads with beans, veggie burgers, veggie sandwiches (check for mayo and cheese), or pasta with veggies.

> ✔ **Lounges, airline clubs, and bars:** These types of places usually offer crackers, pretzels, nuts, fruit, wine, water, and hot beverages. Some may even offer a menu of freshly prepared dishes and may be able to specially prepare a vegan pasta dish for you.

No matter where you are, don't be afraid to ask for what you need and want. But, of course, do so with complete politeness. Be sincere and ask your waitress if your special dietary needs can be accommodated. From truck stops to fancy French bistros, I have always received help from the server when I gently explain my situation. A little smile and a kind voice go a long way. Don't forget to tip a little extra too, to say thank you, and to pave the way for the next hapless vegan who comes through town!

Healthy traveling vegans

Even with the best vegan diet, the onslaught of travel stress, loss of sleep, or foreign germs can be too much for the human immune system. Staying healthy on the road starts with eating well and ensuring your diet includes enough protein, complex carbohydrates, clean water, and veggies.

To ensure you don't get stuck in the hotel with the flu for the whole trip, stay hydrated, avoid overconsumption of sugar and alcohol, abstain from illegal drugs, and know your physical limits. Make your own little travel pharmacy that includes the following:

✔ Vitamin C packets that can be added to juice or a glass of water as well as a multivitamin to tide you over in case you can't find nutritious food choices on your journey

✔ A hot water bottle, which can be filled with hot water from the tap in the airplane or hotel bathroom (A water bottle is perfect for a cramped neck, stomach pain or bloating, or cold feet.)

✔ Hand sanitizer wipes and bandages

✔ Sunscreen

✔ Pain medication like aspirin, ibuprofen, or acetaminophen

✔ Tweezers, nail clippers, and a nail file (stored in checked baggage, if you're flying)

✔ An ample supply of your regular medicines in their original containers, along with extra prescriptions for them just in case

A couple more tips:

✔ Contact your health insurance company to find out the procedure for visiting a doctor in another country.

✔ If you're going to a country that's known for "traveler's diarrhea," be sure to order your vegetables cooked and steaming hot. Peel all your fruit yourself, and don't eat precut fruit; this will help you avoid anything cut with an unclean knife or cross-over contamination from nonvegan foods. Avoid raw salads, and drink your water from commercially-sealed water bottles.

✔ Be sure to eat substantial protein and complex carbohydrates throughout your day while traveling. Walking all day and seeing the sites can lead to exhaustion if you don't eat properly.

Traveling Together: Cruises and Group Trips

Seemingly built to serve your every desire, today's cruise ships are like enormous floating mall-spas. Most ships offer a huge variety of food made available around the clock. Certain cruise packages may be more vegan friendly, so if you have the opportunity, do your research and find a boat that will cater more specifically to you and your vacation dreams.

In this day and age any cruise ship will be familiar with and offer many vegetarian options. Talk with the travel agent or your cruise contact well in advance about your special food needs. This will give them time to come up with better and more varied options for you. These professionals may be able to provide you with sample menus and standard examples of what's available.

When you first arrive on the ship, ask to speak to someone from the kitchen. Tell them you're a vegan, and explain what that means. Ask if there are any items in their kitchen that may not be on the regular menu, like veggie burgers, bean burritos, or tofu dishes. Similarly, if you decide to enjoy a special meal in one of the boat's restaurants, notify that establishment ahead of time. Just like landlocked eateries, most will put something nice together for you if you don't spring it on them during a rush.

Don't be ashamed to take leftovers back to your cabin. If your meal was great but you couldn't finish eating it, you can take it with you and have it for lunch or a snack the next day. Just remember to bring a washable container in your luggage so you have somewhere to store it. When you book your cruise, be sure to ask whether your cabin has a small refrigerator. If not, find out about renting one for the trip. This will allow you a lot more flexibility.

Even if you were somehow plunked down on a cruise ship with no warning, you would certainly be able to find pasta dishes, beans and grains, and lots of fruits and veggies. Again, just ask for what you need and make a meal out of several side dishes if you have to.

Tagging along with a tour group offers the comfort of friendly company and built-in support for many travelers. Vegans will want to talk to the tour leader before signing up for a group tour, because most of the meals will either be ordered ahead of time or scheduled for a specific restaurant along the way. Find out whether the group menu will be preset or whether you'll be able to ask the server for a vegan version. If you're traveling to a country where you don't speak the language, be sure to talk with the tour operator about the likelihood of finding a vegan option. (Tour operators usually frequent the same destinations over and over, so they're knowledgeable and the ones to ask.)

Do your research on the predetermined tour route and search out vegan-friendly restaurants near the group stops. The Internet is full of information on international vegan dining spots. To better communicate with waiters and clerks in foreign lands, get yourself a copy of the *Vegan Passport* by George Rodger (Vegan Society Ltd.), which is detailed in the sidebar "Lost in translation."

Culture-Clash: Staying Vegan in Other Countries

Traveling abroad comes with a special set of considerations. For example, do you speak the language of the country you're going to visit? Do you know anything about the local cuisine? Where will you be staying? But, when you're a vegan, you also have to consider what meals and snacks will be available for you. Most major international and domestic cities will have at least one vegan restaurant, and a few cities are known for being vegan meccas. Portland, Oregon, New York City, London, and Vancouver, British Columbia, are great places to visit as a vegan.

Here are some simple ways to ensure a bon voyage:

- ✔ **Use the Internet or look through vegetarian travel books before leaving home.** These resources offer you ideas for vegan restaurants and health food stores. Don't forget to search out farmer's markets, too.

- ✔ **Make a list of restaurants and health food stores for each country or city you're traveling to.** Compile the address, a small printable map, written directions, business hours, and a phone number for each restaurant or store.

- ✔ **Try to verify that the listings are current before you venture out to eat.** Call ahead and edit your list if they're no longer open.

- ✔ **Ask at local health food stores for recommendations.** The employees there may know of a great, new vegan diner or cafe that hasn't been discovered by the travel guides yet!

- ✔ **Check to see if your hotel, hostel, or other accommodation offers kitchen access or rooms with kitchenettes.** If it does, you're then free to buy food at the store and make your own healthy vegan meals. Research the hotels or hostels in your destination city to see what's offered and which place would be the most vegan friendly.

- ✔ **Search online for local vegan and vegetarian groups by city or country.** They may have an office at your destination or be able to provide further recommendations.

The ultimate travel assistance Web sites for vegans are www.happycow.net, www.vegdining.com, and www.localharvest.org. With these sites, you can research vegan-friendly restaurants, health food stores, and even u-pick farms, farmer's markets, and grocery stores in the United States and abroad. After trying a new vegan diner in Paris, don't forget to return to the site to leave a review, update open hours, and recommend menu items. Pay it forward!

Lost in translation?

Thanks to George Rodger of the Vegan Society, writer and publisher of the *Vegan Passport,* you can now find out how to say "I'm vegan" in 56 languages, which covers 93 percent of the world's population — even Esperanto! You can hand this book to a grocer to find vegan-safe foods at the market, or ask your waiter to show the chef so you can be sure everyone is on the same page. Here are a couple of handy translations for "I'm vegan, so I do not eat . . . ":

✔ **French:** "Je suis vegan, donc nous ne mangeons pas . . ."

✔ **Spanish:** "Soy vegana, por tanto los veganas no comemos . . ."

Vegan Passport by George D. Rodger, used with kind permission from the Vegan Society, UK, 2005

Chapter 18

Dining Out

. . . .

. . . .

*V*egan vixens and gents should hit the town every once in a while! Staying at home makes it easier to ensure that your morals are satisfied, but getting out into the world is fun and often necessary.

Eating in restaurants, cafes, diners, and dives can be tough for an herbivore — unless, of course, the place specifically caters to those who prefer to eat healthfully. However, you can still enjoy going out to eat with friends and family. In fact, you can even survive a cross-country road trip without starving or yearning for a nice bowl of greens, beans, and grains. That's because vegan and vegetarian restaurants are easier to find in this technological age, and several online gems allow you to find what you need.

This chapter leads you through some of the best tips for eating out — anywhere, anytime. Dust off your Emily Post book, because good manners will serve you well with your servers and waiters. Planning ahead and discovering how to get around a set menu can become second nature for any vegan out on the town.

Ask and Ye Shall Receive: Finding Vegan-Friendly Restaurants

Never fear, new vegan, you have hundreds of vegan-friendly restaurants to choose from coast to coast. You just have to do a little homework and look in the right places. I show you how in the following sections.

Doing your research

Finding a vegan restaurant isn't as difficult as you may think, because you have many online resources to help you in your search. For instance, if you're looking for fast-food or fast-casual dining establishments that may have vegan offerings, check out www.veganeatingout.com. This handy resource lists restaurant menus from all over the U.S., including national chains, and notes which items are vegan or can easily be made vegan. To look up vegan-friendly restaurants as well as health food stores, farmer's markets, and co-ops, try these amazing Web sites: www.vegdining.com, www.happycow.net, and www.vegguide.org.

If you're in a city or town that you're unfamiliar with and you don't have a computer handy, stop by a health food store or vitamin shop to ask the employees if they know of any vegan-friendly eateries. These people are usually knowledgeable about local options.

Discovering vegan-friendly ethnic eateries

If you've done your homework (see the preceding section), you've probably realized that ethnic restaurants often are fail-safe options for vegans. And, luckily, the world is full of amazingly unique ethnic cuisines. Many of these cuisines have vegan dishes to choose from, offering new flavors, textures, and experiences.

You should easily be able to find (or request) the following vegan dishes at many ethnic eateries:

- Bean tacos and burritos without lard or cheese
- Chinese bean curd (tofu) dishes with vegetables
- Grilled vegetables with olive oil and olives
- Indian vegetable and bean curries with dahl (lentils) and no *ghee,* clarified cow's milk butter
- Middle Eastern hummus and tabbouleh salad with vegetables and olives
- Thai vegetable curries made with creamy coconut milk
- Vegetable pizza with no cheese

Making the Most of Nonvegan Menus

Dining in a vegan restaurant is ideal, but you may not always be able to find one. If you plan ahead and know the restaurant you'll be going to, you may be able to look at its menu online or call ahead to ask whether it offers any vegan options. If you find that vegan pickings will be slim, plan to eat a hearty snack before going out so you don't have to rely on the bread basket to get filled up.

Even if you aren't armed with a lot of information beforehand, you can usually find things to eat in any restaurant. This section points you to places to try first and also gives you pointers for making the most of nonvegan menus, even if you have picky vegan kids in tow.

Getting what you need wherever you are

Vegans often are faced with choosing their meals from menus that are loaded with meat and cheese. Fortunately, you can make good choices even in these limited situations. Use the following tips to help you make the most of any menu you may come across:

- ✔ **Be as polite and patient as possible when asking for special meals.** The employees at the restaurant may be in the middle of a rush, so your special request could take extra time.

- ✔ **Enroll the help of your server.** Servers often are knowledgeable about what's available and can help you figure out which dishes would be free of animal products. If the restaurant is very busy and your server doesn't seem willing to help, put together a simple meal from vegan-safe side dishes. Most restaurants have a grain, vegetable, potato, or bean side.

- ✔ **Be sure to leave a nice tip for any server who goes the extra mile to help you.** This recognition of a job well done will pave the way for future vegans, especially if you're super nice to boot.

- ✔ **Call ahead to the restaurant as far in advance as possible.** Talk with the manager or chef about your diet and what ingredients you avoid. If given enough advance warning, most chefs will happily accommodate you.

- ✔ **Make the best of your situation and enjoy the company of friends and family.** Order a drink, a salad, and some bread if you aren't able to eat much else. Making a big deal out of the situation will make others uncomfortable and they may think twice before inviting you out again.

- ✔ **Eat before you leave if you know there won't be much available.** Rather than starve throughout the night, you can be digesting while everyone else is eating! Have a cup of tea and fruit to participate in the meal.

Helping vegan kids find yummy choices

Eating on the road with kids can present another challenge to a vegan family. While adults may be more adventurous with ethnic dishes or even satisfied with very simple side dishes, kids can be picky. A vegan-friendly restaurant generally offers more choices for your little veg-head to choose from, but sometimes you can't find such an eatery. This section tells you what to do if that's the predicament you're in.

Often a server can help you by asking the chef to make something vegan (and therefore more familiar) out of ingredients he has on hand in the kitchen. You'll probably be more successful with this tactic if you visit a restaurant during a less-busy time. However, if you do end up at a restaurant during a rush, rather than descending on the already-stressed-out waiter with a list of special requests, try making a meal out of some of these common dishes:

- Bean and rice burritos with salsa and avocado
- Chips, salsa, guacamole, and lard-free beans
- Edamame with vegetable or avocado sushi
- Home-fried or baked potatoes topped with steamed broccoli and a little olive oil
- Hummus with pita bread or vegetables for dipping
- Lentil soup (without chicken or beef stock)
- Minestrone soup without cheese or chicken or beef stock
- Noodles with Thai peanut sauce
- Peanut butter and granola wrap: whole-grain tortilla spread with peanut butter and banana slices and then sprinkled with vegan granola or raisins and crushed nuts
- Pizza toast: whole-grain toast spread with tomato sauce and topped with veggies and legumes, such as mushrooms, tomatoes, olives, white beans, and so on
- Pureed vegetable soups (without dairy or beef or chicken stock)
- Roasted beets, carrots, or sweet potatoes drizzled with olive oil
- Steamed artichoke leaves dipped in olive oil that's been mixed with minced garlic and a little bit of salt
- Steamed corn sprinkled with a little olive oil and salt
- Three bean salad
- Tomato-based pasta sauce with zucchini and mushrooms mixed in
- Tomato soup with a side of rice and peas
- Vegetable pizza without cheese

Cafeteria conundrums: School and work lunches

Let's face it. Unless we're independently wealthy and home-school our kids, we all have to go to school and work. And when we're away from home for that long, we have to eat lunch somewhere. Finding a healthy (and tasty) meal in a school or work cafeteria can be less than fun, and vegans face even bigger challenges. But don't worry; in this section I give you some tips on how to get by without starving.

Navigating the school cafeteria

Eating at school can present a unique set of obstacles for the busy young vegan. Some high schools allow off-campus eating during lunch, but how likely is it that a vegan cafe sits within walking distance of your kid's school? And should they spend that much money on eating out anyway? Even more difficult to maneuver are the elementary and middle school cafeterias. The kids that attend these schools probably aren't making many of their own food choices yet, so they eat whatever is given to them.

Vegan kids can feel pressured by their peers when it comes to eating differently, too. Adolescence is all about acceptance, so some kids may get some teasing for their brown bag option. Help your child feel more comfortable by asking them which vegan options they're most comfortable with for lunch. Leftover tofu stir-fry may draw unwanted attention, but a bean burrito with brown rice and avocado can pass under the ridicule-radar. Lifelong vegan kids feel stronger dedication in their cruelty-free choices, but newer converts may need support from home to make the transition. Help your kid come up with witty jokes about how their food is cool, and remind them of the long list of famous vegans in Chapter 25 to throw out at the lunch table.

When all is said and done, many school cafeteria lunch programs offer a dismal array of menus. So, sending your children to school with homemade lunches is really the best option — unless, of course, your school cafeteria has been made over to provide plant-based options.

Sometimes, you run out of time to put together a vegan lunch for your child. And sometimes your kid may want to fit in every now and then and join the lunch line. Cafeteria settings usually offer a wide variety of a la carte offerings and side dishes. Vegan kids can make a meal out of the salad bar and smaller side options. If a chef is always available in the cafeteria (as they are on Google's campuses), you may be able to request something vegan- and kid-friendly from the staff. It never hurts to ask!

You may not find organic, whole-grain, seasonal foods in every school cafeteria, but you can still often put together a healthy meal. Here are a few ideas:

- Pasta primavera with no cheese
- Tortilla chips, salsa, and guacamole
- Veggie sandwich without the cheese
- Green salads
- Bean salads
- Rice with vegetables mixed in
- Couscous with pita bread and hummus

Eating vegan at your workplace

Eating at work is often easier on the wallet (and on the vegan) if you bring your own lunch instead of heading to the cafeteria. That's not always an option, however, and it can be nice to have someone else take care of lunch once in a while. If your cafeteria currently offers no vegan dishes, talk with the chef about ideas and recipes she can incorporate into the menu. Many vegan dishes would even be appealing to nonvegan employees, including stir-fried Chinese vegetables and tofu, vegan soups, and an expanded salad bar.

Consider organizing a potluck lunch with your co-workers. Every person can bring in a different dish to share, and you can ask that some people try their hand at vegan cooking. This easy activity can encourage camaraderie and can open others up to eating more veggie-based meals.

Incredible Ideas for Eating Anywhere

Even fast-food joints can offer vegans a snack or small meal. In general, these eateries aren't the best option for vegans who care about how corporations treat animals, but sometimes we have to break the rules — especially when driving across the country or when stuck in vegetable-hostile territory.

In this section, I provide you tips and ideas on how to find vegan meals and snacks in national chains, sandwich shops, and fast-food joints. Be sure to ask for exact ingredients from these establishments, because the servers may have limited knowledge of what goes into the food.

Fast-food chains

Veggie burgers at national fast-food chains are often vegan, but make sure to ask about the ingredients first. The patties may include cheese, caseinate (a protein found in cow's milk), or eggs. Many outlets serve potato products like fries, baked potatoes, and hash brown patties that, while fried and greasy, are usually vegan. Salads with a vinaigrette dressing are increasingly available on many menus, but be sure to choose one without grilled meat or added cheese. Many chains offer chili in the colder months, but opt for the veggie chili without dairy. Ice cream parlors often offer dairy- and gelatin-free ices and sorbets, but do be sure to specifically ask about the ingredients before purchasing.

Sandwich shops

Sandwich shops and fast-casual chains offer every kind of animal product imaginable to stuff between two slices of bread. However, you can get by in most places by requesting a veggie-only grinder or hoagie. Some locations may have protein-rich hummus, creamy avocado slices, or guacamole to slather on your sandwich. Just be sure to skip the mayo and cheese. You also can snack on pickles, salads, potato chips, and fruit to fill your belly at these spots.

You also could run down to the health food store and grab a container of fake meat deli slices to bulk up that fast-food sandwich! If a diner has grilled portabellas or other mushrooms on the menu, ask for extra veggies and a couple of slices of toast to make your own mushroom burger.

Pizza parlors and Mexican joints

Many pizza parlors can make a veggie pizza without cheese and load it with extra mushrooms, olives, and peppers. Bread sticks or garlic knots made with olive oil instead of butter can be dipped in vegan marinara sauce for a yummy, filling snack. Ask whether the chef can offer you a side of vegetable toppings like zucchini, mushrooms, or broccoli.

Mexican joints often have rice, tortillas, salsa, and fresh vegetables to create a vegan taco salad. Other options would be to make a taco salad with a fried tortilla as the bowl, beans (for added protein), rice, and diced avocado.

Beware of These Hidden Animal Ingredients

Unless you cook all your own meals and work or go to school next door to a vegan diner, eating according to your values can be difficult in this day and age. Some animal products are used for flavoring foods, and others are used to filter impurities from some alcoholic beverages. Other insect-derived products, such as honey or carmine, are used to sweeten and color foods.

To ensure that you avoid the myriad of animal-derived ingredients used in foods, beverages, and health and beauty products, get familiar with the common additives used. But remember to take it easy on yourself if you find out later that something you ate contained an animal product. Living vegan isn't always easy, but it's worth the effort.

The good people at PETA (People for the Ethical Treatment of Animals), have put together a comprehensive list of animal ingredients to avoid when shopping. You can peruse the list at www.peta.org/mc/factsheet_display. asp?id=72.

Chapter 19

Navigating Tricky Social Situations

*V*egans venture out just as often as "normal" folks, heading to events, gatherings, meals, and celebrations. The danger of ending up hungry during social situations is more common for herbivores, however. You can't count on people to know your dietary preference, but you can take precautions to ensure the best possible outcome for your outing.

Thinking ahead is an important skill for every vegan to hone. Get familiar with the ins and outs of party planning to understand what your options for eating can include. If you're planning a party with a mixed guest list, think about the comfort of everyone you invite. Also accept invitations to events and consider the party plan before you go. Asking for what you want is something you must do from time to time, and the way you interact with the people you're asking a favor of can mean everything.

This chapter explains the different social situations you may find yourself in and how to best navigate them. Considering the lay of the land for large, catered celebrations versus smaller, more intimate gatherings helps you choose the best options whether attending someone's party or planning your next shindig. Creating new celebrations and traditions also is part of being vegan in this culture. In this chapter, I share ideas and resources to help you create a truly luscious life and enjoy the company of others, regardless of everyone's diet.

Hosting Parties, Traditional Meals, and Celebrations

Just because you're a vegan now doesn't mean you can't enjoy the same historic family gatherings you did in years gone by. You'll still be hearing the same old stories about your brother squirting milk out of his nose when Uncle Paul told a funny joke, or the time (50 years ago!) that the same Uncle Paul purposefully scratched your mom's Yellow Rose of Texas record. You'll just be laughing along with a glass of soy nog or a plate full of Tofurky instead.

As a vegan, hosting parties and traditional meals can be tricky (but by no means impossible). After all, you'll likely be inviting some nonvegan family members or friends to your fete. The main decision you need to make is whether you're willing to allow nonvegan food at your party. If not, you need to make sure your vegan dishes will be appealing to everyone's tastes (or at least as much as possible). This section provides you with tips and advice on choosing occasions to celebrate, setting your menu, and more.

Planning your event

Planning a vegan party really is the same as planning any nonvegan event. In both instances, you have certain tasks to tend to depending on how many and what types of guests are coming, how formal it is, and how elaborate the celebration and scheduling becomes. If your event is casual and you'll be doing most of the cooking, the plan will be as easy as vegan pie: Create a menu, invite the guests, buy your supplies, and get to work. More formal events require more thought about the scope and size of a menu as well as what it takes to host a more diverse crowd.

Here are some things to remember for the different types of parties you may have:

- **Kid parties:** Planning parties for children and teenagers requires a few extra steps. Make sure the kids or teens have a say in how the party will look, what music will be played, what the entertainment will be, and what the menu will entail. Buffets are generally the easiest method of feeding a group of kids, so make sure the food isn't too messy. Offer plenty of ways for the kids to have fun while also making sure they know the rules.

- **Mixed-age gatherings:** These parties need a few extra safety plans. For instance, make sure that any alcohol that's served is in plain sight at all times. Don't allow curious kids the chance to sneak into a bar area. Offering snacks and some kind of games or activities for little people can help them feel like treasured guests.

✔ **Adult soirees:** Adult-only parties can range from totally casual game nights to sit-down multicourse dinners. Be sure to invite guests well in advance so they have time to plan their calendars (and so you have time to make sure you've thought of all the supplies you'll need). Decorating can be as simple or over-the-top as you like; just be sure you give yourself plenty of time the day before the party to clean, set up, and cook your menu.

Here's a tip that works for any of the preceding types of parties: Rather than cook several different courses, prepare large amounts of a few, great dishes. Doing so can help make your event easier. In fact, many dishes can be made the day before your event, which will ensure that you have enough time to prepare everything. Spend more of your party budget on fresh flowers to add a dash of sophistication.

Figuring out your menu

If you've reached your limit on going to parties where you can't eat anything but raw broccoli and carrot sticks, funnel your frustration to create your own fabulous vegan party menu. Depending on your level of cooking experience, you can prepare simple or complex dishes. Every host and hostess can use the following tips to plan a well-rounded soiree.

Getting started by gathering some recipes

Whether you're throwing a birthday party for your best friend or having a vegan Thanksgiving dinner for your family, you have countless recipes and menu plans to choose from. Don't feel hindered by tradition, because any good recipe can be included at any event. Still, you can offer more traditional-style meals to help people feel more comfortable if they're unsure of vegan food.

If you take a look at a few vegan cookbooks, you're sure to find at least a dozen recipes suitable for any occasion. Start planning your event by making a list of recipes that you would like to offer. Then look through the vegan cookbooks available at your local bookstore or library. Or check out the Internet, which has countless vegan recipes to choose from.

It's best to choose an online recipe that has positive reader comments or that's published on a well-known Web site. You don't want to try a recipe for a party that wasn't well written or tested. At the very least, be sure to try a recipe a few times before serving it to guests.

Sticking with traditional and familiar foods

Thanksgiving and traditional larger holiday meals are easier to tackle than you may think. Tofurky has been around for years and offers a full vegan meal, including the turkey-shaped tofu filled with a delicious vegetable and bread stuffing. Most side dishes for Thanksgiving are already vegetable based and shouldn't be difficult for you to veganize.

Making a vegan version of a food that's familiar to most people will ensure that your guests are comfortable and enjoy tasting your dishes. Some ideas to offer are a Mediterranean menu of falafels, hummus, tabbouleh, stuffed grape leaves, olives, and baba ghanouj. Another idea is to offer a diner-style menu with homemade veggie burgers, Mac n' TeaseCheese (recipe found in Chapter 14), and baked sweet potato fries. (Flip to Chapter 10 for more on veganizing some all-time favorite foods.)

Keeping some general menu tips in mind

When putting together a menu, think of the overall look and feel you want to create. The taste, color, and texture of each dish should be considered. Create a nice flow from dish to dish by choosing a certain spice profile. You can make a plethora of menus using Italian, French, or Asian ingredients, herbs, and spices. Use pops of color in each dish with garnishes of freshly chopped herbs, grated carrots, or diced bell peppers of several colors.

If you're serving a buffet or multicourse meal, use the following combinations to provide a well-rounded meal: one soft dish, one hard or chewy dish, two savory dishes, one spicy dish, two crunchy dishes, and one sweet dish. For a smaller meal, you could offer one soft dish, two crunchy dishes, two spicy dishes, one savory dish, and one sweet dish.

Dessert is an important part of any party, so choose something fantastic and memorable. Not everyone likes chocolate, and some people are allergic to nuts, so consider offering a fruit-based dessert instead of or alongside the chocolate offering. Chapter 15 provides some recipes for you to experiment with.

Dealing with the age-old question: What can I bring?

If your guests ask to bring dishes to share, it's okay to ask that they bring vegan dishes. They may welcome the challenge, or they may decline — but there's no harm in asking! If someone wants to bring "an old family favorite" that includes meat or dairy, perhaps she has another vegan dish she enjoys and wouldn't mind bringing. If bringing a vegan dish is too complicated for a guest, tell her she can bring bread or wine to add to the celebration.

There's no need to get into a tense situation over dinner, so offer alternatives and be open to your guests' ideas. After all, the reason for getting together is to acknowledge your shared love for each other and to create new memories. If you feel that a more conservative friend or family member is hesitant to "go vegan," even for one night, ask if she'll bring her favorite nonvegan specialty. If you're comfortable having nonvegan food at your event, it could help that guest feel like she's a part of the party rather than an outsider — after all, you know how that feels!

Celebrating grilling season vegan-style

Warm weather brings out the grills and barbecues across America. Vegans often have a difficult time finding anything edible or substantial at these outdoor events. You can get by eating a burger bun with mustard, lettuce, tomato, and pickle slices, but by the end of the night you'll be starving. And it can be tough to reconcile your hopes for the planet while hungry and surrounded by smoking plates of carnage.

Planning your own vegan celebrations allows you to share the barbecue season with friends without competing with the big meat-grilling days like July 4th or Memorial Day. Summer solstice is a nice, alternative holiday that many vegans prefer to celebrate. Held around the 22nd of June, the longest day of the year, this warm first day of summer offers the perfect opportunity to celebrate Mother Nature's bounty and seasonal produce. (See "A summer solstice celebration" for more details on throwing this type of party.)

Parties can be created around any anniversary, upcoming event, or life change. Use these times to bring family and friends together and share with them your love for healthy, delicious vegan food.

Sample party plans and menus

Putting together a plan and menu well in advance can help you work out any kinks as you get ready for your feast. If you're at a loss for ideas, but you're sure you want to gather the gang, look to the themes in the following sections to get the party started.

A build-your-own-burrito party

Who doesn't love Mexican food — chips and salsa, burritos, and vegan-style refried beans? A Mexican-themed build-your-own-burrito party is sure to be a hit with vegans and nonvegans alike. Offering plenty of burrito toppings will distract guests from the fact that there's no meat or dairy on the table.

Serve steamed tortillas or corn chips with a buffet table laden with some of these fillings: shredded lettuce, diced tomatoes, shredded vegan cheese, tofu sour cream, thinly sliced green onions, diced red onions, guacamole, several kinds of salsa, vegan refried beans, crumbled tempeh seasoned with soy sauce and sautéed in olive oil, canned jalapeños, and cooked brown rice. (Check out Chapters 13 and 14 for recipes for Tofu Sour Cream and Seitan Burritos, respectively.)

Here are some ideas to liven up the Mexican theme:

  ✔ Decorate the buffet tables with the colors of the Mexican flag: white, red, and green. Candles and novelty chili pepper light strings will add to the theme as well.

✔ Put together a playlist of music to match the food: The Gypsy Kings, Salsa, Tejano, or Mexican pop can easily lend a festive atmosphere to the party.

✔ If you're serving alcohol, choose vegan Mexican beers like Corona and homemade margaritas with lime or lemon slices.

A summer solstice celebration

The summer solstice, the longest day of the year, deserves a party that lasts well through the afternoon and into the night. This pagan celebration was full of ritual and debauchery back in the ancient days, so encourage your guests to let their hair down, dance, and have a ball. Here are some great ideas for throwing your own summer solstice celebration:

✔ **Incorporate the ancient tradition of wearing flower or leaf crowns.** Making crowns or headbands with ribbons, flowers, and floral wire doesn't take too much crafting skill and really gets guests into the mood of the party.

✔ **Choose refreshing drinks.** Homemade lemonade, iced tea, and white or rosé wines will fit right in with the warm-weather theme.

✔ **Serve seasonal vegetables and fruits to incorporate the bounty of the summer harvest.** Visit your local farmer's market two weeks before the party to ask which foods the farmers will offer the week of your party. Asking in advance gives you time to come up with a menu incorporating those ingredients.

✔ **Entertain your guests with group games.** Plan a few games that involve shouting out answers and teamwork. Trivia competitions or singing games are popular party games.

✔ **Include fire, which is an important part of any pagan ritual.** If you have a large outdoor space, build an outdoor fire pit, a bonfire, or a campfire surrounded by stones. Or just light a bunch of candles if you're short on space.

✔ **Cook foods on the open flame or grill.** You can grill all sorts of food, including seitan skewers, marinated mushrooms, vegetables, peaches, and pineapple slices.

✔ **Prepare some hearty salads to round out the summer menu.** For instance, try a basil tomato salad with tofu chunks that have been marinated in olive oil, red wine vinegar, and salt and pepper. Or put together a chickpea salad with olive oil, fresh parsley, and garlic. A vegan Caesar salad with fried tempeh croutons is sure to be a crowd pleaser.

✔ **Plan to tell stories after the eating is over.** Ask people to share a special event that they were in, a scary thing that happened, or a disaster they survived. Or ask guests to recount the funniest things that have ever happened to them.

> ✔ **Dress up and play.** Draw inspiration from Shakespeare's *A Midsummer Night's Dream* and ask people to come dressed as any character from the play.
>
> ✔ **Light up the party.** Once the sun goes down, offer sparklers to the guests, turn on twinkling outdoor Christmas lights, or light some tiki torches.

Being a Guest at an Omnivorous Table

It's rare to live in a vegan bubble. Most of us still have friends and loved ones who choose to eat meat and dairy products. Shunning the entire nonvegan human race isn't an option — they're still good people and they can be pretty fun! So do accept invitations to celebrate and dine with nonvegan friends and family.

If it seems appropriate, offer to bring one or two vegan options to share with the other party members. Consider yourself warned, however: If your dishes are extra tasty, eat plenty of food before you head to the party. This vegan chef has been left hungry more than once when the other party attendees realized how yummy the vegan food was — and ate it all!

Graciously accepting dinner party invitations

You have two possible scenarios to choose from with any invitation: to go or not to go. Of course, only you can decide the best option for you.

Perhaps you don't want to go, but you're worried about how to nicely decline. Rather than admitting that you don't want to encounter all the meat and dairy at the party, politely respond that you aren't able to attend because of a conflict. Let the host know that you would have loved to attend, if only your calendar had been free. The super polite vegan will go the extra mile and check back to inquire how the party went afterward.

Assuming you've decided to accept the invite to a friend's party, the following sections give you some ideas to keep in mind when attending a nonvegan event.

Talk to your host politely before your meal

Contact your host in person as soon as possible after receiving an invitation. Warmly accept the invite and mention that you don't eat certain foods and that you were wondering whether you could talk about the menu with him. If he offers to include a vegan dish for you, politely gush about how gracious he is. If he doesn't, accept the invitation anyway and plan accordingly.

When a host has been kind enough to include a vegan diet for you at his celebration, be sure to thank him for his consideration at the event. Sending a thank-you note in the mail or via e-mail after the party shows truly lovely vegan etiquette.

Contributing to the feast

Bringing a vegan dish to a party is a great way to break the ice. Make sure you talk with the host or hostess well in advance to ensure that you can appropriately work your food into the evening. If the dinner is built around a certain theme, bring a vegan dish that works well with that cuisine and its aromas. It could be offensive to the other guests' senses if you brought a spicy Chinese dish to a dinner based on milder French herbs and foods.

If the meal is small and casual, putting a couple extra dishes on the buffet won't be a big deal. If the dinner is slightly more formal with servers or courses, plan in advance to bring the dish and work it into the flow of the meal. Check with the hostess about serving dishes, too. She may not have enough platters or serving trays for your extra dishes. In that case, you could bring something with similar colors to work your food into the night seamlessly.

Keeping cool in a crowd of nonvegans

When dining with omnivores at an event, be sure to keep your judgments to yourself. While you may be disgusted with their lobster carcass or bloody steak, making comments about their choices only draws negative attention to yourself and opens the door for a verbal sparring match. Most people don't like being told what to eat or how their choices are "wrong," and nagging rarely wins converts to the vegan lifestyle.

If you're offered a nonvegan dish, you can politely pass with a simple "No, thank you," and leave it at that. If a vegan option is offered to you, reinforce the party planner's decision by commenting on how much you liked the dish and how nice it was to find something so yummy and vegan that you could enjoy. This compliment reminds the host to continue offering vegan dishes at future events.

If anyone gives you a hard time while you're out in mixed company, keep your cool and remember the following:

- **Count to ten and breathe deeply.** Think about whether this is truly the time or place to freak out or offer a finely placed verbal comeback.

- **Laugh the comment off amiably and change the subject to someone else.** People like others who can take a joke.

- **Take the high road and refuse to be rude in return.** Setting a good example for behavior encourages others to keep a rude person in line.

- **Don't take it personally.** The other person may have had a rotten day, or he may just be socially inept.

Little party animals: Helping your vegan kid enjoy the event

When kids are younger and haven't been exposed to a lot of party food, you can easily steer them away from junk food and sugary desserts. As they get older, however, they develop lightning-fast radar to zero in on the cakes, candy, and snacks being offered. Get prepared before the event to help ensure an easier feast.

Sometimes you just have to say no to a food that your little vegan wants, but if you're honest with her from the beginning, the conversation should be easier. Explain why you don't eat milk, dairy, and meat. Talk with your child about how cow's milk, eggs, and other meats require that an animal be hurt or killed. If your child makes an emotional connection with animals, she won't want to eat food made from them. (Chapter 22 provides more information about raising vegan kids.)

Here are some tips for making parties more fun for your vegan kid:

- ✔ **Touch base with the party giver and ask whether any vegan options will be served.** If not, offer to bring a couple of dishes that go with the party theme that your child can enjoy and share. For example, if the party will have chocolate cake and pigs-in-blankets, make a vegan chocolate cake and tofu pups wrapped in vegan pastry dough. You can then all enjoy the party and your kid won't feel left out.

- ✔ **Fill up on favorites before the party.** Eat some delicious food before leaving, and talk about the food that your kid *can* eat at the party. Offering a favorite menu before the party encourages your kid to fill up on healthier foods, making her less hungry when you arrive at the event.

- ✔ **Sneak in snacks.** Take something your family loves to snack on in case enough filling options aren't being offered. Simple rice milk boxes, vegan cookies, and a vegan deli meat wrap can save the day.

- ✔ **Celebrate!** Build up the fun activities and games to participate in, the friends to play with, and the meaning of the party to the host. This is a chance to really enjoy a fun time together and share a special moment with friends.

Fancy functions: Weddings, bar/bat mitzvahs, and galas

Attending a big blast gives you a chance to break out your hottest vegan duds. And showing off your vegan etiquette ensures that you'll be asked to the next elegant event. As with any event, standard rules apply for every guest.

Be sure to act as politely as possible in every interaction with the hosts, staff, party planners, and other guests. Sending a handwritten thank-you card to the host within a few days of the event is good etiquette. If the person who invited you made a special effort to provide you with vegan food, be sure to thank him specifically for his consideration. Good behavior gives all vegans a good name!

In the following sections, I provide advice for enjoying all types of fetes, from small events to grand affairs.

Small events

Cocktail parties often present a vegan dilemma. Passed hors d'oeuvres are often heavy with meat or dairy, and it isn't easy to bring your own vegan recipes to a swanky cocktail party. So be sure to eat something substantial before attending.

Often held in the evening before dinner, cocktail parties can challenge a vegan's alcohol capacity. Imbibing booze on an empty stomach can lead to tummy trouble and drunken party fouls. If you don't have time to eat a light meal before attending, only drink nonalcoholic beverages like juice mixed with soda water.

When attending a cocktail party in someone's home, be kind and polite to the staff. They may be hired for this specific event, or they may be regular employees of the host. Rather than making special food requests of the staff, speak with the person throwing the party well in advance.

Buffet brouhaha

Buffet events, including weddings and award ceremonies, sometimes offer vegetarian options. These dishes could be made vegan if you avoid the egg or dairy, but sometimes those ingredients are completely mixed in.

When you know you'll be attending an event with a buffet, contact the party planner or host to ask whether a vegan-friendly option will be available. She may be able to work something in for you. If not, plan on eating a substantial meal before attending, and try to make a snack out of the side dishes, salads, and bread offerings.

Seated dinners

Formal events, including weddings and bar and bat mitzvahs, have specific three- to five-course seated meals planned far in advance. So planning ahead is imperative for vegans who want to enjoy longer evenings such as these.

Is that alcohol truly vegan?

Many alcohol companies use animal products to create their beverages. Breweries still use *finings,* or filter applications, made from fish bladders called *isinglass.* Gelatin also is used in some brews, as are milk and honey. Some wines are clarified with the same ingredients as well as *caseinate,* a milk protein, or albumin from eggs or dried animal blood. Here's a partial list of vegan beers, wines, and hard alcohols to choose from:

✔ **Beer:** B.J's, Bridgeport, Corona, Deschutes Brewery, Dogfish Head, Fish Tail, Full Sail, Grolsch, Hair of the Dog, Heineken, Henry's, Killian's Irish Red, Miller, Mt. Hood Brewing, Moosehead, Pilsner Urquell, Portland Brewing, Redhook Ale, Rolling Rock, Sapporo, Sierra Nevada, Terminal Gravity, Tuck's Brewing, most Widmer brews, Woodchuck Draft Cider

✔ **Wine:** Albet i Noya, Alderbrook Winery, Avery Lane, Barrelstone, Big Sky, Blossom Winery, Bully Hill Wine, Calamus Estate Winery, Carmel Winery, Casa Barranca Winery, Castle Rock Winery, Cave Springs, Cherry Creek Wines, Cline Cellars, Colchester Ridge Estate Winery, Coturri Winery, Desert Wind Winery, Duck Pond Cellars, Fetzer Vineyards (whites only), Four Chimneys Organic Wines, Frey Vineyards, JoieFarm Wines, Lakeview Cellars, Luna Vineyards, Manischewitz, McManis Family Vineyards, Moet Champagne, Namaste Vineyards, North River Winery

✔ **Liquors:** Absolute, Bacardi, Beefeater, Bombay Sapphire Gin, Captain Morgan, Crown Royal, Cutty Sark, nonflavored Smirnoff

Note: *Thanks to* www.barnivore.com *for this list. The masters of this great site list and update vegan and vegan-friendly booze regularly.*

As soon as you receive the invitation for a seated dinner, contact the host about your vegan diet. Rather than insist that a vegan option be made available, politely ask whether a vegan dish will be offered. If the host hadn't planned on a vegan dish and doesn't offer to provide one, simply thank him for letting you know so you can prepare accordingly. These events can last several hours, so you'll want to eat a substantial meal before attending. Keeping a hearty snack in your purse or pocket can help you get through the party without an attack of low blood sugar.

If you're feeling hungry and no more cruelty-free food options are available, stay away from alcohol; the effects of it will be stronger and faster on an empty stomach.

Event facilities, hotels, and conferences

Attending a conference or event held in a hotel, conference center, or other event facility offers vegans similar challenges to those at large weddings. The event coordinator will be planning meals for hundreds of guests and may not have considered vegan dietary needs.

When confirming your attendance at an event like this, talk with the planner or host committee as soon as possible. Tell the planner your dietary restrictions and ask whether she could arrange for a vegan option to be provided at every meal. This usually can be accommodated. As in all cases, be polite and friendly.

Even though you ask in advance, it's wise to confirm the week before an event that your vegan meal option has been accounted for. No matter what, however, you'll be better off bringing a wrapped sandwich, thermos of soup, and other snacks just in case. Some event facilities aren't as well versed in vegan catering, so the offering provided may be simple veggies and pasta, which isn't very filling. You could get hungry later, so having hearty snacks on hand can get you through the day.

If you'll be staying overnight at a hotel, call ahead and ask to speak to the room service manager or a chef in the hotel's restaurant. Talk with these folks about your dietary needs, and ask whether the hotel would be willing to provide a vegan tofu dish during your stay. You can even offer to bring a new container of tofu as long as the chef is willing to cook it for you. This method is especially useful for business travelers who stay in the same hotel repeatedly.

Dating a Nonvegan: Does True Love Really Conquer All?

Vegans young and old make the choice to live a cruelty-free life based on their morals, emotions, and hopes for their health and the health of the planet. These high personal standards can become difficult to maintain in the face of love with a nonvegan. Whether you're single and have just met the nonvegan love of your life or you're already in a relationship where your partner has chosen not to join you in your dietary endeavors, this section can guide you.

Single vegans must make a choice as to whether they will date nonvegans. Speaking from experience, I can tell you that holding an ideal partner in your mind while on the search for that certain someone may not always become your reality. One night, quite unexpectedly, you'll meet someone totally fabulous who rocks your world — and then you'll find out they've ordered a steak for dinner. For some of us, that's a deal breaker. For others, love will conquer all, and we'll decide to develop an intimate relationship with our carnivorous interest. At least we'll be helping them be healthier in the end — vegan lovers can always get their partner to eat more kale!

If you're already in an intimate relationship with a nonvegan, keep in mind that as time goes on you may have to make sacrifices for each other. Consider the value of the other person in your life and how much he truly means to you. Everyone has faults, and your food choices don't make you better than anyone else. Many nonvegan partners are happy to eat plant-based meals at home and then order whatever they like when they're at work, at school, or on the road. Other partners may want to cook meat or dairy foods at home, but will most likely be willing to use separate cookware. (Chapter 8 provides more information about living with omnivores.)

Occasionally, the love of your life will totally rebel and put up a fuss about not being able to eat meat at home. Perhaps the person picks fights on a regular basis about your choice to avoid animal foods. He may even sabotage your efforts. These actions show that your carnivorous partner is truly scared of change underneath it all. Being clear with each other about what this change means for each individual is important. Share your concerns about your health and that of your partner. Be honest about your commitment to this style of living. If you find that your best efforts are hampered by the other person, it may be time to evaluate the core shared values of the relationship.

If you've been dating a nonvegan and decide to take the next big step and get married or move in together, have a conversation about what will be acceptable in your shared home. Do you not want any meat or dairy in the home? Will the vegan allow the nonvegan's favorite leather easy chair to move in as well? Will your children be raised vegan? Cover as many areas of living together as you can think of before you make the move. Get it all out in the open as early as possible to build an honest, stress-free life together.

Carrying Your Vegan Lifestyle to the Workplace

Working 9 to 5 can be stressful enough without the added intricacies of vegan politics. So be sure to leave them at home unless someone specifically asks you for your opinions or for reasons why you eat a certain way. Creating a professional atmosphere at work, in most settings, means staying clear of conversations that revolve around politics, religion, and the reasons why you shouldn't eat animal products.

What if you're really adamant about not wearing leather shoes and accessories, but your office has matching leather chairs for everyone? You can consider talking with your employer about your beliefs, concerns, and preferences. You may have access to a more earth-friendly option like fabric or wood with an appropriate cushion.

If your employer won't allow other chairs to be used, don't lose your job over it. Take a nice set of fabric cushions to sit on so you aren't in direct contact with the leather. Keep earning that paycheck and use part of your income to fight for animal rights to ease your discomfort.

Similarly, if the company you work for has a cafeteria with no vegan options, it's acceptable to ask that a vegan dish be available — as long as you plan to eat there regularly. Be polite, considerate, and have your case well thought-out before going to human resources or your boss. Offer suggestions and resources so you can be part of the solution. Try not to get emotional about the subject, because you could wind up presenting yourself as unprofessional. Be sure to have healthy, filling food choices for yourself every day in case you aren't able to find an acceptable meal. Bringing your own lunches and snacks from home is often the best option for your health and your budget anyway.

You should be able to eat whatever you like at work without having to worry about the repercussions on your employment status. If you find that other people you work with are hazing you or making repeated jokes about your food and lifestyle choices, you should stick up for yourself. Tell them that you don't think their jokes are funny and that you want them to stop. Keep your responses as professional as you would hope your working environment would be. If the behavior continues, you can go to your human resources manager to talk about the harassment. If you work for a small company with no human resources department and your boss is participating in the joking that makes you uncomfortable, start documenting the incidents. Write down times, what exactly was said, and who was present. After you've gathered some specific evidence, you can then calmly present the information to your boss and mention that you consider this treatment to be harassment and would like it to stop — or else further steps will be taken.

Part VI
Veganism for All Walks of Life

The 5th Wave   By Rich Tennant

"We've thought about living a vegan lifestyle, but
Barbara is stuck in a squeamish lifestyle."

In this part . . .

Every stage of life brings different nutritional needs, but all these needs can be met healthily and vibrantly with a vegan diet. Babies, nursing moms, and pregnant women, for example, have different requirements than a teenaged track star or dancer. Even Grandma and Grandpa may start noticing that they feel a lot better and have a lot less pain when they eat more plant-based foods.

If you aren't sure how to get all the nutrients you need from this "bird food," this is the part for you. It leads you through the various nutritional needs for people who require special diets whether due to age, level of physical activity, or developmental stage.

Chapter 20

Pea in a Pod: The Healthy Vegan Pregnancy and Postpartum Period

*M*otherhood is a wonderful, crazy, bizarre, and magical part of a woman's life. Each woman and her partner should think ahead about their personal views on health and living before welcoming a baby into the world. Embarking into parenthood shouldn't be a light decision. You have much to consider, and the health of the baby and mother rank at the top of the list.

Countless women have brought healthy babies into the world while eating a vegan diet, so you don't need to feel like you're venturing into unknown territory. A vegan pregnancy can be extremely healthy, but you need to think about several areas of nutrition and self care.

This chapter covers the basics that any vegan embarking into the wild world of pregnancy and motherhood needs to know. Proper nutrition before and during pregnancy is important, as are the menus for any mama who wants to breastfeed her baby. I discuss extreme self care, the issues of proper weight gain, and morning sickness. I also give you some tips for taking care of yourself in the postpartum period.

Early Education and Proper Planning

Preparedness is a skill to be encouraged in anyone about to have a baby — heaven knows that once the baby arrives, just leaving the house will require packed bags, extra clothes, sunscreen, toys, extra wipes, food, beverages, and a Sherpa to carry everything. You and every other expecting woman — vegan or not — need to plan ahead for your nutritional and health needs. You also need to plan on many people chiming in about everything in your life — especially your diet.

Family and friends will almost certainly express their concern, either with questions or outright demands, about whether a vegan diet is healthy for a pregnant woman. Begin to familiarize yourself with the standard nutritional recommendations for pregnancy, do your research, and take a deep breath. Your loved ones have your best interests at heart, but only you can make the right decision for your health and that of your growing child.

In this section, I help you educate yourself and your surrounding friends and family about your decision to remain vegan throughout your pregnancy. I also emphasize the importance of eating well before becoming pregnant and of exercising appropriately during your nine months.

Educating your loved ones about your dietary choices

I remember my loving mother-in-law recommending that I should eat some meat when I told her I was tired during my third trimester. I tried to explain that my exhaustion had more to do with the fact that I couldn't sleep because I had leg cramps, a constant need to go to the bathroom, and a baby that kicked incessantly throughout the night. But she still was pretty sure that a steak would help me feel better.

You can choose one of two paths to a healthy and sane relationship with your friends and family during your vegan pregnancy: total silence or calm, educated responses. Sometimes you can use a combination of the two. Read up, as every mother-to-be does, on the various recommendations for proper nutrition. Educate yourself about which vegan foods provide the necessary requirements for you and your baby. Be prepared to answer questions about protein, iron, and nutrition.

Leave books on healthy vegan pregnancy lying around so your aunt and cousins can skim through them during your baby shower or family dinner. Not only will the books show your loved ones that you're doing your homework, but they also may ease any of their concerns.

Studies have proven several times over that vegan women can and do have healthy pregnancies and babies. One of the longest-standing studies on vegan pregnancy comes from the Farm community based in Tennessee. Members of this group eat a vegan diet and give birth attended by trained midwives. As reported in the scientific journal *Pediatrics,* this group of vegan women has a remarkable record of delivering babies of normal, healthy weight without the need for interventions or cesareans. Printing out a few studies like this can help you and your family feel better about your choice to remain vegan throughout your pregnancy.

Your own nurse-midwife or obstetrician may have little experience with pregnant vegans, and she may question your choices or even pressure you to change your diet. This is another good opportunity to share your knowledge with others and dispel the myths that vegans aren't healthy.

Begin keeping a detailed record of what you're eating so you can show everyone how good your nutrition actually is. This record can come in handy to show your healthcare provider that you're getting everything you need. You may even be able to help other pregnant vegans down the road by showing them your nutritional information and recounting your successful pregnancy.

Eating well before you're even pregnant

Ensuring that you're getting proper nutrition for yourself before you get pregnant is the best way to ensure a healthy pregnancy. So if you know that you may want to get pregnant in the next few years, or if you're actively trying to conceive, it would be wise to start eating as if you were pregnant now. You don't want to add the extra 300–400 calories a day required by pregnant women if you're not expecting, but you can eat the proper quality of foods to ensure that when your test comes back positive, you're already on the right path.

Imagine finding out that you're going to have a baby and you've been eating nothing but nonnutritious, highly processed junk food for years. Jumping into a healthy diet appropriate for growing a vegan baby would be a tough shift, especially if you start experiencing the fatigue, morning sickness, or weird food cravings associated with pregnancy.

Not only will you avoid common pregnancy pitfalls by eating healthily beforehand, but you also can really do yourself and your future baby a big favor by quitting smoking and drinking in advance. Some women don't realize they're pregnant until well into their second month. Drinking one or two alcoholic beverages a day while pregnant can lead to fetal alcohol syndrome as well as other complications. Smoking during pregnancy, even in the beginning trimester, can lead to low birth weight, which is associated with more health and behavior problems like stunted growth, diabetes, and low IQ for the baby later on.

Vegan foods are naturally high in many of the nutrients pregnant women need. Most pregnant women don't have an ice cream deficiency, but they usually need help getting enough iron, vitamins, and folic acid! Get familiar with the recommended dietary allowances for iron, calcium, and other nutrients (see Chapter 4) for the average woman who isn't pregnant. Eat a varied diet of whole, fresh, and nutrient-dense foods to prepare your body for optimal health. This diet is the best way to get ready for baby making and ensure an easier recovery postpartum for mom!

Get moving, vegan mama! Exercise and pregnancy

Some days during your pregnancy you'll just want to put your feet up and sleep the hours away. That's certainly okay, but keep in mind that regular exercise is good for you and your baby. Entering into pregnancy in fine shape helps ensure a healthier gestation, and staying physically active throughout the nine months will help you on many levels. Most important, exercising improves your health, and helps you handle mental stress, which in turn improves the health of your baby.

Physically, your body goes through a lot of changes during moderate exercise. You probably shouldn't do extreme sports or rigorous training during pregnancy, but moderate exercises like walking, yoga, Pilates, lifting light weights, and swimming can all help you stay in shape.

The blood flow to your uterus can change depending on the kind of exercise you're doing. Lying flat on your back isn't recommended, because it can decrease the blood flowing to your baby. Also remember that your body needs more oxygen during pregnancy, even when you're resting, so focus on regular, slow and steady exercise. Because your ligaments are looser at this time, be careful with any form of exercise; you don't want to pull or put too much pressure on certain joints.

Prenatal yoga classes can teach you exercises that help to stretch and strengthen muscles that you'll use during labor. These same exercises can help tone the muscles after labor, so you can get your body back into shape after the baby arrives. These yoga classes also bring together women going through the same remarkable phase of life and can help you create a community of support. Often the yoga teacher will have been through at least one pregnancy herself, and so she may be able to offer assistance with health questions you may have.

Emotionally, exercise provides a healthy release for tension or worries that you may be stewing over. Pregnancy is an incredible life-changing time, and it may bring up worries and concerns that you hold in your body. Use your exercise time to really focus on your growing love and your desires for a healthy baby. Use walking as a meditative time to breathe relaxation into your body.

As long as you're properly hydrated and fed, regular healthy exercise poses no risk to your baby's health. Be sure to drink more water during exercise and eat plenty of carbohydrate- and protein-rich snacks. Fueling your body with extra, nutritious food should be part of your exercise routine. Any kid with a mother who values healthy food and regular exercise will grow up better for it!

Eating for Two

Just because you're eating for two doesn't mean you can completely throw caution to the wind — although being a little bit generous won't hurt. And don't forget that eating for two doesn't mean eating for two adults — that little bump in your tummy is a very small person!

Your growing baby requires that you consume between 100 and 450 extra calories a day. In the first trimester, you only need up to 100 extra calories a day, if your morning sickness will allow you to eat that much. In the second trimester, the National Academy of Sciences recommends that you increase your daily intake by 300 to 340 calories. By the time you're breastfeeding, the increase goes up to a total of 450 to 500 extra calories a day.

Your total calories should be increased even more if you're pregnant and breastfeeding at the same time or if you're pregnant with more than one baby at a time. Every woman is unique and has her own special circumstances, so adjust your caloric intake accordingly. Perhaps you work on your feet all day, or maybe you're starting off your pregnancy under- or overweight. Talk with your obstetrician, midwife, or doula about your weight gain to get her help to ensure a healthy pregnancy.

The most important thing to remember is that your extra calories need to be nutritionally dense and not empty. Sure, some good-quality dark chocolate or potato chips are okay occasionally, but they shouldn't become their own separate food group during pregnancy. Instead, use those extra calories wisely and focus instead on truly supportive foods. Choose the following, for example:

- Dark, leafy greens and beans for iron, calcium, vitamin K, and folic acid
- Avocados, nuts, and seeds for healthy fat and protein
- Seasonal fruits for natural sweetness, antioxidants, and healing vitamins

Nutritional know-how: Getting enough of what you need

Now that you're pregnant (or seriously thinking about getting pregnant), you can expect even more questions from nonvegans about your nutrition. Become familiar with the important recommendations in the following sections for folate, protein, calcium and vitamin D, iron, B12, and omega-3 fatty acids. Commit these vegan nutrition basics to memory and share them freely with others. Be assured that a vegan lady with baby can get everything she needs for a healthy, vibrant pregnancy.

Use the helpful list in Table 20-1 to plan your daily meals during your amazing 40 weeks as a pregnant vegan.

Table 20-1	Recommended Servings of Various Food Groups	
Food Group	*Number of Servings*	*Examples of Servings*
Whole grains, breads, and cereals	9 or more servings	1 slice of bread; half a bun or bagel; ½ cup cooked cereal, rice, or pasta; ¾ cup to 1 cup ready-to-eat cereal
Legumes, soy products, and nondairy milks	5 to 6 servings	½ cup cooked beans, tofu, or tempeh; 8 oz. fortified soymilk or other nondairy milk; 3 oz. meat substitute
Vegetables	4 or more servings	½ cup cooked or 1 cup raw vegetables (choose at least one dark green vegetable daily)
Fruits	4 or more servings	½ cup cooked or 1 cup raw fruit; 1 piece of fruit; ¾ cup fruit juice; ¼ cup dried fruit
Nuts, seeds, and wheat germ	1 to 2 servings	2 Tbsp. nuts or seeds; 2 Tbsp. nut butter; 2 Tbsp. wheat germ

Source: Physicians Committee for Responsible Medicine, Vegan Pregnancy

Folate and folic acid

One of the first — and most mysterious — nutrients that comes up in pregnancy discussions is folate, which is also known as folic acid. It's mysterious because no one seems to know what it is or worry about it until they get pregnant. *Folate* is a B vitamin that's found naturally in many vegan foods. *Folic acid* is the synthetic form that people take in supplements.

This nutrient gets a lot of press because it helps the body produce new cells, especially during the rapid cell division and growth of pregnancy. A lack of folate can lead to birth defects, but luckily it's easily avoidable with proper nutrition and a well-chosen prenatal vitamin. You don't want to overdo it though, so don't exceed 1,000 micrograms of folate per day during pregnancy and breastfeeding.

Table 20-2 lists some of the best natural vegan sources of folate to help you reach the recommended minimum of 400 micrograms per day during pregnancy.

Table 20-2	Natural Vegan Sources of Folate	
Food Source of Folate	*Serving Size*	*Micrograms*
100-percent-fortified break-fast cereals	¾ cup	400
Black-eyed peas, cooked	½ cup	185
Spinach, raw	1 cup	110
Asparagus, cooked	4 spears	85
Green peas, raw	¾ cup	65
Vegan baked beans	1 cup	60
Green peas, frozen, cooked	½ cup	50
Broccoli, frozen, cooked	½ cup	50
Broccoli, raw	2 spears, each 5 inches long	45
Avocado, raw	½ cup	45
Orange	1 small	30
Banana	1 medium	20

Source: The National Institutes of Health: Office of Dietary Supplements

Take a vegan prenatal vitamin to ensure you're getting all the necessary vitamins and minerals you need, including folate. Deva Nutrition and Freeda both make a complete prenatal vitamin for vegan women.

Protein

Few concerns are more often expressed to pregnant vegans than whether they're getting enough protein in their diets. Most recommendations for protein hover around an extra 25 grams a day for pregnant ladies. For the first trimester, you want to get about the same 45–50 grams a day that you aim for when you aren't pregnant. During the second and third trimesters, just add 25 grams of protein for a total of between 70 and 75 grams. This level of protein is easily attainable — even for a vegan. You can either eat larger portions of the protein you're already eating, or you can add other protein-rich foods that may also help amp up your other nutrient needs, like calcium and iron.

Table 20-3 shows you some easy ways to get an extra 25 grams of protein along with some other great nutrients in fell swoop.

Table 20-3	Options for Extra Vegan Protein (and Other Important Nutrients)				
Protein Source	Serving Size	Protein (g)	Calcium (mg)	Iron (mg)	Zinc (mg)
Lentils	1½ cups	25	0	9.5	4
Garbanzos	1½ cups	19	60	6.7	0
Black beans	1½ cups	21	180	6.5	4
Enriched pasta	2–4 oz.	7.4–11	8	1.7	2
Enriched soymilk	16 oz.	22	734	5	1.5
Hemp protein powder	4 Tbsp.	11–13	35–50	5–7	5

Sources: USDA tables and manufacturer's information

Calcium

Getting enough calcium for a growing baby and healthy mom shouldn't pose any problems while maintaining a vegan diet. The current U.S. recommended daily allowance (RDA) for pregnant and breastfeeding women above the age of 24 is 1,200 milligrams per day. For women under the age of 24, the RDA is 1,200 to 1,500 milligrams per day. The World Health Organization recommends similar levels to prevent complications during pregnancy and early labor and to promote proper fetal development.

Focusing on healthy sources of calcium, such as leafy greens, tofu, enriched soy, rice, or hemp milk, and nuts, grains, and beans, can help you reach your daily goal. (Flip to Chapter 4 for a list of vegan foods that supply calcium.) And keep in mind that pregnancy likely benefits women by improving calcium absorption! Most prenatal vitamins contain some calcium, so talk to your medical team to find out whether taking a supplement makes sense for you.

Calcium doesn't work alone; it needs vitamin D. Our lovely bodies not only create life and deliver kicking, screaming babies, but they also turn sunlight into vitamin D through the conversion of UVB rays. So, pregnant mamas should get regular, short doses of sun exposure. A good portion of your skin needs to be exposed to natural sunlight, without sunscreen, or safer sun lamps to create vitamin D. Getting 15 to 30 minutes a day of sunlight either in the early morning or late afternoon allows you to produce what your body needs without the danger of sunburn. Your body then uses the vitamin D to properly absorb calcium. So having enough is imperative.

Your body absorbs calcium and iron best when they're taken separately, so plan your vitamins accordingly. Calcium citrate is easier to absorb than calcium carbonate, so get a supplement with this form. Take no more than 500–600 milligrams of either calcium or iron at a time for best absorption.

Iron

Getting enough iron is important to ensure a healthy rate of development for your baby and to ensure a strong and energized pregnancy for you. Your body is making extra blood for the baby now, so you need more iron than ever, about 49 milligrams a day. Focusing on iron-rich foods like dark beans and leafy green veggies, as well as a prenatal supplement that contains iron, helps make blood production go smoothly.

Most vegan prenatal vitamins provide 100 percent of the iron you need, so talk with your healthcare provider about which supplement to take. And be sure to include lots of vitamin C–rich foods to help your body absorb the extra iron you're consuming. (To read more about iron, including a list of great vegan iron food sources, check out Chapter 4.)

B12

Because every vitamin and mineral is needed in higher quantities during pregnancy, it's no surprise that the B12 requirements are higher too. Pregnant and nursing mothers are encouraged to get between 2 and 2.8 micrograms per day. Focusing on enriched soy foods, nutritional yeast, and a good vegan prenatal supplement during pregnancy and breastfeeding can help you reach the recommended daily intake.

B12 helps the pregnant mother maintain a healthy nervous system and create enough blood for herself and her baby. This vitamin crosses the placenta into the baby and is needed to help make DNA and other cell material.

Breastfed babies get their B12 through breast milk, so it's important that a vegan mom continues to get optimal amounts of B12 during nursing. That way both she and the baby are sure to get what they need. Infants can store enough B12 to last 6 months to 1 year from what they get in the womb, so optimal intake during pregnancy is key. For more on B vitamins, including B12, refer to Chapter 4.

Oils and fats

The oils and fats that build and protect our brains, organs, and eyes are necessary in greater amounts for pregnant women. Essential fatty acids like *DHA,* an important omega-3 oil, are needed by every cell in the body and are sometimes referred to as *essential oils.* In other words, it's essential that you get them from your food! DHA is important for proper fetal and infant development.

Vegans can get these oils, which are often found in high concentrations in fatty fish, by eating certain vegetable oils instead. Oils from flax, sesame, sunflower, and evening primrose seeds are sometimes combined in vegan supplements. Products made from microalgae also are good sources of DHA. An added benefit of taking vegan DHA supplements or formulated omega-3 oils is that you avoid the mercury and other toxins that are found in dangerous concentrations in fish.

An easy way to integrate certain omega-3-rich oils, like flax, or combination oils, like Udo's DHA 3-6-9, is to drizzle your daily serving on salad, popcorn, or soup, or whisk it into nondairy yogurt. Heat damages the health benefits of these oils, so don't cook them.

A word on supplements

Adding well-chosen supplements to your well-rounded diet ensures that you and your growing fetus are getting everything you both need in the way of nutrients. Take a realistic look at your diet and talk with your healthcare provider about what you may be lacking. Safeguard your and your baby's health with a few easy vitamins and minerals or take an all-inclusive prenatal.

For example, if you're concerned about your iron intake, discuss it with your midwife or doctor. Many pregnant women, vegan and nonvegan alike, experience anemia during their 40 weeks of baby-making duty. You can choose from three types of iron supplements: iron sulfate or ferrous sulfate, chelated iron bisglycinate, and ferrous fumarate. *Iron sulfate,* also listed as *ferrous sulfate,* can cause upset stomach, black stools, and constipation. The easier types of iron to digest are called chelated iron bisglycinate, ferrous succinate, and ferrous fumarate. If you take separate calcium and iron supplements, take them a few hours apart, because calcium and iron can interfere with each others' absorption.

Similarly, if you aren't getting sufficient sunlight on a daily basis, talk with your healthcare provider about taking a vegan vitamin D2 supplement. While some orange juice and soymilk is fortified with vitamin D, it may not be enough to reach the levels required during pregnancy to ensure proper calcium absorption.

In general, vitamin and supplement tablets and oils should be kept away from heat and sunlight and be stored in opaque containers to prevent oxidation and breakdown. Liquid supplements usually are easier for pregnant women to digest and absorb, but chewables seem to be second best. If you're having a difficult time digesting whole supplements, feel free to cut them into smaller pieces or grind them up and separate the entire dose throughout the day. Chapter 4 provides more detail on choosing vegan supplements.

Awesome snack list for amazing mamas

Snacking is one of the fun parts of pregnancy — you're encouraged to do it often! Nibbling throughout the day while pregnant can help you maintain a healthy weight and avoid heartburn. If you snack on smaller meals throughout the day rather than gorging on three large meals, your digestion may be easier. Snacking also can help you maintain a steady blood sugar rate, avoid dizziness, and keep nausea at bay.

Choosing nutrient-dense snacks can help you meet your daily requirements for protein, calcium, iron, and other vitamins (see the earlier section "Nutritional know-how: Getting enough of what you need." Stock your fridge, car, and workplace with several items from this list to snack more healthfully:

- ✔ Cans of low-sodium vegan bean soups
- ✔ Carrot sticks and hummus
- ✔ Dolmas (stuffed grape leaves)
- ✔ Fortified cereal with berries
- ✔ Hemp milkshakes with frozen bananas and cashews
- ✔ Individual boxes of soy, rice, or almond milk
- ✔ Miso broth
- ✔ Mixed nuts and seeds, raw or roasted (try to avoid too many salted nuts)
- ✔ Olives
- ✔ Organic fruit
- ✔ Rye crackers with sesame seeds, hummus, and olive tapenade
- ✔ Soy yogurt with organic dried fruit and slivered almonds
- ✔ Toasted nori sheets
- ✔ Whole-grain crackers with mashed avocado and grated carrots
- ✔ Whole-wheat bagel with almond butter and apple butter

Eat organic fruits and vegetables during your pregnancy. Pesticides and herbicides linger on conventionally raised produce, and they can travel across the placental barrier to your developing fetus.

Discussing the Weighty Issue of Weight Gain

Gaining a healthy amount of weight is truly important for your health and that of your baby. It's another subject that may cause you grief as a vegan lady who's got a bun in the oven. Friends and family may worry that you aren't gaining as much weight as they think you should. Many vegan women are on the skinny side when they conceive so they may not seem as plump as other pregnant women. Whatever you do, don't let these loved ones guide you. The guidelines set forth by government and health agencies should be your number-one source. Those guidelines, along with healthy vegan foods, can help you maintain a steady, healthy weight gain.

Understanding healthy weight gain

The Institute of Medicine offers reasonable guidelines for U.S. women to aim for when tracking their pregnancy weight. Your midwife or doctor can help you track your gain and offer advice if you feel you're gaining too much or too little. It's better for you and the growing babe in your belly if you main-tain a steady weight gain.

During your first trimester, a total gain of about 3 to 5 pounds is considered healthy and average. After that, through the second and third trimesters, a gain of about 1 pound per week is recommended. However, these guide-lines all depend on your weight when you started your pregnancy. If you were underweight — according to your *BMI,* or body mass index — you may need to gain extra weight, from between 28 to 40 pounds total. If you were at a normal weight to begin with, you should gain between 25 to 35 pounds. Women carrying twins should gain a bit more weight and continue regular visits with their healthcare providers to keep an eye on their weight gain.

One-third of women in their child-bearing years are considered obese. Babies born to these women have a much higher chance of being insulin resistant than babies born to women of a healthy weight. Women who gain too much weight also are more likely to need a cesarean section to deliver their larger-than-normal babies, and they generally have a more difficult time losing their pregnancy weight.

Fighting media images of "skinny" mamas

Recent baby booms among celebrities, coupled with the pervasive media images provided by paparazzi, have created a new image of the perfectly skinny pregnant woman. These women seem to gain just a "baby bump" and not an ounce more. Within a few weeks after giving birth, they're seen again in a bikini or even modeling underwear on the catwalk. This image can make your pregnancy miserable if you try to attain some unnatural, supposedly perfect body and weight.

Gaining too little weight during pregnancy can cause health problems for yourself and your baby. The extra weight you're putting on is a combination of the baby's weight, amniotic fluid, extra blood volume, larger breasts, and a larger uterus. An underweight pregnancy can result in a premature, smaller baby who may suffer from delayed development and the increased likelihood of heart or lung problems.

Just remember that it's totally natural to gain weight all over your body and get a little puffy. And, despite popular belief, it may take several months to lose the weight you acquire during pregnancy. Some women are naturally skinny and lose their baby weight quickly. Some don't. No matter what your body type is or how your body responds to pregnancy, it's more important that you're eating healthy food and providing ultimate nutrition for yourself and your growing child. Revel in the amazing power that your body is capable of, and, if at all possible, avoid any media images of celebrity moms.

Easy Meal Prep and Sanity-Saving Ideas

Pregnancy and modern living are sometimes incompatible. You may need to work until a few days before your due date, you may be a soon-to-be single mom, or you may already have children to care for. Whatever your situation, it can be difficult to maintain a healthy diet during this time. Ordering takeout is sometimes an option to save time on cooking and shopping, but restaurant food is rarely as healthy as home-cooked meals, and the expense is too much to regularly indulge.

Use these tips to keep healthy food readily available and easily accessible so that meals are more manageable to cook for yourself:

- ✔ **Cook once and eat twice (or thrice!).** When preparing meals like home-made soup, pasta, casserole, stir-fry, or curry, make a double batch. Eat the leftovers for lunch or save individual servings in the freezer for easy reheating later.

- ✔ **Start a cooking co-op with vegan friends.** Ask friends to cook extra servings of their favorite meals and trade once or twice a week. This gives you a variety of vegan meals to choose from and it takes away some of the prep work.

- ✔ **Go to your freezer section occasionally.** Freshly prepared foods are certainly best, but some great, vegan frozen meals are available for those times when you're just too tired to cook. Choose hearty frozen dishes like whole grains with vegetables and tofu, bean burritos, and lasagna. These easy meals offer great nutrition and convenience.

✔ **Ask a friend to be prep chef for you.** After a big shopping trip, ask a family member or friend to come and do some of the prep work for you, such as washing, drying, and chopping vegetables. Bagging prepped veggies, lettuce, and chopped fruit cuts down on cooking time later in the week and provides grab-and-go snacks.

✔ **Treat yourself to an in-home vegan chef once or twice during your third trimester.** Hire an expert to come over and prepare a freezer and fridge full of meals to get you through the last week of pregnancy and the first week of parenthood.

Smart Tips for Common Pregnancy Problems

Bizarre issues that you didn't expect can pop up over the course of your pregnancy. Your morning sickness can last all day, as mine did for the first 20 weeks. Or you may be drinking plenty of water and never feel truly quenched. Bizarre food cravings also can take you by surprise.

Starting your pregnancy in great shape is the best way to deal with problems that may arise. Playing catch-up to get in shape while pregnant can be tough, so think ahead and make your own health a priority before getting pregnant. In the following sections, I provide you with some areas to consider and tips to help you through the bumpy times of baby bumps.

Staving off pregnancy woes with fresh foods

Certain problems can arise during pregnancy, including an uncommon condition called *pica* and a pregnancy only form of hypertension called *preeclampsia*. Luckily, eating a healthy diet of fresh foods can stave off problems.

Pregnant women with pica crave strange, usually nonnutritive foods like dirt, clay, or ice. Sometimes this craving is a sign of low minerals or iron anemia. If you start craving these or other strange foods, talk with your healthcare provider. Even though some of the foods craved during a pica episode aren't dangerous, they may take the place of truly nourishing foods that a pregnant woman needs.

Preeclampsia is a combination of protein in the urine and high blood pressure that occurs only in pregnancy. Developing after the 20th week of pregnancy, the symptoms of preeclampsia include headaches, swelling of the face and hands, sudden weight gain, abdominal pain, decreased urine, nausea, and vomiting. The causes of preeclampsia aren't well understood, but one study that followed the women who gave birth at the Farm in Tennessee, under the guidance of midwife Ina May Gaskin, found a much lower rate of this serious condition among these vegan women. They chalk this success up to a diet of whole, fresh foods.

Choosing whole, natural, freshly prepared foods can help you maintain a healthy weight gain and avoid common pregnancy problems, such as pica and preeclampsia. Fruits and vegetables, whole grains, beans, and sea vegetables protect your overall health and ensure that your growing baby is getting everything he needs.

Taking in plenty of water and electrolytes

Staying hydrated by drinking enough water is a good way to ensure a healthy pregnancy. Avoiding caffeinated and chemical-laden beverages like diet and regular soda is definitely a good idea. Why expose your growing baby to these chemicals?

Electrolytes, which are found in sports drinks, are salts like sodium and potassium. These salts are important for true hydration because they're used by your body's nerves, cells, heart, and muscles to create and carry electrical impulses. Without these salts, your body wouldn't function at all. Just as your body needs more iron during pregnancy, you also can feel relief and create better energy by consuming extra electrolytes throughout the day.

Sports drinks have a few added electrolytes, but they also come with troublesome artificial colors and sweeteners. Natural electrolyte drinks, such as young coconut water, are naturally sweet and offer better nutritional support. Sea vegetables and natural sea salt also are healthy sources of electrolytes and minerals. Naturally sweetened electrolyte concentrates like electroBlast are becoming more widely available.

Dealing with food cravings

While pickles and ice cream may not be your normal snack of choice, you may crave unusual combinations or develop an obsession with a certain food during your pregnancy. You may even suddenly hate certain foods you normally love. Not much scientific study is available covering cravings during pregnancy, but we do know that they are natural and normal. For the most part, cravings can be indulged moderately. Enjoying a certain texture or taste won't be harmful unless taken to excess.

Your body may be using cravings to tell you that it needs certain minerals or nutrients, such as calcium or protein. However, emotional cravings may be involved as well. Explore your cravings and get emotional support from other moms and pregnant friends. Talking about your fears and concerns with understanding listeners can help you release tension, which can decrease your desires for unhealthy foods that you've been using to sooth your emotions. You're certainly not alone if you feel overwhelmed or anxious and eat certain foods because of it.

Dairy and meat cravings during a vegan pregnancy can be disturbing to you, especially when you're working hard to stay on the vegan bandwagon. These cravings may signal a need for more iron, calcium, or protein. If you want to continue with your vegan diet, you should eat foods rich in those attributes normally found in the food you're craving. Refer to the earlier section "Nutritional know-how: Getting enough of what you need" for the scoop on eating vegan foods that provide you with the proper nutrients.

If you're craving a certain texture, such as creamy, rich, crunchy, or buttery, keep in mind that many vegan foods are available to satisfy any of those desires. If you're craving any of the following nonvegan foods, don't worry, I've provided some vegan suggestions that are sure to satisfy:

- **Cheese:** Air-popped popcorn drizzled with melted vegan margarine or olive oil and sprinkled with nutritional yeast flakes.
- **Ice cream:** Nondairy ice cream made with soy, rice, or hemp milk.
- **Chicken:** Frozen vegan soy "chicken" nuggets, which you can find in many health food store freezers.
- **Beef:** Cook up some vegan "beef" strips, prepare a rich shiitake mushroom and bean stew, and add more iron-rich foods to your diet in case your body is craving the mineral.

Managing "morning" sickness

I had to laugh when I started feeling morning sickness — all day for weeks on end! Some women have no nausea and other women have endless queasy feelings no matter what time of day it is. This upset stomach may be accompanied with slight headaches, a sour taste in your mouth, and vomiting.

These symptoms are all normal during the first trimester, but if you can't eat at all or have excessive vomiting, talk with your midwife or doctor. Ask her for advice if you seem dehydrated, lose weight, or feel lightheaded. These symptoms can all lead to complications if not addressed quickly.

As with everything else to do with pregnancy, each woman is different. During this time, you may not be able to stomach some foods that you used to love and rely on. And certain times of day may be better or worse for you. Here are some tips that can help you get through the yucky times:

- ✔ Eat small snacks and meals more often throughout the day to help your sensitive stomach.

- ✔ Keep a plate of plain crackers next to your bed and eat a few if you wake up in the middle of the night and immediately upon waking in the morning.

- ✔ Avoid upsetting smells like gasoline, cooking food, perfumes, and heavily scented products.

- ✔ Drink small amounts of natural electrolyte beverages, such as young coconut water, throughout the day to replenish your salts. (The earlier section "Taking in plenty of water and electrolytes" explains more on electrolytes.)

- ✔ Stay cool during the day and avoid overheating. Soaking your feet in a bucket of cold water can help during summer.

- ✔ Relieve your nausea by eating watermelon and drinking naturally sweetened ginger-lemonade. Fresh mint also is known to calm an upset stomach. Ginger tea, either iced or hot, can be made by steeping freshly cut pieces of ginger in water.

- ✔ Exercise moderately and regularly.

- ✔ Keep windows open to keep fresh air inside your home.

- ✔ If at all possible, don't skip meals, even if you only have a few bites at a time.

- ✔ Eat mild foods that are free of excessive spices and flavorings, such as plain whole grains, tofu, avocado, or toast.

- ✔ Soothe minor heartburn and upset stomach by drinking 1–2 tablespoons of aloe juice. You can mix it into apple juice if you need to.

- ✔ Avoid lying down for at least 15 minutes after eating to allow gravity to help your food digest downward.

- ✔ Find your acupressure points on your wrist to help stave off nausea. Seeing an acupuncturist also can have benefits.

- ✔ Speak with a homeopath to determine which of the several available homeopathic remedies will help with your morning sickness.

Caring for Yourself Postpartum

After your bundle of joy has finally made his or her debut into the world, most of the attention will shift from you to the baby. However, it's important to remember that you have just been through a major physical, emotional, and hormonal shift. Whether you're able to begin breastfeeding easily or not, had a cesarean birth or a natural one, encountered complications, or made it through the labor with no major upsets, it's very common to experience major emotional swings, exhaustion, and disorientation due to a whole new life being in your care.

Plan ahead and think about how to make your entrance into motherhood as smooth and supported as possible. Talk with your friends and family beforehand to line up assistants to help take care of your older children, cook and clean, or even hold the new baby while you take a shower. If your family and friends will be helping with meal preparation, be sure to go over vegan menus and ingredients to help them cook for you and your needs. There are many ways to ensure that you feel supported and cared for as you begin to provide for your new baby and grow your family. The following sections will fill you in.

Choosing certain vegan foods for strength

Recovering from childbirth and labor can be a slow process, but having the best foods planned in advance offers an easier transition. By having prepared foods ready for the whole family, you can avoid temptation to resort to less healthy options like takeout and snack foods. Plan to make a few meals that can be frozen in the two weeks before your due date. Stock your cupboards and refrigerator by going on a big shopping trip shortly before the due date as well.

If your partner or husband will be taking over the cooking duties in the weeks after the birth, be sure he or she knows how to prepare healthy vegan meals that will support your energy needs. The meal-planning chart included in Chapter 9 can help to plan the days after your labor.

High-energy foods like whole grains, avocados, nuts, and bean soups are filling and provide you (and your family) with excellent nutrition. If you lost a lot of blood during labor, plan to have more iron-rich foods to replenish your blood supply. (Chapter 4 includes a list of foods that can boost your iron intake.) Stay hydrated with plenty of water, raspberry leaf tea for uterine health, and enriched soymilk for your protein and nutrient intake.

Supplying yourself with foods that encourage good milk production

If you choose to breastfeed your baby, you need to fortify your body regularly with quality water and food. Continue to consume extra calories every day to ensure a steady supply of nourishment for your baby. It can really be helpful to keep a glass of water next to you when you nurse.

Natural foods that have been used in traditional medicine to promote and increase breast milk production are fenugreek, which can be found in special tea combinations (check out health food stores), lettuce, dill, caraway, basil, marjoram, and millet. Drinking several glasses of mixed soy and rice milk a day can be helpful as well. Prepare a millet porridge with caraway seeds, sprinkled with marjoram for a delicious dish. Basil, dill, and lettuce combine for a simple salad. Basil and marjoram can be added to any Italian dish for tasty results.

Certain foods can cause your baby to experience gas and stomach discomfort. Little scientific research is available to prove this, but centuries of motherhood experience show that removing these foods can help your baby feel more comfortable and even avoid colic. Cabbage, chocolate, coffee, garlic, chili, curry, and other spicy foods have been known to affect a mother's breast milk. Some babies show signs of improved digestion when their moms stop eating dairy while nursing, which is another good reason to maintain a vegan diet. Soy, wheat, citrus, and nuts also can cause stomach problems for babies, so try eliminating each food for one to two weeks at a time to narrow in on the culprit.

Meeting calorie and other nutrient requirements

Breastfeeding requires 200–500 extra calories a day and can help you burn off that extra weight gained during pregnancy, but you will do well if you're mindful to continue to eat regular meals of nutrient-rich foods (instead of filling up on foods that have empty calories). Just like when you were pregnant, it's important to choose foods that offer good protein, calcium, iron, B vitamins, zinc, and other nutrients so both you and your baby get everything you need. (See the earlier section "Nutritional know-how: Getting enough of what you need" and Chapter 4 to find out what foods provide you with these important nutrients.)

Many children develop quite well on a diet of only breast milk past their sixth month, and breastfeeding for 1 to 2 years is recommended by most experts. This vegan's son enjoyed "mama milk" until his 22nd month and didn't have an ear infection once during that time. As long as you're breastfeeding, continue to supplement your own diet with omega-3-rich oils like flax and healthy fats from olive oil, unrefined coconut oil, avocados, nuts, and seeds. These oils and fats protect your own health and ensure that your baby gets everything needed for healthy brain and eye development.

Chapter 21

Bouncing Baby Vegans

Starting your kids on a vegan diet from the very beginning offers them a lifetime of healthy habits and benefits. What a person eats in her first few years can set her eating habits for life. So offering your children a healthy diet of various whole, plant-based foods will ensure that they grow up healthy and loving their veggies.

This chapter discusses infant and toddler nutritional needs. By covering the various ways to feed babies and toddlers, I show you that you have healthy vegan options and that cruelty-free menus offer a terrific, nutritious diet. Babies and toddlers can receive complete nutrition from a vegan diet, and a little planning and creativity can make the job of vegan parenting easier and more successful.

Nourishing Your Newborn

Because a new baby's digestive system is still quite immature and sensitive, for the first six or so months, nutrition is pretty straightforward: You should provide either breast milk or formula.

A baby is designed by nature to be breastfed. Vegan mamas who are able to nurse their kids naturally need to ensure that their milk is rich, ample, and providing the necessary nutrients (see Chapter 20 on postpartum nutrition and care). Not every woman can breastfeed successfully, however, and some babies have a difficult time suckling. Luckily, vegan mothers who aren't able to breastfeed their children can provide healthy nutrition by using various plant-based formulas. This section discusses the ins and outs of both breast-feeding and formula feeding.

Whether you're breastfeeding or using formula, if you notice that your infant is experiencing rash or low or no weight gain, talk with your doctor about possible food allergies. Cow's milk products are the most common foods known to upset a nursing baby, but other foods also may cause a negative reaction. Depending on how sensitive your baby is, and how much of the problematic food you ate, the reactions may be mild to severe. Rash, eczema, wheezing or asthma, ear infections, fussiness, colic, and constipation or diarrhea are all possible signs of sensitivity. It may take a little time and some detective work to discover a sensitivity. Food reactions can occur within a few minutes or over the course of a 24-hour period. If you notice a pattern of feedings and reactions, start writing down what the baby ate or what you ate before nursing the baby, and what the reaction is. Talk about the pattern with your midwife, doula, lactation consultant, or doctor.

Breastfeeding: So perfectly vegan!

The female breast is designed to provide milk for the human baby. The first milk women produce is immunity-building *colostrum,* which pregnant women start producing late in their pregnancies. Easy to digest and high in carbo-hydrates and protein, colostrum is also low in fat, making it the perfect first food for a baby. This rich milk is full of the mother's antibodies, which help a mother share her stronger immune system with a baby (who hasn't yet developed its immunity). Your body will provide the exact nutrients your baby needs for proper growth and development — an example of how amazing the human body truly is!

Because breastfed babies receive vitamin B12 through milk, vegan moms should remember to supplement appropriately. Vegan babies still need vitamin D2 (D3 is made from animal ingredients), which can be produced through daily sun exposure or supplementation of 5 micrograms a day. Once the baby starts eating solid foods, be sure to include legumes and whole grains to provide the zinc necessary for proper growth and development.

How long should I breastfeed?

The longer you're able to breastfeed your baby, the better. The American Academy of Pediatrics (AAP) recommends nursing your child for at least one year, and the World Health Organization (WHO) and the United Nations Children's Fund (UNICEF) both recommend at least two years. Why? More than 100 components contained in breast milk protect babies from infections and disease. Many studies prove that significant health risks arise for both the mother and child if breastfeeding doesn't occur. Breastfed babies have fewer incidents of ear infections, allergies, diarrhea, and possibly asthma than formula-fed babies.

Breastfeeding benefits for mama

Breastfeeding isn't just a great choice for baby; moms receive plenty of health benefits, too. Lactation causes the mother's uterus to contract to its original size after expanding during pregnancy. Breastfeeding also reduces a woman's risk of developing breast cancer, osteoporosis, and ovarian and uterine cancers later in life. Nursing also helps her lose the extra weight gained during pregnancy.

Breastfeeding provides the perfect opportunity for the new baby and mother to connect on a deeper level as well. A newborn infant can only see objects 12 to 15 inches from its face — the distance to its mother's face while nursing. This constant visual contact allows a baby and mother to imprint each other's faces.

The good news about vegan moms is that most of us tend to breastfeed our babies — well into their first year, and even into their second year. Consider this: Up to 60 percent of all mothers in the U.S. nurse their babies in the hospital immediately following the birth, but only 25 to 39 percent of those mothers are still breastfeeding at 6 months. Some vegan communities like the Farm in Tennessee, on the other hand, report breastfeeding rates of 95 percent. This amazing fact shows that vegan mothers are pretty hip to the outstanding benefits of mother's milk. They realize that it trumps all other options.

Prepare for successful breastfeeding by choosing a pediatrician who is pro-breastfeeding. Ask how they support new mothers who have difficulties nursing and whether they recommend formula as a last resort. A *lactivist,* or pro-breastfeeding pediatrician, should also have a certified lactation consultant to recommend to you should you need more expert help.

I'm having trouble with breastfeeding — now what?

New breastfeeding moms often become concerned about their infant's growth because they can't tell how much their baby is taking in. Also, formula-fed babies often put on weight faster from ages 6 to 12 months, leading some people to believe that breastfed babies aren't getting enough milk. To make things worse, many growth charts provided to pediatricians and doctor's offices haven't taken into account the differences in weight gain between formula-fed and breastfed babies, leading some parents to feel pressured to switch to formula to help their baby gain weight faster. Even though "breast is best," many doctors have unwittingly been complicit in pressure to wean too early or to supplement with formula due to the misguided and misinformed focus on weight gain.

Luckily the World Health Organization has collected data from around the world to help develop a new set of international standards and growth charts for infants and children through the age of 5 years. The new charts were created using growth information on both exclusively and predominantly breastfed children, and can be found at www.who.int/childgrowth/standards.

Considering using another mom's milk

If breastfeeding is not going well for whatever reason, another alternative is to search out mothers who have extra breast milk that they're willing to share with you. Using another woman's breast milk is preferable to many vegan women who would prefer that their children not be exposed to highly processed cow's milk formula or refined soy products at such an early age. You have two options within this "borrowed" milk model:

✔ You can casually share milk with a mom you know and are comfortable with. You may even find other vegan moms who are willing to pump extra for you, although a nonvegan mom is preferable to canned formula.

✔ You can contact the Human Milk Banking Association of North America (www.hmbana.org) to see whether your baby qualifies to receive donated milk. This group connects parents all over the country who need milk for their babies with prescreened human milk supplies.

Donated milk offers your baby the wonderful immunity and disease prevention that your own milk would have provided. It's a useful and safe way to help mothers who have postoperative problems or infection diseases that stop them from breastfeeding.

Besides concerns over baby's weight gain, most women are tempted to stop breastfeeding because it's painful (usually due to improper latch) or because they don't feel comfortable with the functional aspect of handling their breasts. Women's breasts have become overly sexualized in our culture, so some moms are uncomfortable nursing in public. Plus infants require milk every two to three hours, and that can be exhausting for a new mother.

If you haven't decided whether to stick with breastfeeding, try it for a few weeks before switching to formula (it's very difficult, if not impossible, to change back to breastfeeding from formula-feeding). Get expert help and support through your local La Leche League or hospital-sponsored breastfeeding support group. The lactation consultants are trained to help guide you through the learning stages of nursing — even though breastfeeding is natural, it doesn't always come naturally. They can also help you if you begin to feel postpartum depression.

Thinking about formula as a last resort

If you're a vegan who's considering formula for your baby, you should know that at this time you can't buy commercially made organic, vegan infant formulas. Several soy-based formulas contain no dairy but aren't vegan due to the added vitamin D3, which comes from animal sources. Baby's Only organic soy-based formula is widely available but isn't 100 percent vegan.

Your baby has to eat, though, and if breastfeeding just isn't possible for you, the soy-based formulas are certainly acceptable alternatives. Your little one can be 100 percent vegan a little later on in life.

Soy and rice milk aren't the same as soy and rice formula. These milks that you may use on your cereal don't contain the proper nutrition for babies to thrive. And while you can find some recipes online for homemade formula, which can be made with vegan ingredients, no studies have been performed to discover the long-term effects of these homemade formulas, which may not provide the required fats, protein, and calories for infants.

Also, toxins could be lurking in toddler and infant formulas, so it's wise to research the manufacturing and packaging of each product. The major organic soy and dairy formulas claim that *hexane,* a volatile solvent used to manufacture some of their ingredients, isn't present at all in the final product. Still, parents worry that any product made with a dangerous chemical isn't healthy for their children. Similarly, canned foods, including formula, may contain *Bisphenol-A* (BPA), a resin used in packaging materials. Overexposure to BPA can be harmful to an infant's reproductive system and can alter hormone levels. Even organic formulas can be packaged in containers with BPA. Liquid formula tends to leach higher amounts of this chemical, so it's safer to choose steel cans of powdered formula.

Starting Older Babies on Solid Foods

After your baby reaches the age of 4 to 6 months, you may decide to start offering him food in addition to breast milk or formula. Not only must the baby's digestive system evolve slightly to allow for some food, but the baby's mouth muscles also need to develop enough to move food around and swallow. Around 4 to 6 months, your little one also will begin to hold up his head, developing stronger neck muscles for swallowing as well as sitting up with some help. These milestones are all important on the way to solids.

Current recommendations state that the main source of calories should be coming from breast milk or formula until a child is at least 6 months old. Some parents decide to wait until their child is even older, perhaps not introducing solid food until he's 8 to 10 months old. As long as your baby is still gaining weight and meeting developmental milestones, you have no reason to start feeding your baby solid food too early. Whenever you and your baby are ready, this section is here to help.

Even though your baby may be ready to begin trying some solid foods, hold off on introducing any type of milk. The American Academy of Pediatrics recommends that cow's milk not be fed to children under the age of 1, because it can cause digestive problems and allergies. As a vegan, you aren't likely to be buying cow's milk anyway, but you still need to hold off on giving your baby soy or rice milk until after they're 1 year old. Stick to breast milk, formula, or a bit of water to wash down solids for now.

Slow and steady wins the race

If your little vegan has reached those pivotal milestones of development and starts grabbing for your dinner, you can start experimenting with different foods. Take it slow and introduce foods one at a time. Experts have several theories about which foods are best to serve first, so you can simply go with what makes the most sense for your little one.

Choose only one food at a time, giving each a trial of a few days. For instance, feed your baby a few mashed spoonfuls of avocado a couple of times a day for up to a week. If the baby has no noticeable reactions, try mashed banana the next week, on its own. If she still has no reactions, you can move forward in this manner with a different food every few days. If your baby has a reaction to any certain food, you know not to use it again for a while. Keep in mind that if you were to make a mash of several foods at once and the baby reacted, you wouldn't know which food was the culprit. So always introduce one food at a time.

Deciding what and how to feed your growing baby

What should you choose for your baby's first solid foods? Iron-fortified rice cereal is a popular first food for vegan and nonvegan babies alike. Rice is a great first grain because it rarely causes digestion problems, is gluten-free, and is low in protein. These rice cereals can be mixed with a little breast milk or formula to make a thin gruel. You can use your finger or a spoon to tip the cereal into your baby's mouth.

Miniature wooden or bamboo spoons are excellent choices for your infant's first feeding tool. Rather than relying on plastic-coated spoons, which can chip off microscopic bits into your baby's mouth over time, try bamboo, which is totally natural and nontoxic. These spoons can be found in most health food stores, natural baby stores, and online.

Some health experts have expressed concern that starting babies off with a refined carbohydrate cereal can lead to food sensitivities and obesity later on. Other experts state that introducing grains actually prevents these same issues. Clearly the jury is still out, so the choice is yours. Iron fortified grain cereals are often recommended as a first food since baby's iron reserves start to decline after 6 months.

If you would rather choose a fresh whole food, try mashed organic natural foods for the first forays into eating. Ripe, mashed avocado or bananas are easy on the digestive system for most kids. Natural, unsweetened apple-sauce, mashed sweet potatoes, or ground whole grains like millet are other options. You may prefer serving mashed vegetables first to encourage your babe to develop a taste for healthy veggies before being exposed to sweeter fruits.

Buying baby food in jars or frozen containers is an option, but it isn't neces-sary. Before the mid-1800s "baby food" didn't exist — infants just ate what-ever mom and dad were eating in a mashed up form. Most babies around the world are still fed like this today; it's cheaper and generally easier (and more environmentally friendly) than buying hundreds of little jars of premashed food. If you do need or choose to buy baby food, choose an organic variety.

You can use a fork to mash your own meal into a paste. Just be sure to remove anything spicy or otherwise difficult for a baby to digest. Low-cost baby food mills that grind your adult food into a consistent paste are available online, at health food stores or at larger children's mega-stores. These mills are easy to clean and transport.

Watch Them as They Grow: Food for Toddlers

Toddlers develop their personalities quicker than you may expect — they express their likes and dislikes for foods with no reservations. After the explosive growth that most babies experience, the slowing weight gain of tod-dlerhood can cause a decrease in appetite. When this decrease in appetite is coupled with a child's innate pickiness, you can easily become frustrated. But don't allow this to upset you — most parents experience a similar situation. By simply offering the healthy choices and nutritious snacks that I discuss in this section, your vegan kid will eventually develop great eating habits and tastes.

Don't give up on the greens! Most kids need a new food introduced 12 to 20 times before they accept it. Keep cooking healthy foods, show your kids you enjoy them, and don't force your child to eat something in the beginning.

After your baby's first birthday, you can begin to wean him off of formula and switch to fortified soymilk or toddler formula. If you choose fortified soymilk for your toddler, be sure that the variety you choose has appropriate levels of fat, calcium, protein, and vitamins D, B2, and B12. For babies who are 13 months and older, Toddler Health brand offers organic rice- and oat-based nutritional drink mixes that contain no soy, gluten, or dairy. But they still con-tain animal sources of vitamin D. Be sure to discuss your child's growth with your healthcare provider to help guide your decision.

Quieting the naysayers

Be prepared to hear questions and concerns from your family and friends that a vegan diet won't be sufficient for your growing guy or gal. To reassure your well-intentioned loved ones, offer these morsels of truth:

✔ Several studies suggest that vegan children's' growth rates are more gradual than nonvegans. These children often grow slowly at first, and then they catch up later on. The ultimate adult heights reached by vegan children are comparable to those of nonvegans.

✔ Children who grow up without dairy in their diets have less diarrhea, less gas, and less constipation.

✔ Dairy-free kids have less of a chance of developing type 2 diabetes, several childhood cancers, and heart disease.

✔ Vegan children have fewer problems with acne and eczema and encounter fewer cases of asthma.

✔ A Harvard study from 2000 showed that diets relying heavily on animal protein were shown to produce earlier onset of menstruation in girls by 3 to 8 years of age.

Choosing nutrient-dense foods over fiber

The nutritional needs of toddlers are similar to your own, but they're scaled to their smaller body sizes. They need a good variety of healthy fats, protein, calcium, iron, B12, vitamin D, and all the other minerals and nutrients that adults require.

Vegans tend to eat more fiber than the average person, which is great for adults. The problem with vegan toddler food is that kids can fill up on fiber thereby crowding out other valuable nutrient-rich foods. Because kids have smaller stomachs, it's easy for them to fill up with fruit and whole grains. So ensure that your child is getting enough nutrition by focusing on nutrient-dense foods like avocado, nut and seed butters, enriched whole-grain products, and enriched soy or hemp milk. To safeguard against strong reactions to a nut or seed allergy, avoid these foods until after the age of 2 if there are similar allergies in your family. If you would like to introduce nut and seed butters before the age of 2, talk with your pediatrician about testing a single seed butter first for any reaction. Keep track of your child's growth and weight gain to make sure she's getting enough calories and nutrition.

Choosing healthy fats also is important to guarantee proper growth and development. Aim for 1.1 grams of omega-3 fatty acids a day by adding flaxseed, hemp, and vegan omega-3 oils into your child's food.

Outsmarting finicky eaters

The most frustrating thing about kid's tastes is that they change — often. What they like for lunch one day is "yucky" the next. Here are some tips for presenting healthy foods in a way that entices your little one to eat enough without driving you too crazy:

- ✔ Let your little vegan help in the kitchen by dumping premeasured items into a bowl, stirring a pot, or putting napkins on the table. By "helping" to prepare a meal, children get excited to eat the finished dish.

- ✔ Offer several small bowls of different food items. Studies have shown that when given lots of healthy choices, kids will most likely make a healthy meal for themselves.

- ✔ Make food fun by creating faces out of veggies on his plate, using fruit as decoration, or setting steamed broccoli in mashed potatoes as trees. Get creative!

- ✔ Stick with it and continue offering your little guy healthy foods. Experts have shown that a new food can be introduced 12 to 15 times before a kid will accept it.

- ✔ Don't force the issue. If your child won't eat one meal, don't make a fuss out of it. As long as he has access to healthy snacks throughout the day and takes in a variety of foods over the course of several days, he's likely going to get what he needs.

- ✔ Monkey see, monkey do! Setting a good example and loving your own veggies and healthy food makes good habits natural for the whole family.

- ✔ Sneak those healthy greens in by pureeing cooked kale, broccoli, or spinach and mixing it into pasta sauce, soup, or even smoothies.

- ✔ Don't become a short order cook! Make a variety of foods that kids can choose from and let them decide how much of which foods they will eat.

Satisfying your little snacker

Snacks tend to make up a hefty portion of the toddler diet. A small stomach and constant play makes little ones hungry for small, frequent meals. Choosing healthy, safe snacks is important and can be your key to proper nutrition, even if mealtimes are frustrating.

Ensure your child's love for healthy foods by offering fresh fruits and vegetables every day. Even if she doesn't eat them every time, she'll become accustomed to seeing them and will choose them more often in the future. Here are some excellent nutrient-dense foods that toddlers and preschool-aged kids will love:

- Whole-grain or enriched pasta with blended kale marinara sauce
- Oven-baked sweet potato fries
- Soy yogurt mixed with ½ teaspoon flaxseed oil
- Hemp milkshake blended with nut butter and flaxseed oil
- Sunflower seed butter and jam sandwiches
- Raisins and chopped dried apricots
- Pancakes topped with almond or sunflower seed butter and apple butter
- Udon noodles with tahini sauce
- Cucumbers or flax crackers with nut cheese or tofu dip
- Carrot and zucchini muffins
- Mashed potatoes and vegan gravy
- Bagels spread with nut or seed butter or mashed avocado and hummus
- Pudding made from soaked and drained raw sunflower seeds that are blended into a paste with raisins or dried apricots and fortified hemp or soymilk

To avoid choking hazards when providing snacks to your toddler, be sure to do the following:

- Finely grind nuts in a spice grinder or blender instead of offering whole or coarsely chopped nuts.
- Spoon out half-teaspoons of nut butter rather than large globs.
- Chop vegan hot dogs into pea-sized bits.
- Quarter or halve cherry tomatoes, olives, grapes, pitted cherries, and any other large, round foods.
- Grate raw carrots into shreds rather than offering small chunks.
- Avoid popcorn and gum until the child is older.

Chapter 22

Vegan Diets for Kids, Tweens, and Teens

• •

In This Chapter

▶ Understanding what the experts think of vegan diets for kids

▶ Discovering kid-friendly vegan food choices

▶ Ensuring proper nutrition for all ages and stages

▶ Setting a solid foundation for healthy eating for life

▶ Helping kids deal with commercial and media messages

▶ Ensuring that kids eat well when away from home

• •

*R*aising vegan children from infancy is pretty easy with a little education and planning. On the other hand, transitioning children, tweens, and teens from the standard American diet can be more difficult, especially if they've grown accustomed to dairy, meat, and processed snacks and meals.

You don't need to worry when it comes to nutrition for kids; whether they're active athletes or cerebral book worms, vegan kids can and do get everything they need for proper development. The research is in, and experts agree that vegan kids are healthy and avoid many common health problems. The trick to raising a child vegan is doing it in a kid-friendly way and avoiding the common pitfalls.

Exploring strategies and shopping and cooking tips for families who decide to go vegan is the goal of this chapter. I discuss what to do when your kids will be traveling away from home, and I help you deal with shopping and media messaging. Arming kids with proper nutrition and the information to back up their decision to go vegan prepares them for a successful vegan life in the modern world.

This chapter covers the topics of nutrition and health benefits of a vegan diet for people between the ages of 3 and 19. This group of humans has the most to gain from living vegan — a lifetime of health and responsible action.

Is a Vegan Diet Safe? The Experts Weigh In

Gathering scientific proof on the safety and health of a vegan diet is easy — numerous studies and books detail the benefits of this style of eating. Experts — from the old-school professors to the cutting edge researchers — have been giving a well-balanced vegan diet for children rave reviews for years.

For example, second only to the Bible in terms of worldwide sales, Dr. Benjamin Spock's classic book *Baby and Child Care* is on most parent's shelves. Most people don't know it, but Dr. Spock went vegan in his later years — and he recommended it for children, too. After seeing his own chronic bronchitis disappear at the age of 88, Dr. Spock began to research this miracle diet and came to realize that a dairy- and meat-free diet would offer optimal nutrition for the children he was famous for writing about.

Similarly, Dr. Neal Barnard, the head of the Physicians Committee for Responsible Medicine (PCRM), recommends a vegan diet for children as a way to avoid serious health problems now and in the future. PCRM, which says that about one-third of American children are lactose intolerant or have a dairy allergy, advocates for vegan meals and dairy alternatives in the nation's school lunch programs. Dr. Barnard, a prolific author and speaker, presents research proving that kids of all activity levels can get the protein and nutrition they need from a plant-based diet.

These doctors and health gurus recognize the benefits of a vegan diet for children and teens, and they have done the legwork to prove it. Now it's up to parents and children to do the smart and tasty thing — go vegan!

A vegan diet based on a variety of whole foods ensures that a child's daily nutritional requirements are met and protects the health of that child for her entire life.

Understanding normal growth rates

Don't assume that vegan kids will be scrawny and poorly developed. They may be skinnier than the other kids in class, but considering the obesity epidemic in the United States, this trimness is probably good. Vegan children turn out just fine when offered a healthy diet. Just because your kid doesn't eat cheeseburgers doesn't mean he won't be able to play basketball — vegan kids grow tall too!

If you need some scientific proof, consider the following:

✔ A 1988 study by T.A. Sanders published in the American Journal of Clinical Nutrition showed how a group of vegan kids raised in England grew up just fine. These kids were actually taller than the other children studied and weighed just slightly less. You can search the journal's archived articles for vegan studies at www.ajcn.org.

✔ A study in *Pediatrics* (the official journal of the American Academy of Pediatrics) from 1989 revealed wonderful results from vegan children at the Farm community in Tennessee. Most of the more than 400 kids who were raised vegan from birth were slightly shorter than normal between the ages of 1 and 3, but by age 10 their heights had all evened out. Visit pediatrics.aappublications.org to search the journal's archived articles for this vegan study and many others.

Most American pediatricians, as well as the Centers for Disease Control and Prevention, use a standard set of growth charts to determine whether a child's growth is within the standard healthy trajectory. These charts have been used for years and have been updated according to shifting population information. However, all contain one fatal flaw: Every child is different. Tracking your child's height, weight, and head measurements can help you determine the rate at which they're growing, but you need to take many factors into account to get a true picture. These current charting standards don't tell you how much a child should grow to ensure a healthy life; they only describe how they're growing in comparison to the average child.

While these standard growth charts are somewhat useful, they also can cause unnecessary concern. Some kids hit growth spurts later than others. It's helpful to know the possible medical causes, such as hyperthyroidism, food allergies, kidney problems, and growth hormone deficiency, for a child being shorter than expected. However, if a child's parents are short, the kid will likely be shorter as well.

The bottom line is this: There are healthy kids, vegan and nonvegan alike, who fall within the "normal" rate of growth on doctor office charts. There also are kids who fall below and above normal. If you have concerns that your child's growth has slowed or stopped, talk with your healthcare provider about the possible factors. You're the parent, and you know more about your children than anyone — trust your intuition. If you notice that your child is experiencing any developmental delays or that he's withdrawing, lacking energy, or has lost his appetite, it may be time to talk with a medical professional.

Looking at a new kind of growth chart

In 2006, the World Health Organization (WHO) released its Child Growth Standards. The first charts of their kind, these standards show that children born anywhere in the world, Amazonian Pygmies aside, can grow into the same range of weight and height no matter their upbringing.

These new charts were based on a years-long study, which began in 1997. This study showed that, given healthy conditions and proper nutrition early in life, children from countries as diverse as Brazil, Ghana, India, Norway, Oman, and the United States show similar growth patterns.

Taking into account that the children followed over the course of this study included every kind of religious, ethnic, and nutritional background, it goes to show that vegan children develop into healthy teens and adults the world over. For the first time, these growth charts show how children should grow for optimal health rather than just describing how they're growing compared to the average child. To discuss these WHO charts with your doctor, print one at www.who.int/childgrowth/standards/en/index.html.

Discovering a Bounty of Choices for Your Little Vegan

Your kid's vegan menu can and should offer more variety than her omnivorous classmate's. Creating breakfast, lunch, and dinner to mimic what "normal" people eat is simple. Your family may be worried that a vegan lunch will draw stares or unwelcome comments in the cafeteria, but that's uncommon — and it can be avoided if it does happen.

Plan ahead and do a little research into what the natives are eating at school and at birthday parties. For instance, is pizza being served as the hot lunch item on Friday? If so, make a vegan pizza for dinner on Thursday and send a few slices as leftover lunch. To help your kid feel included at the next birthday party, find out what food the host is offering. Purchase or make a vegan version of that party food and have your kid take it with her. Colors, shapes, and sizes are important here: Ask whether the pizza will be cut into squares or pie slices. If nonvegan cupcakes will be the treat of the day, send your child with vegan cupcakes (rather than baking a full cake). The idea is to help your little vegan blend right in.

In this section, I provide you with some information on choosing kid-friendly meals and snacks for your growing vegan.

Offering kid-friendly vegan fare

American kids eat little real food these days. A normal day includes many highly processed junk foods, some disguised as being healthy. Breakfast may be cereal with hidden sugar, frozen pastry strudels, and even soda or other caffeinated beverages. Lunch will likely contain chips, more soda, cookies, french fries, and perhaps a burger or hot dog. Dinner with the family often means a fatty and heavily salted and sweetened fast-food meal purchased from a drive-through. When parents offer choices like these for their children, kids will take them up on it.

If you want your kid to eat healthy foods, you should only offer appropriate choices. Provide real foods for every meal and eliminate the processed junk food entirely. They may complain at first, but most kids won't starve themselves. Stock up on whole grains, low-sodium canned soups, fresh fruit, and healthy snacks. If you only offer healthy foods, your kids will begin to eat (and willingly choose) those healthy foods whether you're around or not. However, keep in mind that some kids are picky, and it can take up to a dozen times for a new food to be tasted and enjoyed.

Here's a sample list of kid-friendly vegan meals that most parents can whip up whether they went to culinary school or not:

- Baked potato fries with fruit juice-sweetened ketchup
- Baked potato with steamed broccoli and either olive oil or vegan cream cheese
- Barley and vegetable soup
- Burgers, hot dogs, and sandwich slices made of tofu and other meat substitutes
- Grilled soy cheese sandwiches
- Oatmeal with apples and cinnamon
- Pancakes spread with almond butter and pure maple syrup
- Peanut butter and jelly sandwiches (try 'em grilled, too!)
- Rice and beans with a side of salsa and guacamole
- Romaine lettuce salad with cherry tomatoes
- Sautéed seitan with mashed potatoes
- Spaghetti with tomato sauce (mix in some cooked lentils for extra protein)
- Spinach lasagna
- Vegetable stew
- Veggie pizzas with vegan cheese and shredded zucchini
- Waffles with fresh or frozen berries

Excitotoxins in your meals and snacks

Important foods to avoid are those that contain *excitotoxins,* chemical flavorings and preservatives that are added to processed foods. Common excitotoxins include MSG, food coloring, aspartame, and flavoring systems used by fast-food restaurants and packaged-food producers to addict consumers to their brands. Avoid any foods that contain these chemicals, because they can result in brain damage with excessive exposure. Baby food and children's snacks should be screened closely, because young brains are much more sensitive to damage from these additives. As you're studying ingredient labels, look for these key words, which indicate hidden excitotoxins:

- ✔ Autolyzed yeast
- ✔ Calcium caseinate
- ✔ Corn oil
- ✔ Hydrolyzed oat flour
- ✔ Hydrolyzed plant protein
- ✔ Hydrolyzed protein
- ✔ Hydrolyzed vegetable protein
- ✔ Malt extract
- ✔ Malt flavoring
- ✔ Monosodium glutamate
- ✔ Plant protein extract
- ✔ Sodium caseinate
- ✔ Textured protein (including TVP)
- ✔ Yeast extract

If your child has been raised on chemically flavored foods, it may take him a little while to appreciate the more subtle tastes of real, whole foods. Have a discussion with your kid and explain the serious ramifications that his diet is having on his health, mood, and future. Ask for his opinions and concerns. Whatever you do, don't make sweeping changes to the family menu without first discussing your reasoning behind it. If you're straight with your child, perhaps he'll see the value in what you're attempting and can help make the transition easier by participating more fully.

Dealing with kids' snack attacks

Most kids love to snack, and they can develop really scary food habits by relying on sugary, salty, and fatty offerings. Kids will still have access to unhealthy snacks when they're outside the home, but if you provide them with some of the following healthy options, they'll start making better choices most of the time:

- ✔ Applesauce sprinkled with ground cinnamon
- ✔ Brown rice pudding made from leftover brown rice mixed with blackstrap molasses, hemp or soymilk, cinnamon, berries, or raisins
- ✔ Calcium-fortified apple or orange juice

- Calcium-fortified soy, hemp, rice, or nut milk

- Coconut date rolls (fresh Medjool dates blended with unsweetened shredded coconut and formed into balls)

- Corn chips served with salsa, guacamole, and heated black beans

- Falafel patties served in a whole-grain pita with hummus and olives

- Fresh berries and all-fruit sorbet (without sugar)

- Fruit smoothies

- Fruit that's precut into bite-sized pieces

- Homemade popsicles made from blended hemp milk, berries, cashews, and a banana

- Hummus and crackers or veggies

- Organic apple slices dipped in unsweetened, unsalted almond butter

- Pickled cucumbers and other vegetables

- Pitted olives

- Popcorn drizzled with olive oil and nutritional yeast flakes

- Raisins mixed with nuts or seeds

- Spelt pretzels dipped in mustard or tofu dip

- Veggie sticks with tofu cream cheese or nut cheese

- Whole-grain cereal with soy, hemp, rice, or nut milk

Making Sure Your Growing Vegans Are Getting the Nutrition They Need

Every day seems to bring new growth to a child's mind and body. One day she's asking to hold your hand and play with you in the sandbox, and the next day she's boldly running off with her friends. Because each developmental stage brings new challenges, both physical and emotional, it's wise to plan ahead for the nutritional needs of your child.

Consulting traditional food charts isn't especially helpful for a vegan family. The amount of space taken up by meat and dairy on these guides is really large. Instead, rely on this section, which provides sound food options to ensure that your growing vegan family has access to all the food groups it needs.

Including the four vegan food groups in your kid's diet

Relying on the USDA food pyramid hasn't created a healthy nation. We die earlier and are sicker and more overweight than previous generations. Our children need a healthy food guide that takes full advantage of the best foods Mother Nature has to offer.

The healthy food groups to include in a vegan diet are

- ✔ Fruits

- ✔ Seeds, nuts, beans, legumes, and soy foods

- ✔ Vegetables

- ✔ Whole grains

These general guidelines include plenty of healthy fats from vegetable oils like olive, sesame seed, canola, and unrefined coconut oils. Also important are omega-3-rich oils like flaxseed oil. Natural fats also can be derived from nuts, seeds, avocados, nondairy milk, and nondairy yogurt.

Be sure also to include a source of vitamin B12, such as a typical children's multivitamin or vitamin-fortified cereals or soymilk.

The nutrition experts at the Physicians Committee for Responsible Medicine, or PCRM, have put together an outstanding outline for directing food choices for kids, tweens, and teens. See Table 22-1 for a rundown of these choices.

Table 22-1	Serving Recommendations for Kids, Tweens, and Teens			
Age Group	Whole Grains, Breads, Cereals	Vegetables	Legumes, Nuts, Seeds, Nondairy Milks	Fruits
1–4 years	4 servings	2–4 Tbsp. dark green vegetables ¼–½ cup other vegetables	¼–½ cup legumes 3 servings breast milk, soy formula, soymilk, or other enriched non-dairy milk	¾–1½ cups
5–6 years	6 servings	¼ cup dark green vegetables ¼–½ cup other vegetables	½–1 cup legumes 3 servings soymilk or other nondairy milk	1–2 cups

Age Group	Whole Grains, Breads, Cereals	Vegetables	Legumes, Nuts, Seeds, Nondairy Milks	Fruits
7–12 years	7 servings	1 serving dark green vegetables 3 servings other vegetables	2 servings legumes 3 servings soymilk or other nondairy milk	3 servings
13–19 years	10 servings	1–2 servings dark green vegetables 3 servings other vegetables	3 servings legumes 2–3 servings soymilk or other nondairy milk	4 servings

Source: www.pcrm.org/health/veginfo/veg_diets_for_children.html

Getting kids to think about calci-yum!

Cow's milk and other dairy products contain calcium that kids need for growing bones, but plenty of natural vegan foods also are rich in this mineral. Beans, grains, greens, vegetables, seeds, and nuts can supply everything your child needs for ultimate nutrition and proper growth. If cows can get their calcium from greens to grow big and strong, so can humans. Table 22-2 lists the calcium requirements for children (amounts are the same for both males and females):

Table 22-2	Calcium Requirements for Children
Age	Amount (mg/day)
1–3 years	500
4–8 years	800
9–18 years	1,300

Source: American Academy of Pediatrics

The human body absorbs calcium more efficiently from vegetables than it does from cow's milk products. Eating 100 calories of bok choy gives your body 435 milligrams of calcium, or 53 percent of the total available calcium. Drinking 100 calories of skim milk gives your body 107 milligrams of calcium, or 32 percent of the total available calcium. You obviously get some calcium with the milk, but you get more from the bok choy — and you also get the fiber, chlorophyll, iron, and other minerals available from this delicious green.

Chapter 4 provides a list of vegan foods that are great sources of calcium. Be sure to give your child a variety of these foods so he can reach the proper calcium requirements for his age group.

Ensure the bone health of your growing child, tween, or teen by eliminating all sodas from his diet. Most sodas, diet and regular, contain phosphoric acid. This acid has been shown in studies to deplete bones of their calcium. When the body is overly acidic, it leaches calcium out of the bones to alkalinize the blood. Strong evidence suggests that girls who drink more soda are more prone to fractures and broken bones. The soft drink industry vehemently denies that soda has anything to do with bone health, but parents should draw their own conclusions. You can offer your kids many other healthier beverage options, including calcium-fortified juices and vegan milks, iced herbal teas, and plain ol' water.

Iron's in it: Fitting iron into kids' menus

Growing kids need iron-rich food to ensure consistent energy levels and healthy blood production. Table 22-3 provides recommendations for how much iron kids need at various stages. Include in your child's diet items from the list of iron-rich vegan foods in Chapter 4.

Because girls in their tween and teenaged years are likely to be having their menstrual cycles, they require more iron starting at *menarche,* or their first period.

Table 22-3	Iron Requirements for Kids, Tweens, and Teens	
Age	*Males (mg/day)*	*Females (mg/day)*
1–3 years	7	7
4–8 years	10	10
9–13 years	8	8
14–18 years	11	15

Source: National Institutes of Health

Iron-containing foods that also contain a source of vitamin C, which enhances the body's ability to absorb the iron, are the best kind. And kids often like these options (without knowing their health benefits). Broccoli is one of these perfect foods. You also can pair foods to gain the same effect. For example, pair black beans with tomato salsa for a burrito topping or dip for tortilla chips. Or blend tomato sauce with steamed kale for a great pasta dish.

If necessary, children also can take a daily, chewable vitamin that ensures that their iron and mineral intake is sufficient. VegLife and Freeda both make good vegan chewable vitamins for kids.

Emphasizing the power of protein

Growing bodies need protein to create muscle, build blood, do work, and repair tissues. Luckily, protein deficiency is extremely rare. A varied diet can help everyone in your family meet their daily protein requirements, including the kids, tweens, and teens. Use Table 22-4 to create family-friendly menus based on your family's changing protein needs.

Table 22-4   Protein Requirements for Kids, Tweens, and Teens

Age	Males (g/day)	Females (g/day)
1–3 years	16	16
4–6 years	24	24
7–10 years	28	28
11–14 years	45	46
15–18 years	59	44

Source: National Institutes of Health

Focus on offering a variety of protein-containing foods throughout the day, and your kid's body will accumulate all the amino acids it needs to create complete proteins. Daily doses of whole-grain products, different kinds of beans or legumes, and a variety of nuts, seeds, and soy foods all ensure that your child meets her protein needs. Flip to Chapter 5 to see a list of vegan sources of protein.

Gaining essential vitamins and minerals from food

Vegan kids need the same vitamins and minerals that adults need. They may need a bit more or less at certain stages and ages, but a well-balanced, whole-food vegan diet and proper life habits provide them what they need.

The following vitamins are needed on a regular basis for proper development:

- **Vitamin A:** Colorful vegetables like carrots, sweet potatoes, kale, and spinach are great sources of vitamin A. The body uses this vitamin for eye and bone health, growth, and reproductive functions, just to name a few.

- **Vitamin B12:** Red Star Vegetarian Support nutritional yeast, fortified soy or hemp milk, and vegan multivitamins are all reliable sources of B12.

- **Vitamin C:** This is one of the vitamins vegans don't have to worry much about. Fruits and veggies are the best sources of vitamin C, which aids the body in absorbing iron, increasing immune function, and repairing tissue. Papaya, red bell peppers, broccoli, Brussels sprouts, and countless other fresh vegan foods provide this useful vitamin.

- **Vitamin D:** You can find this vitamin in fortified vegan foods. Getting regular doses of sunlight keeps your vitamin D levels high.

- **Vitamin E:** Almonds, avocados, hazelnuts, olive oil, safflower oil, sunflower seeds and sunflower seed butter, and wheat germ all supply good quantities of this antioxidant-rich vitamin.

- **Vitamin K:** This vitamin is found in green leafy vegetables, parsley, avocados, and kiwi fruit. Because it's a fat-soluble vitamin, sautéing greens with olive oil or another fat helps the body use the K better.

Besides vitamins, you also need different amounts of minerals, such as calcium, iron, phosphorus, sodium, potassium, chloride, sulfur, manganese, copper, iodine, zinc, cobalt, and selenium. These minerals are necessary for countless bodily functions every day. A varied diet of whole grains, beans, nuts, seeds, vegetables, and fruits provides what kids' growing bodies need. To ensure a wider and more plentiful source of minerals, start using more sea vegetables like nori, kelp, kombu, or dulse in soups, casseroles, salads, and grain dishes. These vegetables are excellent sources of trace minerals.

Because some kids may not adhere to the best eating habits every day (or while they're out of your sight and control), offering a daily vegan multivitamin is good health insurance.

Encouraging Kids to Eat Healthily

Children who begin living vegan from day one will probably have less trouble sticking to the game plan. If you're transitioning to vegan living after kids' taste buds and attitudes are well formed, however, it may be more difficult to convince them to participate.

No matter what situation you're in, this section provides you with tips on easing your growing family into veganism. I include lists to help you stock up your pantry, sample menus, and information on how to encourage participation from everyone.

Some kids go through periods of smaller-than-normal appetites. It's important not to force your kid to eat everything on his plate. Creating struggles around eating specific portions of vegetables, beans, or whole grains can cause children to rebel against the healthy food habits you're trying to instill. If you consistently offer only healthy foods at home, they'll eat enough of what they need.

Easing kids into enjoying a vegan diet

Creating a healthy environment at home is a must if you want your family to adopt better eating habits. Removing the junk food, meat, and dairy from your house can be done in consistent steps to make the transition easier and more subtle. As you run out of cheese, meat, and eggs, replace them with nondairy substitutes.

For example, if your family eats scrambled eggs for breakfast, try making a tofu scramble every other day until the eggs are gone. I include a recipe for Hungry Man (or Woman) Tofu Scramble in Chapter 12.

To ensure that your kids sign on to the healthier eating style that you're suggesting, make sure everyone is held to the same rules and expectations. Kids don't respond well to rules that are only directed at curbing their behavior. In other words, if you're allowed to have chocolate chip cookies after dinner, they should be too.

Here are several ways to help your children live vegan with less protest:

- ✔ **Allow your kids to splurge (veganly) every once in a while.** Many cities host pastry shops, ice cream parlors, or coffee shops that offer vegan treats. By visiting these special places once or twice a month, your kid will be excited about his new diet. Holding your son's birthday party at a vegan restaurant and preplanning a spectacular cake and treats will help your child feel "normal." Plus he'll have the added benefit of introducing delicious vegan foods to his friends.

- ✔ **Encourage your family to do some research on famous vegans.** Going to a concert performed by a famous vegan (or group of vegans) like Moby, Fiona Apple, The Red Hot Chili Peppers, or André 3000 can help your kid feel proud of his lifestyle. Renting movies with vegans like Woody Harrelson, Daryl Hannah, James Cromwell from *Babe,* or Casey Affleck also can help kids feel cool and represented.

✔ **Take your family to a farm animal sanctuary or other animal rescue shelter.** Doing so offers your child an opportunity to talk about animal rights, cruelty-free living, and vegan food. You don't need to graphically detail the horrors of what happens to animals, but sharing a loving connection with animals solidifies the reasons for not taking advantage of other creatures.

✔ **Plan ahead to ensure that your home is an easy, fun place for your children to get the food that they need and love.** Offer delicious vegan alternatives to old favorites. Remind them that they can eat something fun because it *is* vegan. Stock your pantry with lots of great, healthy foods, and allow everyone in the family some say in what's available.

Making kid-friendly meals out of healthy ingredients isn't as challenging as it sounds; you can make veganized versions of thousands of favorite nonvegan recipes. (Check out Chapter 10 for more information on veganizing old favorites.)

Keeping a well-planned and well-stocked pantry and fridge

Offering healthy snacks and meals at home is the first step in creating a lifetime of great eating habits for kids, tweens, and teens. If you don't have junk food in the house, your children will have to work much harder to get it. And sooner or later they'll instead opt for the natural flavors that are readily available.

By providing constant access to fresh, healthy treats, you're offering a valuable lesson in how to plan and succeed in being a healthy vegan. Use these guidelines to help stock your kitchen:

✔ Whole grains, including brown rice, quinoa, millet, and oats, need to be stocked regularly. These are filling go-to products when time is scarce.

✔ Whole-grain flours like whole-wheat pastry flour, buckwheat flour, brown rice flour, and cornmeal help you whip up special healthy treats for your little vegans.

✔ Nuts and seeds, including almonds, cashews, pecans, walnuts, sunflower seeds, sesame seeds, and pumpkin seeds are protein-filled snacks that kids can reach for any time. Nut butters help make healthy snacks even tastier.

✔ Beans and legumes can be dried, frozen, or precooked in cans. Keep a selection of different types on hand, including black beans, kidney beans, chickpeas, lentils, white beans, peas, edamame, soybeans, and green beans.

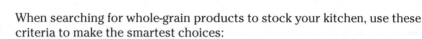

✔ Fruit should be plentiful and fresh. Offer a variety of seasonal whole fruit. To encourage kids to eat it, always make it available either washed, dried, and in a bowl on the counter or cut up in a fruit salad (which is always accessible in the refrigerator for snacking). If kids come to you hungry for a snack, send them to the fruit bowl!

✔ Vegetables can be frozen or fresh. Cutting up a variety of raw veggies for snacking — cherry tomatoes, jicama, bell peppers, carrot sticks, celery, and cucumbers — offers a healthy treat for hungry children.

When searching for whole-grain products to stock your kitchen, use these criteria to make the smartest choices:

✔ **Focus on fiber.** Cereals and breads should have 5 grams or more of fiber per serving.

✔ **Bring in the bran.** Even though bran cereals and wheat germ aren't officially whole grains (because they're missing the endosperm of the grain), they're still an excellent healthy option for filling up hungry tummies.

✔ **Grab some granola.** Make your own muesli (see Chapter 12 for a home-made recipe) or granola and keep it on hand. These snacks allow you to incorporate more whole grains easily into your child's diet. If time is short, you can find excellent naturally sweetened, organic granola in health food stores.

✔ **Search out the hidden sugars.** Minimize the sugar in your kid's diet by choosing whole-grain products that don't include any sweetener or that are sweetened with blackstrap molasses, agave, or brown rice syrup.

Promoting equal participation when feeding the family

Every member of the family can help plan menus and shopping lists. Ask each person to participate in filling out a weekly menu chart found in Chapter 9. After you figure out which ingredients you need, your kids can help you go through your cupboards and refrigerator to see what should be added to the shopping list.

Children as young as 2 or 3 years old can help plan meals in this way. If they're asked what they want, help in the planning, and participate in the shopping, kids are more likely to be invested in the meals after they're prepared. This method works really well over time to help children understand what's necessary in feeding a family. Life skills like these are invaluable and sadly lacking in many young adults. By training your kids early on how to plan, shop, and pre-pare healthy meals, you're ensuring that they experience a lifetime of health.

If your family is vegan and your teen wants to eat meat or dairy products, you can accommodate everyone. Be aware that consuming occasional animal foods can cause stomach problems, gas or indigestion. Providing only healthy foods at home, as well as one or two high-quality, organic nonvegan items may be a good alternative to forcing your kid to leave the house and get the less nutritious foods that she desires. (Flip to Chapter 8 for more information on coexisting with nonvegans.)

Cooking in the kitchen with the kids

Start cooking with your kids at a young age to ensure that they're comfortable preparing meals. It's one of the most important life skills any human can develop. Kids as young as about 2 years old can start helping with meals by picking out fruit at the grocery store, pouring premeasured ingredients into a bowl, or stirring and whisking recipes with adult supervision.

Every person in the house can help plan a menu and participate in some way in its creation. By looking through recipe books, writing a shopping list, going to the grocery store and farmer's market, and preparing the meal with you, your young person will have a vested interest in each healthy, vegan meal he eats.

As kids get older, they can take more responsibility in the kitchen and help more with cooking meals. Tween-aged kids can even get involved with food on a more intimate level by helping to grow a few herbs or vegetables in the garden. Even a potted tomato plant can be a wonderful source of pride for a young person.

Media Watch: Teaching Your Kids to Decode the Messages

Our kids may as well have big bull's-eyes on their backs when it comes to advertisers. Tweens and teenagers are two of the most desirable target markets, leading most global brands to have a "tween strategy." The average American kid is exposed to more than 100 media messages and commercials a day from television, radio, billboards, magazines, and the Internet. We live in a consumer culture, and the effects on children are maddening.

In this section, I help you deal with this advertising. I show you how to develop a healthy media strategy for your home by linking the vegan ethics of cruelty-free living with the commercial messages that children are inundated with. Uncovering the hidden costs of all those advertised foods and products can help everyone in your family be mentally and physically healthier.

Decoding eating disorders

Dieting to lose weight has become an epidemic in our modern culture — and with good reason. We're one of the fattest, most unhealthy countries on earth. However, pre-teens and teenagers are especially vulnerable to the family and media messages about the benefits of being thin, and their behavior can have dangerous consequences. For example, *anorexia,* which affects mostly young girls and women, is an eating disorder where the person stops eating and loses an excessive amount of weight. They do this because they're overly concerned about their body shape and "getting fat."

Teenagers may choose to adopt a vegan diet for many reasons. Animal rights are one of the top concerns of these young people, and health may be another issue. The American Dietetic Association (ADA) has expressed the opinion that vegan and vegetarian diets could be more prevalent among anorexic teens because they offer a way to hide eating disorders. However, the ADA states that being vegan (or vegetarian) doesn't cause people to become anorexic.

While eating a vegan diet doesn't in itself lead to eating disorders, a tween or teen who's constantly dieting and decides to go vegan may be using this new diet as a way to further restrict her calories. Keep an eye on the child's health and appearance. If you feel that she's developing an eating disorder, seek the advice of a trained professional.

For the health of your entire family, it's wise to avoid overt media images from magazines, television, and movies that push the idea that being thin is the only way to be beautiful and loved. Find healthy images of women, including athletes, confident public figures, and female leaders, to populate your home. Being too far overweight can be unhealthy, but loving your body no matter your size is the best attitude to maintain.

Deflating kids' commercial interests (or at least explaining what they see)

Parents' best efforts to get their kids to eat healthy foods like broccoli and beans are frustrated by commercials and advertisers. Commercials for foods aimed at kids are mostly for junky, processed snack foods, not natural, healthy items. Sodas, chips, and candy are sold in brightly colored, animation-adorned packages. Lettuce is not. It's a tough battle when Shrek is shilling Twinkies instead of green beans.

By making it clear to your children, even at a young age, that these packaged snack foods aren't healthy, aren't vegan, and aren't an option, you can raise a more savvy child. Keep in mind that I said "more savvy," not perfect. They may still ask for these foods when they see friends with them. In these instances, talk with your kids about what advertisers are doing — selling unhealthy food to make money. My mother's rule was "if you see something on TV and ask for it — you'll never get it!" She stuck to it, so we never did.

Eliminating the pressure of the press

Sadly, peer pressure and marketing messages are powerful in getting kids to second-guess themselves. Many studies reveal that children and teens feel better about themselves when they buy certain products that they see on television. The pull to own items that their friends already have is so strong that kids will badger their parents dozens of times for a single item until they give in and buy it for them.

Vegan kids will be less likely to pressure parents for items if they understand the relationship between products and animal welfare. A company that sells a game or toy may be the same company that tests makeup on animals for its other products. Most junk food items in advertisements aren't vegan and contain dairy, meat, or gelatin products. If a processed snack happens to be vegan, it's most likely made by a company that uses nonvegan ingredients in its other foods. Help your kids see the links between their purchases and the health of the environment and the animals they love.

Coming up with responsible responses to media-induced panic

Make your home a healthy haven away from advertising by teaching your kids how to question the messages they see. Talk about them together. When you see a beloved character like Shrek, the Simpsons, or Spider Man selling junk food, help your child call or write the company to complain that you don't like the way they're doing business. Take a stand for your child's health by working together to stop these insidious practices.

Get involved with your child to create positive changes in his everyday life. School lunch programs can be improved and advertising messages can be removed from the classroom. The USDA has created a program called *Fruits & Vegetables Galore: Helping Kids Eat More* to help school food-service teams create healthier lunches. The Physicians Committee for Responsible Medicine has resources available on its Web site about making healthy eating easier and more accessible to kids. Visit www.healthyschoollunches.org/resources/parents.cfm to take a look at these resources.

Creating game nights, dinner party nights, or other themed events for the family keeps the TV off and the media at bay. According to a 2003 poll by the nonprofit group The New American Dream, 57 percent of kids aged 9–14 would rather do something fun with their parents than go shopping. The point is this: Find creative ways to spend time together that don't require shopping, money, or television.

Taking Care of Your Children When They're Away

Parents and kids aren't together 24/7 — and thank goodness for that! When school, trips, and sleepovers are on the calendar, it's time to think ahead and make some strategic decisions. As the old adage goes, "If you fail to plan, you're planning to fail." Going away from home as a vegan kid requires more forethought to ensure that nutritional needs are met.

The strategies in this section can help to make time away from home easier and more stress free for your little vegan. Parties, away games, and competitions can all be healthy adventures with a little preplanning.

Planning ahead

When your child is going away from home, whether it's for a day of school or an out-of-town event, it's important to plan ahead. For daily school planning, it's as easy as packing a lunch with a couple extra snacks and a juice box. For longer weekend trips or special events, you need to find out more information. Ask where your child is going, for how long, what meals will be provided, who else is going, and what the group's expected schedule is.

Many events and trips can be successful for vegan children if they have a packed cooler of snacks and sandwiches. If your child will be staying overnight with access to a kitchen, send a vegan frozen entree in the cooler with ice packs.

Some kids love to try new things, and others want the comforts of home while they're away. A lot of these feelings depend on age. An older teenager, for example, may feel confident enough going to dinner in another state with her soccer team. She can look at a restaurant menu and pick out vegan-friendly options or ask the server to help. However, because they aren't yet making their own decisions, younger kids need prepared meals for the trip. Either way, make sure to pack lots of extra snacks and some fun foods that your kid loves. Placing a package of vegan cookies, muffins, or homemade banana bread in your child's bag will ensure that she has a nice time.

Touching base with chaperones

If your kid is going away without you, talk with his chaperones well beforehand. Make sure these chaperones understand what a vegan diet is, and find out as much as you can about planned mealtimes and locations.

If your child's group will be stopping at a specific restaurant while on a trip, call ahead and speak with the manager about preparing your child a vegan dish. Keeping everyone in the loop will ensure that your growing vegan has an excellent experience.

Chapter 23

The Vegan Athlete

The human body can attain incredible levels of fitness on a vegan diet, and hundreds of competitive and professional athletes prove it. For instance, Carl Lewis, the nine-time Olympic Gold Medal track star, is often quoted saying "My best year of track competition was the first year I ate a vegan diet."

Visiting a gym or professional sporting event doesn't usually bring to mind beans and vegetables. "Meat head" is a term more often given to weight lifters and their thick physiques. People committed to working hard physically to attain personal records, running at the top of their game, lifting more, and pushing their bodies to the ultimate edge of endurance can and do thrive on vegan diets.

Transitioning to a plant-based diet as an athlete can bring many benefits as well as a few challenges. Raising a vegan child who wants to participate in any type of sport — from tennis, swimming, and soccer to running, football, or ballet — should present few problems with proper planning. This chapter addresses the various nutritional hurdles that a vegan runner, or any other sports star, may encounter.

Macronutrients for Strength and Stamina

Whether running, biking, playing with a ball, or stretching to yogic nirvana on a daily basis, athletes need to include healthy meals as part of their training and avoid foods that can decrease stamina. Proper snacking and quality foods will improve your energy levels and physical ability, and still maintain your body's ability to fight off disease.

Every athlete's training should include vibrant, naturally energizing foods that help build the body's muscle and stamina. To create this kind of energy, the body needs *macronutrients* — protein, fats, and carbohydrates — in proper amounts. In the following sections, I give you the lowdown on each of these macronutrients that athletes need. Head to Part II for more on the nutrient requirements for nonathletic vegans.

Powerful vegan protein for performance

The World Health Organization has stated that a vegan diet can provide all the protein humans need during every phase of life. And that's a good thing, because our bodies use protein to do all sorts of things, including making muscle, repairing tissues damaged during training, and building healthy hair and nails. Protein, of course, also is used as energy.

Vegan athletes need extra protein to keep up with their active lifestyles. These increased protein needs can easily be met, however, by adding more of the same great protein-containing vegan foods already found in the normal vegan diet.

Meeting these daily amounts is easy, and exceeding them for muscle building and more strenuous workouts isn't a problem. Following are some recommendations, depending on your level of workout:

Standard: 1.0–1.2g/kg

Endurance 1.2–1.7 g/kg

Power/speed 1.2–2.0 g/kg

Early training 2–2.3g/kg

By choosing larger portions of protein-rich meals, vegan athletes can meet their needs. Eating a protein-rich snack every few hours can help the body recover from regular, strenuous workouts.

Natural vegan foods that are rich in protein include the following:

- ✔ Bean burgers
- ✔ Black bean chili
- ✔ Hemp seed butter
- ✔ Hummus on whole-rye crackers
- ✔ Mashed potatoes smothered with vegan baked beans
- ✔ Mixed nuts, seeds, and dried fruit

✔ Peanut butter and jelly on whole-grain bread

✔ Seitan kabobs grilled or baked with vegetables

✔ Soy or hemp milk

✔ Tempeh burgers

✔ Tempeh cubes in vegetable stew

✔ Vegan baked beans on whole-grain toast

Fueling your muscles with fat

Vegan athletes need to include high-quality plant sources of fat in their diets. The body uses fat to cushion organs, lubricate joint movement, and carry out the thousands of operations needed to jump a hurdle or throw a ball. Eating too little fat while training can lead to muscle fatigue, and fat is needed to utilize certain vitamins, minerals, and phytochemicals.

One of the ways the body uses fat during exercise is to save carbohydrates, which are used up as energy first, in longer workouts. Endurance sports or long training exercises actually increase the ability of muscles to use fat for fuel. This doesn't mean that a vegan athlete needs to pile on the oil to increase fat intake; even leaner athletes have enough fat stored in their tissues to meet their needs.

To shake or not to shake: Some thoughts on protein powders and bars

Athletes of all ages use protein powders as a way to bulk up and meet their daily protein needs. You have many vegan options if you choose to add a powder to your diet. Drinking a smoothie with a scoop or two of soy, hemp, or rice protein added can ensure that your body has the protein it needs to build muscle and recover from hard workouts.

Soy powders contain more grams of protein per serving, but many people want to avoid using too much processed soy in their diet, because a vegan diet can already rely heavily on soy foods. Hemp is considered by many to offer the best plant source of protein, because it also offers a higher amount of complex carbohydrates and quality fats. Rice protein powders tend to have fewer calories per serving and can offer another choice if you want to switch things up in your morning smoothie.

Note: Although uncommon with a vegan diet, too much protein in your diet can lead to dehydration and can be converted into fat. Watch your protein intake by keeping a food diary.

Eating a high-fat diet can result in the burning of more fat during exercise. However, this diet would ultimately limit the amount of carbohydrates the body can store and use. Because carbohydrates are the easiest form of fuel for the body to use for energy, a high-fat diet can end up limiting an athlete's endurance.

Vegan athletes should stick close to the normal recommended daily allowances for fat for nonathletes. Fat should comprise less than 30 percent of your total caloric intake.

Selecting high-quality vegan sources of fat ensures that the body gets what it needs. In fact, vegan sources of fat also offer two-for-one benefits, such as protein from nuts and seeds and anti-inflammatory properties from flaxseed oil and olive oil. Avocados offer a powerhouse supply of good-quality fat while also offering needed nutrients and minerals like potassium, vitamins C and K, folic acid, copper, sodium, and fiber.

Taking in carbohydrates for endurance and brain power

Whether you need to run away from a leaping lion or throw the winning pass, carbohydrates fuel your forward motion. Playing an important role in giving your body and brain the power needed to complete the multiple movements and reactions during training and competing, complex carbohydrates are the best fuel for athletes.

The body stores carbohydrates as *glycogen,* an easy-to-use form of glucose or sugar, in the liver and muscles. During workouts the body taps the reserves of glycogen in the liver to maintain blood sugar levels, which keep the brain and nervous system in working order. If you want to stay sharp and keep your mental agility in tiptop shape, eat a diet rich in complex carbohydrates.

Focus on eating enough complex carbohydrates, as opposed to simple ones like refined sugar and white bread, to ensure that you have a steady supply of fuel for endurance and repetitive strenuous training exercises. If you don't eat enough carbohydrates to replenish the stores that are used up during each workout, you'll burnout and experience fatigue more quickly.

When getting ready for a big event, focusing on complex carbohydrates to build your body's supply of easily accessible fuel is helpful for another reason: Because these foods are digested easily and absorbed into the bloodstream, you avoid a heavy stomach or indigestion during the main event.

Including complex carbohydrates in your diet is so easy as a vegan that you'll have a head start over your competitors. Choose items from this list on a daily basis to ensure you can go the distance:

- ✔ Beans
- ✔ Corn
- ✔ Lentils
- ✔ Muesli (see Chapter 12 for a homemade recipe)
- ✔ Peas
- ✔ Potatoes
- ✔ Udon noodles found in the Asian food aisle
- ✔ Whole, fresh fruit rather than fruit juice
- ✔ Whole grains, including brown rice, oats, millet, quinoa, barley, and wheat
- ✔ Whole-grain flour products, including multigrain, yeast-free breads; high-fiber breakfast cereals; whole-wheat pastas; and wheat bran
- ✔ Yams

Many exercise experts recommend that serious athletes aim for a diet comprised of 50 to 70 percent of total calories from complex carbohydrates.

Avoid simple carbohydrates like refined sugar, white breads, and white pasta. While they may supply a quick fix of energy, they don't last as long as the complex carbohydrates and can lead to faster burnout. Not only will you hit the wall faster if you eat more refined carbohydrates, you also won't be getting the other essential nutrients that complex carbohydrates provide, such as vitamin C, protein, and fiber.

Pumping Iron . . . and Calcium and Other Minerals

Those tiny, trace minerals that the average person needs for daily living are even more important to an athlete. You can't pump iron if you don't eat enough iron to produce healthy blood. And strong bones for contact sports need a diet rich in healthy calcium sources. Despite popular belief, you don't need meat and dairy products to get iron and calcium. (Refer to Chapter 4 for more on getting iron, calcium, and other minerals into your diet.)

Maintaining healthy blood with vegan iron sources

Vegan athletes need to consider their iron needs carefully. According to the National Institutes of Health, iron needs may be 30 percent greater in those who engage in regular exercise because their blood needs to have proper levels of iron to aid in the transport of oxygen to the tissues. To keep training regularly and maintain consistent performance, healthy iron levels are key.

If you start feeling lethargic or your times or performance start to decline, consider having your iron levels checked out by a doctor. Vegan iron supplements are available to help make up the difference, but natural vegan sources of iron-rich foods should be a daily part of your training regimen.

Because it takes the body some time to recover from anemia, it may be useful to have a simple blood test before you begin training to accurately gauge your blood iron levels, red blood cell size, and iron storage. Iron overdose is very serious, so always have a blood test before taking a supplement.

Vegan sources of iron that athletes should include in their daily diet are

- ✔ Beans and legumes, including black beans, lima beans, lentils, and kidney beans
- ✔ Blackstrap molasses
- ✔ Dried fruits, including prunes, raisins, and apricots
- ✔ Iron-enriched whole-grain cereals
- ✔ Leafy greens like spinach, broccoli, kale, collards, and dandelion greens
- ✔ Seeds such as almonds and Brazil nuts
- ✔ Tofu

Female athletes especially need to be careful of their iron levels and daily intake. *Amenorrhea,* or the temporary loss of menstruation, is a relatively common concern for female athletes — vegan and nonvegan alike. In September 1999, David Nieman published a study in the American Journal of Clinical Nutrition that showed low calorie intake, not the vegan diet itself, was the major cause behind female athletes developing amenorrhea. In short, eating enough calories from healthy vegan foods can provide what a female athlete needs.

Vegan sources of iron, the nonheme variety, are better used and absorbed by the body when ample vitamin C is available. So boost the power of these iron-building foods by eating them with papaya, red peppers, oranges or orange juice, or other vitamin C–rich foods. Remember, broccoli has both iron and vitamin C!

Protecting your bones by staying on track with your calcium

Calcium supplies the building blocks for the strong, flexible bones that athletes need for running, throwing, jumping, and falling on a daily basis. Ensure that you're reaching the daily minimum requirement by including natural, calcium-rich foods in your meals. Male athletes need 800 milligrams per day and female athletes should aim for 1,200–1,500 milligrams per day. If you can't get enough from the foods you eat, vegan supplements also are an option.

Female athletes especially need to keep on track with their calcium intake. Excessive training, which is defined as more than seven hours a week, can lead to a decline in hormone levels. These lower hormone levels can compromise bone health and lead to premature osteoporosis, a weakening of the bone matrix.

These simple vegan foods should be a part of your daily calcium strategy:

- Almonds
- Calcium-fortified cereals
- Calcium-fortified orange juice
- Enriched hemp, soy, and rice milk
- Greens like broccoli, kale, and spinach
- Soy yogurt
- Soy-yogurt dip mixed with a tablespoon of blackstrap molasses as a topping for fruit
- Tofu processed with calcium sulfate

Avoiding calcium-depleting foods is just as important as including calcium-rich foods. Coffee and sodas, both caffeinated and caffeine-free, have been shown to leech calcium from the bones to balance the acidity of these beverages.

Remembering your vitamins and minerals

Because of their training and constant exercise, athletes need to consume more minerals and vitamins than their nonathletic counterparts. Keep in mind, however, that the human body best absorbs nutrients from fresh foods as opposed to supplements. So vegans should mine their mineral needs from healthy whole foods on a daily basis.

Magnesium

Magnesium is one mineral that athletes need to focus on when designing their diets for performance. Magnesium helps the body regulate muscle tone and is necessary for metabolizing carbohydrates and protein. Fortunately, most of the foods that contain the highest amounts of magnesium are vegan, including black beans, pumpkin seeds, sesame seeds, soybeans, spinach, sunflower seeds, and Swiss chard.

Chromium

Chromium is used by the body to regulate insulin, metabolism, and blood sugar levels. Athletes need slightly more chromium on a daily basis during training. Table 23-1 shows the recommendations for chromium.

Table 23-1	Recommended Levels of Chromium	
Age	*Males (mcg/day)*	*Females (mcg/day)*
9–13 years	25	21
14–18 years	35	24
19–50 years	35	25
50 years and older	30	20

Source: National Institutes of Health

Broccoli, grape juice, whole grains, potatoes, and fortified nutritional yeast flakes are good vegan sources of chromium.

Copper

Copper is an athlete's ally, as this mineral creates cellular energy and strong connective tissue. Copper also allows the body to metabolize iron better, so be sure to get your recommended daily allowance from cashews, almonds, hazelnuts, lentils, mushrooms, and even vegan chocolate. Table 23-2 lists the various copper recommendations.

Table 23-2	Recommended Dietary Allowance (RDA) for Copper	
Age	*Males (mcg/day)*	*Females (mcg/day)*
4–8 years	440	440
9–13 years	700	700
14–18 years	890	890
19 years and older	900	900

Zinc

Zinc levels may be lower in athletes, and it's needed for healthy skin and wound repair. You can easily meet the daily requirements of 8–10 milligrams a day with good food choices. Vegan sources of zinc include fortified cereals, fortified nutritional yeast flakes, wheat germ, legumes, nuts, tofu, and miso.

Eating for Excellence in Your Sport of Choice

Choosing nutritious, whole foods on a regular basis during athletic training is the best way to prepare for the main event. Eating well consistently every day ensures a better outcome for your future athletic goals. Hundreds of professional athletes have used a plant-based diet to increase their intake of truly energizing foods.

Preparing your diet before an athletic event

Getting ready for a physical competition requires both mental and physical focus. Choose your foods for physical focus as wisely as you choose your thoughts to get psyched up for your event.

Beware of the naturally high fiber content in vegan foods. Too much soluble fiber can lead some athletes to experience stomach cramps or other digestive problems like diarrhea. You don't want the runs while you're running!

If you know you have a more sensitive stomach (or a nervous stomach before competitions), reduce your fiber intake 24 to 48 hours before the big game or meet. Instead, try choosing other high-calorie foods, such as potatoes and whole-grain pasta, that will fuel your energy needs. A larger meal of about 800 to 1,000 calories can be eaten about four or five hours before the start of an event, and a smaller, high-quality snack of 150 to 200 calories, such as cereal and soymilk, can be eaten an hour or two before. You want to give your digestive system time to absorb the nutrients and energy from the meal, while giving the stomach time to empty out.

The most important aspect of nutrition that athletes need to consider is their water intake. Staying hydrated before and during training and competitions can make or break your record. Some athletes rely on artificially flavored and sweetened sports energy drinks. These drinks provide *electrolytes,* or salts, that the body sweats out during exercise. The artificially flavored drinks have too many chemicals and too much unneeded sugar.

Looking for a natural electrolyte drink to guzzle during your next game or meet? Try R.W. Knudsen's Recharge sports drink, made with natural fruit juices, or electroBlast's Power Concentrates, which come naturally flavored with essential oils and stevia. Young coconut water, naturally rich in electrolytes, can also be found in delis, health food stores or on the Internet.

Looking at long-term nutrition goals

The success of many vegan athletes in the professional sports arena proves that a plant-based diet can lead to goal-setting performances. Brendan Brazier, a vegan professional triathlete, and 2003's Ultra Marathon National Champion, has proven that this diet works well for even the hardest-working human bodies.

The amazing Dr. Ruth Heidrich also has proven that a vegan diet can be a part of healthy, long-term nutrition goals. Dr. Ruth has completed six Ironman Triathlons and has won more than 900 gold medals in various distance races. She also has completed more than 60 marathons and holds 3 world fitness records. Ruth has been vegan for more than 25 years.

What you eat is as important as what you avoid eating. Stay away from empty calories that many athletes rely on for quick energy. Slurping down energy drinks full of sugar and chemical colorings won't truly support long-term health. Crunching salty, fried meals may make you feel full, but they still can clog the arteries of someone who trains every day. Instead of wasting valuable energy eating junk, focus on eating natural, vital foods that give you more healing energy than a dozen donuts or a bottle of soda.

Chapter 24

Aging Gracefully and Veganly

In This Chapter

▶ Understanding the nutritional needs of vegan senior citizens

▶ Maintaining a healthy metabolism as you age

▶ Using a vegan diet to heal your body

▶ Eating veganly without complication

*H*aving watched grandparents, and now parents, retire and settle in to the golden years, many people realize that senior nutrition is vitally important to creating a high quality of life. While most vegan books and Web sites tend to focus on nutrition and lifestyle advice for infants, children, and families, mature adults definitely shouldn't be left out. The health benefits available to aging adults through a vegan diet can address most of the illnesses and woes they develop as time marches on. As the baby boomers are now entering retirement, the vegan diet and lifestyle becomes even more popular with those fabulous folks over 40.

Adults of the baby boomer generation are showing signs of being less healthy than their parents as they enter retirement. Even though they smoke less, this new crop of seniors has a higher rate of obesity, more chronic illnesses like hypertension and diabetes, and a more sedentary lifestyle. The American dream of owning a house in the suburbs and driving a big car to the office has been realized, but now many older citizens also are living the nightmare of health complaints and higher stress levels.

In this chapter, I discuss the nutritional needs of people over 40 as well as the best ways to make the vegan transition later in life. I make suggestions for simple food plans that can help guide you through a dietary shift, perhaps on a smaller budget. This shift will improve the quality of your life as you enjoy your middle and later ages.

The beauty of taking on the vegan ethos later in life is that the resulting health benefits can help you feel years younger. A well-planned vegan diet supports decades of good health and even provides insurance against our country's top three killers: heart disease, cancer, and stroke. According to the American Dietetic Association, vegans have lower rates of heart disease, type 2 diabetes, and prostate and colon cancers; lower blood cholesterol levels; lower hypertension; and lower blood pressure. The question is, why *wouldn't* you go vegan after 40?

Boomer Bottom Line: Nutritional Needs after 40

Focusing your attention on quality nutrition in your later years protects you from disease and gives you the energy to play with the grandkids and do all those things you saved up a retirement account for.

A well-planned vegan diet that's based on whole foods, including whole grains, beans, nuts, seeds, vegetables, and fruit, provides a strong foundation for those in and beyond middle age.

The nutritional needs for vegans over the age of 40 are similar to younger adults, but there are a few important differences. To ensure that your body has enough of every necessary nutrient, it's important to be educated about the sources and quantities necessary. So in the following sections, I show you some of the most important nutrients you need as a senior vegan.

Sun + greens = healthy bones

According to the National Institute of Arthritis and Musculoskeletal and Skin Diseases, 10 million people already have osteoporosis in the United States. And apparently another 34 million people have low bone mass, which places them at an increased risk for developing the disease. Baby boomers have lived an entire life being marketed to about how dairy is the optimal source of calcium and that milk is the best way to build bones and avoid osteoporosis. This simply isn't true.

While Americans consume more dairy than most nations on earth, we also have one of the highest osteoporosis rates. The real culprits behind this degenerative bone disease are diets that are too high in acidic animal protein, too high in sugar and salt, and too low in vitamin D.

To ensure healthy bones, eat a vegan diet that's devoid of traditional dairy products and that's full of green leafy vegetables. Because the human digestive system doesn't digest dairy well (lactose intolerance, anyone?), it makes sense that, according to the Heaney and Weaver article in *The American Journal of Clinical Nutrition* in April 1990, "[leafy] greens such as kale . . . [are] at least as good as milk in terms of calcium absorbability." These same greens also contain the other minerals that make up strong bones that taking a lot of calcium supplements won't give you.

The impact of impact exercise

Bones aren't just static stalks holding up our bodies like scarecrows. Like muscle, bone is an ever-changing, living tissue that responds to proper exercise by becoming stronger. Weight-bearing exercise that encourages bones and muscles to increase strength is the best kind for preventing osteoporosis. In addition, many experts believe that the cushioned athletic shoes we often wear may actually decrease the stress we put on our bones — and that's not a good thing. The mild impact of walking in bare feet may actually improve bone health because of the low-impact vibrations that travel up the skeleton. Try a combo of weight lifting for upper and lower body, biking, and walking around your house or safe outdoor area in bare feet. While you're at it, try carrying those bags of groceries up the stairs one at a time. Talk about an excellent — and free — weight-bearing exercise!

Make certain that your body uses calcium properly by getting enough vitamin D from sunlight on your skin. The top layers of your skin make vitamin D (which is actually a hormone) when exposed to sunlight or special light boxes. If you live in a Northern climate, and you don't get daily sun exposure for at least 20 minutes, consider taking a vitamin D supplement.

Even though many vegan products like soy, rice, and hemp milk are fortified with vitamin D, many health experts and doctors think that the recommended daily allowance (RDA) isn't high enough to ensure proper bone health. Researchers recently found that even higher recommendations of 2000IU a day were too low. Consider having your vitamin D levels checked with a blood test to determine what level of supplementation you need.

B healthy — get your B12

Despite occasional food recalls and outbreaks of food-borne illnesses, we live in an age of unparalleled food safety when it comes to cleanliness. This sanitation is necessary when one factory or processing plant is manufacturing thousands of pounds of food from hundreds of sources every day.

The flip-side of this rampant disinfection and sanitation is that our fruits and vegetables are virtually free of bacteria. I'm not promoting that we go around eating dirty, unclean food, but the truth is that some bacteria is good for humans. B12 is produced by bacteria and is then stored in animal tissues. Because livestock animals have these bacteria in their diet, people who eat animal flesh consume B12 in their food. Of course, vegans don't naturally consume B12.

B12 is necessary for every human in sufficient quantities, and for senior citizens or middle-aged folks it can help protect the nerve fibers in the brain as well as protect the body against anemia and dementia. Muscle coordination, balance, memory, and depression are all helped with adequate B12. Senior vegans can ensure they're getting enough B12 by including fortified soy, rice, or hemp milk as well as Red Star nutritional yeast on a daily basis. Taking a B12 supplement may also be necessary to protect against deficiency.

The right fats are fabulous

Fat makes food taste good. It's that simple. It moves tastes around in our mouths, enabling us to really enjoy the nuances and layers of flavors. In addition, fat is necessary for good health. The right kinds of dietary fat ensure healthy skin, properly lubricated joints, and proper brain function. Senior vegans can rejoice knowing that healthy plant-based fats will help them utilize many vitamins and minerals better, which contributes to better overall health.

The fatty acids *linoleic,* or omega-6, and *alpha-linolenic,* or omega-3, are good for you. These fatty acids are converted in the body to form the long-chain fatty acids needed by the body. Vegans need to be aware of their fat intake so they consume the healthy ratio of 6s and 3s. Increasing daily omega-3 intake to equal twice the omega-6 intake will help protect against immune and inflammatory disorders, chronic diseases, and psychological disorders that are common amongst America's seniors.

The average American diet is heavy in animal fats, which are high in saturated fats as well as cholesterol. These fats also are often teeming with toxins. Most agricultural animals are raised on chemical-, medicine-, and antibiotic-laced foods, which are ultimately stored in their fatty tissues. Including healthy vegetable fats from nuts, seeds, avocados, and olives helps vegan seniors to maintain heart and cardiovascular health.

The most dangerous fats are the *trans fats,* or *hydrogenated oils.* These fats are made by heating oils under pressure and then adding hydrogen to make them thick and stable at room temperature. Steer clear of commercially prepared, packaged, and refined foods, which are the most common sources of these nasty, artery-clogging fats.

Vegan sources of fat are wonderful for overall health, and they help you avoid the dangerous toxins common in animal-flesh fats. To ensure that you consume the right quantity and ratio of the different varieties of fats, it's best to avoid processed and refined foods that can rely heavily on fried or hydrogenated omega-6 oils. The vegan sources of omega-3 fatty acids are ground flaxseeds, flaxseed oil, hemp seeds, green leafy vegetables, and walnuts. Omega-6 fatty acids are found in sunflower, safflower, sesame and grape seed oils as well as corn and soy oil.

Because omega-3 oils are highly sensitive to heat, it's important to use them in warm- or room-temperature applications only. Don't sauté or fry anything in flax or walnut oil. Instead, drizzle these oils on foods after they're cooked. Flax oil can be consumed in blended smoothies as well.

Other vegan sources of health-promoting fats are avocados, raw nuts and seeds, and coconut meat. Eating raw nuts and seeds is more beneficial because roasting degrades the quality of the fats.

Keeping your iron in check

Both women and men in their later years still need to be aware of their iron intake. The main preventable cause of iron-deficient anemia in middle-aged men and postmenopausal women is the long-term use of aspirin or nonsteroidal anti-inflammatory medications (NSAIDS), including ibuprofen.

These anti-inflammatory drugs are taken to remedy many aches and pains like gout, rheumatoid arthritis and osteoarthritis, and headaches and migraines. A whole-foods, vegan diet, especially one that avoids caffeine and refined sugars, has been used to greatly reduce these and other inflammatory conditions. And when you reduce these conditions, you reduce the reliance on the iron-decreasing drugs.

Many natural vegan foods contain iron, so be sure to include a variety of them in your weekly menus. Blackstrap molasses, dried apricots, sea vegetables, whole grains, nuts, green leafy vegetables, seeds, and legumes are good sources. Using iron cookware also increases your daily intake. For more information on iron-rich foods, check out the tables in Chapter 4.

If you aren't taking aspirin or other NSAIDS, it isn't usually necessary to take an iron supplement after menopause, and most men don't need to supplement for this mineral. Before supplementing iron it's wise to consult with your doctor and have a simple blood test.

Metabolic Mayhem for the Mature

Keeping off the muffin top in retirement is a high priority for a lot of baby boomers. One of the great joys of vegan living is that most of us have a lower *BMI,* or body mass index, than meat eaters, fish eaters, and even vegetarians. Because high protein and low fiber consumption are the factors most strongly linked with increased BMI, it makes sense that vegans would naturally weigh less and reap the associated health benefits.

Seniors staying sexier for longer

Switching to a low-fat, whole foods, vegan diet is one of the best ways to deal with women's menopausal symptoms of weight gain, insomnia, hot flashes, fluid retention, vaginal dryness, and wrinkles. Along with greater longevity, lower incidence of heart disease, and osteoporosis, Asian and African women who eat a more traditional diet that's less reliant on meat don't experience the same rates of menopausal symptoms that Canadian and American women do, according to T. Colin Campbell's *The China Study* (Benbella Books). Eating a diet devoid of the hormone-producing fatty animal foods like meat, poultry, and dairy can greatly relieve women's symptoms and help them stay trim and confident.

Mature men also sense a sexier self after going vegan. The increase of fiber and elimination of cholesterol and high-fat meats and dairy products improves overall vein health and circulation. Because Viagra essentially works by increasing and improving the flow of blood in the body, it helps men with circulatory problems achieve erection. Vegans generally have better cardiovascular health, so erectile dysfunction won't be as much of a downer.

As we age, our metabolism slows down and so do we. Not only do the *mitochondria* (every human cell's power source) slow down, but most humans also lose muscle over time and exercise less. When people age and stop working to build muscle through weight-bearing exercise, their ability to metabolize energy and calories is reduced. For these people, it takes longer to burn off a piece of vegan cream pie at the age of 70 than it does at 25.

To improve metabolic response and overall energy, a vegan diet paired with a daily exercise routine that includes consistently increasing weight-bearing activities greatly improves the body's ability to lose weight.

Healing Disease with a Vegan Diet

These top killers in America should be put on big banners right next to the post office posters of the most-wanted criminals: heart disease, cancer, and stroke. These, and most of the next top five diseases, including diabetes, affect the health of most seniors and are often avoidable with proper diet and lifestyle considerations. We've all heard the doctors and seen the special reports: What we eat can kill us — or heal us.

The facts are clear that a whole-foods, vegan diet that avoids processed sugars and over-chemicalized ingredients can help seniors to sidestep and even cure many diseases. Along with heart disease and cancer, osteoporosis and digestive problems plague senior citizens and lead to a greatly diminished quality of life.

Due to overfarming, and the explosion of monocrop agriculture, the actual quantities of nutrients in our food and soil have greatly declined over the past 100 years. Choosing a diet of organic foods that have been raised in healthier, more nutrient-dense soils will increase the nutrition you get from your food, thus helping your body recover from and avoid disease.

Improving cardiovascular health as you age

Sadly, most of the reasons that seniors develop cardiovascular or heart disease are avoidable. High blood cholesterol, smoking, lack of exercise, stress, and being overweight are the main culprits which become more dangerous as humans age.

And there's no denying that a diet rich in meat, refined carbohydrates, and processed foods leads to high cholesterol and ultimately heart disease. Some meat eaters believe that only eating poultry and avoiding red meat will protect their health. What they may not realize is that although chicken has less saturated fat than beef, both have nearly the same amount of cholesterol.

A whole-foods, vegan diet, on the other hand, has been proven to reverse and heal the human body of heart disease. If you need proof that a vegan diet can improve your cardiovascular health, consider these studies:

- According to a study in the journal *Public Health Nutrition* (October 2002), vegans "have a lower prevalence of hypertension and lower systolic and diastolic blood pressures than meat eaters," due in part to the fact that they consume *no* cholesterol from their food and generally weigh less than meat eaters.

- Dr. Dean Ornish received worldwide acclaim in 1990 when he published his classic, best-selling book *Reversing Heart Disease.* In it, Dr. Ornish details how prescribing low-fat, vegetarian, or vegan diets, along with exercise and stress-reduction exercises, was used to stop and reverse heart disease. Without the use of cholesterol-lowering drugs (or any other drugs), Dr. Ornish was able to prove that a plant-based diet can cure heart disease, which is one of the most fatal diseases amongst senior citizens.

- Dr. Caldwell Esselstyn, a cardiologist at the Cleveland Clinic, uses a stricter, exclusively vegan diet where total calories from fat are kept under 10 percent of a total daily caloric intake. Because strokes are essentially brain "heart attacks," this diet has been used to help people at high risk to avoid strokes, the top cause of disability for older adults.

Animal foods are the only source of cholesterol in a diet. They're also the main source of saturated fat, and vegans avoid most of these risky products. The American Heart Association, and most other medical experts, supports the idea that a high-fiber diet decreases the risk of cardiovascular disease. Because a vegan diet is higher in fiber, it will automatically be better for heart health. Other therapeutic diets that include animal products are much less effective, and usually only slow the process of atherosclerosis (rather than stop it altogether).

High dietary consumption of vitamin C also is linked to better heart and cardiovascular health. Eating fresh, seasonal fruits and vegetables naturally increases one's intake of vitamin C. The best sources of this incredible antioxidant are organic red bell peppers, parsley, broccoli, cauliflower, strawberries, lemon juice, mustard greens, Brussels sprouts, papaya, kale, grapefruit, kiwi fruit, cantaloupe, oranges, cabbages, and tomatoes. What a surprise — they're all vegan! They also add a healthy dose of fiber, which helps seniors combat high cholesterol and chronic constipation.

The great thing about switching to a vegan diet to improve your heart health is that you can see results quickly. In the peer-reviewed study found in the *Central European Journal of Public Health* (December 2008), a "low-fat, low-[calorie, vegan] diet, over the course of one week in a stress-free environment, had positive impact on the risk factors of cardiovascular disease."

Eating a whole-foods, vegan diet is an amazing leap toward heart health, but you can't just sit on the couch eating your beans and rice and expect to feel better. It's time to get serious and get moving! You need to make it a priority to work up a sweat, get your heart rate up, and move your limbs with some cardiovascular exercise.

Easing digestion and elimination

Older adults are often plagued with chronic constipation. It can be a symptom of various diseases, including irritable bowel syndrome, diabetes, colon cancer, multiple sclerosis, colonic disorders, and even Parkinson's disease.

Many seniors take a cornucopia of drugs and supplements that also can lead to constipation. Everything from iron and calcium supplements, sleeping pills, antidepressants, painkillers, and antacids can lead to constipation. Combine this pharmacy of medications with a low-fiber diet and low-water intake, and you'll find yourself visiting the old water closet a lot less frequently than you would like.

Chronic constipation is not only uncomfortable and unhealthy, but it also can be dangerous. It can lead to pressure inside the veins, which often leads to painful hernias or varicose veins.

The best ways to naturally avoid and treat chronic constipation involve your diet, movement, and hydration. Before I get to diet, let me emphasize that chronic constipation is much improved with daily physical exercise. Walking, bike riding, swimming, dancing, and weight lifting are all useful for clearing out constipation's effects. And aiming for six to eight 8-ounce glasses of water a day will ensure that you're properly hydrated.

Getting fiber into your diet helps ease constipation and reduces cholesterol levels. And guess what? Animal foods have no fiber! A vegan diet, on the other hand, is naturally fiberfull. The recommended daily fiber amounts for men are 30 to 38 grams a day, and women should get 21 to 25 grams a day. To get to the recommended daily amount, take a look at this sample menu:

Breakfast: Oatmeal with 1 cup raspberries (12 grams)

Lunch: Vegan lentil soup mixed with 1 cup brown rice (19 grams)

Dinner: Steamed Artichoke with Sautéed Tofu (10.4 grams)

You can easily exceed your daily fiber recommendation with little effort. Consider having three or more servings each of high-fiber whole grains and steamed vegetables each day. Starting your day with a breakfast of fruit and oatmeal or a vegan bran muffin is easy and full of fiber.

Some folks may develop dental problems as they age. Painful teeth and gum disease can make eating some high-fiber foods difficult. Raw vegetables and crunchy whole foods may be great for the constipation counterattack, but if eating them is too difficult for you, many other high-fiber vegan foods can be cooked and still offer the fiber benefits. Table 24-1 shows some of these foods.

Table 24-1	Soft High-Fiber Vegan Foods	
Food	*Serving Size*	*Amount of Fiber (g)*
Split peas, cooked	1 cup	16.3
Lentils, cooked	1 cup	15.6
Black beans, cooked	1 cup	15
Lima beans, cooked	1 cup	13.2
Artichoke, cooked	1 medium	10.4
Peas, cooked	1 cup	8.7
Raspberries	1 cup	8
Pearled barley, cooked	1 cup	6.0

(continued)

Table 24-1 *(continued)*		
Food	*Serving Size*	*Amount of Fiber (g)*
Quick oatmeal, cooked	1 cup	4.0
Pear, with skin	1 medium	5.1
Apple, with skin	1 medium	4.4
Broccoli, boiled	1 cup	5.1
Turnip greens, boiled	1 cup	5.0
Brown rice, cooked	1 cup	3.5

For true poop-perfection, aim for one good bowel movement a day. A healthy stool isn't too loose and shouldn't be difficult to eliminate. Pushing and straining can lead to other bowel problems like intestinal obstructions, fainting, or even cardiac attack, so balancing your diet and water intake will be a big help.

The modern sitting position on a toilet often makes going to the bathroom difficult and incomplete, which can lead people to force and strain. The human body releases feces better in a squat position. However, it can be difficult for baby boomers to get into that proper position. So, in order to naturally improve your elimination and ease constipation, consider buying a *squatting platform* for your toilet. Several companies make these chairs that easily fit around a standard toilet.

My sign's not Cancer: Using a vegan diet to reverse cancer

A plant-based diet can help the human body recover from and reverse the course of many cancers, including colorectal cancer which affects mainly seniors. This fact alone should inspire many thousands of baby-boomers to try a whole-foods, vegan diet.

Emmy Award–winning cooking-show hostess and author Christina Pirello often tells her personal story of overcoming leukemia with a macrobiotic-style vegan diet. On the opposite end of the vegan diet continuum, a raw-foods diet also has cured countless people of their cancers. Both the Living Foods Institute in Atlanta, Georgia, and the Tree of Life Rejuvenation Center in Arizona help people who are interested in using the raw foods diet to heal and recover from cancer.

Many studies have shown the healing benefits of a vegan diet for cancer patients and those who want to protect themselves from developing the disease. In *The British Journal of Cancer* (July 7, 2009), the incidences of several forms of cancer were less prevalent in vegans and vegetarians than in meat eaters.

Be aware of the dangers of grilled meats and pass them on to your meat-eating friends and loved ones. The Physicians Committee for Responsible Medicine tested Kentucky Fried Chicken's Kentucky Grilled Chicken products and found "substantial amounts of carcinogenic chemical[s] in all samples tested." Time to start making vegan tempeh "chicken" salad, Grandma!

One of the main reasons plant-based diets work to heal and rid the body of cancer is the high amount of phytochemicals found in edible plant foods. *Phytochemicals* are naturally occurring biochemicals found in plants that are used as protection from disease, oxidation, and insects. These same protective biochemicals are cancer-suppressing in the human body. Thousands of phytochemicals are found in fruits, vegetables, sprouts, seeds, nuts, legumes, and grains. These nutritional gems must be eaten in fresh, whole foods, not just extracted into supplements. Working in concert, the myriad combinations of phytochemicals found in natural vegan foods are truly healing and protect the human body from diseases that affect so many seniors.

Planning for Success with Easy Food Choices

Making major dietary changes may seem overwhelming to older citizens who are set in their ways. However eating well as you age can be easy if you keep in mind the following parameters:

- ✔ **Choose a variety of nutrient-dense foods every day.** These foods are high in nutrition but low in calories — foods such as whole grains, beans, and organic fruits and vegetables.

- ✔ **Avoid all processed sugars, including white granulated cane and beet sugar, high-fructose corn syrup, and artificial sweeteners.** Instead use agave syrup, brown rice syrup, or blackstrap molasses.

- ✔ **Choose whole-grain products.** Whole-grain products, like whole-wheat bread, are made with all the edible parts of the seed. The bran, germ, and endosperm are present to contribute fiber, complex carbohydrates, protein, vitamins, and healthy fats.

- ✔ **Include a variety of proteins every day.** Various kinds of beans, nuts, seeds, whole grains, and soy foods combine over the course of the day to give you all the amino acids you need for complete protein.

- ✔ **Eat smaller, more frequent meals.** Seniors often find that their appetites decrease with age. Eating smaller meals more often throughout the day can help ensure proper nutrient consumption without causing discomfort.

✔ **If chewing or swallowing has become difficult or uncomfortable, make nutrient-dense smoothies with fresh, organic ingredients.** Hemp protein, rice milk, nuts, avocado, organic berries, and even chopped raw greens can all be blended into tasty, easy-to-digest meals.

Eating healthily on a fixed income

Buying healthy food can seem more expensive if you walk down the organic produce section of a health food store. Don't be discouraged. There are many ways to save money and still eat better-quality ingredients.

Buying grains, herbs, spices, nuts, seeds, and beans in bulk greatly reduces the cost of organic ingredients. Many health food stores have bulk bins where you can scoop the desired amount of ingredients into plastic or paper bags. You also can bring your own reusable plastic or glass containers if you want to stop wasting plastic or paper bags. Just be sure to weigh the empty container with the check-out person to find the *tare,* or weight of the empty container, before you fill it with new product.

You also can join a local co-op or food buying club. Most co-ops are run by the workers who spend a few hours a month performing predetermined duties for the store. Other co-ops offer yearly membership fees, and may offer a senior discount. The prices for groceries are much less expensive because the store doesn't have to pay high labor costs.

Local farmers may run *CSAs,* or *community supported agriculture associations.* Members buy a share in a farm and then receive weekly deliveries of fresh, locally grown, and usually organic produce. The cost for these fruits and vegetables is often much cheaper than the local health food store, and you get the added benefit of helping a small, local farmer stay in business while making new friends. To find a co-op or CSA near you visit www.localharvest.org. or call 831-475-8150.

Part VII
The Part of Tens

"First it was the cattle, now it's a tempeh mutilation.
I just wish I knew what these weird other-worldly
vegan aliens wanted."

In this part . . .

Here comes the part of the book you've been waiting for — unless, of course, you flipped here before reading anything else! These handy lists of important and often-used information can get you through cocktail party discussions and family meetings about health and diet.

These last chapters give you the lowdown on why vegan living is so amazing, how to make it more fun and interesting than you ever thought possible, and how to respond to the most common questions you'll hear about your new lifestyle.

Chapter 25

Ten Reasons for Eating a Vegan Diet

In This Chapter

▶ Understanding the health benefits of a vegan diet

▶ Arming yourself with information to support your decision to live a vegan life

*I*f you're unsure about changing your eating and lifestyle habits, this chapter can offer you the most compelling, fact-rich information to help you in your transformation. The justification is different for every vegan, and no reason is better than any other.

It's Heart Healthy and Cancer Protective

The facts are undeniable: Heart disease remains the number one killer of men and women in the United States. Luckily, a vegan diet is good for your heart health. The American Heart Association supports the fact that a balanced vegan diet is lower in fat and is cholesterol-free (because only animal foods have cholesterol), which leads to lower risks for coronary heart disease, high blood pressure, and obesity.

In fact, studies have shown that a vegan diet — rich in whole grains, fruits, and vegetables — can stop and even reverse heart disease. Imagine how many lives could be saved if more people adopted a vegan diet.

The second most common cause of death in America is cancer. Like heart disease, many cancers can be treated or prevented with a vegan diet. The immense amount of cancer-fighting properties in fresh fruits and vegetables is leading scientific researchers to study the benefits of this diet. Chapter 1 discusses these topics in further detail.

It Keeps You Slim

Maintaining a healthy weight is much easier with a vegan diet. Because most plant foods are naturally low in fat, a vegan eats less total fat and very little saturated fat. A thoughtful vegan diet is helpful for overweight and obese people who want to lose weight. That's because they'll naturally consume fewer calories, even while eating good-quality ingredients and abundant nutrition.

A plant-based, vegan diet is full of veggies, fruits, nuts, seeds, grains, and beans, which are all great sources of fiber. A fiber-rich diet is more filling, often leading a person to eat less food and fewer calories. Fiber also helps the digestive system move better and eliminate properly, helping the body to maintain a healthy balance of water.

It Has a Lower Carbon Footprint

The farming and agriculture conditions required to raise animals for food production cause some of the largest uses of fresh water and fossil fuels in the world. Experts state that food production in the U.S. accounts for 19 percent of total energy use. By choosing a vegan diet, your food automatically requires less intensive use of petroleum for transporting animals, running machines, and powering factory farms. Buying local, seasonal produce is even more eco-friendly because it requires less refrigeration and fuel for transportation. Even if you do continue to eat Maine blueberries in your winter muffins, you're still being better to the environment than if you were still eating animal foods.

It's Kind to All Living Creatures

As you know, a vegan eats no fish, fowl, cows, lambs, sheep, pigs, eggs, cheese, milk, butter, or honey. Mahatma Gandhi is credited with saying "To my mind, the life of a lamb is no less precious than that of a human being. I should be unwilling to take the life of a lamb for the sake of the human body." By refusing to take the life of another creature, a vegan allows all creatures to continue on their natural course toward full self-expression, which is the true hallmark of an enlightened soul. I like animals, and I consider them to be my friends. And, well, I don't eat my friends.

It Provides Excellent Nutrition

Fresh plant foods are full of phytochemicals, minerals, vitamins, enzymes, and fiber. These nutritious aspects of a vegan diet are sorely lacking in the standard American diet, and they can help halt, reverse, and cure long-standing health concerns like heart disease and obesity.

A vegan diet that includes a variety of foods will easily provide enough protein, healthy fats, complex carbohydrates, and calories for the average person. A vegan diet also provides a wealth of amazing nutritional support not found in the standard American diet; the vegan's reliance on fresh fruit and vegetables as well as other whole foods, such as beans and grains, provides plenty of vital, nourishing energy.

It Protects Our Natural Resources

Grazing animals, such as cattle and sheep, for food leads to massive soil erosion as well as the loss of precious topsoil. Topsoil is a basic component of a healthy landscape and is necessary for natural plants, agriculture, wildlife, and healthy ecosystems. Forests are constantly being cut down to make room for more grazing area, leading to deforestation and contributing to the greenhouse effect and the loss of precious natural habitat for wildlife. The loss of these natural resources, forests, and soils is devastating to the health of our entire planet and humanity.

Choosing a vegan lifestyle is just as meaningful to the health and future of our planet as using reusable cloth shopping bags or compact fluorescent light bulbs.

It Protects the Food Supply for All Humans

Hundreds of gallons of water and many acres of arable land are required to produce a pound of meat for human consumption. A cow needs to eat hundreds of pounds of soybeans or wheat to produce a small amount of edible animal protein. As the world's resources become more and more strained, a vegan diet takes on more importance than just being kind to our four-footed friends. If we stopped feeding all that edible plant food to animals, much more food would be available for humans around the globe. More than 900 million undernourished people inhabit our planet. Feeding those people the grain destined for factory-farmed animals would end a lot of suffering for both people and animals. What could be more humane than eating simply so that others may simply eat?

It Has Fewer Pesticides, Drugs, and Toxins

Animal foods that are produced by modern conventional methods often come with an unsavory side dish: the residue of antibiotics and hormones used to treat factory-farmed animals. How do these toxins get into the food? Allow me to explain.

These animals generally are raised in densely populated conditions, often without access to fresh air, sunlight, or exercise, and they're fed an unnatural diet of high-calorie foods that are used to fatten them as quickly as possible. These conditions lead to an unhealthy environment in which diseases quickly spread. Then farmers and ranchers must use antibiotics to treat the animals. Cows, chickens, and other animals also are given hormones to speed their growth and produce more meat. These hormones and antibiotics can end up in the final products of milk, meat, and eggs, which are then absorbed into the human body when eaten. The question remains, what do these dangerous drugs do to people when eaten regularly, even in small doses?

Other toxins make their way into meat and dairy by way of what the livestock is allowed to eat. According to the Environmental Protection Agency, StarLink corn, a genetically modified organism, isn't safe for people to eat. However, it has been deemed safe to use as livestock feed. But then those same animals get served up to humans as dinner. Sounds a little iffy to me.

Similarly, the Food and Drug Administration has long advised women and children to limit their consumption of certain types of fish because of the health risks associated with high levels of mercury. By avoiding fish altogether, vegans avoid the dangerous side effects associated with mercury toxicity, including damage to the neurological development of fetuses and infants as well as an increased risk of cardiovascular disease.

A vegan diet, especially one that includes mainly organic foods, contains no man-made antibiotics or hormones and very few chemical pesticides. Because our modern world is already so polluted, it can be a huge relief to the human body to eat only nontoxic foods.

It Can Save You Money!

Most vegan foods are cheap, even when purchased in the organic aisle. Eating a diet of mainly inexpensive commodities, such as beans, whole grains, and veggies, can lead to great savings in the checkout line. These savings are mostly due to the fact that plant proteins are much more inexpensive than meat, poultry, eggs, and fish. Even ground beef averages $3.50 per pound in most U.S. cities, and chicken breasts can cost $3 to $4 per pound.

The same $4 buys more than 2 pounds of organic brown rice and 2 pounds of organic lentils. For a few extra pennies, you can buy some organic sunflower seeds and broccoli. No matter how you look at it, the same amount of money provides more food, more protein, more minerals, more fiber, more nutrition, and less disease-promoting material for your body to digest.

A vegan diet also leads to financial savings by helping you avoid illnesses and long-term diseases, such as heart disease, certain cancers, and dementia. Avoiding unhealthy foods now will save you years of lifespan and countless dollars on unnecessary healthcare costs in the future. Dr. T. Colin Campbell, author of *The China Study* (Benbella Books), believes Americans' overly meaty diets result in $60 to $120 billion in healthcare costs every year — try that on for a national healthcare plan!

Vegans Are Cool! (Famous Vegan List)

In our celebrity crazed culture, the following lengthy list of accomplished, talented leaf eaters can help you convince yourself and others that living a vegan life is a great idea. This list is only partial; more musicians, artists, athletes, politicians, and newsmakers turn to a vegan lifestyle all the time:

✔ **Athletes:** Ridgely Abele (karate champion), Ken Bradshaw (pro surfer), Surya Bonaly (Olympic figure skater), Peter Burwash (pro tennis player), Andreas Cahling (bodybuilder and Olympic ski jumper), Chris Campbell (Olympic wrestler), Nicky Cole (first woman to walk to the North Pole), Mac Danzig (pro mixed martial arts fighter), Tony Gonzalez (NFL player), Ruth Heidrich (six-time Ironwoman), Seba Johnson (Olympic skier turned actress), Scott Jurek (ultramarathon runner), Carl Lewis (Olympic track-and-field star), Cheryl Marek and Estelle Gray (world record holders, cross-country tandem cycling), Paavo Nurmi (Olympic long-distance runner), Bill Pearl (four-time Mr. Universe), Dave Scott (six-time Ironman champion), Art Still (NFL player and Hall of Famer), Salim Stoudamire (pro NBA player), Ed Templeton (pro skateboarder), Ricky Williams (pro NFL player)

- **Musicians, actors, and artists:** "Andre 3000" Benjamin (singer/actor), Bryan Adams (singer), Casey Affleck (actor), Pam Anderson (actress/model), Gillian Anderson (actress), Fiona Apple (singer), Erykah Badu (singer), Anthony Kiedis (singer), Ed Begley, Jr. (actor), Linda Blair (actress), Peter Bogdanovich (film director), James Cromwell (actor), Ellen Degeneres (talk-show hostess/actress), Emily Deschanel (actress), Ginnifer Goodwin (actress), Daryl Hannah (actress), Woody Harrelson (actor), Chrissie Hynde (singer), Tobey Maguire (actor), Peter Max (artist), Moby (DJ/singer), Alanis Morissette (singer), Carrie Anne Moss (actress), Kevin Nealon (actor), Robin Quivers (actress/talk-show hostess), Joaquin Phoenix (actor/musician), Summer Phoenix (actress), Dan Piraro (cartoonist), Natalie Portman (actress), Jason Schwartzman (actor), Alicia Silverstone (actress), Grace Slick (singer), Shania Twain (singer), Alice Walker (author), Gretchen Wyler (actress), "Weird Al" Yankovic (comedian, singer), Thom Yorke (singer)

- **Other notable vegans:** Cesar Chavez (civil rights leader), Coretta Scott King (civil rights leader), Dennis Kucinich (politician), Nicole Lapin (journalist), Howard Lyman (former cattle rancher turned activist and author), John Mackey (co-founder and CEO of Whole Foods Market), Petra Nemcova (model), Benjamin Spock, M.D. (pediatrician)

Chapter 26

Top Ten Questions (and Answers) about Going Vegan

How irritated will you get with the same questions from nonvegans over and over again? Probably very irritated. That's why this chapter is so important. Here, amid the ten most common questions you're likely to hear, you can find all the comebacks, educated information, and succinct points of fact needed to make it through what I call the "vegan third degree."

If you're still sitting on the fence about whether to become a full-on vegan, this chapter can help you make the final decision. The best part about these savory bits of knowledge is that you just may entice the person asking the question to go vegan too!

Why Would You Do Something Like That?

Going vegan is one of the best ways to protect the environment. After all, raising animals for meat is one of the leading contributors to global warming. Because raising animals for human consumption requires huge amounts of clean water, land, and oil for transportation and refrigeration, it's better for the environment to be an SUV-driving vegan than a Prius-driving meat eater.

Similarly, the best way to show that you care about animals and other people is to stop eating animal products. By not eating meat, cow's milk, or eggs, a vegan saves the lives of more than 100 animals a year. Eating meat and dairy takes food and clean water away from starving people around the world. It takes many pounds of grain and hundreds of gallons of water to produce just a small amount of meat or dairy. The more people who live vegan, the more other people can simply eat.

Aside from being an environmentally friendly decision, a vegan diet also will keep you alive! The American Dietetic Association states that vegans are less likely to become obese or develop diabetes, many cancers, or heart disease.

Where Do You Get Your Calcium?

Vegan sources of calcium are everywhere. Dark green veggies, such as broccoli and bok choy, are excellent sources. And soy, rice and hemp milks are all enriched with the mineral — as are many orange and apple juices. Tofu is often processed with calcium sulfate, making it a good source. Soy yogurt, almonds, blackstrap molasses, and tahini also contain substantial amounts.

Several studies have shown strong evidence that people who eat lower-protein, plant-based diets need less calcium than those eating higher-protein diets based on animal foods. Even though vegans may need less calcium to ensure strong bones, they can (and should) get the recommended daily allowance, with natural, cruelty-free foods.

Where Do You Get Your Protein?

A varied vegan diet provides enough protein for both adults and children. As long as you eat enough calories from varied sources of food, it's easy to get your recommended amount on a daily basis. Vegan sources of protein include whole-wheat bread, nuts like almonds and cashews, seeds like sunflower and sesame, peanut and almond butter, soy and hemp milk, whole grains, beans, and soy foods like tofu and soy yogurt.

An 18-year-old male needs between 55 and 60 grams of protein a day. So, if he eats the following foods in one day, he's set on his protein: 1 cup oatmeal, 2 tablespoons flaxseeds, 2 cups hemp milk, 2 slices of whole-wheat bread, 4 tablespoons of peanut butter, 1 cup of vegan black bean chili, 1 cup cooked pasta, 1 cup broccoli, and ½ cup tofu.

Animal foods offer complete protein — they have each of the 22 amino acids present that the body needs to use protein. Luckily, however, tofu and other soy foods also contain the necessary amino acids. Other vegan foods like beans, grains, vegetables, nuts, and seeds will provide, over the course of a day or so, all the essential amino acids that the body needs.

What Can You Eat?

You can eat so much good food as a vegan! Believe me, you won't go hungry. Consider this list, which breaks down just a few of your options by meal:

- ✔ Breakfast may be a fruit and nut smoothie with hemp or soymilk, corn muffins, tofu scramble, blueberry pancakes made with rice milk (and don't forget the maple syrup), toast and jam, soy yogurt with fruit, granola, or hash browns with tempeh sausages.

- ✔ Lunch can include peanut butter and jelly sandwiches, chocolate chip cookies made with applesauce and flaxseeds instead of eggs, veggie burgers, french fries, falafel with hummus and pita bread, or a fake meat and cheese sandwich on whole-wheat bread.

- ✔ Dinner menus offer vegetable and tofu lasagna; pasta with broccoli, tomatoes, and white beans; lentil soup with crusty bread and sautéed kale; bean casseroles; chili with chips, salsa, and guacamole; or curried vegetables with rice and chickpeas.

Flip to Chapter 9 for more on planning your meals to stay faithful to your new vegan diet.

Isn't That a Difficult Lifestyle to Get Used to?

When you're passionate about your health, treating animals kindly, and protecting the environment, it isn't difficult to make a few dietary and lifestyle changes. The first few weeks can be an adjustment, but once you start looking, you see vegan options everywhere! Health food stores are popping up all over the country, providing many vegan products to Americans coast to coast. In fact, there are more than 250 Whole Foods Markets in North America alone! If you don't have a good health food store near you, keep in mind that the Internet is an incredible resource.

If you think you can't get by without some of your favorite nonvegan foods and household items, think again! You can find alternatives for almost everything you may need to buy. Vegan milks, cheeses, meats, shoes, wallets, belts, vitamins, makeup, deodorants, shampoos, candles, pet foods, and baby items abound!

Do You Eat Fish or Dairy Products?

Fish are animals, so vegans don't eat them. Vegans also don't eat dairy products that come from animals, including cow's milk, cow's cheese, goat's milk or cheese, and butter.

Other animal products that vegans avoid eating are honey, eggs, meat, chicken, veal, pork, or turkey (even on Thanksgiving).

Where Can You Go Out to Eat?

Going out to eat isn't difficult — just ask for what you want and kindly request that your server omit dairy and meat from your dishes. I've never had a problem "veganizing" a menu item, especially if you ask sweetly and smile.

You really can eat anywhere as a vegan — even a steak house! Try ordering hummus with vegetables, falafel and pita bread, vegetable pizza minus the cheese, pasta with beans and vegetables without cheese or butter, vegetarian refried beans with guacamole and chips, or coconut curry bowls with rice. You also can make a meal out of side dishes that don't include animal products. Most restaurants offer some bean, green, and grain dish on the side that you can combine to make a complete meal. Just be sure to specifically ask that no dairy, butter, meat, or chicken stock be used in any of the preparation.

Not only are regular restaurants accommodating, but vegan and vegetarian restaurants can be found all over the world. Visit www.happycow.net or www.vegdining.com to find a vegan-friendly dining spot near you.

Can You Be Healthy on a Vegan Diet?

If you want to know whether you or a loved one can be healthy on a vegan diet, the answer is "Heck yeah!" Vegans are often at least 20 pounds lighter than meat eaters who are the same height. Even better is the fact that many people have actually reversed their serious health conditions — including cancers, type 2 diabetes, heart disease, and obesity — by adopting a vegan diet along with increased exercise.

Top government and healthcare organizations, such as the American Dietetic Association, have declared that a vegan diet can be perfectly healthy for every stage of life including pregnancy, infancy, childhood, and adulthood. The competitive sports world even contains many professional vegan athletes. Pro football players, triathletes, ultramarathoners, tennis players, karate champions, and even body builders create their incredible physiques from plant-based diets. Part VI discusses veganism in all walks of life.

Vegans tend to eat more fiber, fresh fruits, vegetables, and whole grains than nonvegans. These are the exact foods that health experts are constantly harping on the public to eat more of — living vegan almost ensures this.

What Do the Experts Think of Veganism?

Some folks can't accept a new line of thinking unless they hear positive comments from leading experts in that field. So, when you're faced with explaining veganism to this type of person, feel free to quote the following expert opinions:

- ✔ "A low-fat, plant-based diet would not only lower the heart-attack rate about 85 percent, but would lower the cancer rate 60 percent." — William Castelli, M.D., Medical Director, Framingham, Cardiovascular Institute

- ✔ "Scientific data suggest positive relationships between a vegetarian [and vegan] diet and reduced risk for several chronic degenerative diseases and conditions, including obesity, coronary artery disease, hypertension, diabetes mellitus, and some types of cancer." — American Dietetic Association

- ✔ The rate of breast cancer among premenopausal women who ate the most animal (but not vegetable) fat was a third higher than that of women who ate the least animal fat. — Journal of the National Cancer Institute

- ✔ "With all the information now available about the long-term health benefits of plant-based diets, there is really no question that the vegan diet is safe — in fact, it offers the most disease-fighting protection of any dietary pattern." — Amy Lanou, Ph.D.

Where Can I Learn More?

Many magazines, books, Web sites, Internet groups, and organizations can provide information on how to live a vegan life. An excellent magazine on vegan living is *Veg News,* which can be ordered online or purchased in health food stores. Some of my favorite books include

- *Diet for a New America* by John Robbins (HJ Kramer)

- *The Vegan Lunchbox: 130 Amazing, Animal-Free Lunches Kids and Grown-Ups Will Love!* by Jennifer McCann (Da Capo Press)

- *Cooking the Whole Foods Way* by Christina Pirello (HP Trade)

- *Breaking the Food Seduction* by Dr. Neal Barnard (St. Martin's Griffin)

- *Veganomicon* by Isa Chandra Moskowitz and Terry Hope Romero (Da Capo Press)

Excellent Web site resources for finding out more about vegan living include The Physicians Committee for Responsible Medicine (www.pcrm.org) and Girlie Girl Army for vegan fashionistas (www.girliegirlarmy.com). For everything else under the sun, check out www.veganessentials.com.

To bone up on how to become vegan, check out these Web sites:

- The Vegetarian Resource Group at www.vrg.org

- People for the Ethical Treatment of Animals at www.peta.org

- American Vegan Society at www.americanvegan.org

- Vegan Family Living at www.vegfamily.com.

Chapter 27

Ten Ways to Make Vegan Living Extraordinary

In This Chapter

▶ Broadening your horizons by joining other vegans

▶ Discovering new skills that promote your values

▶ Acting like a global citizen in your local area

*I*n this chapter, I show you how to turn your veganism into a powerful, productive, and satisfying lifestyle by expanding your horizons and getting off the couch. It's easier to make this diet a lifelong commitment if you begin to create a supportive, exciting community. Reaching out to deepen your awareness and going beyond the normal will be truly satisfying.

Join a Local Vegan Group

Starting any new hobby, lifestyle, diet, or spiritual practice requires you to have a community of people and teachers around you to offer support. Because becoming vegan encompasses all these things, joining a local vegan group can help ensure your success. Membership in a local group gets you in touch with like-minded people who you can share activities and meals with. These folks ideally live close by and can offer you nuts-and-bolts support with vegan living.

To find local groups of like-minded veggie lovers:

✔ Look at your local health food store bulletin board, which may list meetings of local supper clubs.

✔ Ask the local college if it has any student-run vegan groups. Even if you aren't eligible to join, the group may be willing to share some local resources with you.

✔ Ask the servers, owner, and chef at your local vegan-friendly restaurant if they know of any groups, meetings, or experts living nearby.

✔ Check the events sections in your local newspapers and nickel ads. They may list vegan festivals, speakers, or potlucks.

Join a Few Online Vegan Groups

Meeting up with local vegans is only part of your new community. You can find thousands more online! The Internet can connect you to every aspect of veganism: shopping, cooking, dating, political activism, and community building. Here are some of the best resources to get you started:

✔ **MeetUp.com:** vegan.meetup.com

✔ **Vegans World Network:** www.vegansworldnetwork.org

✔ **The Vegan Forum:** www.veganforum.com

Throw a Totally Vegan Birthday Party

Bring your vegan and nonvegan friends together and throw yourself (or someone else) a totally vegan birthday! This winning strategy combines what we love best about living vegan: great food, fun, cool new things, and cake.

By throwing your own party, you can introduce your favorite new recipes to friends and family to show off your burgeoning culinary skills. Here are some things to do to ensure success:

✔ **Choose fun party foods to entice nonvegans to the buffet table.** These are just a few options: tofu chicken fingers, decadent vegan cake or cupcakes with piped frosting, stuffed mushrooms, seven-layer dip, olives, stuffed grape leaves, spiced nuts, fruit salad served in a scooped-out watermelon, hummus, crackers, chips, salsa, and guacamole. The choices are endless. Part IV is your guide to cooking vegan. Check it out.

✔ **Set up a bar with beer, wine, juice, seltzer, and cocktail mixers.** Offer olives, cherries, lemon and lime slices, and lots of ice. Borrow glass tumblers from friends or family or pick up a dozen at your local thrift store. They're reusable and can always be donated, which is cooler and more "free-gan" than throwing out paper cups. (See the later section "Be More Free-Gan with Used Goods.")

✔ **Ask the invitees to dress as nice as they can without wearing any leather, silk, wool, or fur.** Throwing a dress-up party always makes the event more festive, and this little twist encourages your nonvegan friends to think a little bit about what they wear on a daily basis.

Write About Veganism

Every year the Vegetarian Resource Group holds a contest for the best essay written on the topic of vegetarian and vegan living. Entering the contest helps you form your ideas and arguments into a logical, well-formulated framework, and can win you some notoriety and a $50 savings bond! Visit www.vrg. org/essay for more details. You must be under 19 to enter.

Adults can set their pens to paper as well, however. Writing an article or op-ed piece for your local paper is a great way to focus your passion and express a point of view that others in your community may not have considered. Whether you're compelled to write about a recent puppy mill scandal in your home state or the terrible nutrition standards in your school cafeteria, your voice will help to broaden the debate. Make it known within the article that you're vegan, what that means, and why it's relevant to the issue at hand.

Hold a Fundraiser for Your Local No-Kill Animal Shelter

Some animal shelters are dedicated to providing homes for little lost Fidos and Fluffys. These shelters refuse to kill the animals — even if they can't find a suitable adoptive family for them. These shelters are always in need of funding to house, feed, and provide medical services to the animals.

Holding a vegan bake sale, garage sale, or other fundraiser offers you a chance to put your passion to work constructively. You can raise money and gently offer information to customers and passersby about the shelter. You may be able to get copies of a pamphlet from the shelter itself, or you can simply make a homemade flyer listing the contact information, mission statement, and name of the shelter.

Meditate and Set Intentions at Mealtime

Every time you sit down to eat, take a few moments to quiet your mind, take a few deep breaths, and check in with your body. What does it need? Is it thirsty? Is it calm or angry? Are you anxious or unhappy? Bringing that awareness to each meal helps you in deciding what to eat, how quickly to eat it, and how much to consume. This is the simplest meditation for the body and mind.

Eating slowly improves digestion and allows your body to use the nutrients from your meal better. By chewing each mouthful thoroughly and slowing your eating down, your body has more time to communicate with your brain, which leads more quickly to a feeling of fullness. People generally eat less this way and experience less indigestion. Try to make each meal last at least 30 minutes by putting your fork down between bites, chewing until each bite is liquefied. And turn off the television during meals.

Setting an intention at each meal to be kind to yourself and nourish your body in whatever way is best at that moment can bring a new level of awareness to your entire life. Other intentions can be to send out prayers for peace, calm in the world, compassion for all living creatures, or thoughts for strengthening your community.

Vote Your Truth: Compassion in Action

Register to vote, and update your registration every time you move. Get to know the candidates and legislation coming up in each election cycle. For instance, where do the candidates stand on issues that are important to you? What impact would a new piece of legislation have on your life? Do you agree with the values it promotes?

National and state animal rights groups have been successful in changing the laws to better protect farm animals in the last few years through dedication, donors, volunteers, and voters. Be part of the movement and vote! It's your duty as a citizen to take an active role in the democratic process.

Become a Pro in the Kitchen

Cooking basic, healthy meals should be a requirement for every human being who graduates from high school. Can't cook at all, you say? Never fear! You'd be surprised at how many people would be willing to help you, either for free or very cheaply. Here are a few ways to get some help:

- ✔ **Ask an older, trusted adult for his advice.** Tell him that you can't cook and that you want to learn. Then ask whether he knows anyone who can help you learn. Chances are he'll let you follow him around in the kitchen. Or he may even work with you on vegan recipes you want to master — as long as he can share in the finished product, of course.

- ✔ **Get your friends together for a cooking party.** E-mail the recipe to everyone beforehand, have all the ingredients ready, and work together to create a lovely meal. Don't be afraid to ask questions along the way and dive in to help with techniques you haven't tried before.

- **Look around your area for vegan cooking classes.** Community colleges, vegan restaurants, health counselors, and cooking schools may offer just what you're looking for.

- **Look for a knife skills class at your local culinary school or community college.** Discovering how to care for your knives and properly cut and prepare vegetables is amazingly empowering. You'll want to cook more right away just to practice your new skills!

- **Ask a local professional chef (private or from a restaurant you like) to teach you a few private classes.** You can choose the menu and techniques, and you can either have the chef bring the ingredients to your home or hold the class in his kitchen. Get a group of friends together for a group class, which would probably cost less for each person than if you did it on your own.

- **Try something new.** Experiment with a new recipe at least once a week. Countless vegan recipes from every ethnic background are available on the Internet. Many of these recipes have comments from other home cooks, which can help you avoid possible mistakes in the original recipe. If you need some ideas to get started, try recipes from www.vegweb.com, www.veganchef.com, or www.fatfreevegan.com.

Start a Vegan Victory Garden

The idea to contribute to your own health and the environment was given a huge boost in March 2009 when President and Mrs. Obama participated in planning a large organic garden on the White House lawn. Large plots of land like the one at the White House aren't necessary, however; even the smallest apartment can house a mini-farm. Container gardening can produce lettuce, herbs, tomatoes, green beans, carrots, and berries (and virtually any other type of veggie, as long as you choose the proper variety and have a big enough pot).

If you have access to more land and are inclined to get busy in the garden, you can grow a considerable amount of food with a little research and a few seasons worth of patience. An acre of arable land can produce thousands of pounds of strawberries, potatoes, corn, or lettuce. For an amazing selection of organic and heirloom seeds, look around www.seedsofchange.com.

A great resource for getting to know the local land and what you can expect when you start your own Victory Garden are local County Extension offices. Every state has offices staffed with experts who supply useful information to the public regarding planting season, local native varieties, information on soil health, and sources for seeds and tools.

Be More Free-Gan with Used Goods

Vegans can get even more eco street cred by looking for ways to be *free-gan,* or buying, borrowing, and finding used items instead of buying brand-new goods. Start looking for used items that are free — in New York City we call this *dumpster diving* or *trash picking.* Instead of buying new or used items, you often can find a free item that someone else doesn't need anymore. Why is dumpster diving a great thing to do? Picking up that old bookshelf from the curb keeps it out of the landfill, saves you money, and prevents natural resources from being overused to create new items.

Some communities have scheduled "clean out" weekends where people put items out on their curbs or sidewalks. The stuff is then fair game for anyone who wants to pick it up and take it home. Not only does it save everyone money by reducing garbage collection fees, it redistributes goods to people who are in need and can't necessarily afford to buy new things.

You also can go online and join Freecycle.org to post items you want to part with. Other users will then respond and schedule a time to pick up that old sofa bed that's clogging your walking path through the living room.

Index

Business/Accounting & Bookkeeping

Bookkeeping For Dummies
978-0-7645-9848-7

eBay Business
All-in-One For Dummies,
2nd Edition
978-0-470-38536-4

Job Interviews
For Dummies,
3rd Edition
978-0-470-17748-8

Resumes For Dummies,
5th Edition
978-0-470-08037-5

Stock Investing
For Dummies,
3rd Edition
978-0-470-40114-9

Successful Time
Management
For Dummies
978-0-470-29034-7

Computer Hardware

BlackBerry For Dummies,
3rd Edition
978-0-470-45762-7

Computers For Seniors
For Dummies
978-0-470-24055-7

iPhone For Dummies,
2nd Edition
978-0-470-42342-4

Laptops For Dummies,
3rd Edition
978-0-470-27759-1

Macs For Dummies,
10th Edition
978-0-470-27817-8

Cooking & Entertaining

Cooking Basics
For Dummies,
3rd Edition
978-0-7645-7206-7

Wine For Dummies,
4th Edition
978-0-470-04579-4

Diet & Nutrition

Dieting For Dummies,
2nd Edition
978-0-7645-4149-0

Nutrition For Dummies,
4th Edition
978-0-471-79868-2

Weight Training
For Dummies,
3rd Edition
978-0-471-76845-6

Digital Photography

Digital Photography
For Dummies,
6th Edition
978-0-470-25074-7

Photoshop Elements 7
For Dummies
978-0-470-39700-8

Gardening

Gardening Basics
For Dummies
978-0-470-03749-2

Organic Gardening
For Dummies,
2nd Edition
978-0-470-43067-5

Green/Sustainable

Green Building
& Remodeling
For Dummies
978-0-470-17559-0

Green Cleaning
For Dummies
978-0-470-39106-8

Green IT For Dummies
978-0-470-38688-0

Health

Diabetes For Dummies,
3rd Edition
978-0-470-27086-8

Food Allergies
For Dummies
978-0-470-09584-3

Living Gluten-Free
For Dummies
978-0-471-77383-2

Hobbies/General

Chess For Dummies,
2nd Edition
978-0-7645-8404-6

Drawing For Dummies
978-0-7645-5476-6

Knitting For Dummies,
2nd Edition
978-0-470-28747-7

Organizing For Dummies
978-0-7645-5300-4

SuDoku For Dummies
978-0-470-01892-7

Home Improvement

Energy Efficient Homes
For Dummies
978-0-470-37602-7

Home Theater
For Dummies,
3rd Edition
978-0-470-41189-6

Living the Country Lifestyle
All-in-One For Dummies
978-0-470-43061-3

Solar Power Your Home
For Dummies
978-0-470-17569-9

Internet

Blogging For Dummies,
2nd Edition
978-0-470-23017-6

eBay For Dummies,
6th Edition
978-0-470-49741-8

Facebook For Dummies
978-0-470-26273-3

Google Blogger
For Dummies
978-0-470-40742-4

Web Marketing
For Dummies,
2nd Edition
978-0-470-37181-7

WordPress For Dummies,
2nd Edition
978-0-470-40296-2

Language & Foreign Language

French For Dummies
978-0-7645-5193-2

Italian Phrases
For Dummies
978-0-7645-7203-6

Spanish For Dummies
978-0-7645-5194-9

Spanish For Dummies,
Audio Set
978-0-470-09585-0

Macintosh

Mac OS X Snow Leopard
For Dummies
978-0-470-43543-4

Math & Science

Algebra I For Dummies
978-0-7645-5325-7

Biology For Dummies
978-0-7645-5326-4

Calculus For Dummies
978-0-7645-2498-1

Chemistry For Dummies
978-0-7645-5430-8

Microsoft Office

Excel 2007 For Dummies
978-0-470-03737-9

Office 2007 All-in-One
Desk Reference
For Dummies
978-0-471-78279-7

Music

Guitar For Dummies,
2nd Edition
978-0-7645-9904-0

iPod & iTunes
For Dummies,
6th Edition
978-0-470-39062-7

Piano Exercises
For Dummies
978-0-470-38765-8

Parenting & Education

Parenting For Dummies,
2nd Edition
978-0-7645-5418-6

Type 1 Diabetes
For Dummies
978-0-470-17811-9

Pets

Cats For Dummies,
2nd Edition
978-0-7645-5275-5

Dog Training For Dummies,
2nd Edition
978-0-7645-8418-3

Puppies For Dummies,
2nd Edition
978-0-470-03717-1

Religion & Inspiration

The Bible For Dummies
978-0-7645-5296-0

Catholicism For Dummies
978-0-7645-5391-2

Women in the Bible
For Dummies
978-0-7645-8475-6

Self-Help & Relationship

Anger Management
For Dummies
978-0-470-03715-7

Overcoming Anxiety
For Dummies
978-0-7645-5447-6

Sports

Baseball For Dummies,
3rd Edition
978-0-7645-7537-2

Basketball For Dummies,
2nd Edition
978-0-7645-5248-9

Golf For Dummies,
3rd Edition
978-0-471-76871-5

Web Development

Web Design All-in-One
For Dummies
978-0-470-41796-6

Windows Vista

Windows Vista
For Dummies
978-0-471-75421-3

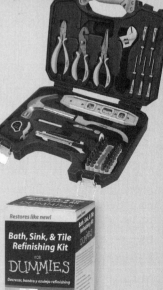